THIS PRESENT MOMENT

CRAFTING A BETTER WORLD

THIS PRESENT MOMENT

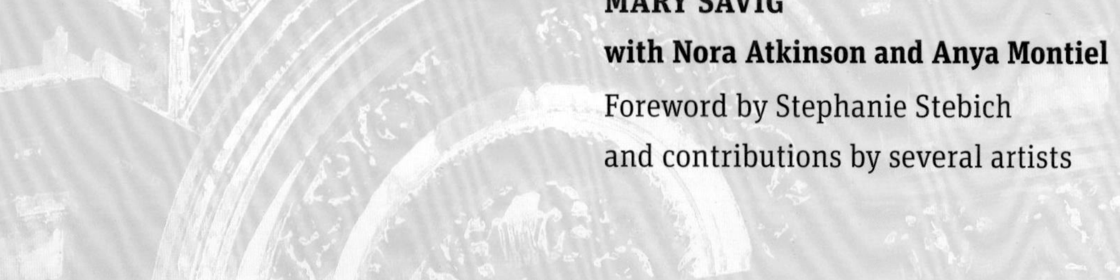

MARY SAVIG
with Nora Atkinson and Anya Montiel
Foreword by Stephanie Stebich
and contributions by several artists

CRAFTING A
BETTER WORLD

Renwick Gallery of the
Smithsonian American Art Museum
Washington, DC
in association with D Giles Limited

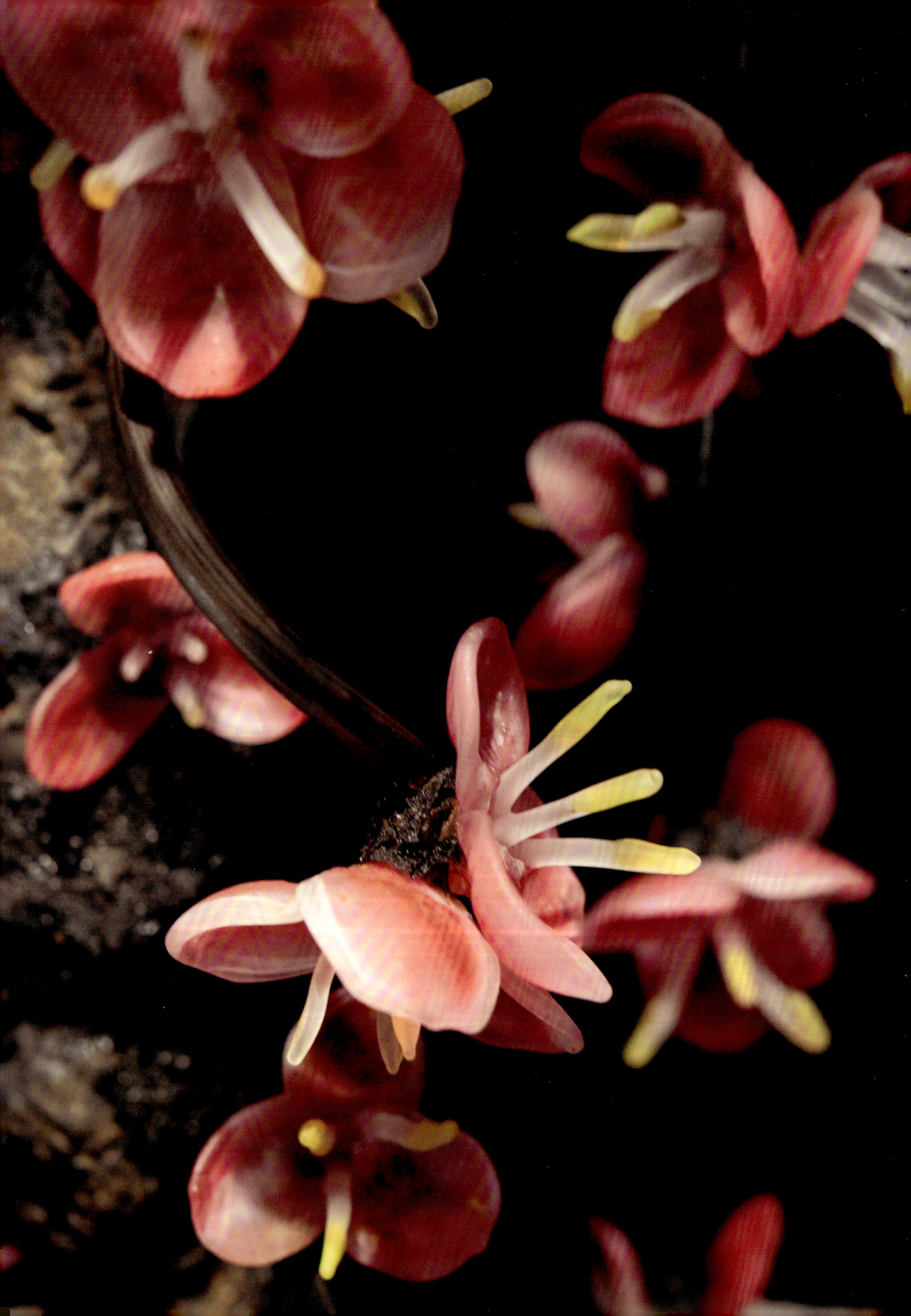

This Present Moment: Crafting A Better World is organized by
the Renwick Gallery of the Smithsonian American Art Museum.

Generous support is provided by Carl and Jan Fisher, Shelby and
Fred Gans, the James Renwick Alliance for Craft, and Ann Kaplan
and Robert Fippinger.

The catalogue is made possible by Cindy Miscikowski.

Additional support is provided by:

Alturas Foundation
Elizabeth Broun Curatorial Endowment
Sharon and Bob Buchanan
Sheila Burke
DLR Group
Mary Anne Fray
Cary J. Frieze
The Galena-Yorktown Foundation
Chris G. Harris
Cecily and Bannus Hudson
Colleen and John Kotelly
Joseph P. Logan
Eleanor T. Rosenfeld
Dorothy Saxe in memory of George Saxe
Maggie and Dick Scarlett
Barbara Tober
Judith S. Weisman
Myra and Harold Weiss
Kelly Williams and Andrew Forsyth
Todd Wingate and Steven Cason

THIS PRESENT MOMENT: CRAFTING A BETTER WORLD

Published to accompany the Renwick Gallery's fiftieth anniversary program and in conjunction with the exhibition of the same name, on view at the Renwick Gallery of the Smithsonian American Art Museum, Washington, DC, from May 13, 2022, to April 2, 2023.

Produced by the Publications Office, Smithsonian American Art Museum, Washington, DC, AmericanArt.si.edu

Theresa J. Slowik,
    Former Head of Publications
Tiffany D. Farrell,
    Interim Head of Publications
Julianna C. White, Editor
Karen Siatras, Designer
Antonio Alcalá, Studio A, Cover Designer
Louise Ramsay, Production Coordinator
Richard Sorenson and Aubrey Vinson,
    Permissions & Image Coordinators
Rosemary Hammack, Proofreader
Jodi Simpson, Proofreader
Elana Hain, Collections Manager
Sue Farr, Indexer

Published by the
Smithsonian American Art Museum
in association with

GILES
An imprint of D Giles Limited
66 High Street
Lewes BN7 1XG
UK
gilesltd.com

The Smithsonian American Art Museum is home to one of the largest collections of American art in the world. Its holdings—more than 43,000 works—tell the story of America through the visual arts and represent the most inclusive collection of American art in any museum today. It is the nation's first federal art collection, predating the 1846 founding of the Smithsonian Institution. The museum celebrates the exceptional creativity of the nation's artists, whose insights into history, society, and the individual reveal the essence of the American experience.

The Renwick Gallery became the home of the museum's American craft and decorative arts program in 1972. The gallery is located in a historic architectural landmark on Pennsylvania Avenue at 17th Street, NW, in Washington, DC.

For more information, contact:

Office of Publications
Smithsonian American Art Museum
MRC 970, PO Box 37012
Washington, DC 20013-7012
AmericanArt.si.edu/books

Typeset in Unit and Unit Slab Pro, Microbrew Soft One, and P22 Sneaky Pro. Printed in Italy by Conti Tipocolor on Condat Matt Périgord 170 gsm paper.

Front cover: Renwick Gallery façade, 2019
Back cover: Alicia Eggert, *This Present Moment* (see CAT. 37)

All artworks are in the collection of the Renwick Gallery of the Smithsonian American Art Museum unless otherwise noted.

A note about the cover:

To honor the Renwick Gallery's fiftieth anniversary, Antonio Alcalá of Studio A created fifty different color variations for the image of the Renwick Gallery's façade. Each variation was digitally printed in a limited edition of sixty. The color combinations were inspired by nature; special thanks to Carol and Basil Brown for access to their glorious gardens.

Library of Congress
Cataloging-in-Publication Data

Names:
Stebich, Stephanie A., writer of foreword. | Savig, Mary. This present moment. | Atkinson, Nora. Foundation for the future. | Montiel, Anya. Respect, reciprocity, responsibility. | Renwick Gallery, organizer, host institution.

Title:
This present moment: crafting a better world / Mary Savig with Nora Atkinson and Anya Montiel; foreword by Stephanie Stebich and contributions by several artists.

Description:
Washington, DC: Renwick Gallery of the Smithsonian American Art Museum; London: in association with D Giles Limited, [2022] | Includes bibliographical references and index.

Identifiers:
LCCN 2021055588 | ISBN 9781913875268 (hardcover)

Subjects:
LCSH: Decorative arts—United States—History—21st century—Exhibitions. | Artists and community—United States—Exhibitions.

Classification:
LCC NK808.2 .T49 2022 | DDC 745.0973/074753—dc23/eng/20220106

LC record available at
https://lccn.loc.gov/2021055588

CONTENTS

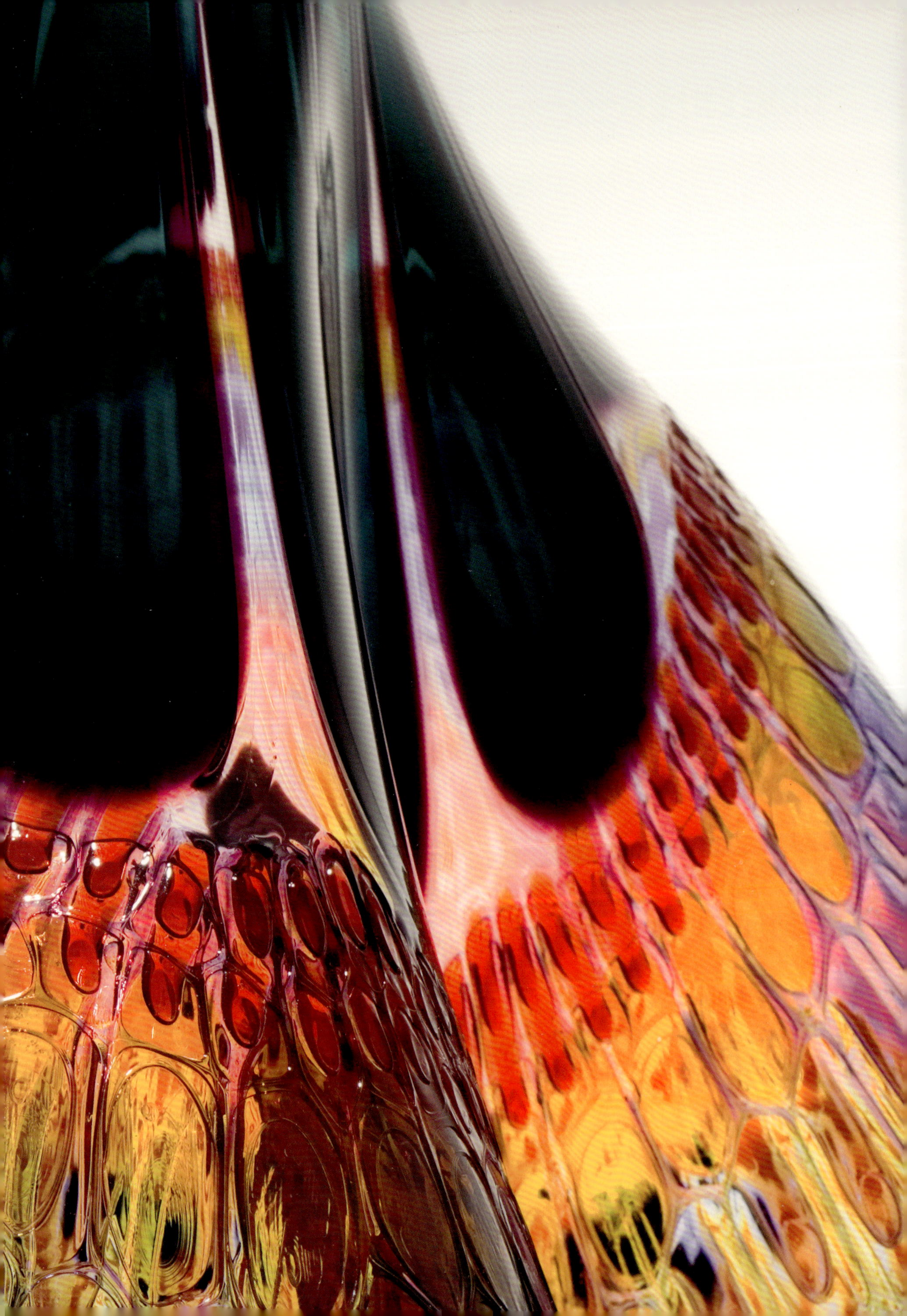

DONORS TO THE CAMPAIGN

Nedra and Peter Agnew

Alturas Foundation

Rebecca Benaroya

David Bonderman

Maureen Fennessy Bousa and Edward P. Bousa

Fleur S. Bresler

Sharon and Robert Buchanan

Judith Chernoff, MD, and Jeffrey Bernstein, MD

Frances Dubrowski and David Buente

Brenda Erickson

Mary Anne Fray

Donna M. Gottlieb

Diane and Marc Grainer

Judy and Stuart Heller

Lloyd E. Herman

Pamela and David Hornik

Cecily and Bannus Hudson

Aiko Iseyama and Family

Jaimianne and Anthony Jacobin

Deena L. and Jerome A. Kaplan

Sharon Karmazin

Colleen and John Kotelly

Lorne E. Lassiter and Gary P. Ferraro

Alida and Christopher Latham

Cliff Lee

Leslie LePere

Tom Loeser

Joseph P. Logan

Wendy MacGaw

Michele A. Manatt and Wolfram Anders

Jane and Arthur Mason

Carolyn L. Mazloomi

Forrest L. Merrill

Alison and Glen Milliman

Clemmer and David Montague

Joel Mulhauser, MD

Merrily Orsini and Frederick Heath

Sheldon Palley, Lisa Palley, Donna Kass, and Kevin Palley

Gwen and Jerome Paulson

The Porter Family

Shelly, Piper, and Oliver Powell

Chris Rifkin

Ted Rowland

Dorothy Saxe

Aaron Schey — Habatat Galleries Michigan

Cynthia Sears

Sally Silberberg

Preston Singletary

Rebecca Anne Sive

Frances Spivy-Weber and Michael L. Weber

Michael J. Stein

Linda and David Stout

Jacqueline D. Urow and Tom Lynn

Paul Villinski

Sara M. and Michelle Vance Waddell

Patti Warashina

Judith S. Weisman

Myra and Harold Weiss

Todd Wingate and Steven Cason

Estate of Nancy Worden

Malcolm Wright

Denise M. Wynn

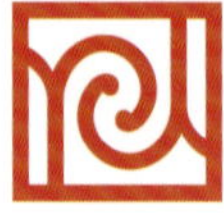

THE JAMES RENWICK ALLIANCE
FOR CRAFT

The James Renwick Alliance for Craft proudly participates in the Renwick Gallery's fiftieth anniversary acquisitions program as we mark our own fortieth anniversary. Founded in 1982, JRACraft has helped the Renwick acquire nearly two hundred artworks for the museum's permanent collection and supported fellowships, catalogues, educational programming, dozens of exhibitions, and the 2015 renovation. We celebrate the Renwick's goals of increasing representation and diversity in its collection, and the generosity of our supporters has allowed JRACraft to help the Renwick achieve this objective. We express our gratitude to all who joined this effort and look forward to fifty more years of exploration, inspiration, and dialogue from this expanded collection.

JAMES RENWICK CIRCLE

Diamond
Nedra and Peter Agnew
Fleur Bresler
Michele A. Manatt and Wolfram Anders
Gwen and Jerry Paulson

Gold
Janice and Harvey Berger
Jan and Carl Fisher
Jere Gibber and J.G. Harrington
Sharon Karmazin
Chris Rifkin
Irene and Bob Sinclair

Silver
Sharon and Bob Buchanan
Miriam and Leon Ellsworth
Brenda Erickson
Anne Mehringer and Terry Beaty
Bonnie and Gil Schwartz
Bobbie Van Haeften
Mikki Van Wyk

Bronze
Char Beales
Barbara and Arnold Berlin
Cynthia Boyer
Susan and Steven Bralove
Diane Charnov
Elizabeth Doyle
Marilyn Falik
Marsha Gold
Carol and Joe Green
Jaimianne and Anthony Jacobin
Mickey and Stephen Kurzbard
Sandy and Norman Mitchell
Michael Monroe
Rebecca Ravenal and Stephen Costello
Karen and Michael Rotenberg
Susan and Fred Sanders
Jeffrey Spahn
Lenel Srochi-Meyerhoff and John Meyerhoff
Jacqueline D. Urow
Pati Young

Partners
Susan Buffone, Rebecca Cross, Leslie Ferrin, Betsy Holland, Randi Jacobs (deceased),
Clemmer Montague, Carol Terris, Andrea and Joseph Uravitch, Barbara Wolanin

The James Renwick Alliance for Craft celebrates and advances American craft and craft artists by fostering education, connoisseurship, and public appreciation through programs, educational trips, publications, and recognition of excellence in the field.

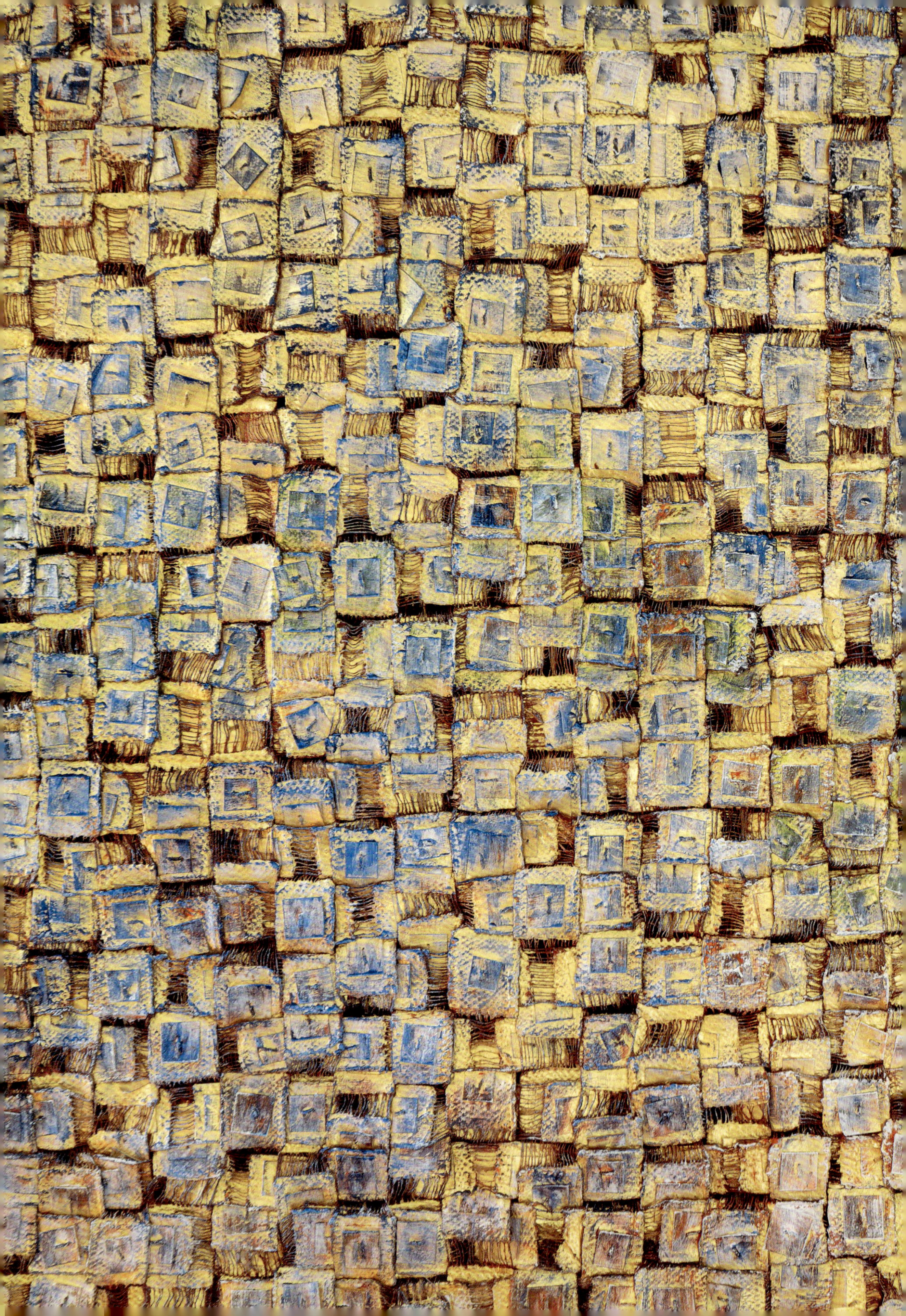

DIRECTOR'S FOREWORD

During this transformative moment in America and American craft, we contemplate the past, present, and future of the Renwick Gallery in its fiftieth year. In 1972, the Renwick opened as a Smithsonian museum dedicated to craft and design, marking an important time in the cultural life of this city and nation. The first purpose-built art museum in the United States was reimagined as a home to "showcase the creative achievements of Americans past and present in design, craft, and the decorative arts," as stated by founding director Lloyd Herman. Today, we push that idea further, to create a more welcoming space for all, and one more fully "Dedicated to Art," as the entablature above the Renwick's entrance proclaims. These goals drove the efforts behind the fiftieth anniversary program, which aimed to further the museum's inclusive and inventive atmosphere through its objects and its craft community.

When the Renwick opened its doors half a century ago, it was a historic structure brought back to life. Just a few years prior, in 1969, it was added to the National Register of Historic Places. It was designated a National Historic Landmark in 1971 and then named the Renwick Gallery in honor of its architect, James Renwick Jr., who designed the Smithsonian Castle and then the Renwick in 1859 in a French-inspired style with American touches that earned it the name the "American Louvre." Here one could find space and quiet to roam, while taking in remarkable architecture and objects that questioned definitions of art and craft. Early special exhibitions focused on a range of design, craft, and decorative arts, from handmade furniture and Pueblo pottery to wide-ranging surveys comprised of objects made by craftspeople from all over the nation. Since then, the museum has highlighted extraordinary work by artists rising to prominence, helping to further the careers of many, including Wendell Castle, Dale Chihuly, Sam Maloof, Maria Martinez, and Judith Schaechter. This defined the character of the Renwick and solidified its importance in the growing national craft conversation. The objects collected and the exhibitions organized over those first fifty years paralleled the development of the American studio craft movement and its communal and pioneering spirit, a spirit that continues today with the ever-changing landscape of contemporary craft.

Now the Renwick Gallery, as the flagship museum of American craft, is a driving force in this conversation. Following the great success of the special exhibition *Wonder* in 2015, which transformed the newly renovated museum into an immersive artwork, the Renwick has continued to surprise and delight audiences while achieving national critical praise. The boundary-breaking vision and leadership of the museum continues today with Nora Atkinson as the Fleur and Charles Bresler Curator-in-Charge and Mary Savig as the Lloyd Herman Curator of Craft. Since joining the museum in 2014, Atkinson has brought creativity and energy to exhibitions and collecting efforts that continue to point to new directions in the field of contemporary craft. In 2018, *No Spectators: The Art of Burning Man* brought cutting-edge artwork created at the annual desert gathering to the nation's capital for the first time, expanding the idea of American craft and attracting record-breaking crowds. *Murder Is Her Hobby: Frances Glessner Lee and the Nutshell Studies of Unexplained Death*, in 2017, explored the unexpected intersection between craft and forensic science while telling the story of how a woman co-opted the traditionally feminine craft of dollhouse making to advance the male-dominated field of police investigation. Since 2000, the Renwick Invitational series has highlighted emerging makers who have encouraged us to think differently about materials and making in the world around us. In her introduction to this catalogue, Atkinson sets the stage for the Renwick's first fifty years and discusses its relationship to the transformation of contemporary craft today. While she puts things in perspective, she recognizes the Renwick's exciting role in shaping the future.

Mary Savig joined the Renwick in the beginning of the unprecedented year of 2020. Bringing a deep knowledge of the field and a fresh voice, she developed *This Present Moment: Crafting a Better World* as an exhibition to showcase the fiftieth anniversary program. The exhibition, and her essay in this catalogue, centers on craft's power to show us more

relational, empathetic perspectives. Needed now more than ever, Savig mindfully focuses on diverse and multivocal points of view to foster an engaging experience with artwork that heightens our sensitivities to each other and to the everyday. In the innovative and welcoming spirit of the Renwick's past, she uses the collection to inspire new ways of seeing "home." Through five thematic spaces, starting with the egg, then the nest, house, nation, and universe, Savig illustrates how craft creates avenues for imagining, persistence, resilience, activism, and more.

The final long-form essay offers a restorative way forward for American craft based in Indigenous knowledges that prioritize respect, reciprocity, and responsibility, written by Anya Montiel. Montiel joined the museum in February 2020 as the first Smithsonian American Women's History Initiative–funded curator of American and Native American women's art and craft. Now at our sister institution, the National Museum of the American Indian, full time, during her time with us Montiel played a key role in expanding the museum's holdings of Native American craft by more than 80 percent and paved the way for future scholarship in this area. In fact, efforts made during the fiftieth anniversary campaign have brought this expansion to approximately 130 percent. Accompanying the curators' essays are written reflections by several artists, who offer us insight into how they feel their work relates to the past, present, and future of craft.

They contemplate the humanity in their work and the people who experience it. Lastly, Savig recognizes the Bernstein–Chernoff Collection of Sculptural Wood Art with an essay that takes us into the collectors' home and offers a glimpse into their meaningful collecting practice. Together, these essays and this catalogue pay tribute to the Renwick's first fifty years, highlight the achievements of the present, and inspire us to imagine a better future.

To help us celebrate this program, it is my pleasure to welcome First Lady Jill Biden in the role of Honorary Patron of the Fiftieth Anniversary of the Renwick Gallery. The Renwick has enjoyed a very special relationship with first ladies over the years, especially given its proximity to the White House. It was First Lady Jacqueline Kennedy who rescued the building from demolition in 1962 by rallying preservationists. Decades later, President George H. W. Bush proclaimed 1993 the Year of American Craft: A Celebration of the Creative Work of the Hand; that same year, under a new administration, First Lady Hillary Clinton invited former Renwick curator Michael Monroe to organize the exhibition *The White House Collection of American Crafts*, on view at the White House and the National Museum of American Art (now the Smithsonian American Art Museum) before touring across the country until 2000. More recently, First Lady Michelle Obama served as Honorary Patron of the Renwick's reopening in 2015. We are grateful for Dr. Biden's endorsement and support from the White House as we move into the Renwick's next half-century of championing American ingenuity and creativity.

We could not have reached this milestone without the support of passionate friends of the Renwick, who have allowed us to build the collection, expand its range and scope, and foster the creativity of artists who are essential to the future of craft. As part of our fiftieth anniversary celebrations, we kicked off an acquisition campaign with a goal of adding at least one hundred significant craft objects to the collection, with a particular aim of increasing representation by women and artists of color. Under the exceptional leadership of our campaign cochairs, Carolyn Mazloomi and Myra Weiss, we made significant strides in diversifying our holdings and exceeded our goal by over 100 percent.

We are grateful to our many donors — artists, collectors, and dealers — from across the country and here in the Washington, DC, area who helped us reach and then exceed this goal. Notable collection gifts were made by many, including Judith Chernoff and Jeffrey Bernstein, whose transformative gift of their sculptural wood art collection joins the remarkable Fleur and Charles Bresler Collection of Turned and Carved Wood, which established the Renwick Gallery as one of the preeminent public collections of contemporary wood art in the United States. Other major donors include Fleur Bresler, Sharon and Bob Buchanan, Deena and Jerry Kaplan, Colleen and John Kotelly, Clemmer and David Montague, and the Nancy Worden Estate.

We are also thankful for the tremendous support of members of the James Renwick Alliance for Craft who, under the leadership of President J.G. Harrington and Director Jaimianne Jacobin, helped fund the exhibition and sponsored several purchases of new works selected by the Renwick curators. Additionally, the generous and enduring Windgate Foundation endowment, dedicated to acquiring artworks by living craft artists, affirms and supports the Renwick Gallery's leadership role in advocating for a diverse and inclusive view of contemporary American craft through its collecting, research, and exhibition program. And, finally, we thank Cindy Miscikowski for generously underwriting this beautiful catalogue. Collectively, our donors and supporters have helped the Renwick build a robust national collection and platform to showcase the best of American craft.

Building on its innovative legacy and embracing the tremendous change encompassing the present, I believe the museum's next fifty years will also astonish. The artwork being crafted and collected now is shaping an even bolder future, one that will help us better understand ourselves, each other, and the world around us. *

Stephanie Stebich
The Margaret and Terry Stent Director
Smithsonian American Art Museum

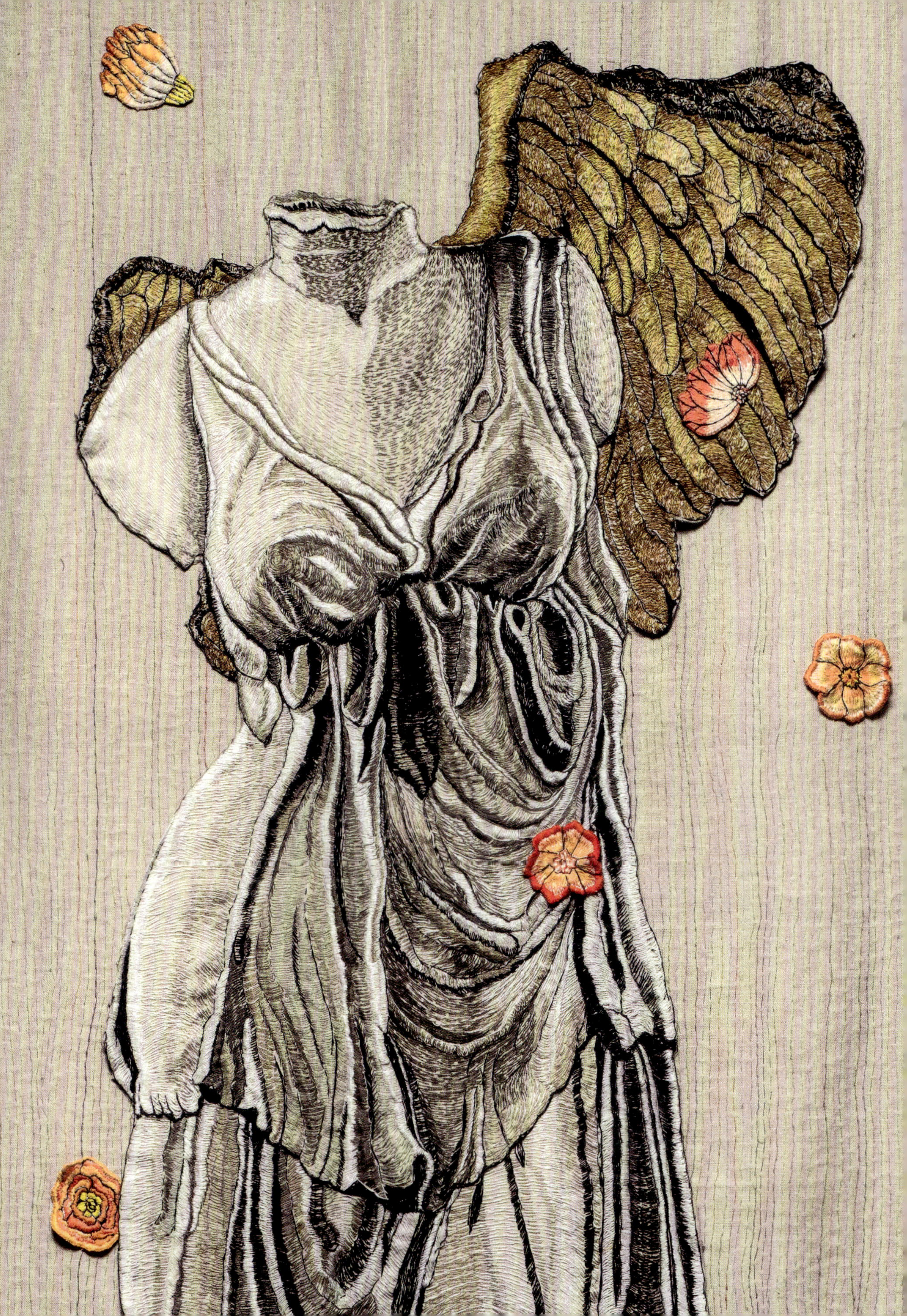

ACKNOWLEDGMENTS

The Renwick's fiftieth anniversary program kicked off in January 2020, just as I was settling into my new job as the Lloyd Herman Curator of Craft. Almost as soon as I began to explore the Renwick's collection and history, the COVID-19 pandemic upended everyday life. From my home office, with my elderly pug, Betty, curled up at my feet, I was able to see the history and possibility of American craft from an unexpected vantage point. Craft has always been a measure of the present moment. This is because craft is inherently a measure of who we are — our labor and our memory. It has been an enormously humbling experience to linger on fifty years of presence and possibility at the Renwick.

Even without a global pandemic, the task of planning an ambitious acquisition campaign to acquire one hundred new artworks, organize an exhibition, and produce a catalogue would have been a difficult undertaking. The process required a backward approach of developing themes around an unknown checklist of artworks. Likewise, we embraced the opportunity to document the contours of the present moment, with acquisitions like face masks, that would have been impossible to anticipate in January 2020. The success of this endeavor relies on the collective efforts of many, many people. Together, our efforts measure our hopes for a better world.

First and foremost, I would like to thank Stephanie Stebich, the Margaret and Terry Stent Director, for her ongoing advocacy and guidance of the Renwick Gallery. It is a privilege to work for a director so well versed in the history of craft in the United States. I am also thankful for my time spent with the inimitable Robyn Kennedy, head administrator, whose institutional knowledge (and personal anecdotes) enlivened my understanding of the Renwick's history. This catalogue is dedicated to Robyn and her remarkable forty years of federal service.

A core cast of bold and astute colleagues helped this complex project take flight. We began with the Renwick's Collection Plan devised by Nora Atkinson, the Fleur and Charles Bresler Curator-in-Charge, to represent the profound diversity, spirit, and relevance of craft in the United States. My heartfelt gratitude goes to Nora for leading our team and entrusting the exhibition to my care. The exhibition checklist was greatly shaped by both Nora and Anya Montiel, now curator of history and culture at the National Museum of the American Indian. Nora and Anya are my dear cocurators whose incandescent ideas are woven into every element of this project. Christie Davis, major gifts officer, helped build and guide our national network of trusted advisors and donors. Eunice Park Kim, an extraordinarily clever designer, heightened the emotional resonance of the exhibition themes and solved a host of practical challenges. Julianna White, editor, is a craftsperson of language who built connections among each of the essays in this catalogue, and vastly improved my own essay. The wondrous Elana Hain, collections manager, was the heartbeat of this entire endeavor — we are all indebted to her scrupulous and compassionate contributions to every single facet of this project.

A small and mighty team warmly welcomed me into the Renwick's fold: Michael Sperow, exhibition specialist, is a multitalented colleague and virtuoso woodworker in his own right; Rebecca Sullesta, operations specialist, has remained mindful of visitor and volunteer experiences; Lonnie Upchurch, the Renwick's assistant building manager, kept the facilities in shape throughout the pandemic; Hannah Owh hit the ground running as our new management specialist; as well as our predoctoral fellows from 2020 to 2022, Allison Robinson, Matthew Limb, and Sara Morris.

The scope of this project was ambitious and contingent on the skill, creativity, and patience of many artists, donors, advisors, and colleagues. It was an honor to build the acquisition campaign with a committee cochaired by fierce craft advocates Carolyn Mazloomi and Myra Weiss. This committee propelled us to exceed our goal of one hundred new acquisitions and led us to unexpected discoveries. Thanks to all of the committee members: Nedra and Peter Agnew, Sharon and Bob Buchanan, Judith Chernoff and Jeffrey Bernstein, Susan Cummins, Fran Dubrowski, Miriam and Leon Ellsworth, Brenda Erickson, Mary Anne Fray, Laura and Todd Galaida, Diane and Marc Grainer, J.G. Harrington and Jere Gibber, Judy Heller, Candace and Michael Humphreys, Jaimianne Jacobin, Jerry Kaplan,

Sharon Karmazin, Colleen and John Kotelly, Lorne Lassiter and Gary Ferraro, Alida Latham, Joe Logan, Wendy MacGaw, Michele Manatt, Alison Milliman, Clemmer Montague, Joel Mulhauser, Merrily Orsini, Gwen and Jerry Paulson, Jerry Peters, Francine Pilloff, David Porter, Chris Rifkin, Ted Rowland, Dorothy Saxe, Sharon and Fred Schomer, Cynthia Sears, Larry Sibrack, Rebecca Anne Sive, Michael Stein, Tim Tate, Barbara Tober, Jackie Urow, Sarah Vance Waddell, Judy Weisman, Patti Warashina, Frances and Michael Weber, Todd Wingate, and Driek Zirinsky.

I am also deeply thankful to Cindy Miscikowski for making this catalogue possible. I am pleased to recognize the Windgate Foundation for providing funds to acquire works as part of the campaign and in honor of one of my curatorial predecessors, Kenneth R. Trapp. I owe much gratitude to the James Renwick Alliance for Craft, especially J.G. Harrington and Jaimianne Jacobin, whose enthusiasm sustained our efforts in countless ways, including the acquisition of some major artworks by Susie Ganch, Roberto Lugo, and Preston Singletary. All these efforts were energized by SAAM's Development team, led by Donna Rim. Michelle Atkins, Christie Davis, and Elizabeth Daoust, along with the Special Events team of Chavon Jones, Mary Beth Maggio, and Andrew Rondinone, have ensured that the Renwick celebrates its anniversary in style and will continue to thrive for the next fifty years.

I am especially thankful for the heroic work of the Registrar's department, led by Melissa Kroning. Christopher Kirages, with the assistance of Austin McNellage and Cassandra Belliston, facilitated the shipments of more than 150 new acquisitions and donations, ranging from a case of 178 acorns to a speedy go-kart, and Jim Concha and Claire Denny, with the assistance of intern Grace Cho, managed several acquisition reviews and provided safe storage for all the new artworks. Richard Sorenson and Aubrey Vinson oversaw the photography and helped secure quality images of the works illustrated in this catalogue. Heather Delemarre coordinated the loans of the promised gifts and Emily Conforto finalized the acquisition paperwork.

The Conservation department, led by Amber Kerr, provided expert care of the wildly diverse mediums represented by the artists, from used Starbucks lids to 3D-printed ceramic vessels, and from a giant neon sign to a spoon made from bison horn. Object conservators Ariel O'Connor and Leah Bright, along with time-based media conservator Daniel Finn, assessed and outlined conservation plans for every artwork acquired.

The Exhibitions team, led by David Gleeson, took on the challenge of a full-building "inhab-itation" made possible with the strength of Eunice's designs and the creative graphic work of Grace Lopez and Nathaniel Phillips. The exhi-bition posed numerous challenges, including the installation of a monumental spiral stair-case and evocative lighting techniques. I thank Martin Kotler, Jenna Michael, Adam Rice, Caleb Plattner, Nick Primo, Scott Rosenfeld, Harvey Sandler, and Lily Winer for bringing to life such a beautiful project.

I unabashedly love the editing process because I get to work with the Publications team, led by Theresa Slowik and Tiffany Farrell. Book designer Karen Siatras took on the challenge of lacing together a diverse range of images and essays into an exciting catalogue that speaks to our present moment. Julianna and Karen received invaluable assistance from Rosie Hammack and Tiffany Farrell, as well as from our copublisher col-leagues at D Giles Limited.

The Education department, led by Carol Wilson, provided insightful feedback on our interpretative strategies. I thank Joanna Marsh and Anne Showalter for their thoughtful reviews of the exhibition script and video pro-duction. Likewise, the department of External Affairs and Digital Strategies, led by Sara Snyder, built the scaffolding for the exhibi-tion's vibrant online presence and an array of virtual and in-person programs. I thank Laura Baptiste, Amy Fox, Amy Hutchins, Howard Kaplan, Gloria Kenyon, Carlos Parada, and Ashley Reese for their persistent advancement of the Renwick's mission to broad audiences.

I thank my lovely curatorial colleagues at the Smithsonian American Art Museum for helping build and providing feedback on our acquisi-tion priorities: Laura Augustin, Saisha Grayson, Eleanor Harvey, Melissa Ho, John Jacob, Karen

Lemmey, Alex Mann, Sarah Newman, E. Carmen Ramos, Leslie Umberger, and Claudia Zapata. Along similar lines, I thank one of my most beloved colleagues and the pillar of research on American Art, Amelia Goerlitz, the interim head of Research and Scholars, for her support of the Windgate Fellowship opportunity.

As with everything, the administrative team, led by Doug Wilde, kept this project on track and within budget. I am grateful for the work and counsel of David Voyles, Kate Fernstrom, and Kelly DeFilippis. I am also eternally grateful for the diligent work of Erin Bryan, perhaps the most organized person on this planet.

Numerous colleagues and initiatives at the Smithsonian helped shape the acquisition campaign and exhibition. The American Women's History Initiative, cochaired by Dorothy Moss and Kate Lemay, provided funds for the Renwick to acquire Sonya Clark's *Monumental*. The AWHI also helped us acquire, with the Cooper Hewitt, the pivotal work by Tanya Aguiñiga, *Metabolizing the Border*. I am especially grateful for Christina De León, associate curator of US Latino Design at Cooper Hewitt, who successfully shepherded our proposal through numerous channels. I would also like to thank Diana Baird N'Diaye and her team at the Center for Folklife and Cultural Heritage for involving the Renwick in its Smithsonian One: African American Summit, which yielded numerous new acquisitions. I am also honored to work for the Secretary of the Smithsonian, Lonnie G. Bunch III, who guided the Smithsonian through the pandemic and created initiatives to advance justice and equity within the Smithsonian and beyond.

So many colleagues and friends shared their wisdom at various points in this project. During challenging times, I took comfort in this wide network: the two anonymous peer reviewers, Lloyd Herman, Michael Monroe, Helen Drutt English, Caroline Kipp, Karen Patterson, Josh T. Franco, Liza Kirwin, Susan Cary, Rihoko Ueno, Erin Kinhart, Leila Cartier, Monica Hampton, Glenn Adamson, Susie Silbert, Elizabeth Essner, Emily Zilber, Donté Hayes, Kevin Pourier, Kit Paulson, Linda Lopez, Julia Kwon, Carolyn Crump, Sharon Kerry-Harlan, David Harper Clemons, Tim Tate, Annet Couwenberg, Bisa Butler, Steven Young Lee, Paul Sacaridiz, Alyssa Erickson, Jennifer Bindman, Julie Mihalisin, Stewart Brand, Gary Snyder, Sharon Massey, Paul Villinski, Leslie Ferrin, Lucy Lacoste, Mindy Solomon, Martha Sielman, Rachel White, Diana Greenwold, Sara Clugage, Jennifer Zwilling, Sharbreon Plummer, Peter Held, Anna Walker, Ben Gillespie, Ayumi Horie, Julie Siglin, Sarah Turner, Kathryn Hall, Erica Collins, Diane Charnov, Faythe Levine, Kayleigh Perkov, Renée Ater, David Smith, Lewis Wexler, Claire Warner, Marilyn Zapf, and Stephanie Smutz Moore.

Finally, I relied on so many family members — near and far — for support during the pandemic. I extend my deepest personal thanks to Will and John for bringing such love, joy, and noise to my life. ✳ MS

THIS PRE
MOMENT
USED TO
THE UNIM
FUTURE

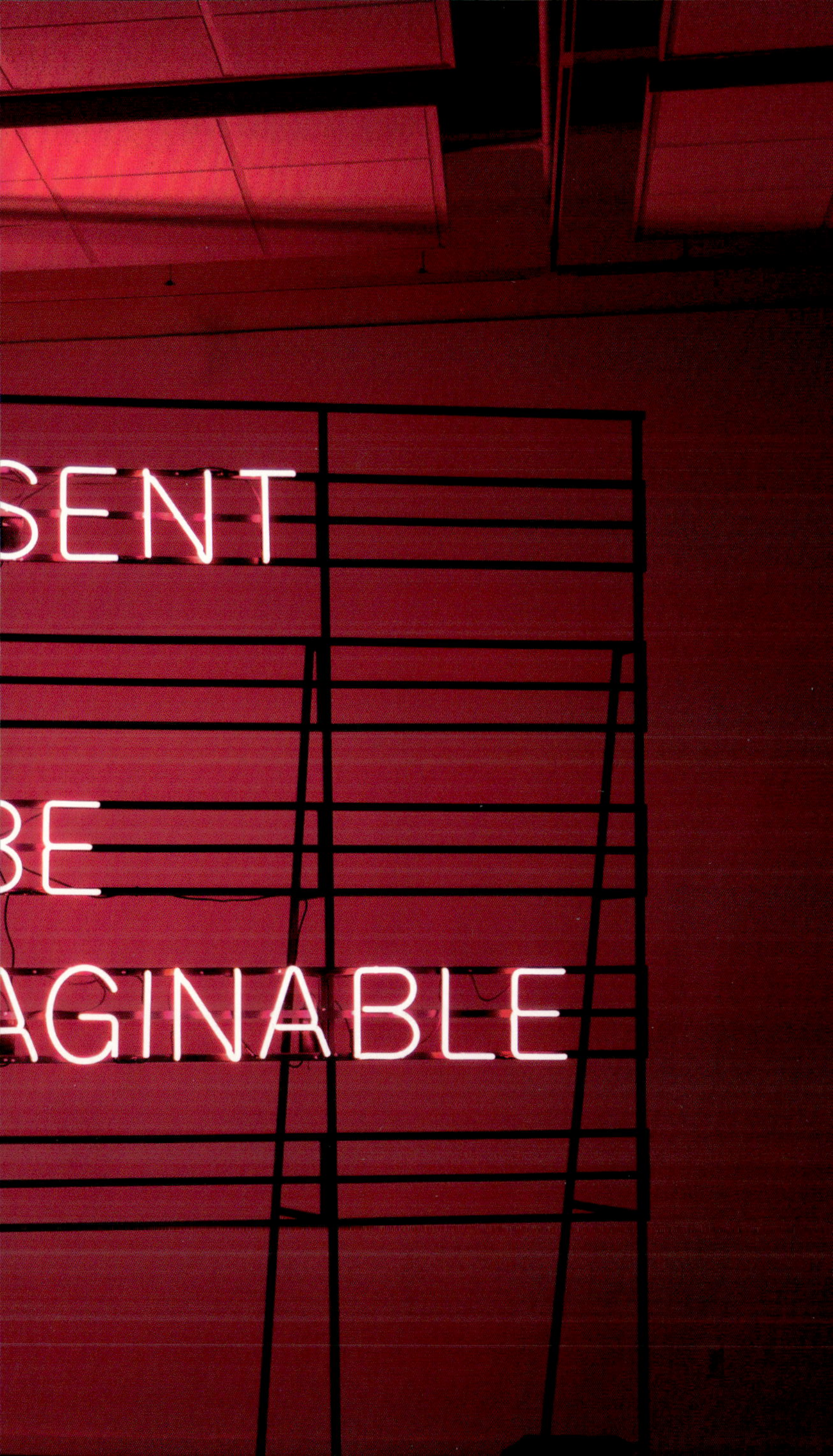
SENT
BE
AGINABLE

A FOUNDATION FOR

BY NORA ATKINSON

This present moment
Used to be
The unimaginable future. — Stewart Brand, from *The Clock of the Long Now*

The profundity of this quote, appropriated by artist Alicia Eggert, enchants me. The words come from Stewart Brand, revolutionary futurist founder of the *Whole Earth Catalog*, taken from his book *The Clock of the Long Now* (1999), which proposes an approach to living intentionally with a ten-thousand-year clock in mind, combatting the fast-paced "twitter feed" frenzy of social media and the anxiety of the twenty-four-hour news cycle.[1] In Eggert's work (CAT. 37; see pp. 114–15), neon words blink on and off revealing only some words, "This / Moment / Used to Be / The / Future," then all, "This PRESENT / Moment / Used to Be / The UNIMAGINABLE / Future," casting brilliant pink light onto the viewer and the surrounds — pink,

the artist explains, as a call out to the Me Too movement of 2017, another present moment that seemed unimaginable once.[2]

Eggert's treatment of the quotation, which owes much to Bruce Nauman's linguistic games in neon, elucidates what I find so compelling about it. In this declaration, Brand manages to weave present, past, and future together indivisibly, into a fabric that wraps around us. The two modifiers (to me essential to its meaning) transform what might otherwise be a mundane platitude into something transcendent: "Unimaginable" may be one of the most imaginative words in the dictionary. Like entreating you not to think about pink rhinoceroses, it dares you to dream. "Present"

THE FUTURE

THE RENWICK AT 50

begs the questions, *Whose presence? Who here is bearing witness in this moment? To whom are we responsible?* It reminds us that time is perceived subjectively, ever malleable—extended or compressed—in our minds. In short, Brand's pithy truism is a meditation not only on the passage and continuity of time, but on our own agency, and the responsibility that comes with it.

In the long now, as the Renwick celebrates its fiftieth anniversary as our nation's craft museum and looks to the future, amid an ongoing global pandemic and time of social reckoning, it feels all the more important to acknowledge that this, in fact, is the great, essential role that artists play in our world: to bear witness and dare us to dream of an unimaginable future. When Sonya Clark presents us with the quiet power of her tour de force, *Monumental* (CAT. 36; see pp. 110–11), the giant white flag inspired by the dishcloth

waved in surrender at Appomattox, woven in the scale of the Star-Spangled Banner, she dares us to dream of an America that discarded the Confederate battle flag in favor of a symbol of reconciliation. This is an America in which humility, not racism and hate, has been cultivated. When April Surgent accompanies research scientists to the farthest and most desolate reaches of the ocean, returning transformed, to share her experience through cameo-engravings (like those so often practiced on seashells), she uses the metaphor of her medium to reflect light on Earth's fragility and our impact on it. And when ceramists like Ehren Tool make cups about war and politics (Fig. 1), or fiber artists like Carolyn Crump (CAT. 87; see p. 178), Julia Kwon (CAT. 1), and Katrina Mitten (CAT. 2) make face masks that simultaneously celebrate their heritage while combatting the "dual pandemics" of COVID-19 and systemic racism, they invite us to have difficult conversations that help us to see each other as people, despite the polarization that divides our nation. As they bear witness, their work personalizes these issues and shows us a more compassionate way of seeing; there is something about craft, particularly about the handmade, that naturally aligns with human empathy. But before we understand how this work is leading us forward, let us first look back to the legacies that have brought us to where we are today.

A BOUNDARY-BREAKING LEGACY

In 1965, shortly following First Lady Jacqueline Kennedy's successful crusade to save the historic character of Lafayette Square, the grand Second Empire building on the corner of 17th and Pennsylvania, which originally housed the Corcoran Gallery of Art, was gifted to the Smithsonian under its eighth Secretary, S. Dillon Ripley. Ripley took office in 1964 with a mission to "awaken all Americans

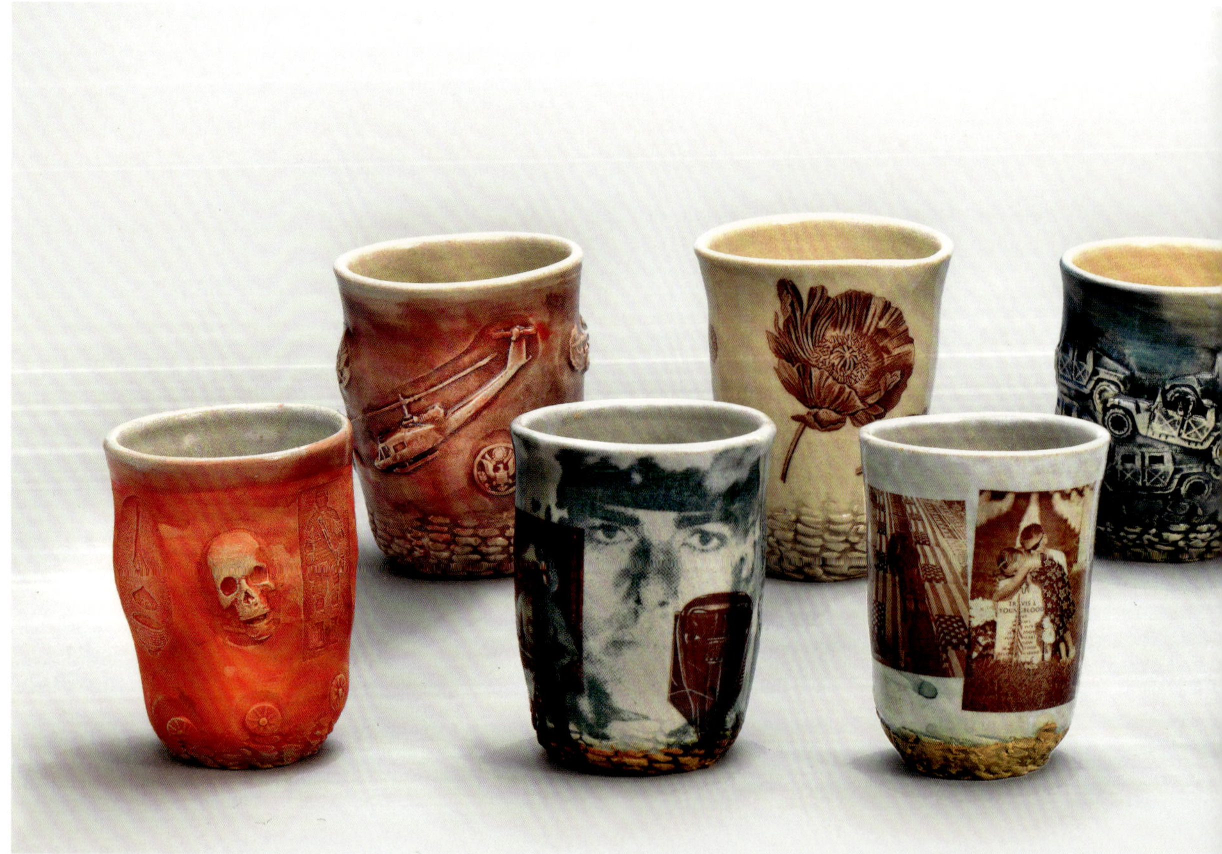

Fig. 1 Ehren Tool, *204 of Thousands*, 2014–15, stoneware with glaze and decals, approx. 5 × diam. 3 ½ in. each, Gift of the artist in honor of the people who give the work meaning, 2015.35

to the fact that the Smithsonian belonged to them, not to a bunch of curmudgeons on Capitol Hill,"[3] during a time of great upheaval and disparity in our country. Like today, our nation seemed to be moving quickly toward an inflection point in the mid-1960s. While Pucci-clad Braniff Airways stewardesses were "air-stripping" their way into the cultural imagination in space-race-inspired ensembles of questionable taste, the American war in Vietnam was escalating. That spring in

Alabama, not far from where the quilters of Gee's Bend would later be "discovered," six hundred civil rights marchers were blocked and beaten as they traveled from Selma to Montgomery in protest of Black voter suppression. It would be 1968 before we would see President Lyndon B. Johnson sign the Civil Rights Act into law, 1969 before Neil Armstrong would walk on the moon, and 1972 before the Senate would pass the Equal Rights Amendment. How far we have come, and yet

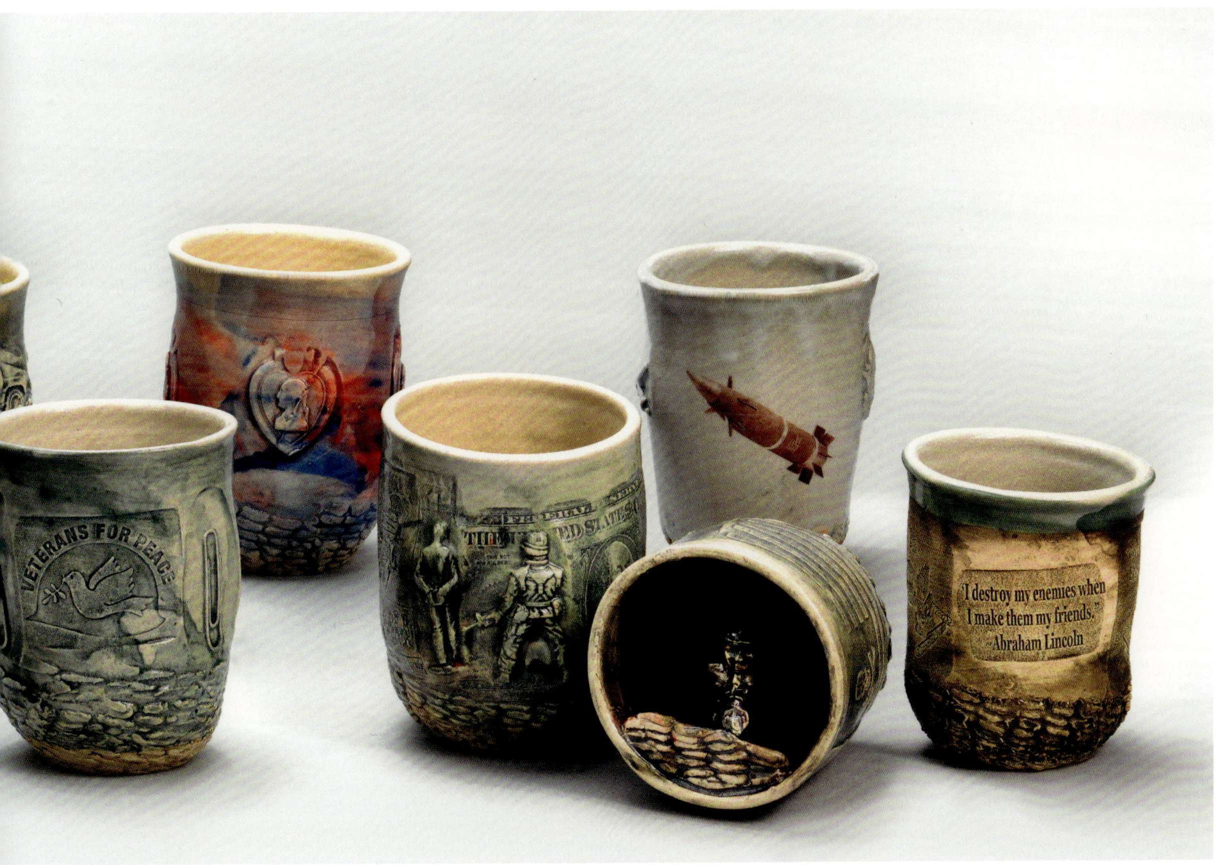

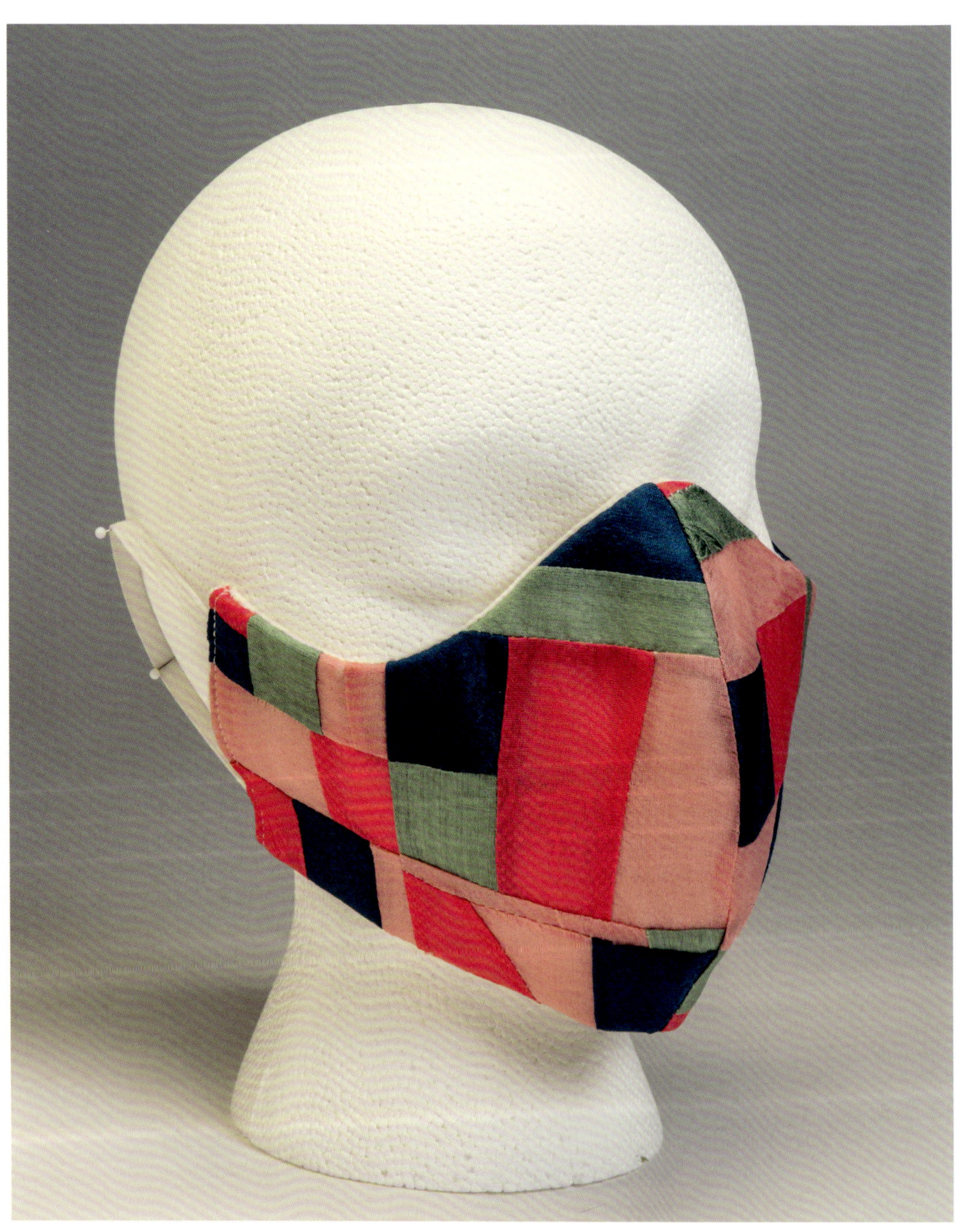

CAT. 1 Julia Kwon, *Unapologetically Asian*, 2020, Korean silk, cotton canvas, muslin, and elastic, overall: 5 × 14 × 1 5/8 in.

CAT. 2 Katrina Mitten, *MMIW*, 2020, cotton with ribbon, Czech seed beads, bone, and shell, overall: 4 ¼ × 41 ⅛ × 1 ⅝ in.

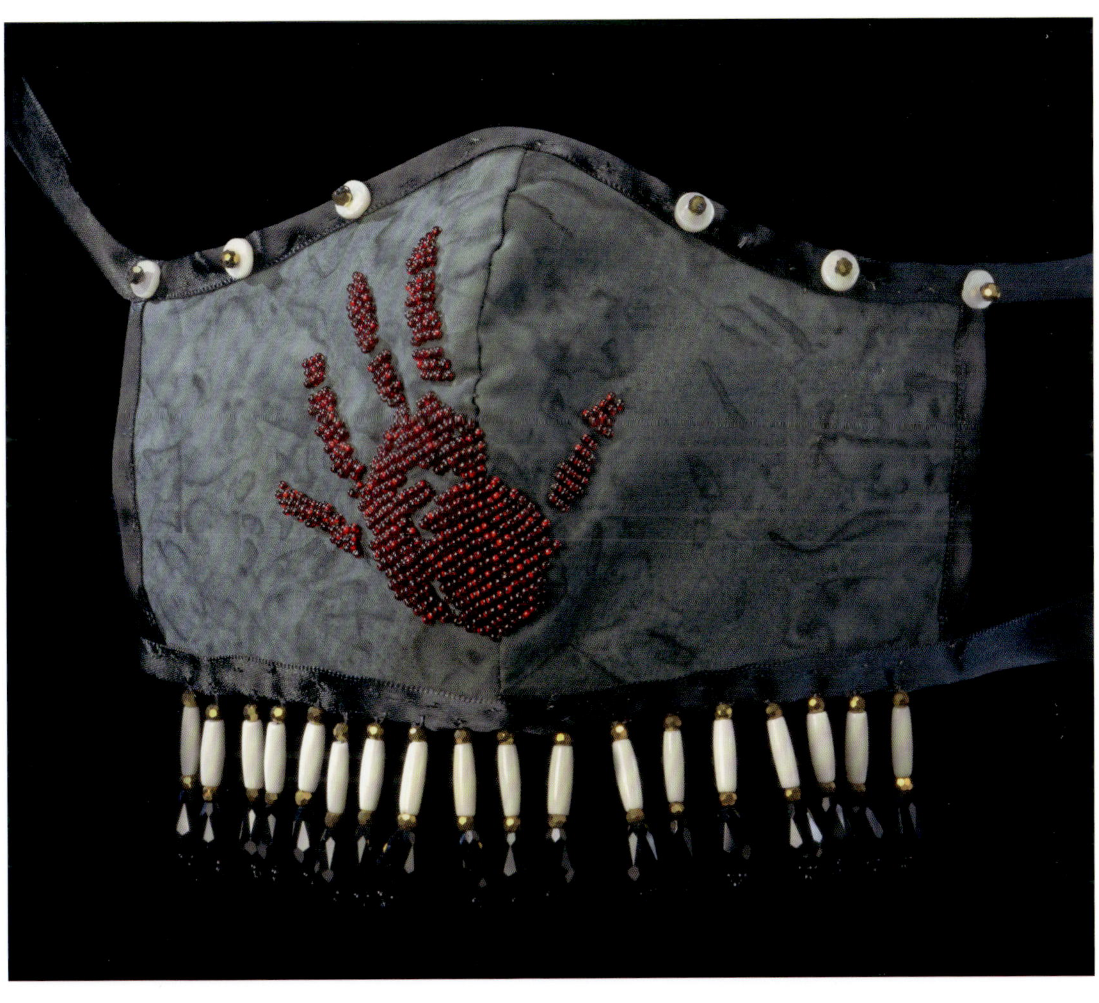

CAT. 3   Pencil Brothers
(Ken Cory and Leslie
LePere), *Egypt*, 1974,
copper, champlevé enamel,
rosewood, graphite
on paper, and glass,
4 × 4 × ¾ in.

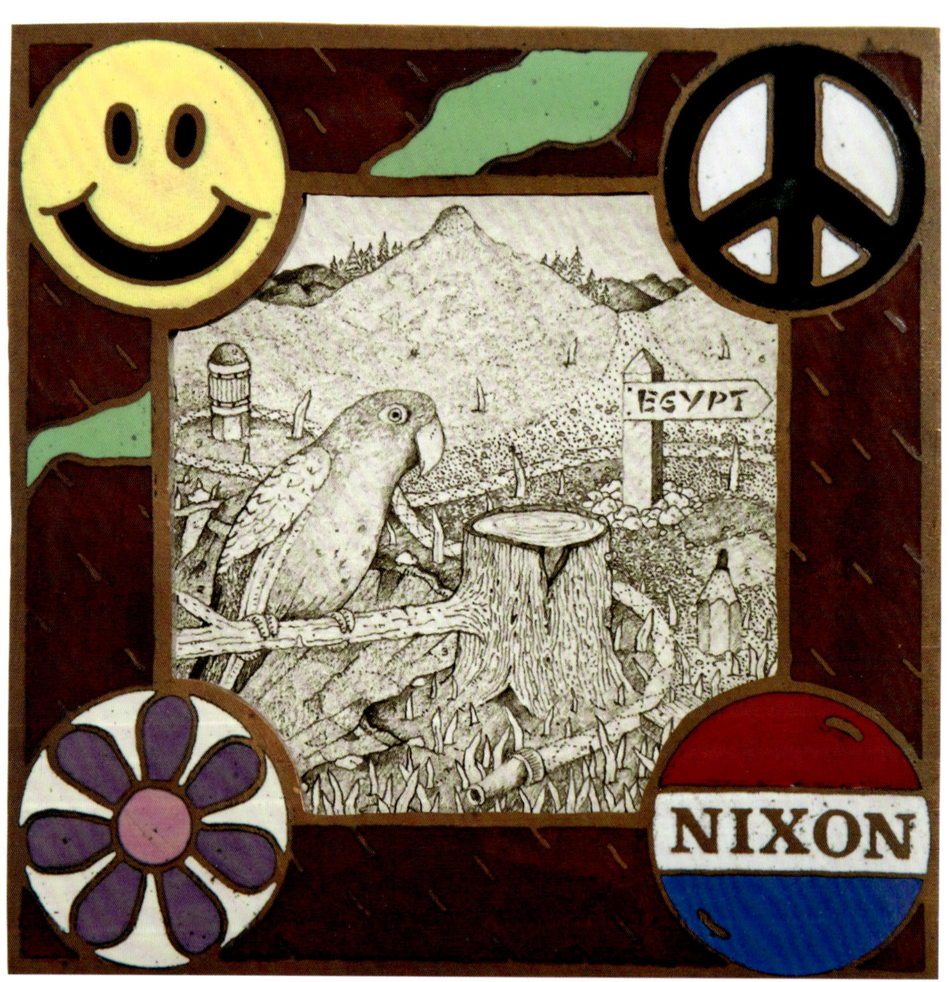
EGYPT
NIXON

how little has changed in the constant struggle toward a better union.

Against that transformative backdrop, in stepped a young curator named Lloyd Herman (then working at the Arts and Industries Building of the Smithsonian), who had a vision for the Renwick, which was under renovation and still in need of a purpose.[4] Herman admired Ripley, who he felt "started really blowing the dust off the place,"[5] and he saw an opportunity in the Renwick's renovation to do the same. Influenced by the 1969 exhibition *Objects: USA*, a wildly popular show that for the first time brought craft into the halls of the National Collection of Fine Arts (now the Smithsonian American Art Museum), Herman submitted a proposal to extend the dynamic program of the Arts and Industries Building to the Renwick, with a focus on contemporary craft, design, and decorative arts. The idea initially met with little interest, tabled in favor of plans for "ho-hum" period rooms, as Herman would later describe. But under director Joshua Taylor at the National Collection of Fine Arts, the proposal resurfaced as the frontrunner. In February 1971, Taylor hired Herman to lead the Renwick's exhibition program, giving him just eleven months to organize the opening shows, without a permanent collection. Herman was up to the task (Fig. 2).

When the Renwick Gallery at last opened its doors fifty years ago in 1972, true to its vision, the inaugural exhibition program resisted easy definitions and boundaries, instead radiating the possibilities of craft and design. In total eight exhibitions graced the galleries within the first few years. The highlighted inaugural exhibition, *Woodenworks*, featured handmade furniture by five now legendary makers: Wharton Esherick, Sam Maloof, George Nakashima, Wendell Castle, and Arthur Espenet Carpenter. Seven other exhibitions included a showcase of objects from Indigenous Peoples of western New Mexico, *Pueblo Pottery: Zuni and Acoma Designs from Smithsonian Collections*; the fanciful *Design Is…*, which explored the nature of design and function, from the nose of the Space Shuttle to fiber art by Kay Sekimachi, presented in towering "futuristic" clear tubes that dotted the gallery (Fig. 3); *The Four Continents*, an exhibition of eighteenth- and nineteenth-century ceramics, glass, porcelain, and metalwork loaned from the Cooper Hewitt Museum of Decorative Arts and Design (now the Cooper Hewitt, Smithsonian Design Museum); *Steuben Glass Works*, a retrospective of the work of Frederick Carder; *Selections from the Index of American Design*; *American Architecture*; *Photographs by the Late Frank Roos*; and, finally, a feature on the building's architect, *James Renwick in Washington*.[6]

This eclectic approach to exhibitions became a hallmark of the Renwick under Herman, who was soon joined by Michael W. Monroe, a young curator with an impeccable eye for design, as the museum developed its identity. Echoing Ripley's vision, Herman

Fig. 2 Renwick Administrator Lloyd E. Herman examines the work of Wendell Castle at the opening of the Renwick Gallery, 1972

Fig. 3 Installation view of *Design Is…*, 1972

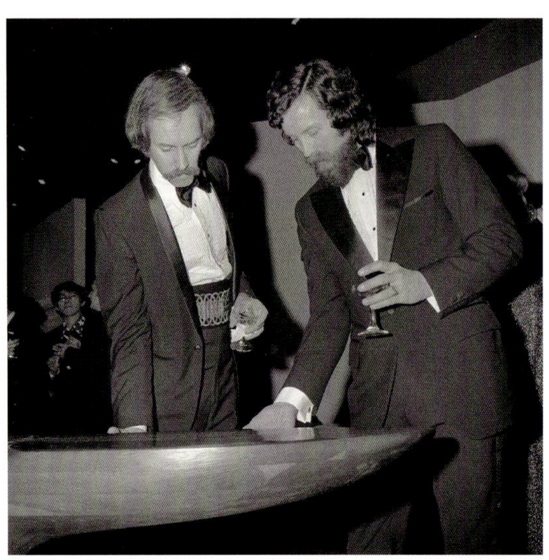

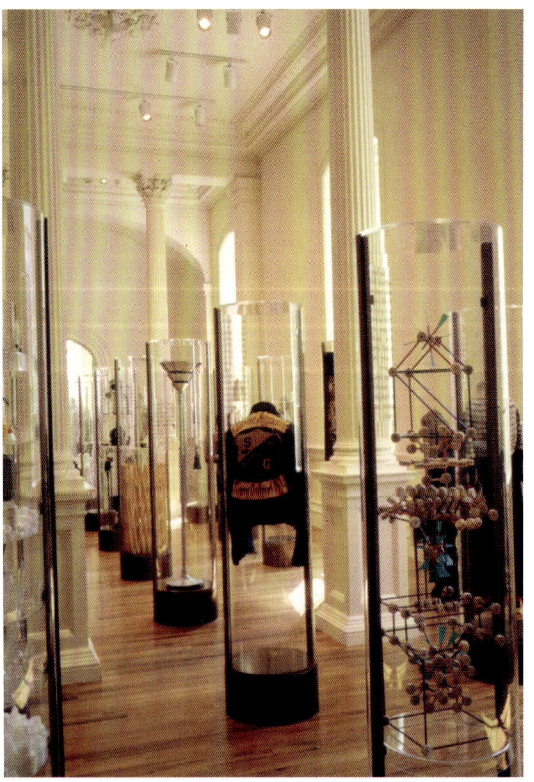

imagined the Grand Salon as a kind of "living room" setting for heads of state and the public and, early on, intended to align exhibits of foreign crafts with state visits by dignitaries at Blair House next door. This, however, proved impractical and was quickly abandoned. When, in 1980, the National Collection of Fine Arts became the National Museum of American Art, the Renwick further honed its program from an international focus to exclusively American work. Though it continued to showcase a mix of craft, design, and decorative arts, craft increasingly took center stage, marking a clearer distinction from its sister institution, the Cooper Hewitt. Yet exhibitions retained the idiosyncratic character Herman charted with encouragement from friend and colleague Paul J. Smith at the Museum of Contemporary Crafts (now the Museum of Arts and Design) in New York. Smith championed the Renwick as a site for "happenings" that often exploited craft's art-world "otherness" to best effect, with explorations that veered into ethnographic, sociological, and poetic territories. Ever pushing the boundaries of its mission, the Renwick showcased art and functional objects, from pieced quilts to playbills to items for preparing food, while promoting the ingenuity and popular appeal of the "American craftsman."

Though originally envisioned as a non-collecting branch of the National Collection of Fine Arts, Herman desired to collect the remarkable craft he saw being created in real time around him. Following *Craft Multiples* in 1975–76, he took the chance to bring this proposition forward with the craftspeople in the exhibition who were eager to donate these inexpensive works to the museum. His efforts were soon bolstered by an external support group he helped to found, the James Renwick Alliance, which celebrates its fortieth anniversary this year as the Renwick celebrates its fiftieth. Today, the Renwick's collection counts more than twenty-three hundred objects, catalogued loosely within the traditional five craft media—wood, fiber, ceramics, metal, and glass—and ranging from time-honored utilitarian forms such as pottery, turned wood, basketry, and quilts, to large-scale sculpture, a staircase, and even a functional go-kart. Most of these are superbly handmade, the output of baby boomers emerging from the rapidly expanding medium-specific MFA programs that proliferated across the nation in the post-war period. Yet as accomplished and truly awe-inspiring as many are, in the contemporary context the vast majority belie an aging definition of craft, and a very narrow field of producers honored in that time. In short, they represent characteristics that perhaps define the American studio craft movement, within a larger field steadily shifting away from an emphasis on skill, bravado, and craft-for-art's-sake toward a contemporary emphasis on social practice, particularly as it regards identity politics, the influence of the Do-It-Yourself movement, and the popularity of Instagram-worthy large-scale installations promulgated by the internet.

A FAREWELL TO THE AMERICAN STUDIO CRAFT MOVEMENT

At the 2019 Haystack Summer Conference, Craft and Legacy, colleagues and I again discussed the loaded question that has plagued the field for seemingly a decade: Can we finally say the American studio craft movement is over? Though the topic never made it to the stage, I would like to put this question to bed once and for all. The studio craft movement was a discrete time in American history, now past. This proclamation genuinely distresses many in the craft community, yet as paradoxical as it may seem to them, as the curator-in-charge of one of the leading craft museums in the nation, this rather excites me.

Why? Because the studio craft movement is only a chapter in the story of craft, not its beginning or its end. As the Renwick Gallery's soaring attendance over the past five years can attest, craft is thriving in America today, though it does so under new terms, having to do with changes to both the means and the ends of the game. The means—the landscape of American secondary education, once the bedrock upon which the studio craft story was built—have shifted. Some will tell you craft programs have died out with the retirement of legendary professors like Mary Lee Hu in the University of Washington's jewelry department, whose position was never filled. Instead, the jewelry program was absorbed into the larger rubric of 3D4M (3-Dimensional Forum), a consortium lumping ceramics, glass, and sculpture together into one framework, emphasizing concept over medium specificity, making study of skilled making possible, but not primary. Leaving the university, degree in hand, undoubtedly there are fewer opportunities today for craftspeople to enter the tenure track, though this should be contextualized alongside countless other liberal arts programs suffering the same fate, as universities push to promote math, science, technology, and engineering programs and face increasing pressure to generate revenue.[7] But, as a result, the current generation has found new avenues to pursue craft skills. And the ends — the reason why artists today practice craft — have also shifted. As provocateur Garth Clark opines, there is an ever-diminishing marketplace for fine craft today; though for the shrewd, there is space to be found in the rich arena of design, or for the lucky few, in his opinion, in art.[8] Students ask, How can I make a living at craft? My answer is simple: Craft is a calling, like teaching, not a money-maker, and that is precisely why it is valuable today. Sure, with a particularly entrepreneurial spirit, there are avenues in which you can succeed, but pursue it because we live a little less richly, a little less fully, without it.

The question, then, is not *if* the American studio craft movement is over, but *when* exactly it ended. Some could easily argue the writing was on the wall around 2002, when the American Craft Museum (previously the Museum of Contemporary Crafts, until 1979) adopted its new identity as the Museum of Arts and Design, or in 2003, when the California College of Arts and Crafts followed suit, trimming craft from its name to become the California College of the Arts (despite artist L. J. Roberts's infamous intervention to re-insert it).[9] Personally, I place the ending of studio craft in 2005, at the symbolic ascendance of a new dominant craft paradigm coming of age with the birth of Etsy, but that is simply one milestone with the convenience of a solid date. Following that, in 2008, Faythe Levine debuted her book (then film, in 2009) *Handmade Nation*, further rooting a new idea of craft in the popular imagination. The same year, Garth Clark voiced his thoughts in the lecture "How Envy Killed the Crafts," given at the Museum of Contemporary Craft in Portland, an institution that closed in 2016 after partnering with the Pacific Northwest College of Art in attempt to extend its existence. The shift was clear in Glenn Adamson's now-comical talk "Goodbye to Craft" in 2012, and at the Candice Groot auction, one of the most comprehensive collections of modern ceramics to ever come to sale, which shook the community in 2016 with its disappointing results.[10]

So here is my appeal to our friends in the craft community: we will continue to collect, study, and showcase studio craft and the wondrous objects it birthed, but let us not mourn its passing! With the end of the historical movement comes its reframing. We now have the distance to shape its stories, question its boundaries, and see this period with clarity, to give it the scholarly context it has always craved and deserved. Yet now, we have the freedom to go forward, to embrace a new vision of craft filled with a chorus of voices that speak to our present moment.

THE CRAFT OF NOW

Today, craft flourishes in myriad forms, from frequent nods to the handmade within the field of contemporary art — "craft-like" work, as aptly described by critic Jenni Sorkin[11] — to the revival of knitting circles. It has returned to utility (if it ever left), infiltrated design fairs, and developed a cult following in reality TV.[12] It has become more socially conscious, more performative, more grassroots and hipster-cool, and it has learned to adapt to the new learning platforms and marketplaces of the internet. True, today it is less about the bravura skill that was its hallmark at the height of studio craft, which has been a bitter pill for some to swallow. But this seems a small price to pay for the popular renaissance the field currently enjoys, as a new generation innovates and develops those skills. For heaven's sake, Great Britain's gold medal–winning diver, Tom Daley, made as much of a splash at the 2021 Tokyo Olympics with his knitting in the stands as with his diving! Craft today is as much about protective masks, protest banners, and humble mugs, about cherished traditions passed down, about the personal experience of making, as it

is about hanging in the hallowed halls of art museums. And perhaps that is what makes it so alive, so beautifully suited to this contemporary moment, in which old barriers of access are being questioned and torn down.

As the Renwick Gallery's first woman curator-in-charge, heading its first all-female curatorial team alongside my esteemed colleagues Mary Savig, the Lloyd Herman Curator of Craft, and, until recently, Anya Montiel, the Renwick's Curator of American and Native American Women's Art and Craft,[13] there is no area of focus I find more compelling than craft today. I believe we are rife for a greater shift to a more inclusive definition of craft, one that regards the often-overlooked histories and contributions of women, people of color, and other marginalized communities to this remarkable field. I think back to the foundations of the Renwick and the American craft field, when visionaries like Herman, Smith, and Monroe were playing outside their trained disciplines, charged with the delicious task of opening up a whole new way to think about objects. I see our role now as continuing that legacy, by looking with a critical lens to break down the barriers further, letting in people of all genders, sexualities, ethnicities, abilities, and creeds, examining all forms of craft practice with genuine curiosity, and reaping the benefits of this multiplicity of stories.

Indeed, though the Renwick's historic program endeavored to be inclusive in its time, in the hindsight of 2022, it is clear it failed to meet its democratic ideals for large segments of the population, particularly women and people of color. Throughout the 1970s and '80s, except for a few exhibitions of Native American craft, diversity most frequently came in the form of international exhibits like *Contemporary Nigerian Art: Craftsmen from Oshogbo* (1974), *Clay Figures from Guerrero* (1978), and *Costumes from the Arab World* (1979), sidelining diverse communities in our own nation. Gender equity was also highly problematic. Founded just as the studio craft movement was reaching its apex, the Renwick's exhibition and collection program reflected (and often asserted) the primacy of the movement's dynamic male stars and the dominant narrative of its founding by artists coming of age under the GI Bill. Only four of twenty solo shows were devoted to women—and only one to a woman of color—in the museum's first decade, overlooking deserving contributions to the field by the likes of Lenore Tawney, Toshiko Takaezu, Judy Kensley McKie, and Marguerite Wildenhain. Like so many museums struggling with these issues, the Renwick has made steady but slow progress over time. From 2012 to 2022, that gender ratio improved to three out of eight. There is still much work to do.

Over the past decade, the museum has been dedicated to this task. With *Thomas Day: Master Craftsman and Free Man of Color* (2013), the museum at last presented its first solo exhibition devoted to an African American artist. With the blockbuster exhibition *Wonder,* which drew nearly one million visitors when it reopened the gallery after a major renovation in 2015, curator Nicholas Bell transformed the gallery into a Wunderkammer, featuring grand-scale works by nine contemporary artists who defied conventional definitions of art and craft (Fig. 4). In doing so, he paid homage to the Renwick's 1972 inaugural shows, hanging as little as possible on the walls, echoing Herman's strategy from so long ago: "We want people to appreciate the architecture. The building is our own biggest exhibit."[14] If the exhibition *Voulkos: The Breakthrough Years* (2017) trod well-worn territory, honoring the legacy of studio craft, *June Schwarcz: Invention and Variation* (2017), shown alongside it, elevated an overshadowed contemporaneous female virtuoso. The exhibition *Murder Is Her Hobby: Frances Glessner Lee and the Nutshell Studies of Unexplained Death* (2017) took the commitment to women's history further, spotlighting a pioneering artist in forensics who used the craft available to her to break the glass ceiling in a field dominated by men. Broadening the field in a different vein, *No Spectators: The Art of Burning Man* (2018–19), which also drew nearly one million visitors, looked back at more than thirty years of maker culture taking place in the desert to trace a utopian movement in craft and technology that challenged the dominant narratives of art and capitalism (Fig. 5); while *Hearts of Our People: Native Women Artists* (2020), organized by the Minneapolis Institute of Art with an advisory panel of Native women artists and Native and

CAT. 4 Einar and Jamex de la Torre, *Ohio Goza y Mas,* 2013, blown glass, resin castings, and mixed media, 67 × 67 × 9 in.

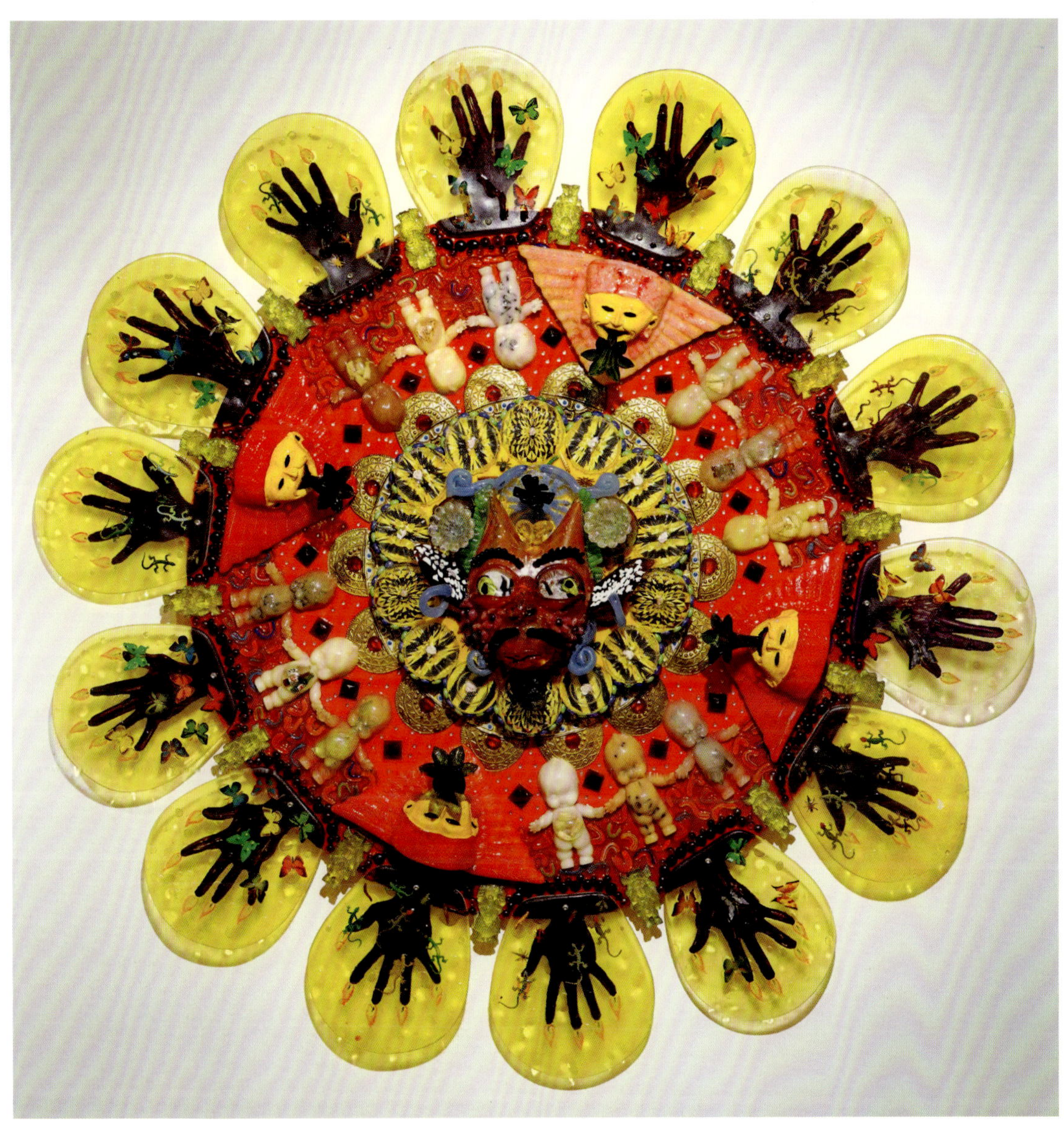

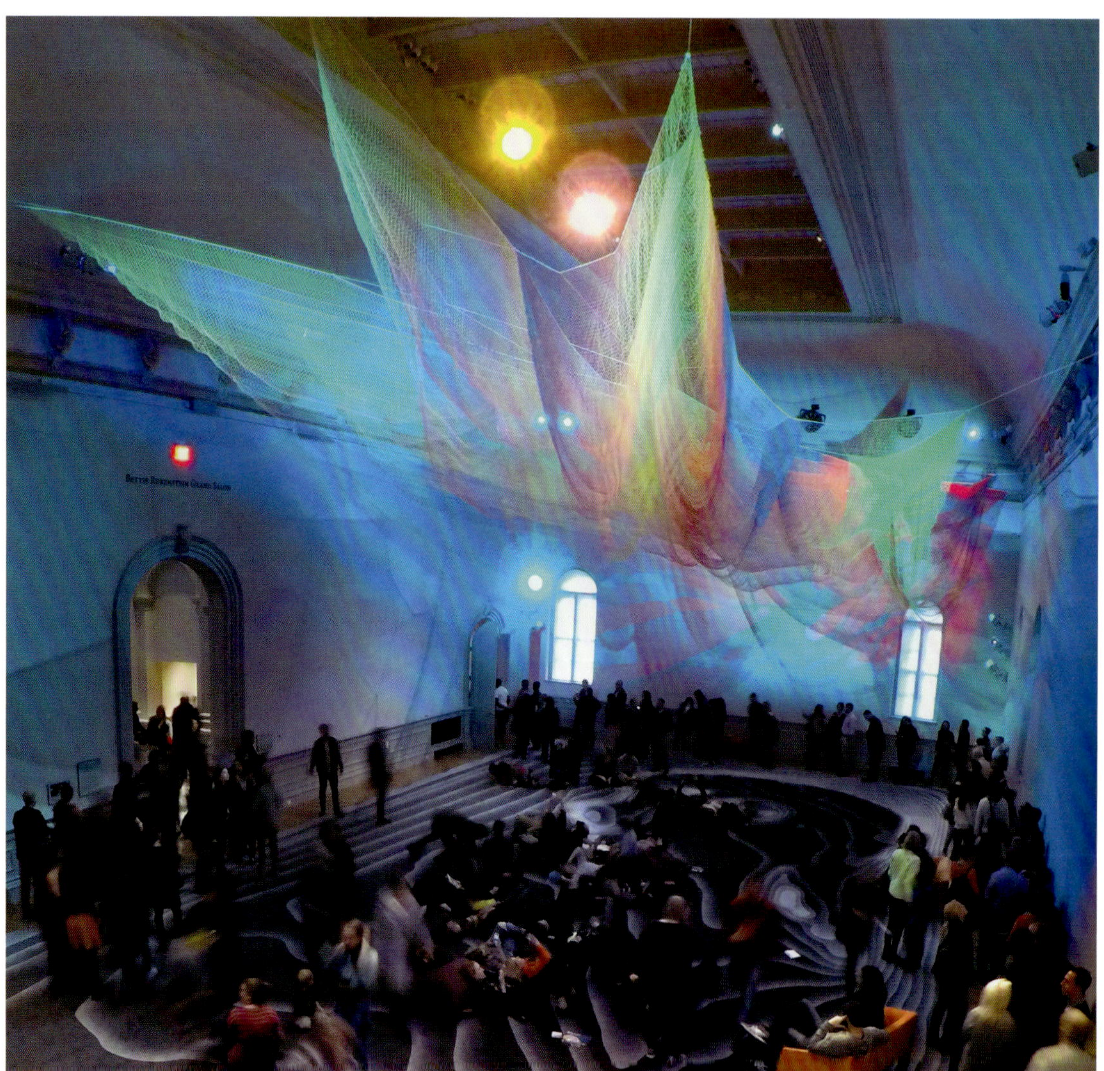

non-Native scholars, celebrated the creativity and strength of Native American women through their own voices.

Mary Savig's *This Present Moment: Crafting a Better World*, the exhibition created to accompany the Renwick's fiftieth anniversary program, builds on these provocations, leading with craft's humanist values and its unusually curative and empathetic character to inch us one step further toward our aim to become a museum for all people. Deeply moved by the unimaginable events of 2020 — the nationwide

Fig. 5 Installation view of *No Spectators: The Art of Burning Man* featuring Marco Cochrane's *Truth Is Beauty* (2017)

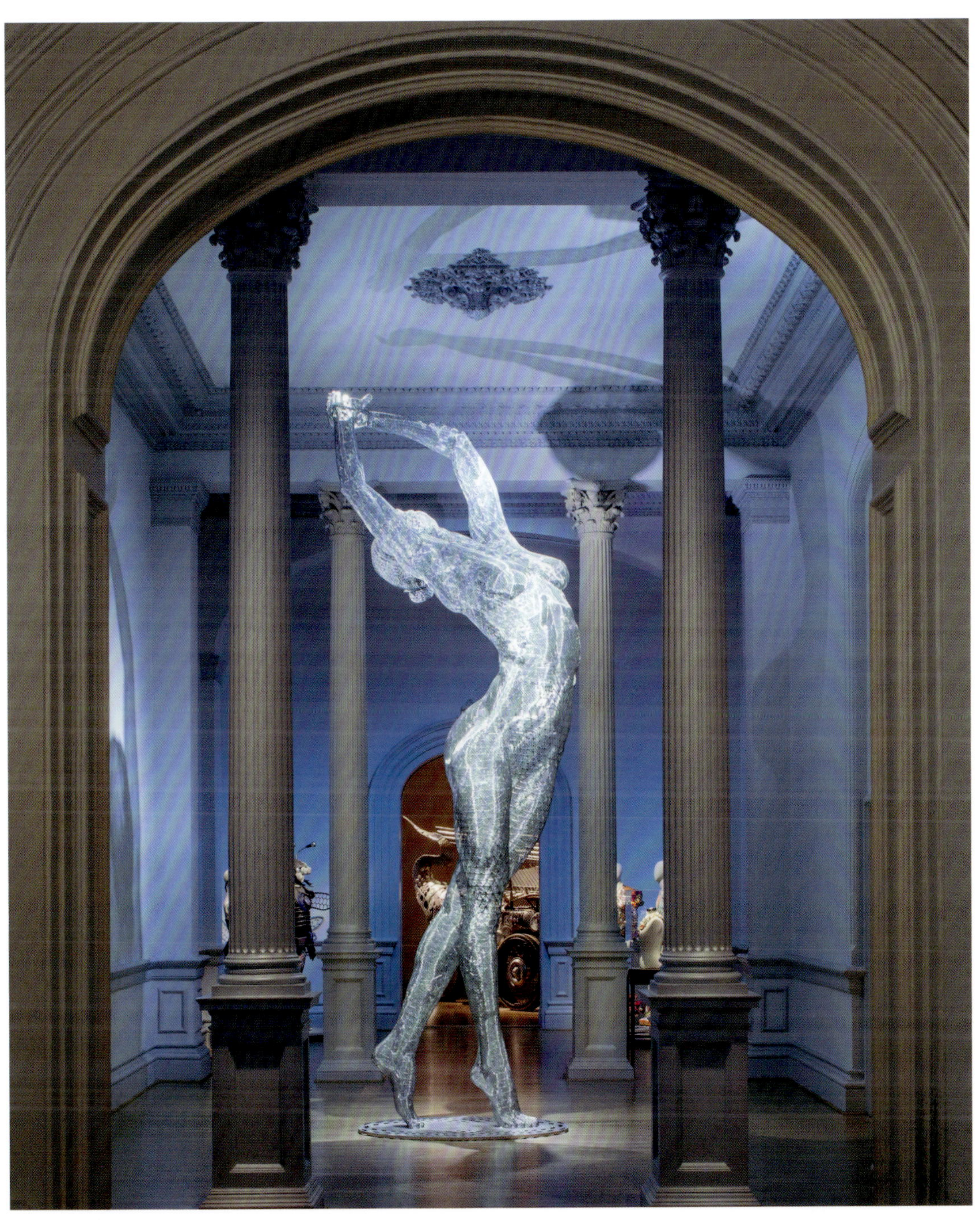

Black Lives Matter protests following the killing of George Floyd, political polarization that led to the storming of the US Capitol, and the grief and isolation of the coronavirus pandemic—Savig turned to French philosopher Gaston Bachelard to make sense of the world. In his treatise *The Poetics of Space* (1958), she found inspiration in his examination of Victor Hugo's *The Hunchback of Notre-Dame* (1831), in which Hugo describes the cathedral where his protagonist, Quasimodo, lives as his "egg, nest, house, country and universe." Through these interpretations, Bachelard reminds us that space, like time, is in our perception and we have the power to transform it. Taking these five themes—egg, nest, house, country, universe—as a point of departure, Savig uses the many manifestations of craft, and its associations with tradition and community, to examine our own notions of home, and who we are as a nation, in this time of crisis. Exploring further, in this volume, Anya Montiel offers a glimpse of what a future of craft, and America, could be. As a counterpoint to prevailing "Western" thought, she proposes a guiding philosophy centered on Indigenous values of respect, reciprocity, and responsibility as a roadmap for the future and illustrates these principles through the contemporary practice of several Indigenous, Black, and Latinx artists. To accompany these long-form essays, several artists share reflections on the past, present, and/or future in their own work.

Change is incremental, but in the *long now*, it is happening, and it is our responsibility to shape it for the future. At fifty years, we have an opportunity to look back at our history, to see where we have succeeded and fallen short, and to humbly begin the course correction for the next fifty years. It is always a work in progress, yet, as I was recently reminded by Jaron Lanier's incisive observation in *The Social Dilemma* (another critique of the particular ailments of our time), "It's the critics that drive improvement. It's the critics who are the true optimists."[15] Through this exhibition and the acquisitions drive that preceded it, we have begun the difficult yet exciting work of acting as our own critics, to recalibrate the story of American craft. If this present moment used to be the unimaginable future, then the stories we tell now, we hope, will help shape the next. ✳

NOTES

1. The epigram comes from the book's final chapter and was inspired by his friend and poet Gary Snyder's epigram, "This present moment / That lives on to become / Long ago." See Brand, *The Clock of the Long Now: Time and Responsibility* (New York: Basic Books, 1999), 163–64.

2. Alicia Eggert, email to Mary Savig, Lloyd Herman Curator of Craft, March 31, 2021.

3. S. Dillon Ripley Oral History Interviews, 1977–1993, Record Unit 9591, Smithsonian Institution Archives.

4. From the time President Lyndon B. Johnson signed an executive order transferring the building to the Smithsonian in 1964 until its opening in 1972, a Renwick Committee met to oversee the renovation and funding, and to plan its purpose. For a more comprehensive history of the Renwick Gallery and its building, see Nora Atkinson, *Craft for a Modern World: The Renwick Gallery Collection* (Washington, DC: Smithsonian American Art Museum, 2015); Charles J. Robertson, *American Louvre: A History of the Renwick Gallery Building* (Washington, DC: Smithsonian American Art Museum, 2015); and "Renwick Gallery Architectural History," Smithsonian American Art Museum, accessed July 31, 2021, https://americanart.si.edu/about /history/renwick-architecture.

5. Oral History Interview with Lloyd E. Herman, September 21, 2010, Archives of American Art, Smithsonian Institution.

6. That Herman invited a researcher from the National Museum of Natural History to curate *Pueblo Pottery: Zuni and Acoma Designs from the Smithsonian Collections* and Paul V. Gardener of the National Museum of American History to curate *Steuben Glass Works* illustrates Herman's inaugural vision for the Renwick as a collaborative *kunsthalle* drawing upon Smithsonian collections and expertise institution wide.

7. Numerous articles substantiate this discourse, within the *Chronicle of Higher Education* and other sources. Here are two: Patricia Cohen, "A Rising Call to Promote STEM Education and Cut Liberal Arts Funding," *New York Times*, February 21, 2016; and Justin Stover, "There Is No Case for the Humanities," *Chronicle of Higher Education*, March 4, 2018.

8. Garth Clark, *How Envy Killed the Crafts Movement: An Autopsy in Two Parts* (Portland, OR: Museum of Contemporary Craft and Pacific Northwest College of Art, 2008).

9. For more on Roberts's work on this, see Jessica Hemmings, "Guerilla Tactics & Feats of Negotiation: Knitted Installations by Lacey Jane Roberts & Sophie Horton," *Surface Design* 33, no. 4 (Summer 2009): 22–27, and Diane Daniel, "Landing Places," *American Craft Council* (April/May 2016), https://www.craftcouncil.org/magazine /article/landing-places.

10. I am especially grateful to Elisabeth Agro, the Nancy M. McNeil Curator of American Modern and Contemporary Crafts and Decorative Arts, Philadelphia Museum of Art, for our long discussions on this topic during the Haystack conference and since. I also extend thanks to the members of Critical Craft Forum for sharing their insights.

11. See Jenni Sorkin, "Craft-Like: The Illusion of Authenticity" (lecture, Nation Building: Craft and Contemporary American Culture symposium, Smithsonian American Art Museum, November 8–9, 2012, https://americanart.si.edu/videos /session-7-symposium-nation-building -post-craft-154203).

12. Several examples include *Ellen's Design Challenge*, HGTV, debuted 2015; *Framework*, Spike TV, debuted 2015; *Making It*, NBC, debuted 2018; *Blown Away*, Netflix, debuted 2019; *Rough Cut with Fine Woodworking*, WGBH Boston, debuted 2010; *Forged in Fire*, The History Channel, debuted 2015, and many more.

13. At time of publishing, Anya Montiel, who had been sharing a joint temporary post between the Renwick Gallery and the Smithsonian's National Museum of the American Indian, has left the Renwick to accept a permanent, full-time position at that sister institution.

14. "A New Era for the Renwick Gallery," *New York Times*, January 25, 1972.

15. Jaron Lanier, in *The Social Dilemma*, directed by Jeff Orlowski (Netflix, 2020), 1:34, https://www.netflix.com/title /81254224.

THIS PRESENT

BY MARY SAVIG

i can't stop being in the present

noticing how the past tells me what i should care about and the future
tells me what i should fear
and the past tells me what we forgot
and the future tells me what we must dream
but here

i breathe in

—adrienne maree brown, excerpt from "this is the only moment (species love poetry)"[1]

The Renwick Gallery's fiftieth anniversary program was planned under unimaginable circumstances.[2] When the museum closed to help stop the spread of COVID-19, I planned to work from home for a few weeks. A month at most. After more than a year, the indefinite timeline of "sheltering in place" changed my perception of the very meaning of home.

Disruption of everyday life coincided with an eruption of protests for social justice at the White House and an insurrection at the US Capitol. In this cascade of current events, my colleagues and I considered how to make an anniversary project relevant and meaningful. In her introduction, Nora Atkinson presents a fuller picture of the Renwick's first fifty years,

MOMENT

while Anya Montiel in her essay offers a restorative framework for American craft's next fifty years. This essay lays out major themes that emerged for *This Present Moment: Crafting A Better World*, the exhibition accompanying the Renwick's fiftieth anniversary, inspired by the idea that craft, now more than ever, offers possibilities for a more relational and empathetic world. The first theme considers the uses of craft in the present tense. A selection of artworks, all new acquisitions, indexes creative moments held in the tension between the past and the future. Such examples, perhaps unsurprisingly, begin at home. The second theme explores how craft inspires new ways of imagining the shapes of home, from a protective egg to the expansive cosmos. Together, the artworks eschew grand narratives in favor of personal experience and collaboration, convening new conversations in the "grand public living room"[3] that is the Renwick Gallery.

MOMENTS OF PRESENCE: THE USES OF CRAFT

The whirlwind of now has provided profound moments of humility, prompting questions on the very use of craft. Several new artworks acquired during 2020 and 2021 bring focus back to the basics. A quilt, a storage case, a pot, and eating utensils are seemingly everyday, useful comforts, but they are crafted to show us a deeper, wider perspective of the world around us. Artist Sharon Kerry-Harlan's 2020 quilt, *Portrait of Resilience* (CAT. 6), pieces together social issues exacerbated during a time that once again tested and continues to test the resolve of Black women. Kerry-Harlan, who made this quilt within her home in Milwaukee, Wisconsin, depicts a girl with a youthful bubble braid. Each bubble is haloed with the crownlike appearance of a SARS-CoV-2 virus particle. The girl's blouse

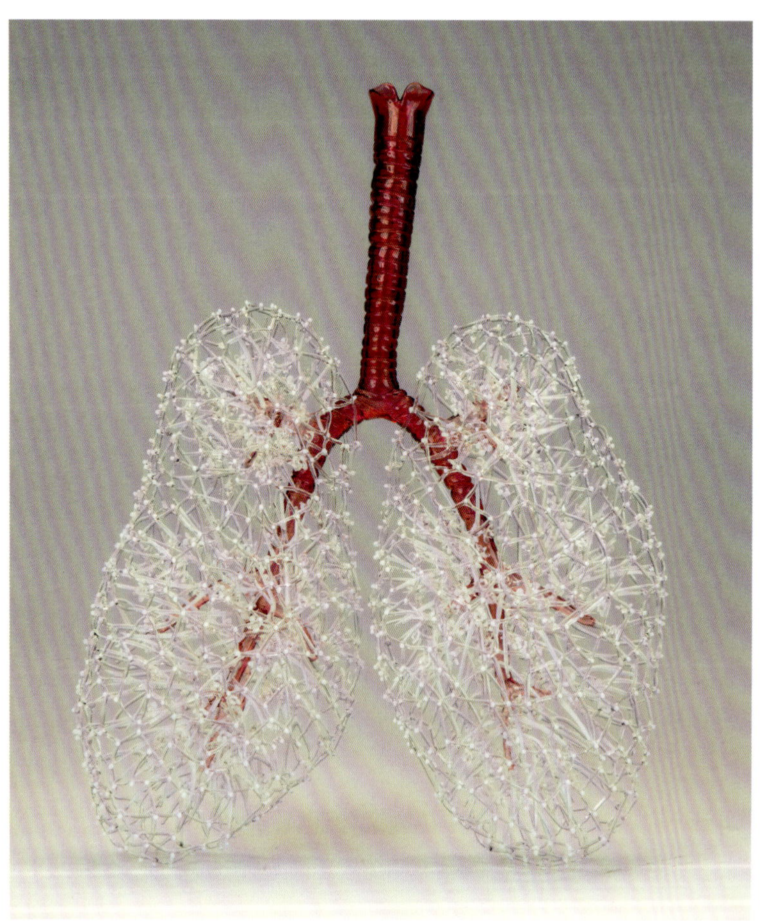

is constructed of an antique patchwork quilt, adorned with a 2020 golden necklace made with faux leather. Her lips and nose are made of a commercial cotton American flag, and the bows accenting her braid are made of kente cloth. With these materials and symbols representing past and present Black and American culture, this portrait is a window into the experience of a Black American woman during this current moment. The pandemic has disproportionately impacted Black, Indigenous, and other people of color, all of whom have died from COVID-19 at a higher rate than white people throughout the United States.[4] Along other fronts, the killings of Black Americans, like medical worker Breonna Taylor, who was shot and killed in her own home by Louisville police officers in March 2020 during a botched raid, as well as violent attacks on people of Asian descent, have affirmed deep structures

CAT. 6 Sharon Kerry-Harlan, *Portrait of Resilience*, from the *Flag Series*, 2020, machine-quilted, dye-discharge fabric designed by the artist and antique quilt, vinyl, American flag, and African print fabrics, 86 ½ × 73 ½ in.

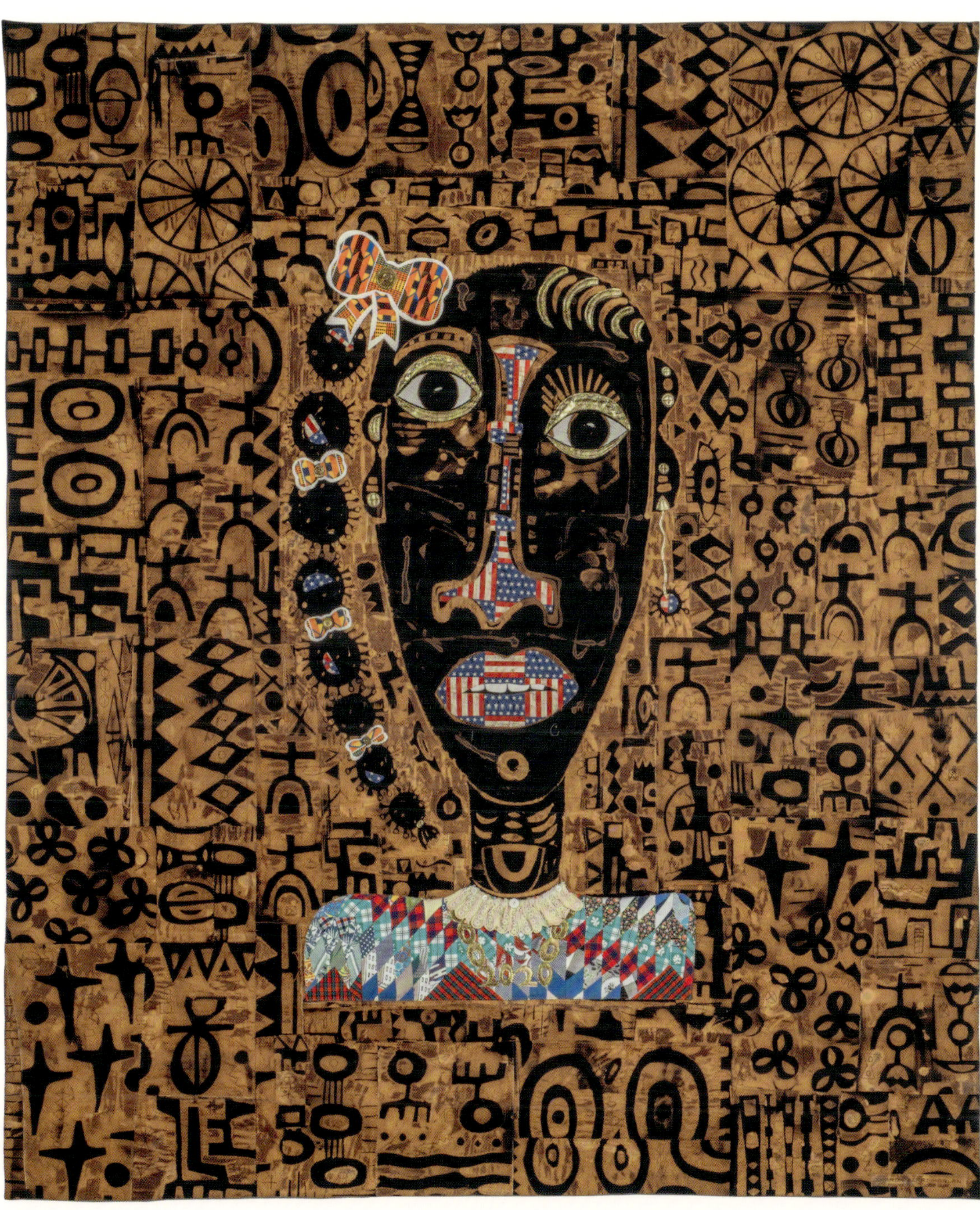

of racism in American society. Additionally, as Kerry-Harlan indicates in her artist statement, many states attempted to suppress Black voters during the 2020 election and continue to enact racist voting laws for future elections.[5] Kerry-Harlan writes, "despite these dire situations, resilience remains among African Americans and their allies to realize a better future."[6] The artist's relational quilting process inspires a cooperative way forward, empowering the young girl with the strength of the community.[7] The stitches carry the stories of pain, but also mend and bring comfort. After all, quilts conjure feelings of home, beginning in the cradle. Carolyn Mazloomi, founder of the Women of Color Quilters Network, states that this connection to the comfort of home and family is what gives quilts such power. "Cloth is the first thing we are swathed in upon birth, and the last thing that touches the body upon our death," and such a deep familiarity can be used as a tool to tell a story that elicits emotion and empathy and advances social change.[8]

In thinking of a craft object as a tool, its outward usefulness is just the beginning. Cultural theorist Sara Ahmed argues in *What's the Use? On the Uses of Use* that the use of an object animates our relationship to space — how we interact with the object and the environment around it — but not always in the expected way.[9] Often, a "useful" object implies the means to an end: a hammer, shoes, a blanket, a cup. And yet, such objects sustain longer stories and

memories than we do. This reorients our idea of an object's use in space and time and complicates our relationship to these objects. Ahmed considers a pot owned by Silas Marner in George Eliot's eponymous 1861 novel. At first glance, the pot is just a vessel to bring water from a well to his home. But this is just the beginning of the pot's story. "Use is also represented here as companionship; the pot is reliable, kind even, standing there, ready for him."[10] Of course, the emotional value of a pot is central to the work of many ceramists. Consider the large double-walled cauldron, *Communion* (CAT. 7), by artist James C. Watkins. Watkins created the cauldron from memories of his childhood on a farm in Athens, Alabama. His mother and grandmother cooked and cleaned in black cast-iron pots reminiscent of *Communion*, and the repeating rim motif emulates the pickets of a cattle fence built by his father.[11] Watkins has transformed a pot from an essential farm tool into an expressive reminder of shared family experiences.

Craft can alter our perspective of use further by its deviation from use. To misuse or queer the use of an object is both a radical and tender act. Ahmed suggests that "To queer use can be to linger on the material qualities of that which you are supposed to pass over; it is to recover a potential from materials that have been left behind."[12] Consider furniture maker Katie Hudnall's poignant sculpture with reclaimed wood and found acorns (CAT. 8). In 2017, she began to fill her home with acorns

CAT. 7 James C. Watkins,
Communion, 1998, raku-
fired, double-walled
earthenware with glaze,
20 ¼ × diam. 22 in.

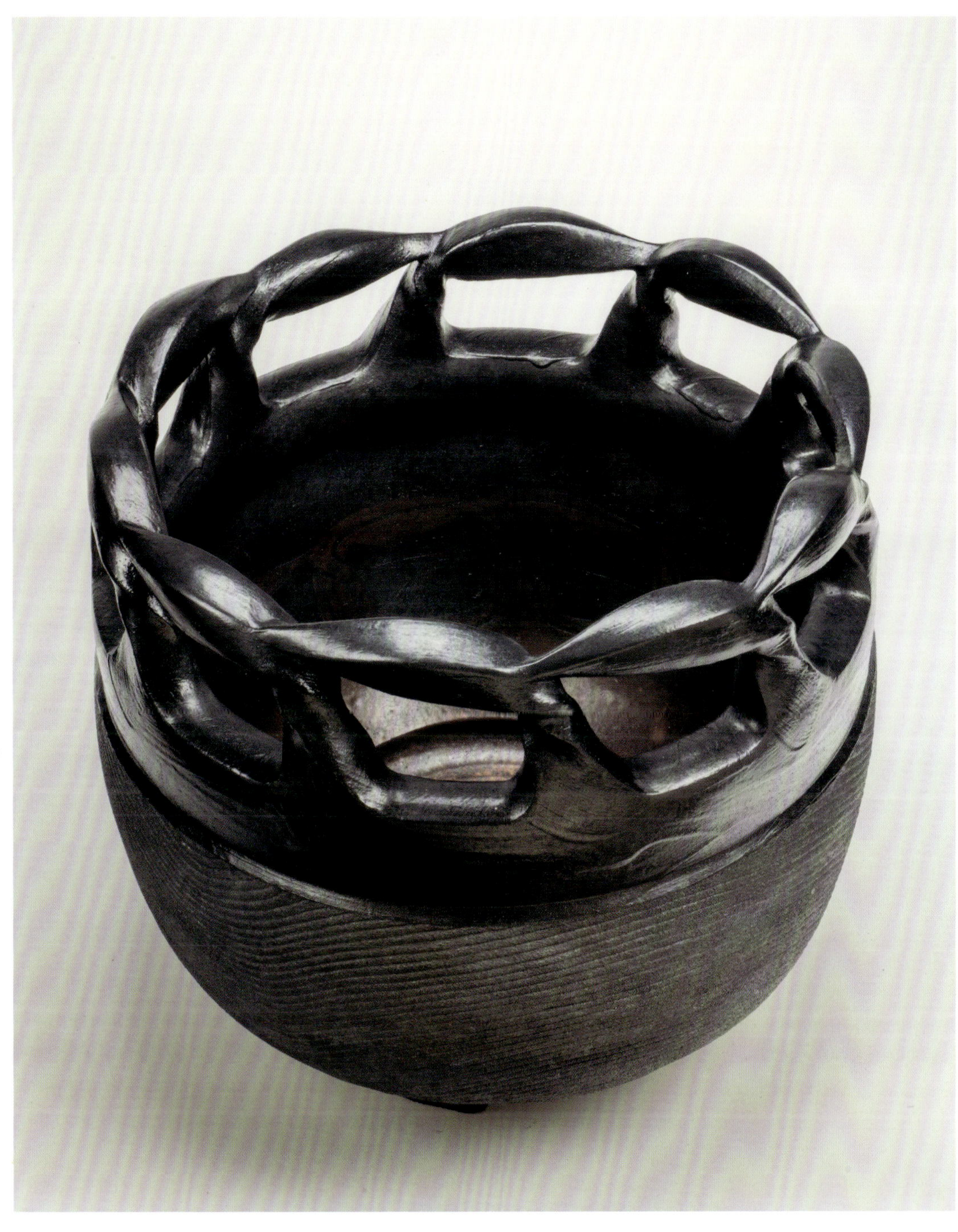

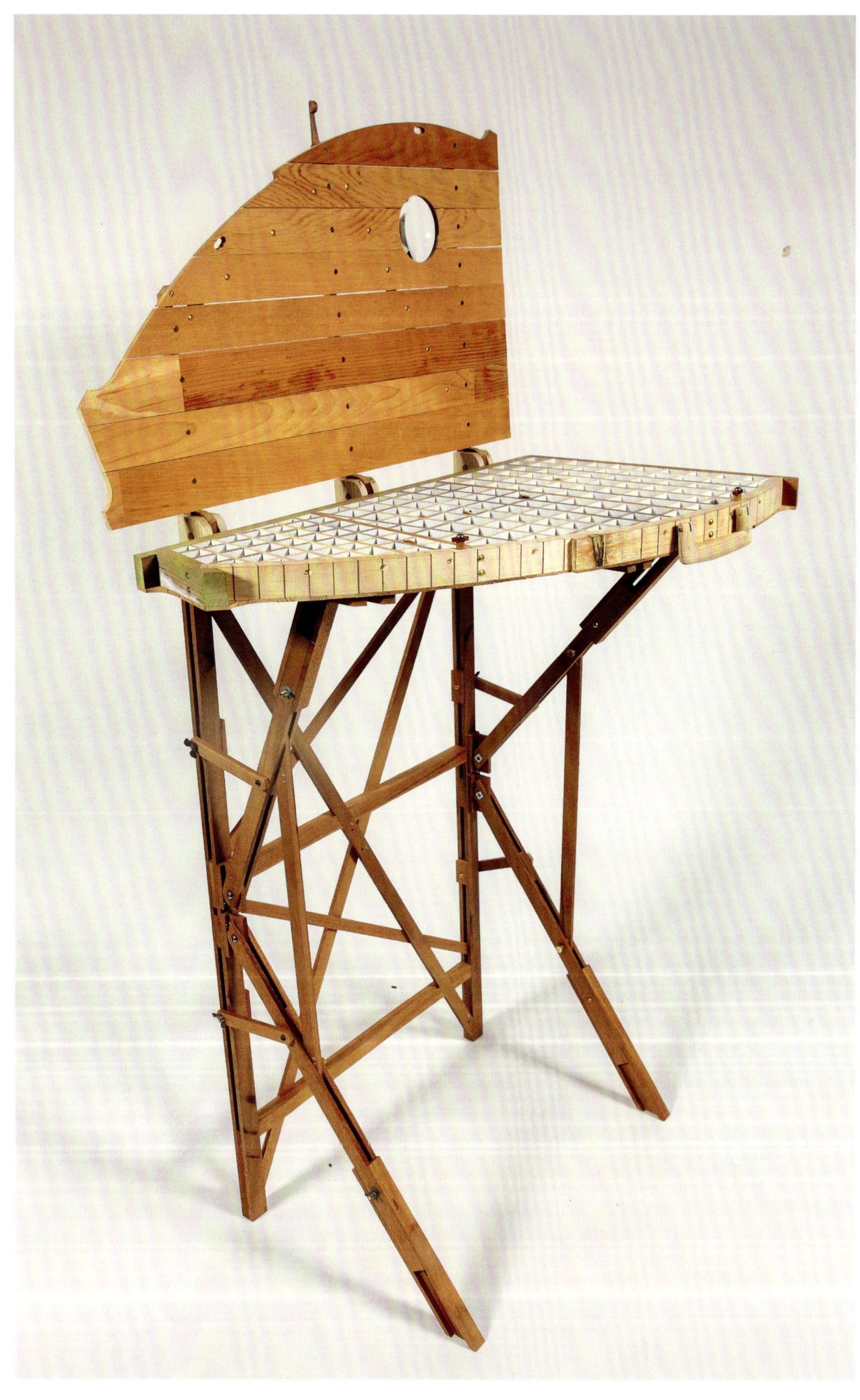

collected on long walks. At first, the walks and
the collecting were not intentional. Dealing
with difficult life circumstances, Hudnall found,
"The walks became a way to find myself back
to my mind and body again and to be really
present."[13] As she walked, she filled her pock-
ets, and then her home, with acorns. Hudnall
realized that the acorns needed their own
special shelter, which materialized as a curvilinear suitcase featuring a square — a home — for
each one. As a whole, the 178 acorns trace the
ongoing journey of the artist. A mature oak tree
produces about two thousand acorns a year,
but only one in ten thousand acorns reaches
maturity. Hudnall relates:

**I think the idea of constant, repeated, tiny
attempts for success, with the understanding
that most will go nowhere, became a way
for me to think about slow progress toward
health in my own life.**[14]

The artist renders a playful case of acorns into
a powerful call to action: slow down and linger,
seek alternative paths, and accept failures.

Metalsmith David Harper Clemons stretches
the expected use of utensils with *The Weight of
Deferred Gratification* (CAT. 9). While imagining
a better future, Clemons looked to the past,
specifically to the 1939 World's Fair. The fair,
staged in Queens, New York, celebrated the

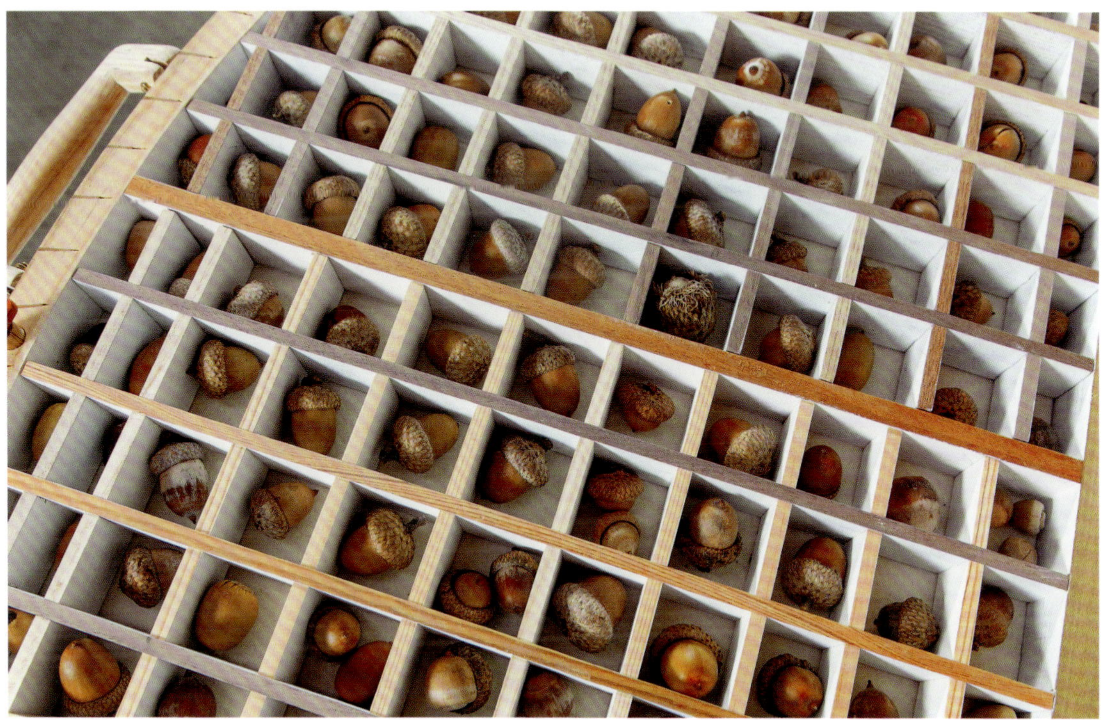

CAT. 9 David Harper Clemons, *The Weight of Deferred Gratification*, 2019, sterling silver, stainless steel, brass, glass, and mahogany with corn, wild rice, and wheat, overall box, closed: 15 × 9 × 5 in.

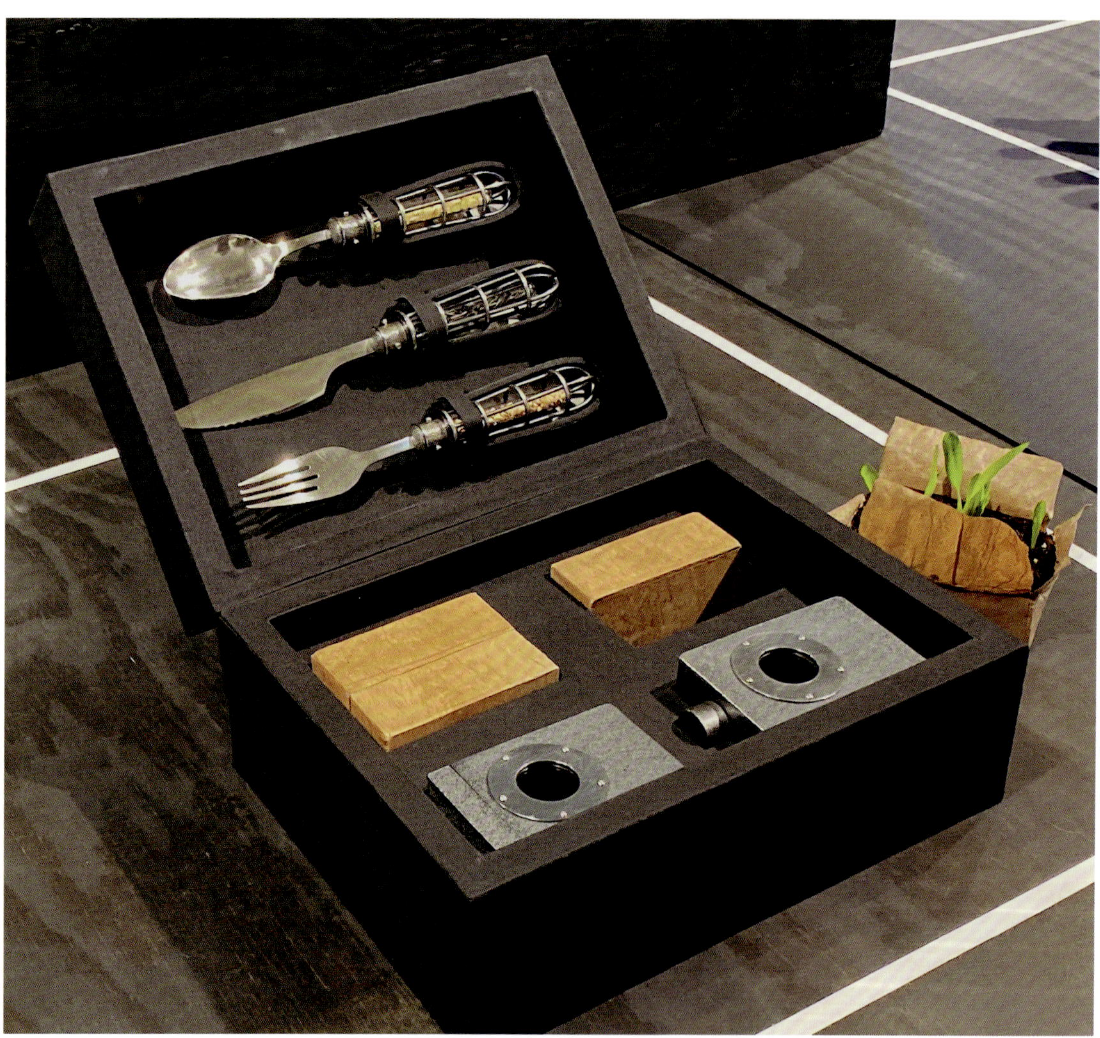

speed of development and consumerism of the agricultural industry, which favored immediate gratification over long-term environmental and social impact. Clemons created a functional knife, fork, and spoon that are also vessels for grains, soil pods for planting the grains, and water flasks for nourishing the sprouts. The artist states, "The tools become vehicles to convey the extended relationship between germination, production, cultivation, preparation, consumption, and even sharing and distribution."[15] To use the utensils, from seed to table, requires a commitment to nurturing the present; they encourage the user to avoid repeating the mistakes of the past.

The utensils, along with a quilt, a cauldron, and a nutcase, bring new perspectives to what (and who) makes the world. The artists show us how to be more in touch with the present moment in order to think through past use and gain purchase on new uses. Next, I offer how artists have reimagined the world as seen through spaces of comfort, from the small and intimate to the immense universe.

HOMES FOR DREAMING: FROM AN EGG TO THE UNIVERSE

Artists who work with craft materials and processes have long aspired to make the home more comfortable. In *The Poetics of Space*, philosopher Gaston Bachelard contemplates the metaphorical and poetic possibilities of a house as both an escape and a shelter for troubling times.[16] "For our house is our corner of the world. As has often been said, it is our first universe, a real cosmos in every sense of the word," Bachelard asserts.[17] The basic architecture of a house provides a sense of stability and security. Over time, a shelter becomes integral to one's own conception of self. Bachelard laces his text with poems to describe how domestic things—a folded family blanket, a shelf of trinkets, or a chest of drawers—have been wielded by poets to "move the very depths of our being."[18] A home illuminates the imagination. While Bachelard turns to poetry, I offer craft as the physical relation. Like poetry, craft holds the most intimate impressions and memories of its maker; it is a material trace of the artist's presence.[19] A handcrafted artwork can also elicit notions of shelter, providing a sense of belonging in everyday life.

There are many scales of shelter, from the contentment of snuggling under a handmade quilt to looking up in wonder at the Milky Way galaxy. Bachelard uses novelist Victor Hugo's story *The Hunchback of Notre-Dame* (1831) to elucidate this incredible range. He states, "In one short sentence, Victor Hugo associates the images and beings of the function of inhabiting."[20] The sentence from this gothic novel turns around the multipole modalities in which Quasimodo, kyphotic bellringer, inhabits Notre-Dame de Paris:

"In the course of time there had been formed a certain peculiarly intimate bond which united the ringer to the church.... Notre-Dame had been to him successively, as he grew up and developed, the egg, the nest, the house, the country, the universe."[21]

EGG

I do not live happily or comfortably
with the cleverness of our times.
The talk is all about computers,
the news is all about bombs and blood.
This morning, in the fresh field,
I came upon a hidden nest.
It held four warm, speckled eggs.
I touched them.
Then went away softly,
having felt something more wonderful
than all the electricity of New York City.

—Mary Oliver, "With Thanks to the Field Sparrow, Whose Voice Is So Delicate and Humble"[22]

Toshiko Takaezu expanded the possibilities of landscape art with her nonfunctional sculptures, questioning enclosures and establishing thresholds within which nature and the built environment remain enigmatic, fluid places. For much of her career, she created iconic closed forms in varying sizes and colors (Fig. 6). The artist intuited the vibrancy of nature in her calligraphic strokes of gorgeous glazes. When recalling her childhood in Hawai'i, she thought of the tall shadows of long sunny days and spotting a blooming lily flower in her pond.[23] The pond, her gardens, and even the sunlight all defined her image of home. Her home was inextricable from her pots. As she noted, "there is no difference between your work, your cooking and the garden. They're all the same. You have to put

yourself into it."[24] Accordingly, her ceramic process was as direct as nurturing a garden. She used an ancient technique of coiling, handbuilding, and wheel-throwing to shape large pots. As she moved upward, coil by coil, she slowly pinched and pressed the clay into a nearly closed spheroid. She then applied her signature glazes—earth tones and shocks of cobalt blue and canary yellow—and fired them to completion. Inside many of these forms she placed pieces of paper and clay that became ceramic beads that would rattle when fired. The interior cavity, described by art historian Ezra Shales as "a space to which we will never gain access except by breaking into it," distinguished her forms as an evocation of cocoons, caves, and of course eggs, an articulation of the fragility of life.[25] Takaezu explains:

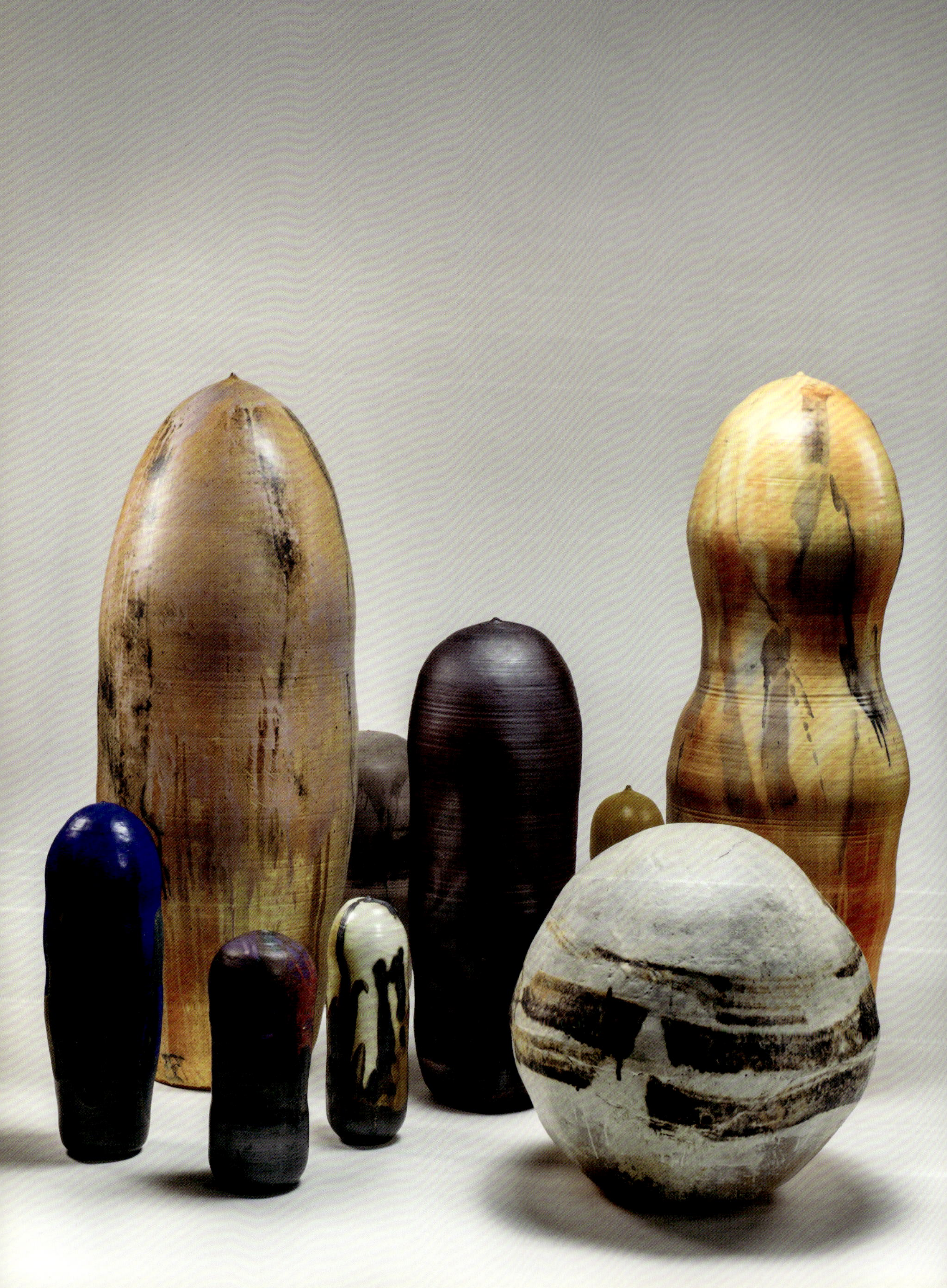

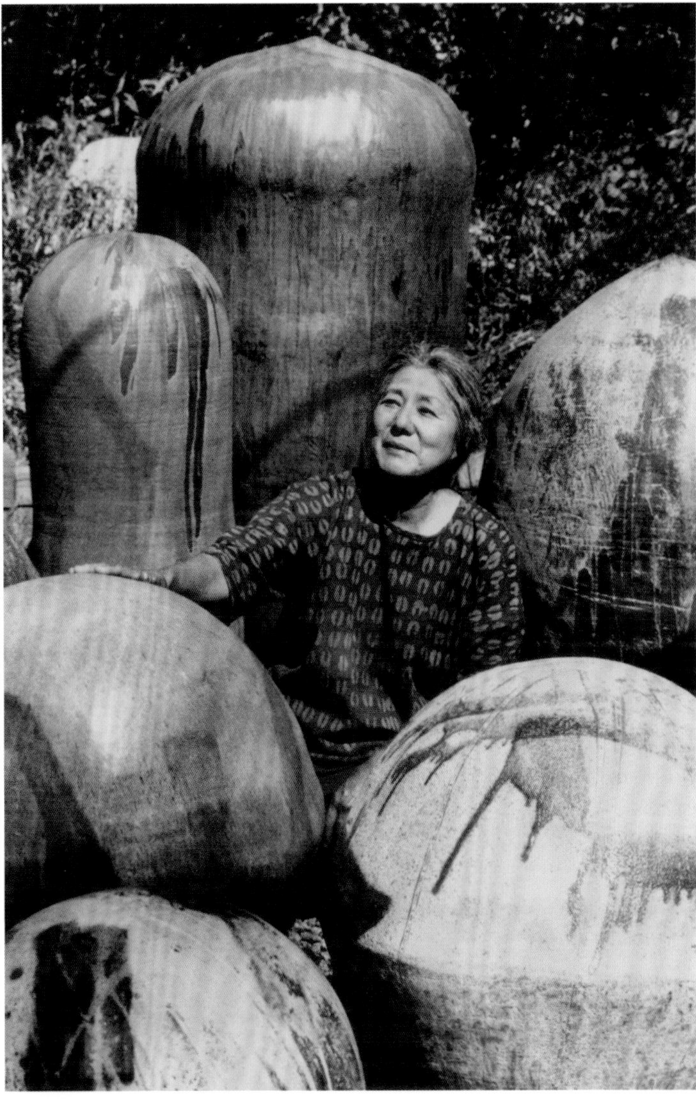

One of the best things about clay is that
I can be completely free and honest with it.
And clay responds to me. The clay is alive
and responsive to every touch and feeling.
When I make it into form, it's alive, and
when it is dry, it is still breathing! I can
feel the response in my hands, and I don't
have to force the clay. The whole process is
an interplay between clay and myself, and
often the clay has much to say.[26]

Indeed, ornithologist David Allen Sibley
explains that many species of birds, like
mallards, communicate with each other before
they hatch: "the young start peeping and click-
ing inside the eggs about twenty-four hours
before hatching, and this may help synchronize
hatching. It is usually just a few hours from
the time the first egg hatches until the entire
family is ready to leave the nest together."[27]
Takaezu often arranged her closed forms in
a natural setting (Fig. 7), marking an important artistic shift from mere representations of
nature toward the process of nature itself. Like
chattering eggs, these forms conjure new imag-
inings about the tenderness of home.

NEST

—Aimee Nezhukumatathil, excerpt from "Potoo: Nyctibius griseus"[28]

Countless poets have attempted to put into words the magic and perfection of nests.[29] Birds busily build them for care and comfort from the resources of their environment. Sibley posits that nests are not merely created out of instinct, but that birds make crafty choices in response to any given moment, including absorbing the detritus of humans.[30] Nests might be made with plastic ribbons and nets and built on structures like barns, doorways, and mailboxes. According to Ahmed, a nest constructed on a mailbox elucidates the multitudes of use.[31] From a human's perspective, the mailbox is temporarily unusable. From a bird's perspective, the mailbox is home sweet home. The avian vantage point might expand notions of utility, perhaps in directions that are more inclusive and collaborative. Along similar lines, baskets reveal alternative stories of containment, such as the labor of their makers and the environments in which they are made.

Contemporary baskets thrive on the tension between tradition and adaptation, use and poetry. Leona Waddell began learning to make egg baskets from white oak splints when she was seven years old. In the 1940s, she and her fifteen siblings grew up in rural Hart County in southeastern Kentucky. The Waddell family used their baskets for household functions, traded them for food, and sold them along the highway for sixty-five cents apiece.[32] As Waddell grew more skilled, she brought her personal touch to her family's traditional style. In the latter half of the twentieth century, the market shifted away from a local economy toward a fledgling tourism and collecting market. Today, Waddell's exquisite egg baskets rarely hold eggs (Fig. 8). Along similar lines, Polly Adams Sutton arduously strips and weaves the bark from the logged forests of the Pacific Northwest into voluminous forms. "There is no preconceived notion as to the purpose of my sculptural shapes, except perhaps, a quest for pleasing curvilinear forms," she explains.[33] *Facing the Unexpected* (CAT. 12) comprises nine cedar-bark baskets arranged into an undulating sculptural group. No longer useful, the baskets disclose the ephemeral nature of nests.

Fig. 8 Leona Waddell,
Squared Egg Basket,
2011, white oak,
12 ¼ × 16 ⅛ × 12 in.,
Gift of Martha G. Ware
and Steven R. Cole,
2011.47.68

Artists continue to weave their presence into baskets, especially as use changes over time. Gullah artists have coiled sweetgrass baskets for generations, maintaining basket techniques from Africa used for fanning (processing) rice and storing food. According to historian Fath Davis Ruffins, this remarkable continuity was born out of physical isolation, and then maintained by choice. Weavers today, like Elizabeth F. Kinlaw (Fig. 9), enjoy exposure to "contemporary" art as they continue the tradition of centering African baskets in their American lives.[34] Indigenous basket makers also share intergenerational knowledge through basketry. Artist and poet Gail Tremblay (Mi'kmaq and Onondaga) learned how to gather sweetgrass from her grandfather and how to braid the grass from her great-aunt. In 1985 she began adapting split ash and sweetgrass techniques to weave baskets with strips of vintage film (CAT. 13). Tremblay explains that the material marks a new function of the basket: to show the violence of settler culture as it advances stereotypes in popular media of Indigenous Peoples as perpetually primitive. She states, "the dominant culture romanticizes the traditional lifestyle while at the same time destroys the traditional lifestyle."[35] For many basket makers, their practice is a meditation on time, change, and resilience. From the ground up, they weave ever-expanding Networks of Care in the movement toward a more relational world.

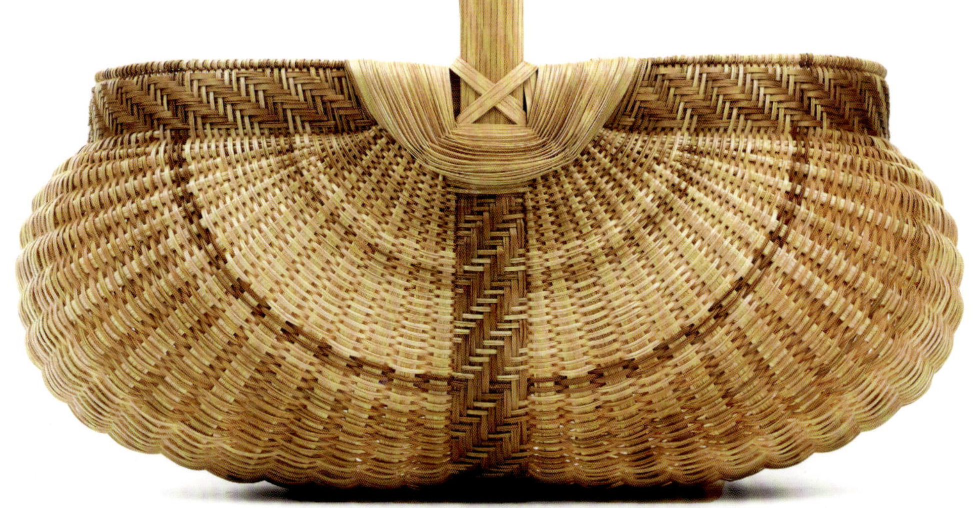

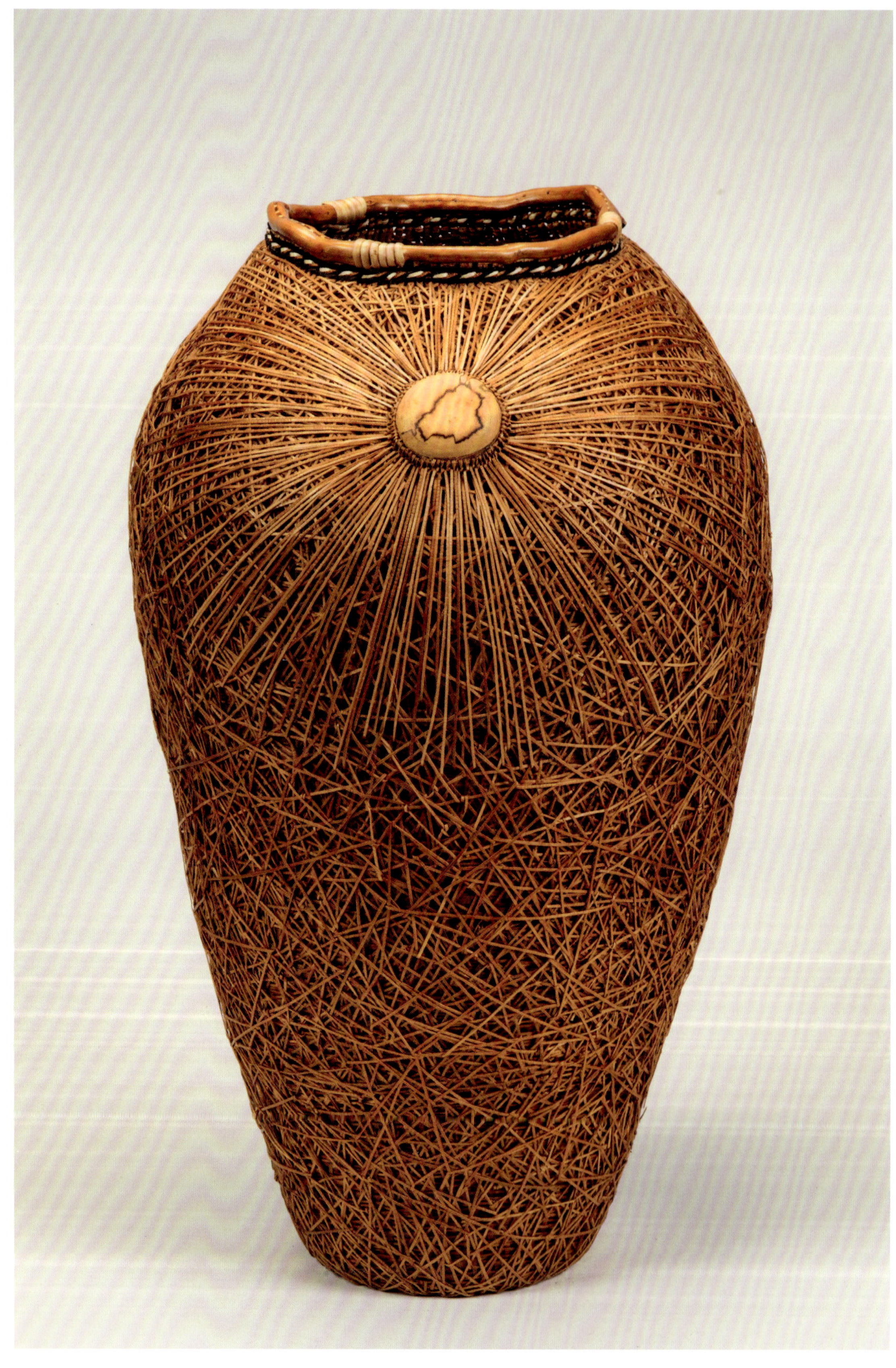

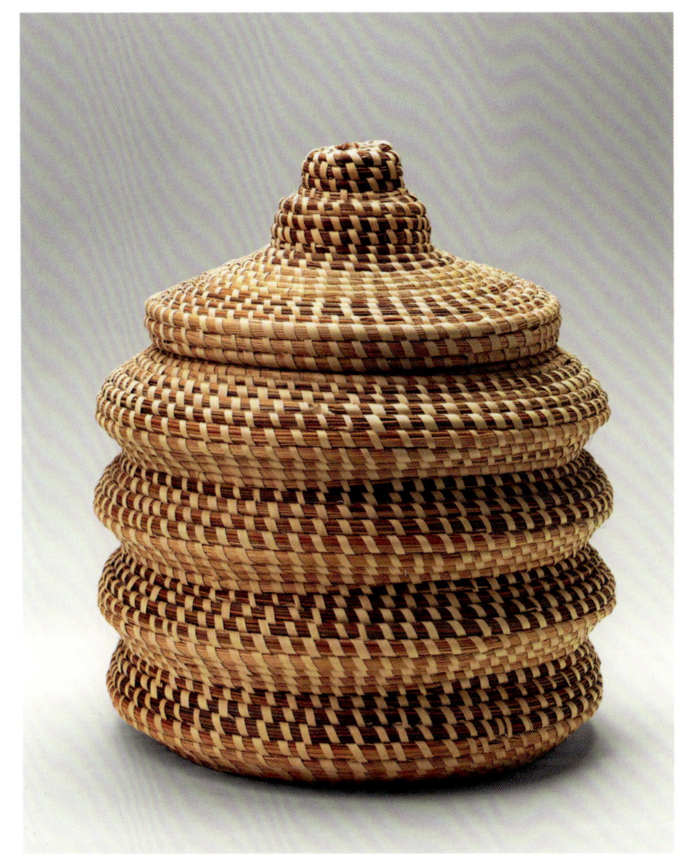

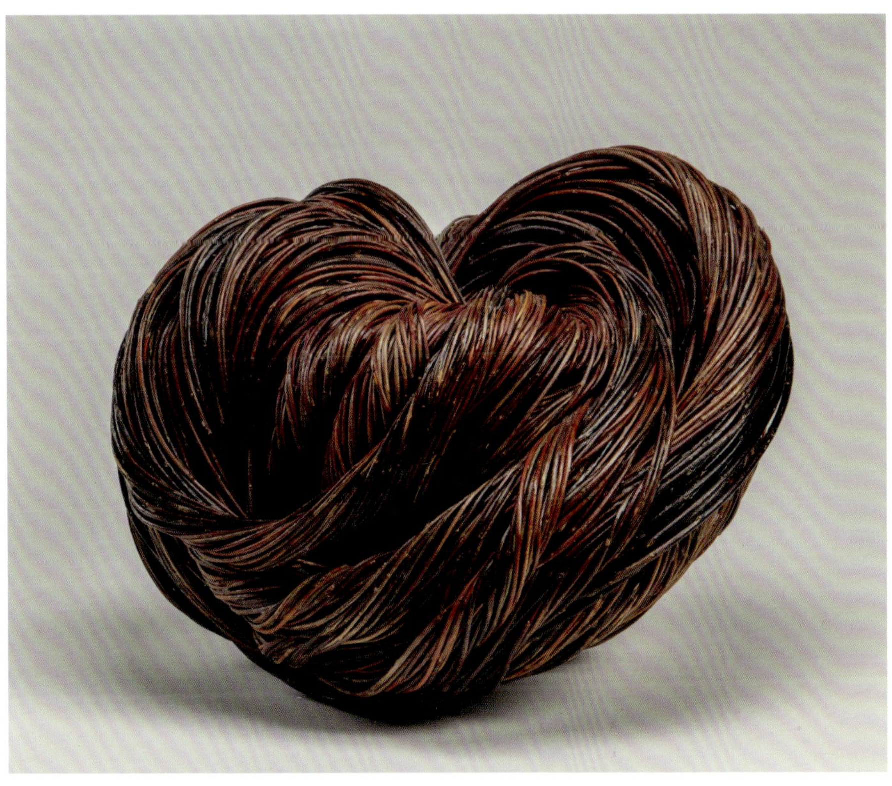

CAT. 10 Dawn Nichols Walden, *Random Order XIII*, 2006, cedar bark and roots with beargrass, 23 ¾ × diam. 14 ½ in. (irreg.)

Fig. 9 Elizabeth F. Kinlaw, *In and Out Basket*, 1991, bulrush, sweetgrass, palmetto fronds, and pine needles, 12 ⅛ × diam. 11 in., Gift of Martha G. Ware and Steven R. Cole, 2011.47.32A–B

CAT. 11 Christine Joy, *Small Dark Cloud*, 2012, willow and Rocky Mountain maple with encaustic finish, 15 ¾ × 20 ¾ × 15 ½ in.

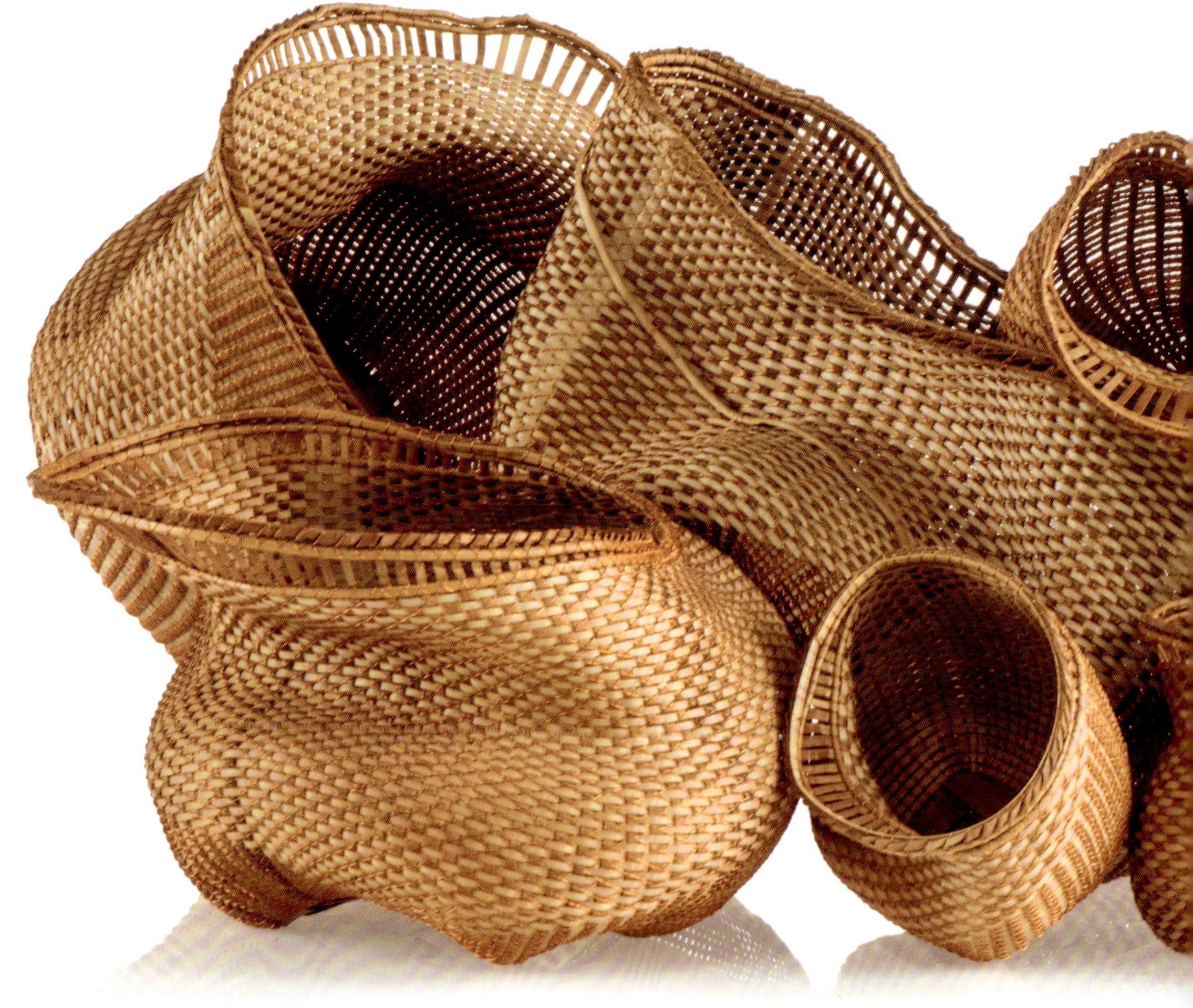

CAT. 12 Polly Adams Sutton, *Facing the Unexpected*, 2013, western cedar bark, ash, spruce root, and coated copper wire, overall: 11 ½ × 18 × 32 in.

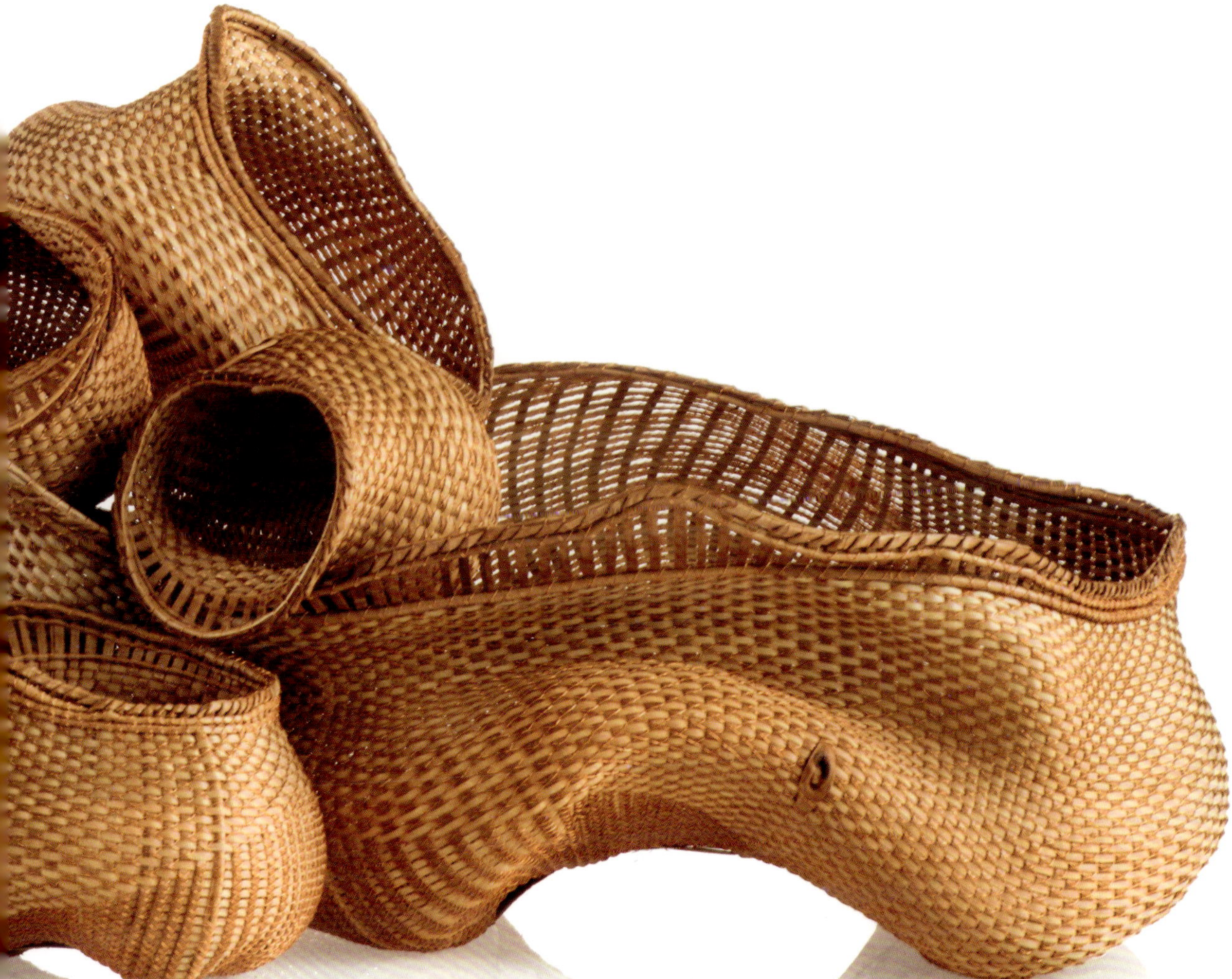

CAT. 13 Gail Tremblay, *When Will the Red Leader Overshadow Images of the 19th-Century Noble Savage in Hollywood Films that Some Think Are Sympathetic to American Indians*, 2018, 35mm film from *Windwalker* (1981), red and white leader, and silver braid, overall: 15 ½ × diam. 14 ⅞ in.

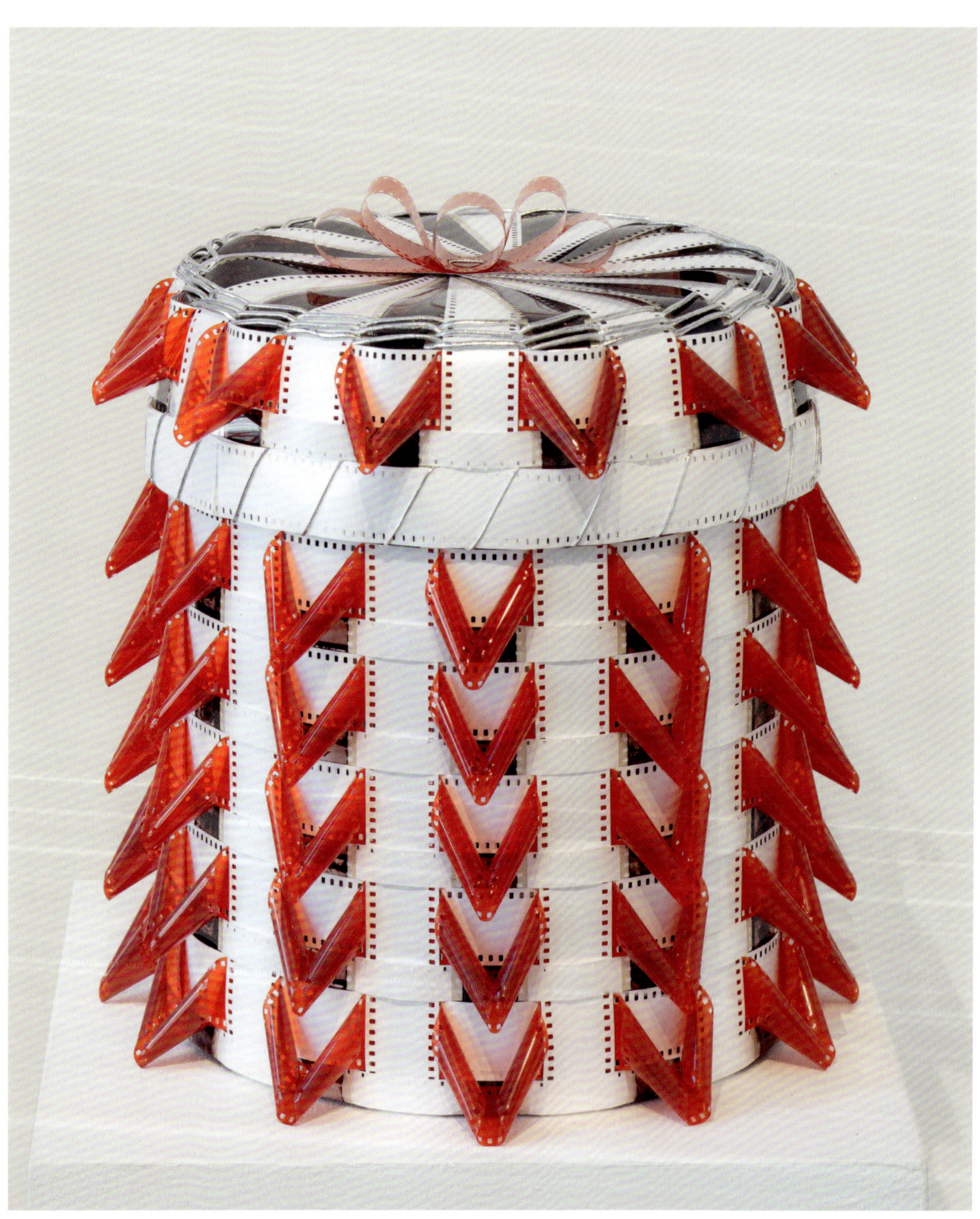

CAT. 14 Jeremy Frey, *Large Turquoise Urchin Basket* (top view), 2019, brown ash and sweetgrass, overall: 5 ¼ × diam. 11 ½ in.

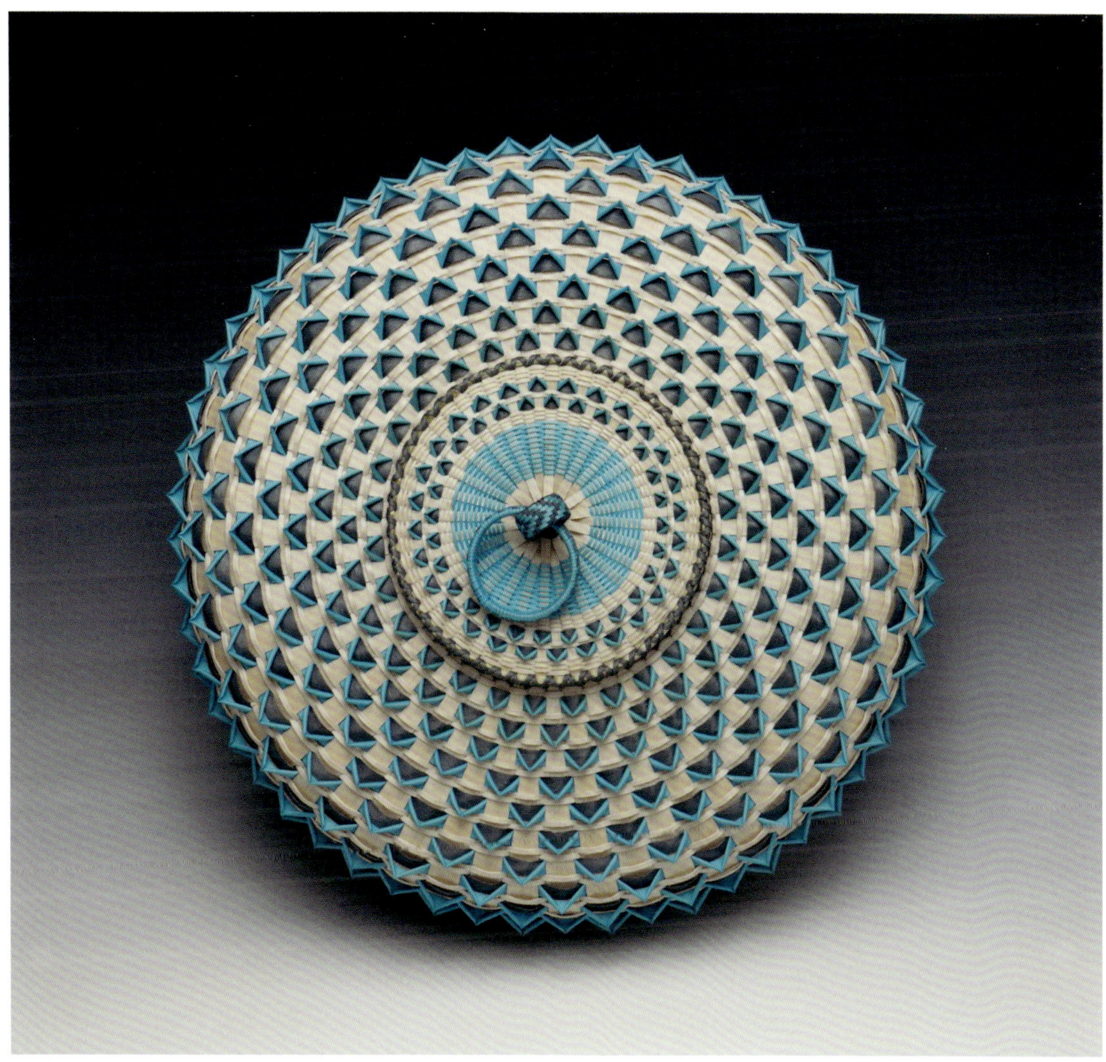

Fig. 10 Arthur Espenet
Carpenter, *Staircase*, 1969,
hyedua and oak, sight:
192 × 84 in., Gift of David L.
Davies and Jack Weeden,
1998.15A–S

HOUSE

*The inhabitant gives the room its purpose. Your actions
are mightier than any architect's intentions.*

—Carmen Maria Machado, from *The Dream House*[36]

A house is a physical place that serves the most basic of human needs. A home might be an abstraction of memory and sentiment that carries us through life. While a roof and walls provide some measure of safety, the contents of the home dovetail poetry and utility. Bachelard explains the shimmering possibility of smaller spaces within homes, the "transcendental geometry" of niches, furniture, and drawers that model nonhuman dwellings, particularly those of invertebrates, birds, and burrowing mammals. Spaces that feel like shells or nests invite us to curl up into a daydream. A particularly striking example is a 1969 spiral staircase by Arthur Espenet Carpenter (Fig. 10). The graceful structure comprises eleven curved, interlocking steps radiating around a center post. As Carpenter intended, the intrinsic warmth of the wood and the organic forms demand interaction along multiple fronts, including movement up and down the steps and pushing and pulling the propeller-like treads. Carpenter crafted a virtual staircase for imagining: the spiral steps register with curved forms of nature, pushing against the grain of right angles and square rooms.

Homes are complex spaces for displaced people. According to Mazloomi, "memories of home and family have sustained us during difficult times and encouraged us in happy ones. Without this strong bond, it is difficult to say whether the horrors of slavery and the ensuing years of racial bigotry and oppression could have been survived."[37] Artist Chawne Kimber stitches her experience as a Black woman in the United States on her monumental quilt, *still not* (CAT. 15), beginning with the declarative *i*.[38]

> i am
> i am still
> i am not still
> i am still not free

While working on this quilt, Kimber wrote, "I am paralyzed with fear, slowed down by obstacles, and overflowing with rage borne from inhabiting this society as a person who is not a white man."[39] While attesting to her lived experiences of racism and sexism, Kimber nevertheless communicates her anticipation of future erasure, a terrifying awareness. She continues, reinscribing both despair and empowerment:

> **I am** told I don't understand....
> **I am** told not to make these quilts....
> **I am** told that things are much better now.
> **I am** told just to let it go.[40]

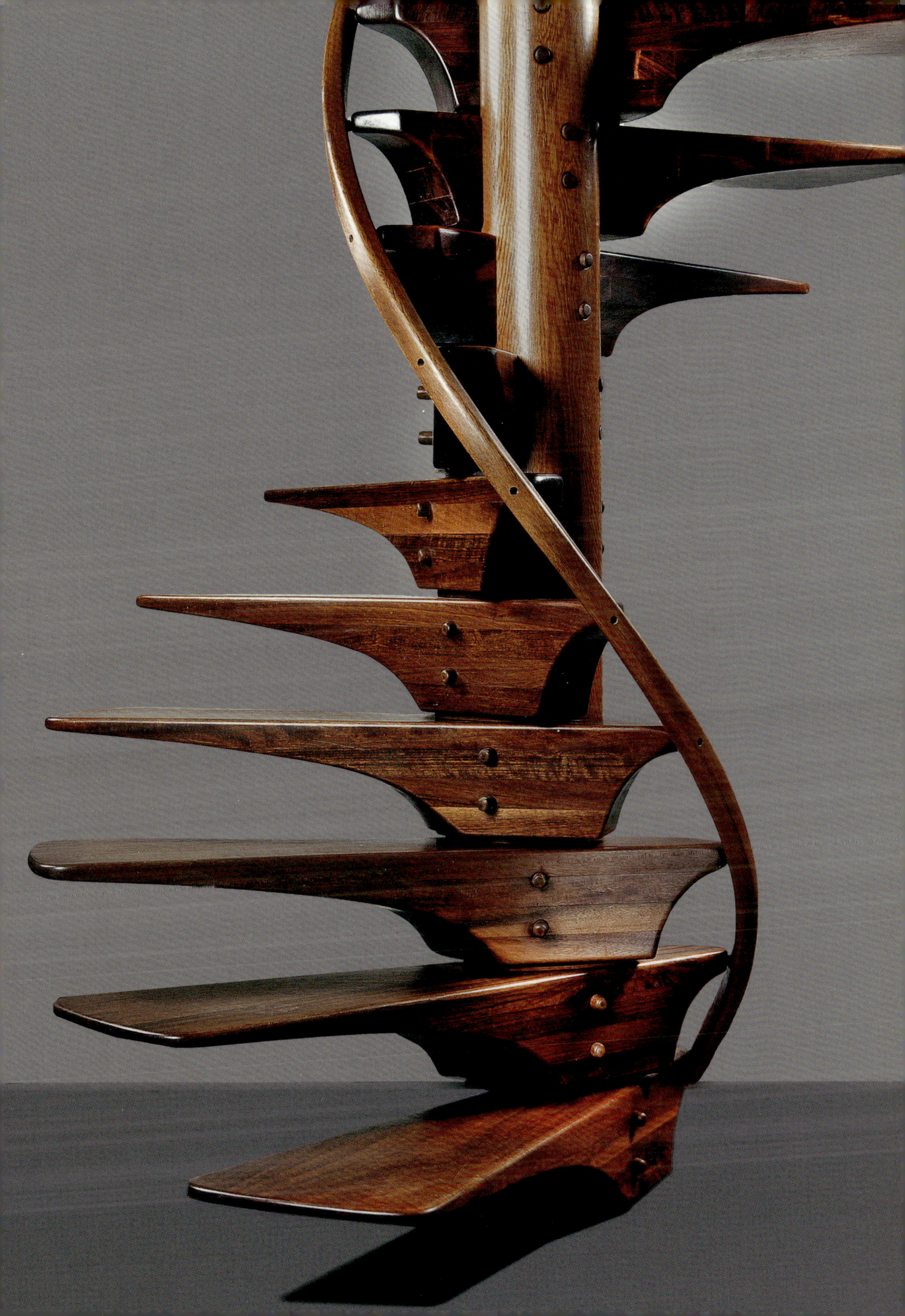

CAT. 15   Chawne Kimber, *still not*, 2019, machine-pieced, hand-quilted, hand-bound mid-century fabric, quilting cotton, and denim with cotton sashiko thread, 71 ¼ × 69 ⅛ in.

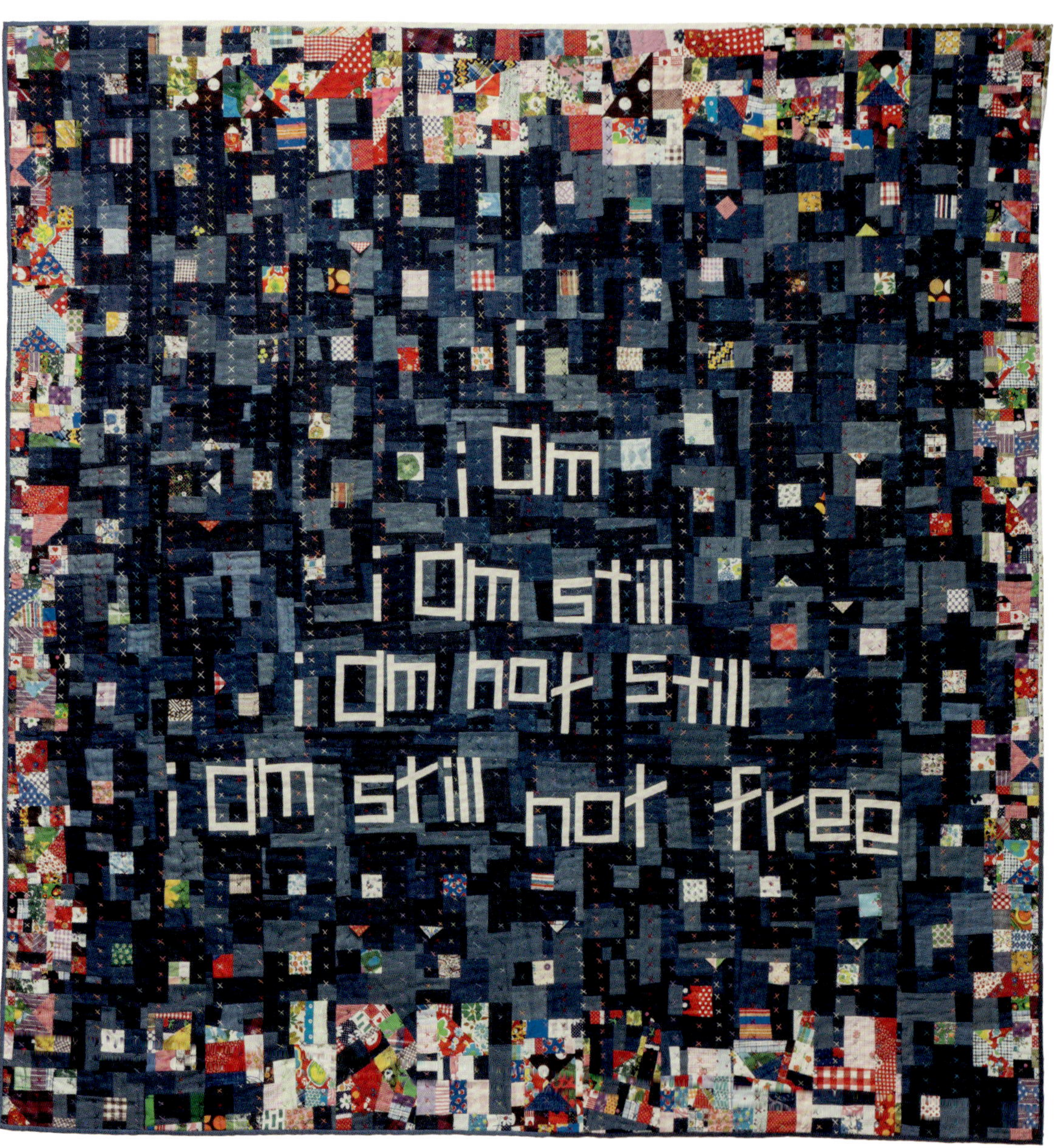
i am
i am still
i am not still
i am still not free

The backdrop of Kimber's text is a body of bluesy denim patches, framed by pops of colorful fabric—all sourced from mid-century textiles.[41] Kimber's choice to use vintage cloth, improvisational patterns, and kantha stitches draws on her memories and family history. Many of her enslaved ancestors in rural Alabama cultivated and ginned cotton. Her great-grandmother, Mamo, and other relatives expressed themselves through quilting.[42] Kimber's father cherished Mamo's quilts because he remembered their creation. As a young boy, he helped Mamo's quilting circle by sitting under the quilts, returning the needles to the surface as the women stitched.[43] The movement of the needle not only becomes a physical reflex, but a reflexive memory passed from family member to family member. The

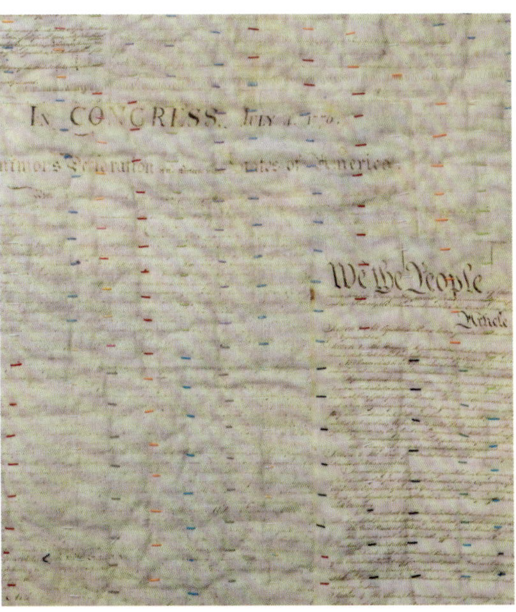

family participated in quilting circles to chat, cry, laugh, think, and mend—to be present together. Mamo's story is told through her quilts, and Kimber continues the thread. Kimber's stitched *i* is a declaration to march on.[44]

Philosophizing about use, Ahmed places pressure on the assumptions that a home is useful and welcome to all. Many homes are sites of dysfunction or trauma, or they entirely displace their inhabitants. They firmly close the door on bodies—like that of Quasimodo—that do not comply with physical and cultural norms. Ahmed explains, "When doors are closed to some people, they are also closed to our stories, which include our stories about closed doors. When a door is closed, you have to find other ways to get information out."[45] This can be through a series of tiny deviations that helps crack open the door that leads to a new shelter, just as the birds made a nest on an urban mailbox.

At a larger scale, L. J. Roberts knitted and sewed a map of queer community building in Brooklyn, New York (Fig. 11). The large-scale work is a vibrantly colored collage of knitted rectangular poufs, reminiscent of both hand-made patchwork quilts and the brickwork of Brooklyn brownstones. Hot pink triangles (a symbol of LGBTQ self-identity) mark the homes with open doors, exemplifying Ahmed's claim that "creating our own dwellings becomes necessary given how queerness can be squeezed out of spaces."[46] *Queer Houses* continues the work of radical community organizing that changes the home, not the inhabitants.[47]

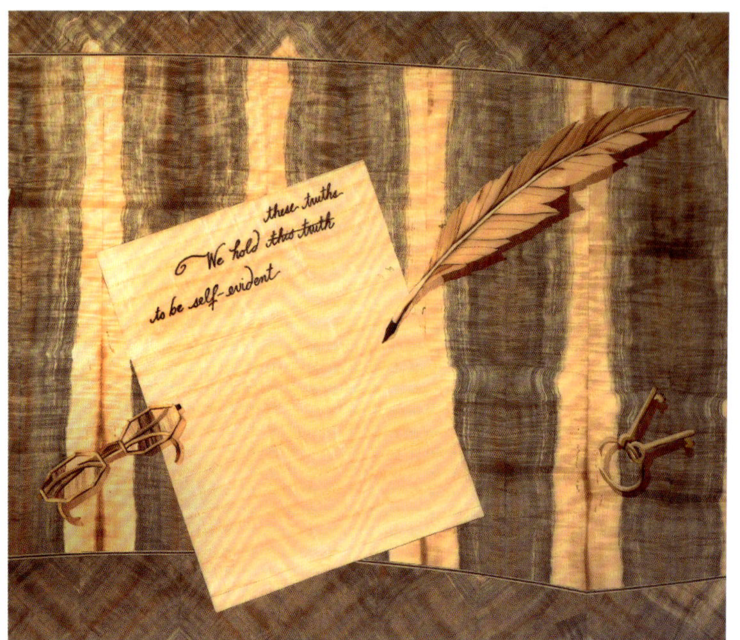

CAT. 16 Silas Kopf, *Founding Fathers Writing Table* (detail and overall), 2010, wood from historic estates of George Washington, Thomas Jefferson, James Madison, Patrick Henry, and James Monroe, 29 ⅞ × 49 ⅛ × 12 ½ in.

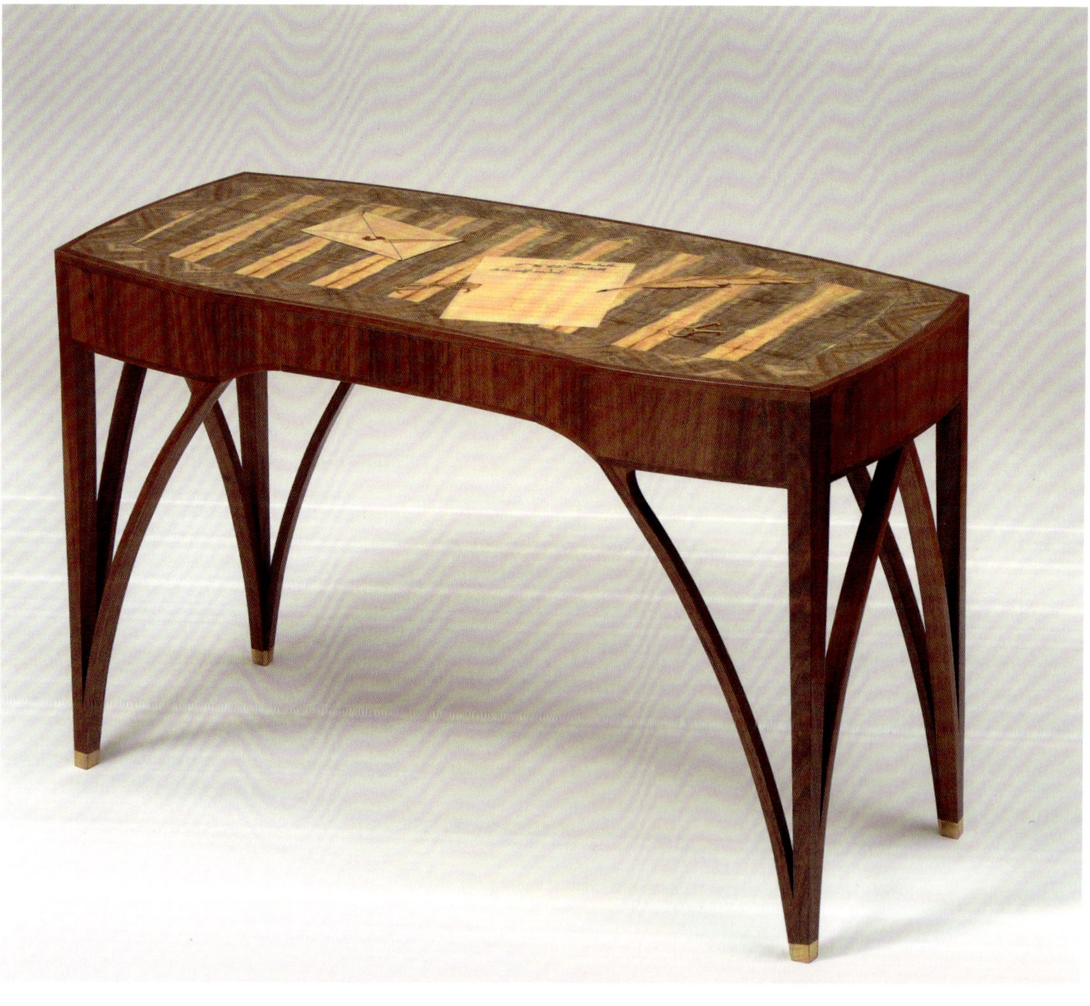

CAT. 17 Thomas Hucker, in collaboration with Silas Kopf, *Dearest Sally Chair* (overall and detail), 2010, walnut, ash, and cherry with marquetry, 32 × 20 × 20 in.

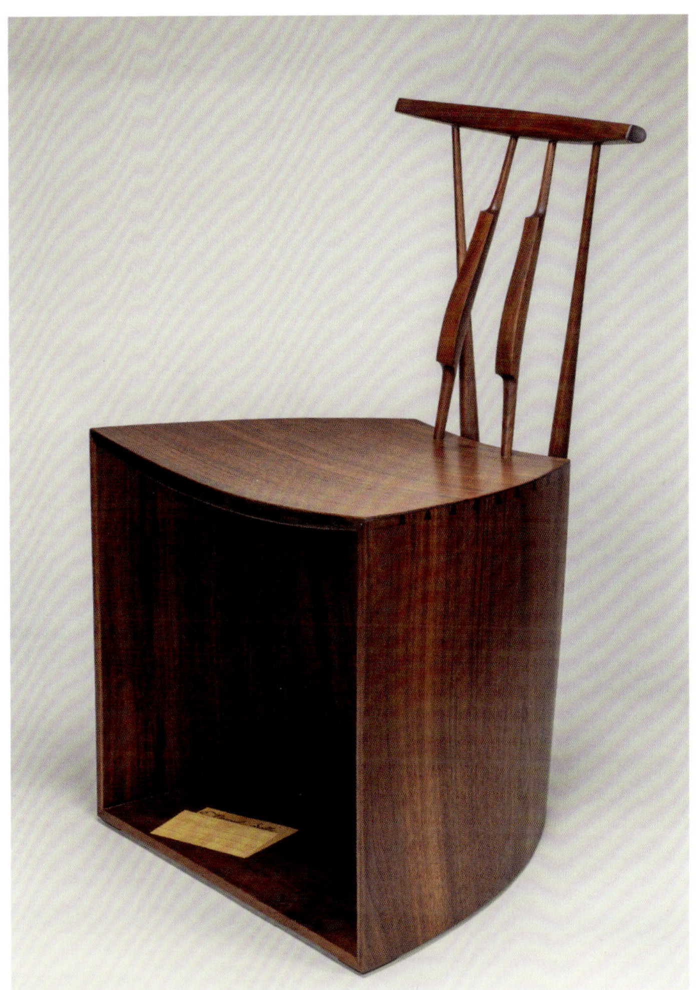

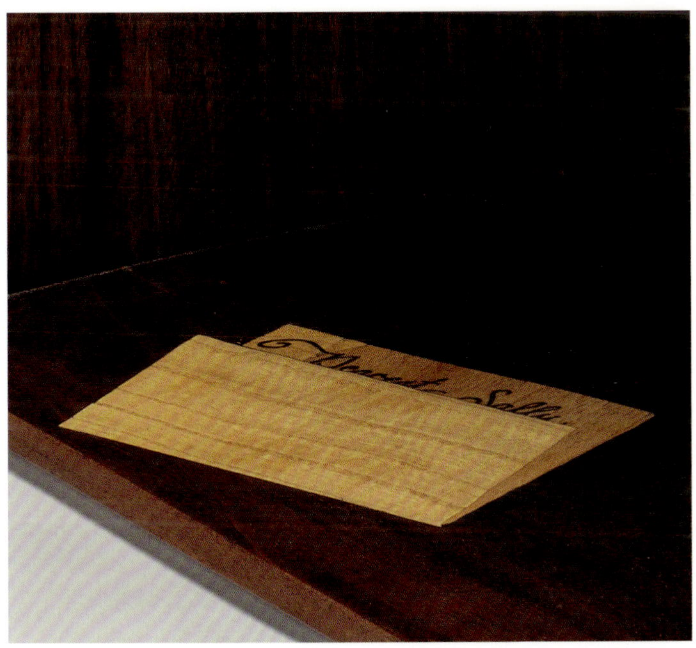

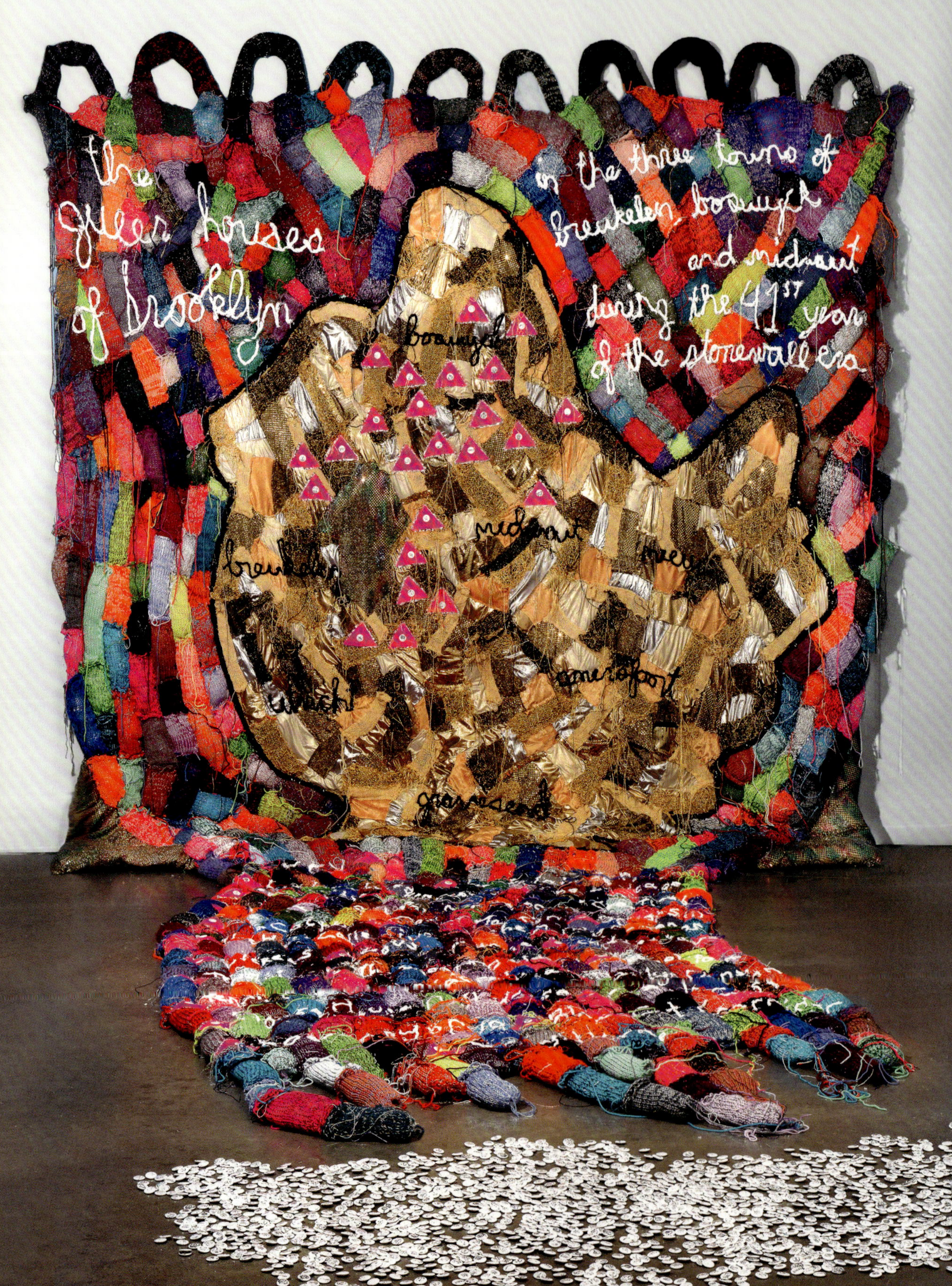

the queer houses of brooklyn
in the three towns of breukelen, boswyck and midwout during the 41ST year of the stonewall era
boswyck
breukelen
midwout
which
amersfoort
gravesend

Fig. 11 L. J. Roberts, *The Queer Houses of Brooklyn in the Three Towns of Breukelen, Boswyck, and Midwout during the 41st Year of the Stonewall Era*, 2011, Poly-Fil, acrylic, rayon, Lurex, wool, polyester, cotton, lamé, sequins, and blended fabrics with printed pinback buttons, 138 × 114 × 108 in., Gift of Elaine Reuben, 2012.43

CAT. 18 Roberto Lugo, *Juicy*, 2021, glazed stoneware with enamel paint and luster, 19 ⅞ × 13 ⅜ × 9 ⅜ in.

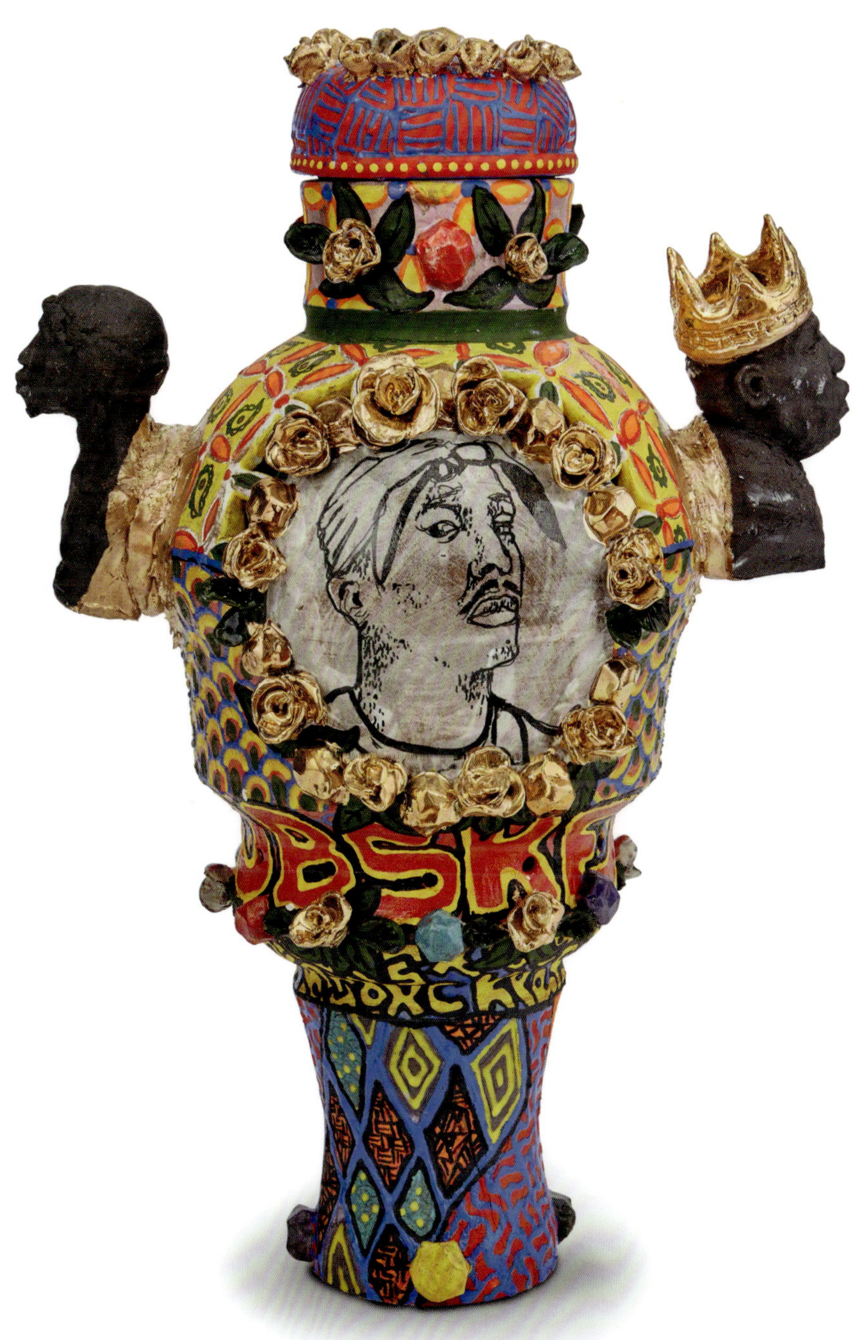

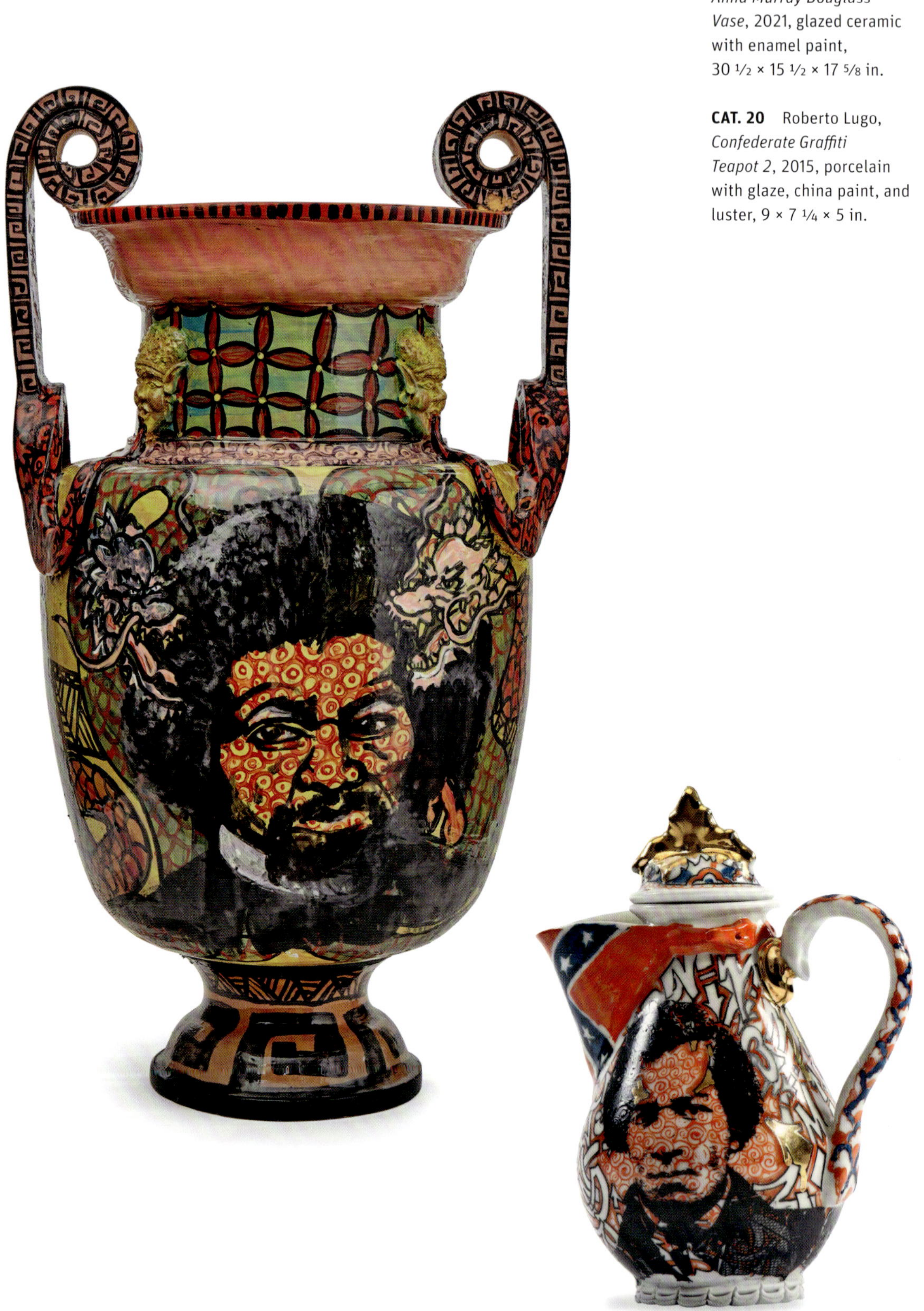

CAT. 19 Roberto Lugo,
*Frederick Douglass and
Anna Murray Douglass
Vase*, 2021, glazed ceramic
with enamel paint,
30 ½ × 15 ½ × 17 ⅝ in.

CAT. 20 Roberto Lugo,
*Confederate Graffiti
Teapot 2*, 2015, porcelain
with glaze, china paint, and
luster, 9 × 7 ¼ × 5 in.

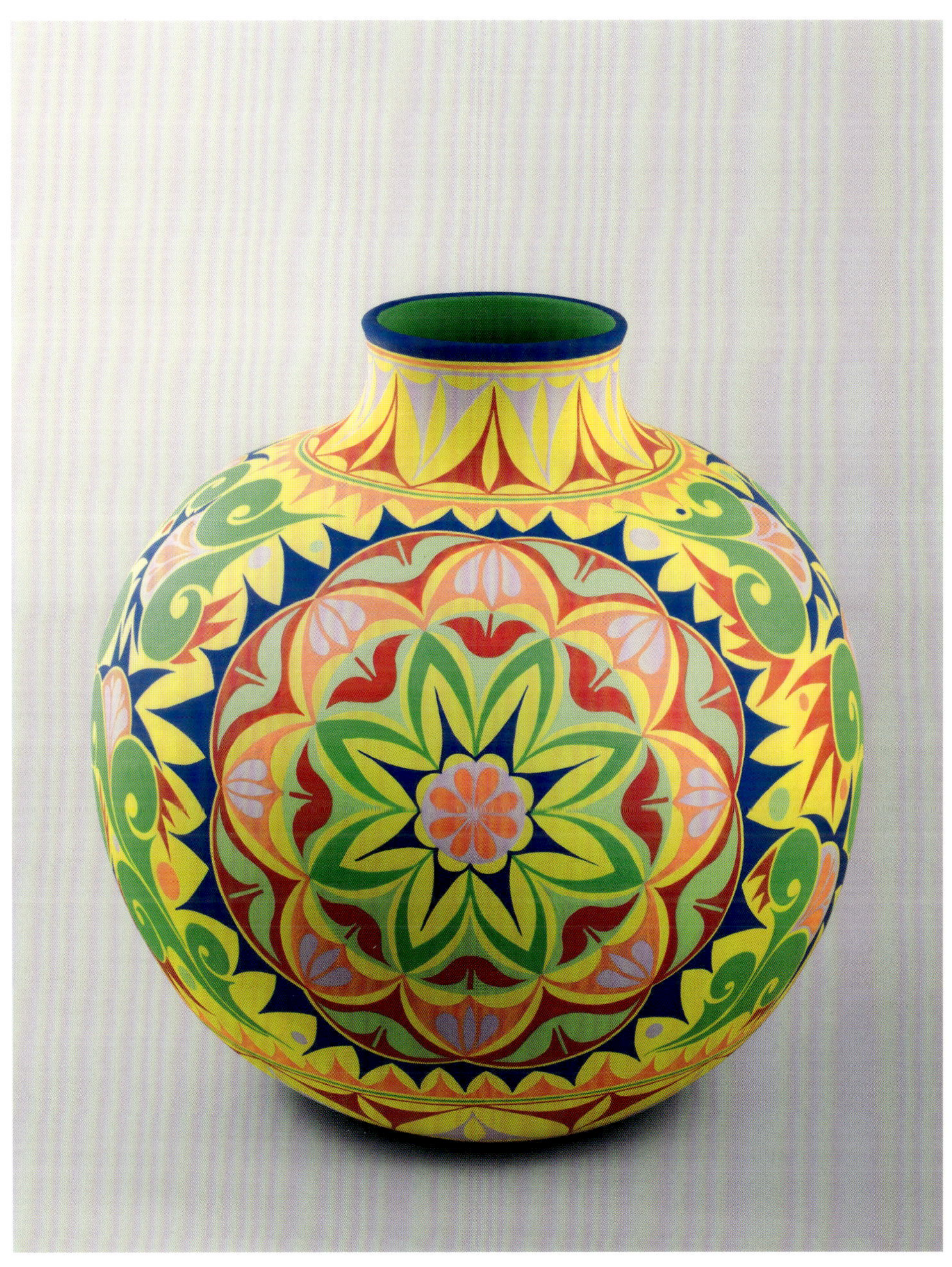

CAT. 22 Janel Jacobson, *#505 Oak Savanna Sentinel*, 2014, boxwood with acrylic paint, gold and silver leaf powder, and nail lacquer, 6 × 3 × 2 1/8 in.

Fig. 12 Tim Jerman, *Hermit Crab*, 2000, flameworked glass, 5 3/4 × 5 3/8 × 6 3/4 in., Museum purchase through the Renwick Acquisitions Fund, 2000.26.1

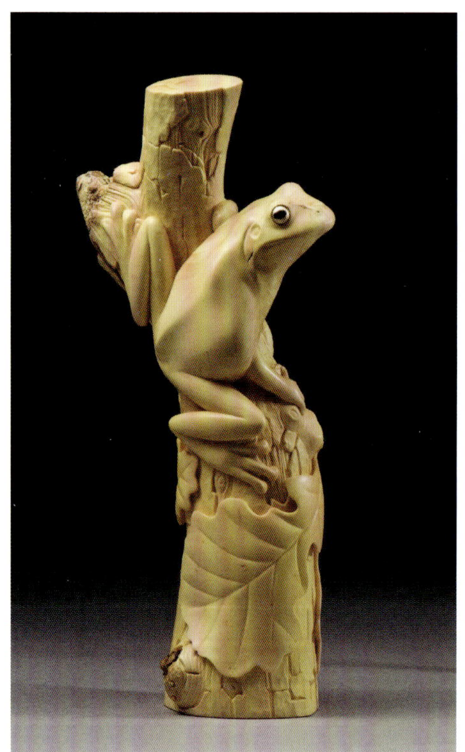

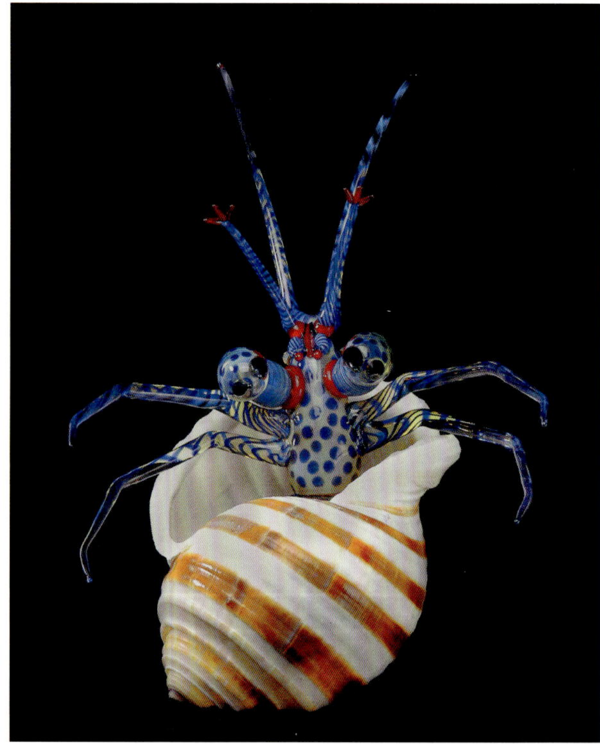

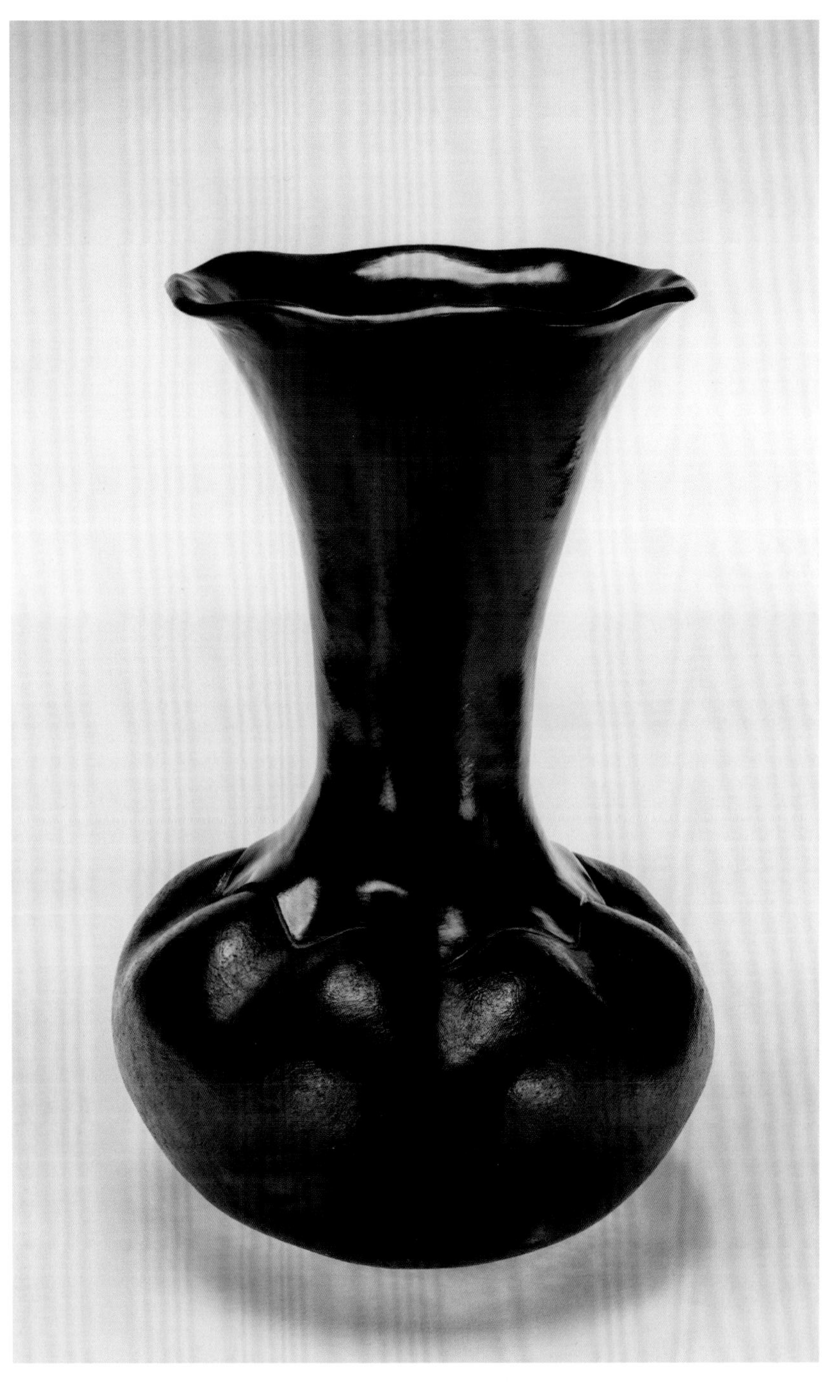

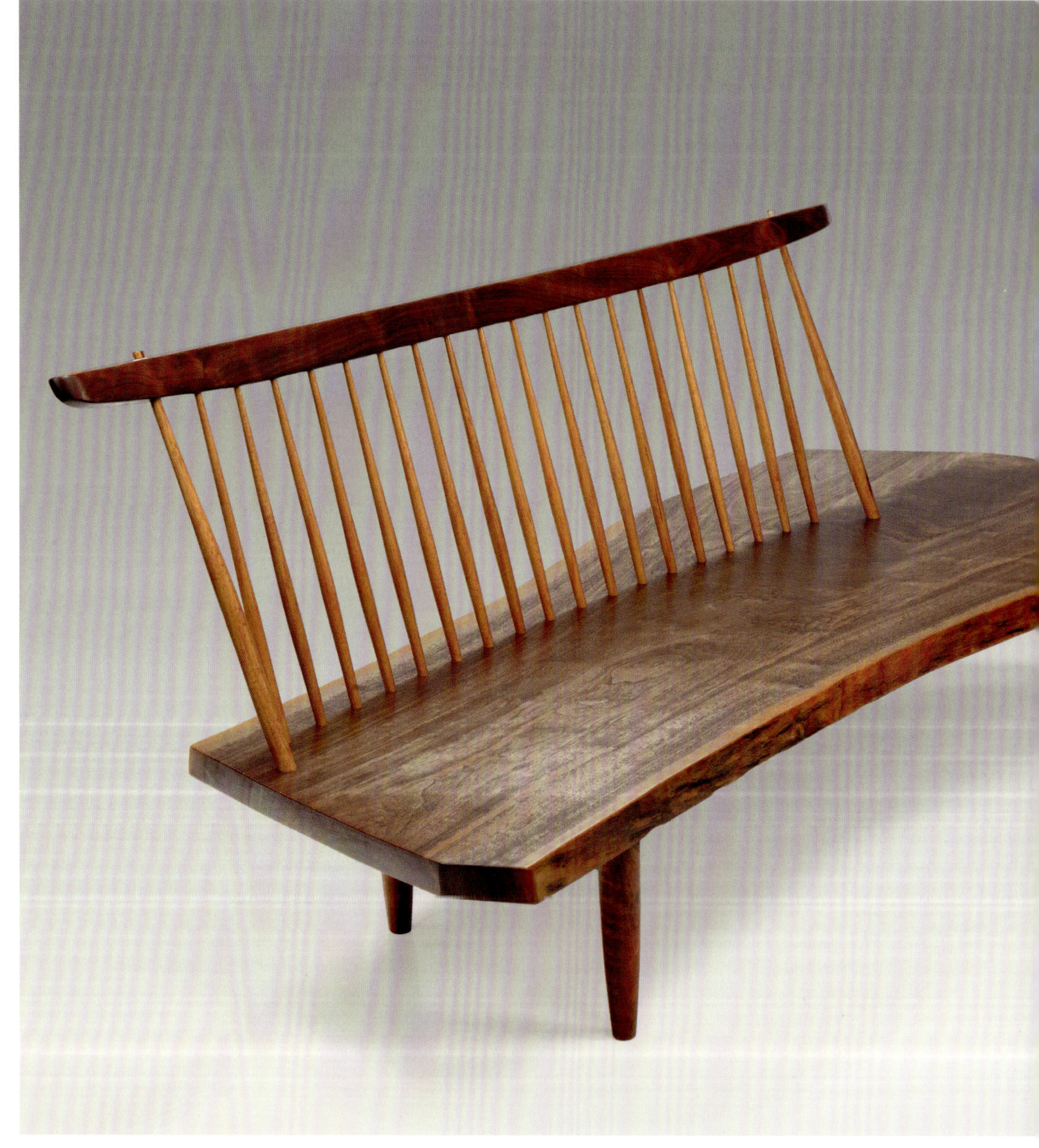

Fig. 13 George Nakashima, *Conoid Bench*, 1977, black walnut and hickory, 31 1/8 × 84 1/2 × 35 5/8 in., Gift of Dr. and Mrs. Warren D. Brill, 1991.121

CAT. 24 Laura Andreson, *Bowl*, 1939, earthenware with uranium glaze, 4 × diam. 11 7/8 in.

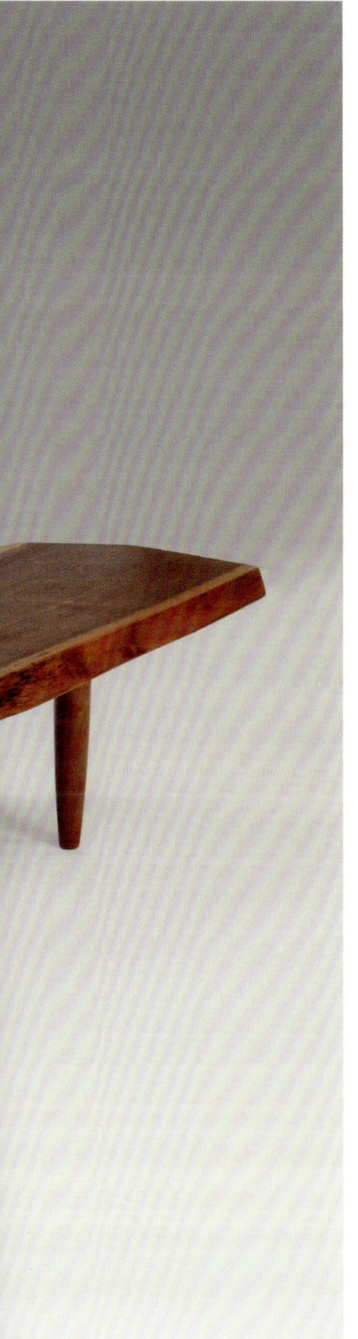

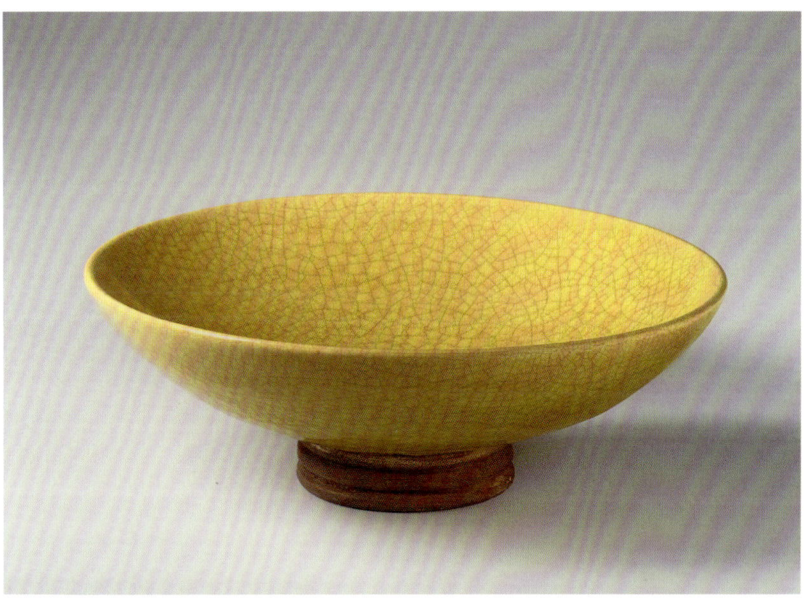

CAT. 25 gwendolyn yoppolo,
scoopbowl service, 2010,
porcelain with micro-
crystalline glaze, bowl:
6 × diam. 14 ½ in., 10 spoons:
2 × 5 ¼ × 3 in. each

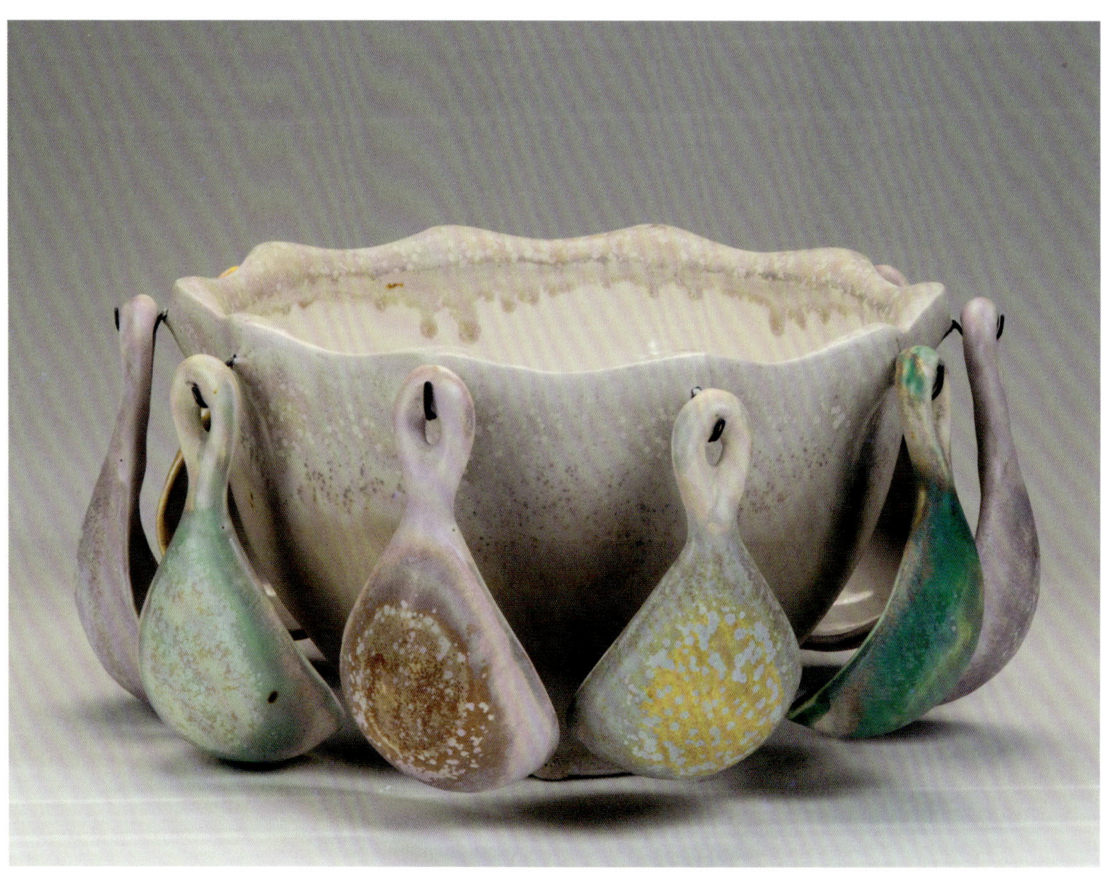

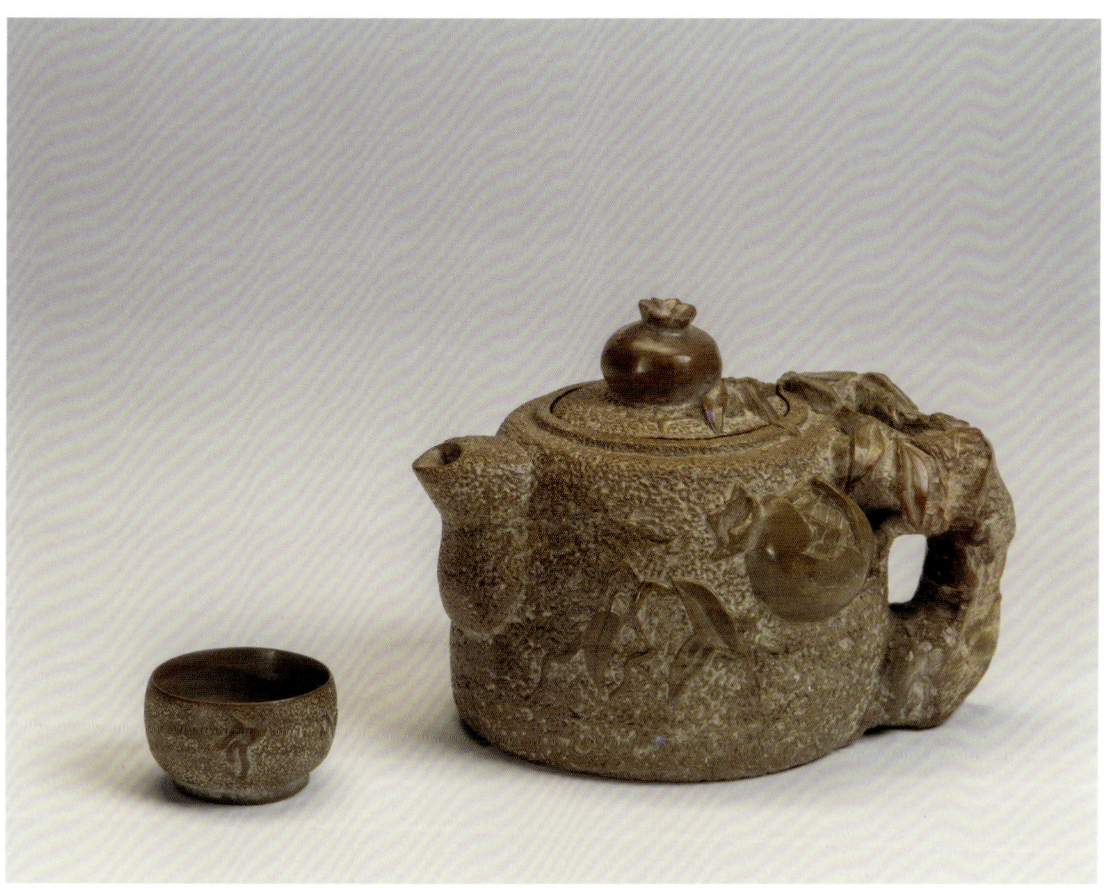

CAT. 26 Homei Iseyama, *Teapot and Cup*, 1939–45, carved found slate, teapot with lid: 4 5/8 × 6 7/8 × 5 in., teacup: 1 1/4 × diam. 2 in.

Fig. 14   Margarita Cabrera, *White Coffee Maker*, 2011, vinyl, copper wire, and thread, 12 ¾ × 8 ¾ × 10 ½ in., Museum purchase through the Luisita L. and Franz H. Denghausen Endowment, 2012.35.2A–D

Fig. 15   Margarita Cabrera, *Black and Grey Toaster*, 2011, vinyl, copper wire, and thread, 7 ¼ × 10 ½ × 7 ⅛ in., Museum purchase through the Frank K. Ribelin Endowment, 2012.36

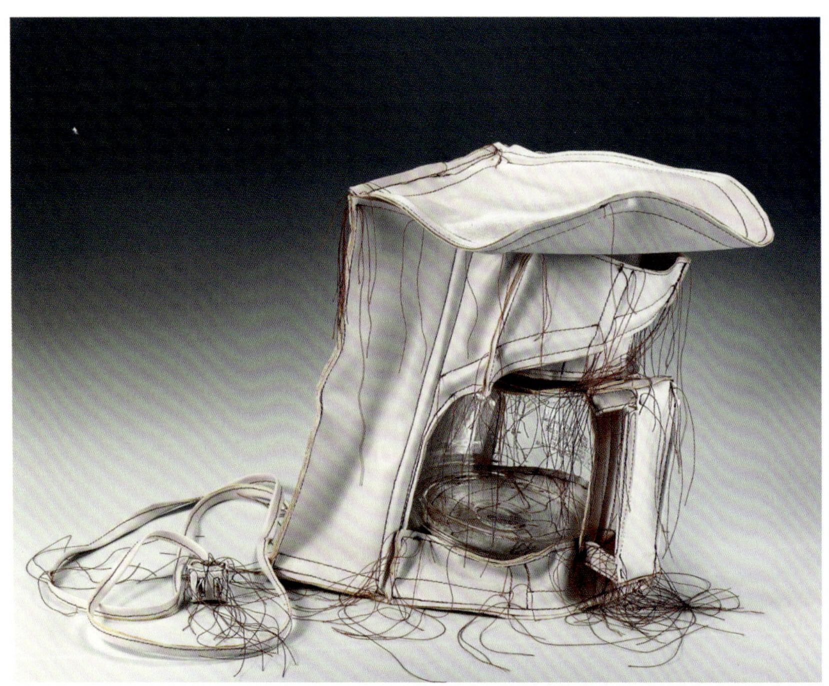

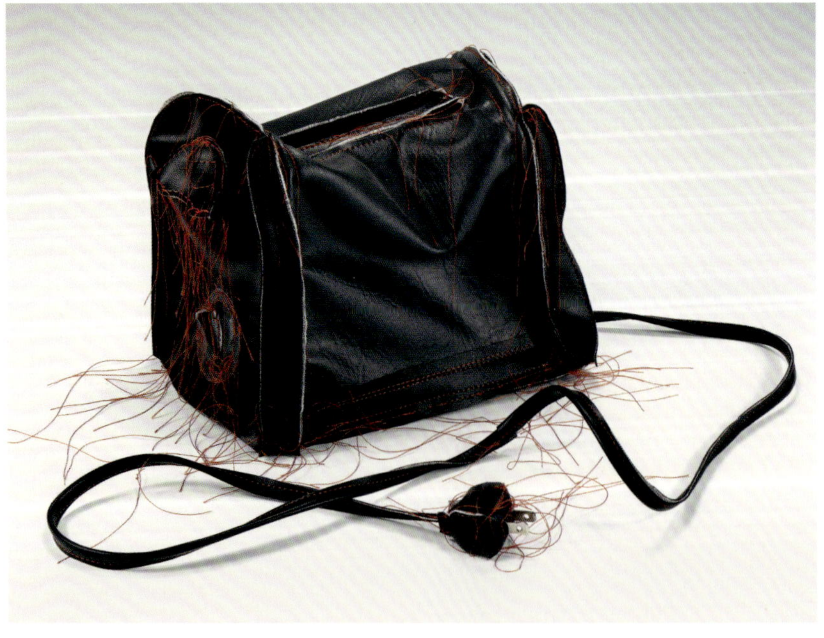

Fig. 16 Margarita Cabrera, *Brown Blender*, 2011, vinyl, copper wire, and thread, 14 ¼ × 6 ½ × 9 ⅜ in., Museum purchase through the Luisita L. and Franz H. Denghausen Endowment, 2012.35.1A–D

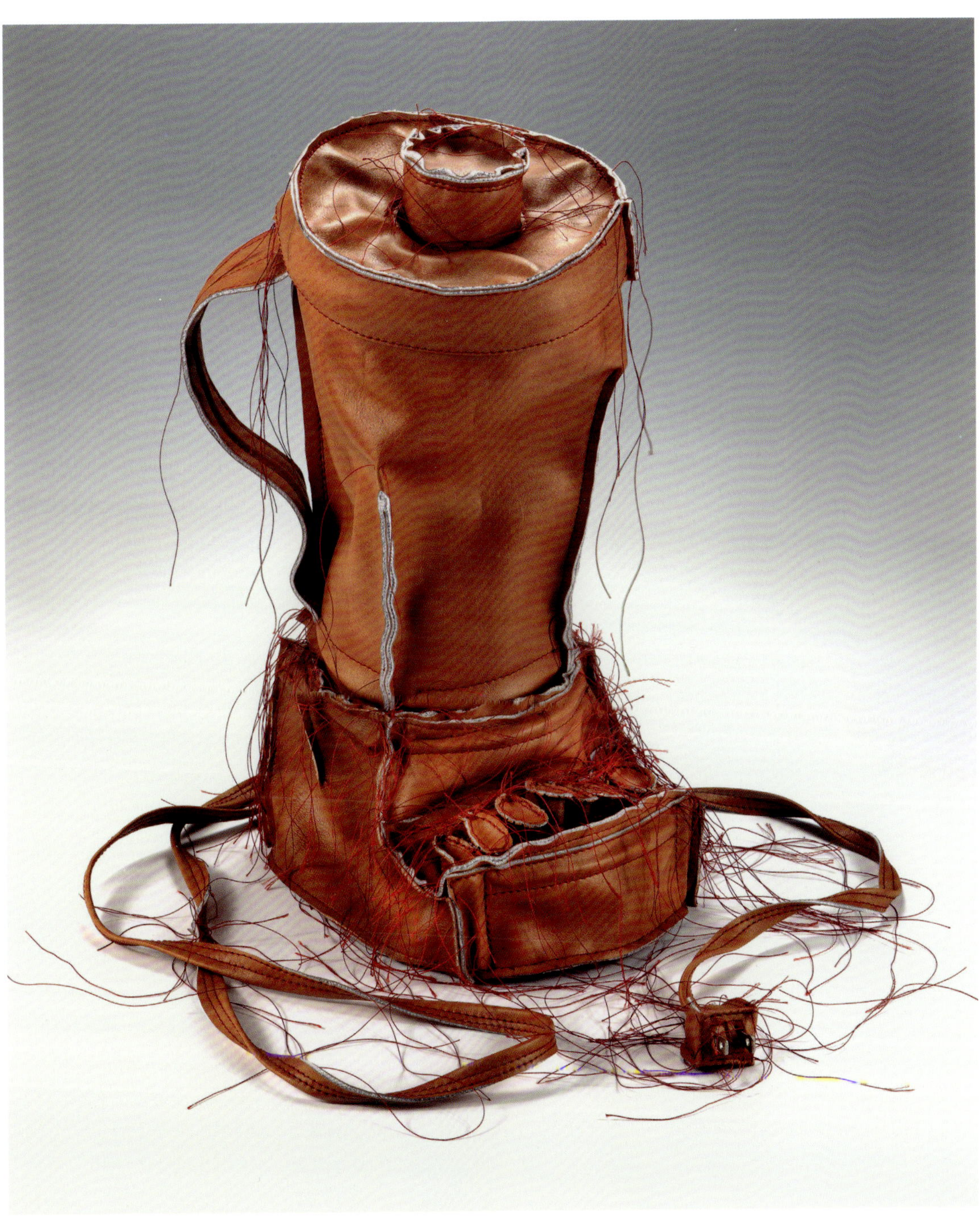

*I press my hand to the steel curtain—
chainlink fence crowned with rolled barbed wire—
rippling from the sea where Tijuana touches San Diego
unrolling over mountains
and plains
and deserts ...*

*1,950 mile-long open wound
dividing a pueblo, a culture,
running down the length of my body,
staking fence rods in my flesh,
splits me   splits me
me raja   me raja*

—Gloria Anzaldúa, excerpt from *Borderlands/La Frontera: The New Mestiza*[48]

Nations are defined by their borders, the dividing lines between lands and the people who are contained or excluded. The first barriers between the United States and Mexico were installed in the early twentieth century. Later, under the leadership of President Bill Clinton, the looming fences separating California from Tijuana were constructed with surplus corrugated steel used as helicopter landing pads in the American war in Vietnam. Successive administrations continued building barriers in the borderlands, which were notably intensified by the anti-immigration rhetoric of 2016 Republican presidential candidate and eventual president Donald J. Trump.

Fiber artist Consuelo Jiménez Underwood has made weavings about immigration at the US-Mexico border for much of her career. Her father was an undocumented field worker in California, and her family regularly crossed the border. In the early 1990s, while driving along the 405 Freeway in San Diego, Jiménez Underwood became distraught at the sight of an "Immigrant Crossing" sign. "I almost braked. I was appalled, angry and shocked that the citizens of our nation were asked to accept this image of a running family crossing the 405 Freeway. Plus, I totally identified with the little girl," she later recalled.[49] Jiménez Underwood began depicting this motif

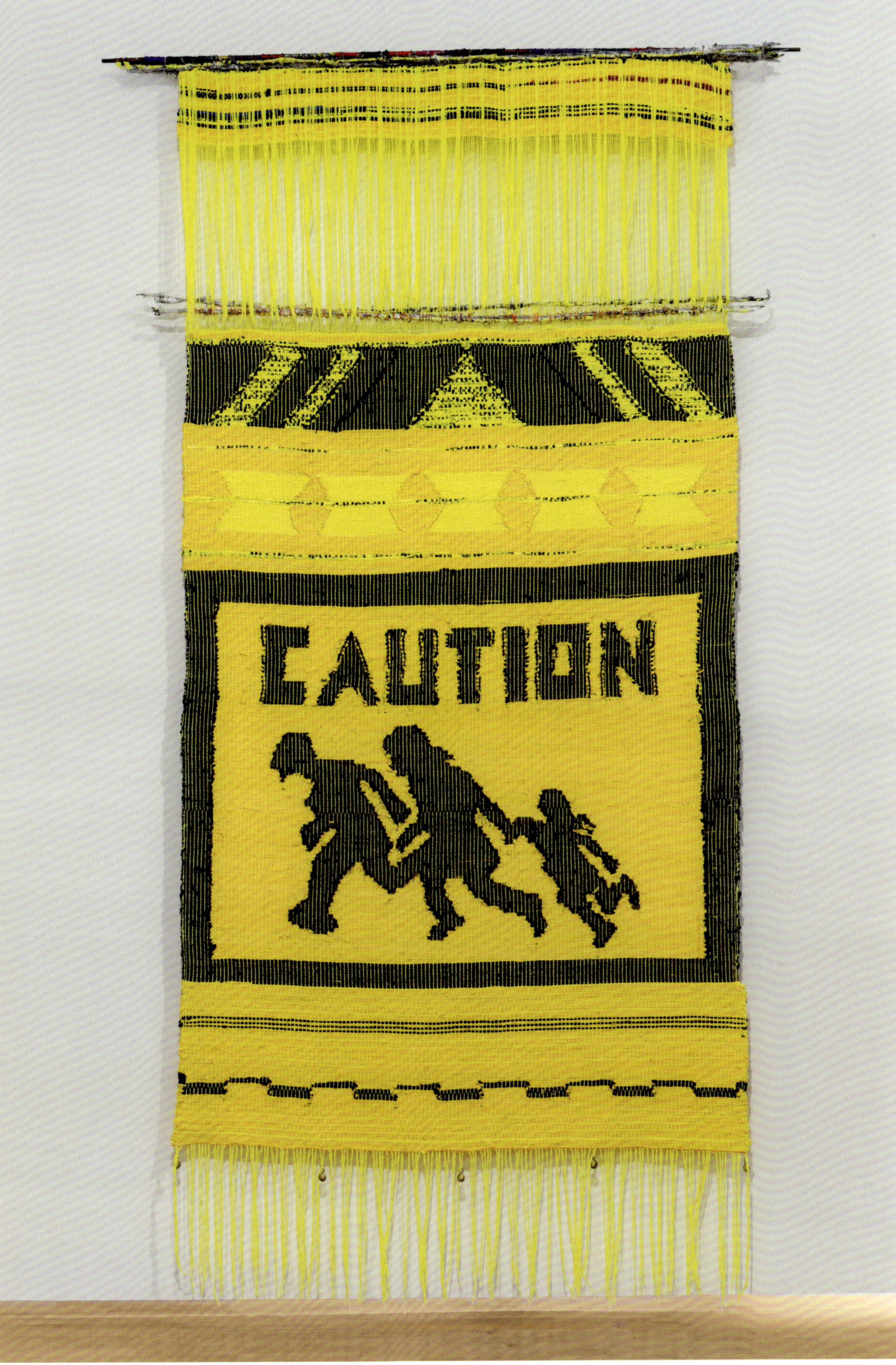

CAUTION

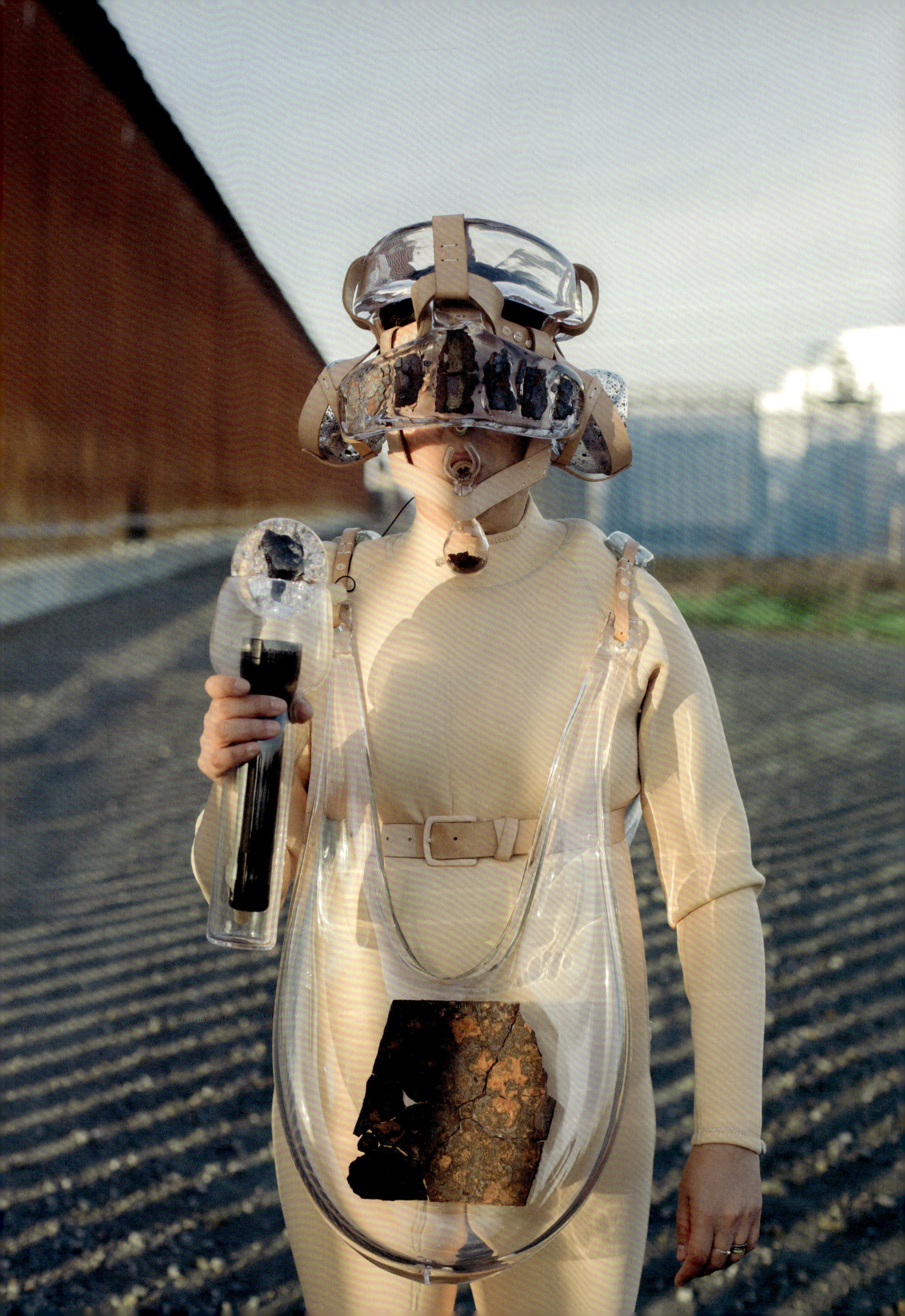

CAT. 28 Tanya Aguiñiga, *Metabolizing the Border*, 2018–20, analogue VR headset, breath distiller, sound amplifiers, Maglite border torch, "Saint Juan Diego and Our Lady" cloak, water backpack, and huaraches made of blown, cast, and sculpted glass with rusted metal pieces of US-Mexico border fence, leather, and cotton twine; neoprene wetsuit

Aguiñiga walking along the US-Mexico border fence

threaded with barbed wire, caution tape, and yellow cotton into many of her weavings. The monumental work *Run, Jane, Run!* (CAT. 27) pays homage to the migrants killed on the highway and makes visible their humanity.

Artist Tanya Aguiñiga affirms alternative stories about the border fence. Her project *Metabolizing the Border* (CAT. 28) explores the corporeal and psychological experiences faced by migrants while crossing the borderlands. In 2019 she gathered rusted fragments of the steel fence between Tijuana, where she grew up, and San Diego, where she traveled to school every day. Aguiñiga brought the fence fragments to an artist residency at the Pilchuck Glass School in Washington state and embedded them in several blown-glass and mixed-media wearable elements for a 2020 performance at the border fence. The wearables processed the border through her five senses. The headpiece, its design inspired by a virtual reality headset, focuses the sense of sight through the ocular lens, the sense of sound through the ear amplifiers, and the senses of taste and smell through the breath distiller. Huaraches, a border torch, and a "San Juan Diego and our Lady" cloak exaggerate the sense of touch and movement. The cloak references the tilma of San Juan Diego, a significant spiritual and national symbol of Mexico. The sandals are modeled after tire-soled

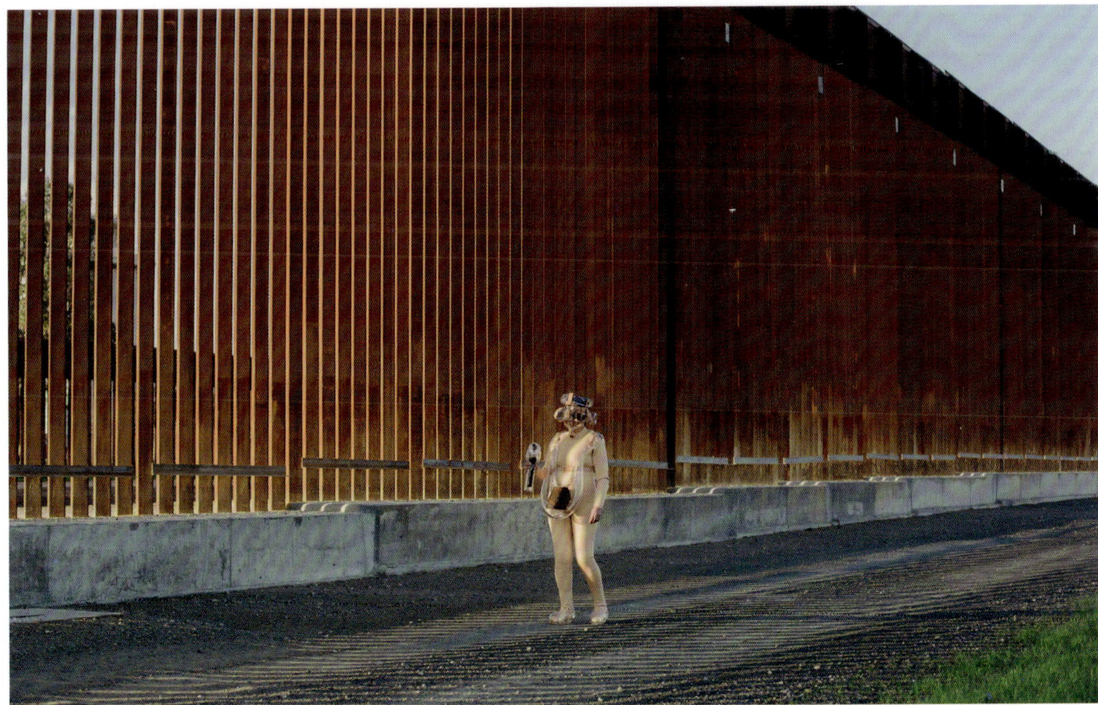

huaraches that Indigenous Peoples and others wear in Mexico and Central America. The artist also wore a neoprene suit for protection and a water backpack for hydration. In January 2020 Aguiñiga walked along the US-Mexico border wall wearing each element of the suit; thirty minutes in, the glass huaraches began to break beneath her feet.

Aguiñiga's performance was arduous and intimate. There was no moment of victory because the fence itself remains insurmountable. And yet, her burden of the scraps of steel countered the dominant narrative of the wall. Each step offered a new path toward justice. Just as the fence came to overpower the borderlands over the course of a century, activism can undo it.[50] As Aguiñiga has explained, histories of craft, many learned from her family, pave the way for collaboration and regeneration.[51] *Metabolizing the Border* embodies many of the struggles and perils migrants face throughout their journey for a better home.

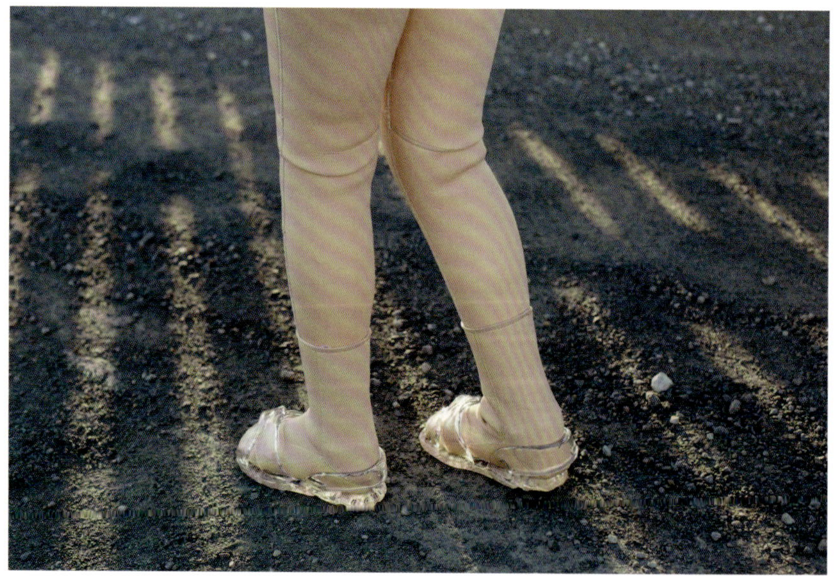

CAT. 29 Ronald Rael and Virginia San Fratello, *Bad Ombrés v.2* (full set and detail), 2017, six 3D-printed ceramic vessels, overall: 23 × 51 × 35 in.

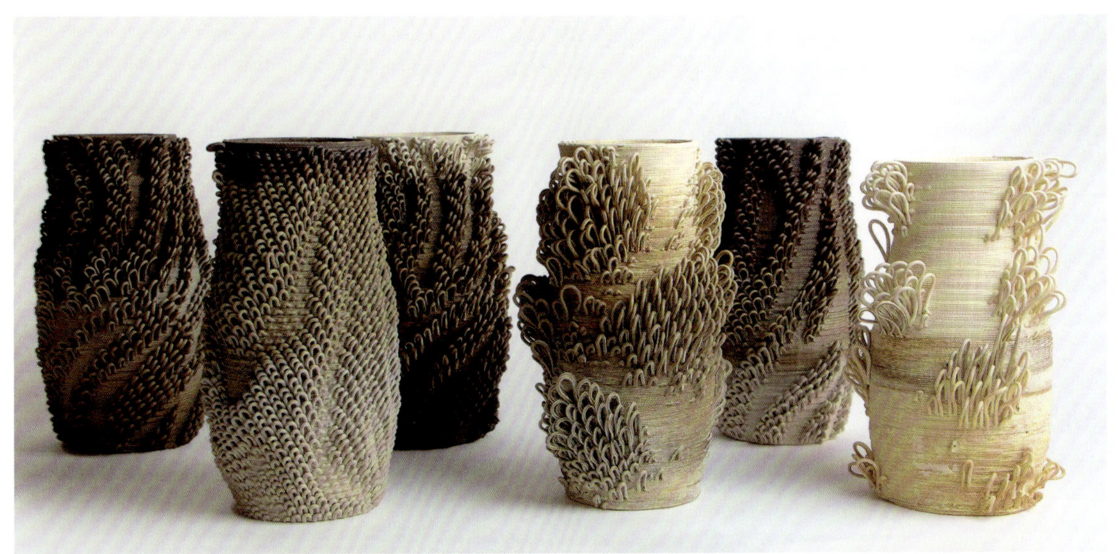

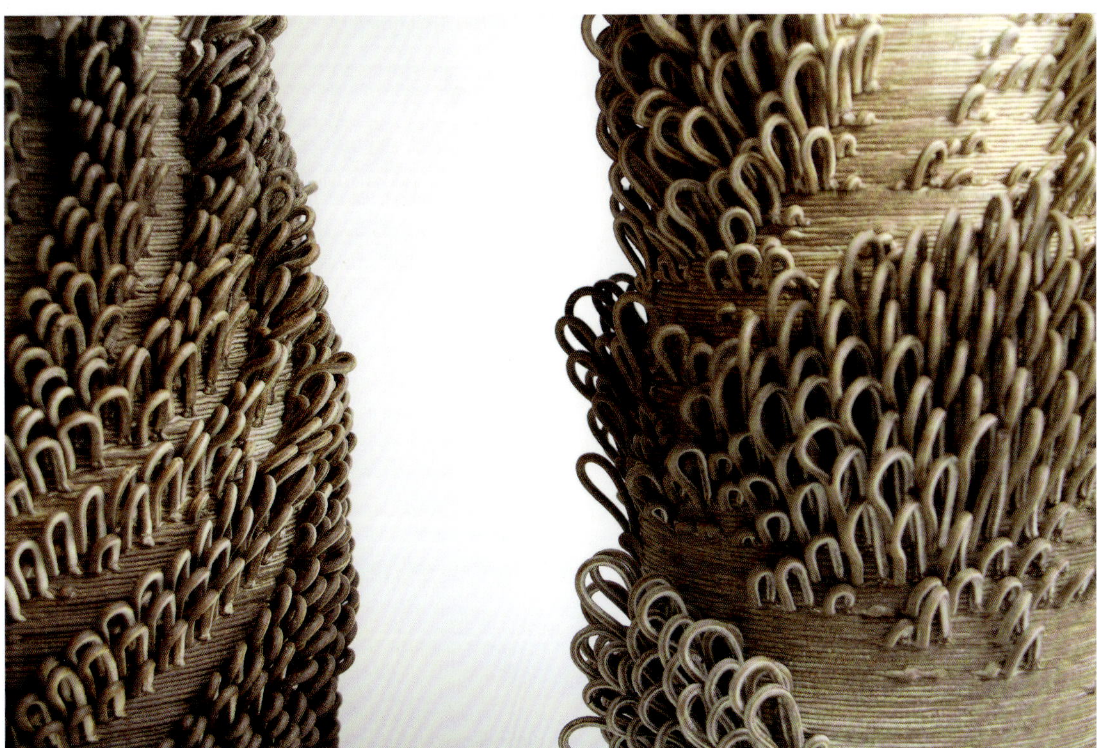

What's the function of a galaxy? I don't know if our life has a purpose and I don't see that it matters. What does matter is that we're a part. Like a thread in a cloth or a grass-blade in a field. It is and we are. What we do is like wind blowing on the grass.

—Ursula K. Le Guin, from *The Lathe of Heaven* [52]

Perhaps the only constant of the universe is that there is no constant. It is an infinite exhale into immeasurable space and time. Many artists draw inspiration from the poetic and scientific expanse of the cosmos. Glass artists in particular have used the language of light to characterize the sky, sun, and beyond. Howard Ben Tré's *Wrapped Light* (CAT. 30) seemingly transcends time and space. Light diffuses through the semiopaque glass and gold-leaf surface, creating a transfixing glow — an allusion to the mystery of life beyond the ordinary.

Artist Therman Statom alludes to the night sky in his wall sculpture *Arabian Seasons* (Fig. 17). Even more, he calls attention to the contradictions of the universe. The strokes, dots, and daubs of paint are both brilliant and intimate. Clear glass panels contain an assemblage of found objects, including a playing card, a rock, maps, a tree branch, a magnifying glass, and glass rods. Each object surely contains a memory of the artist, but he holds his cards close to his chest. With the dreamlike shapes and inchoate objects, the work traverses the depths of the imagination. Like the universe, the stories of *Arabian Seasons* have no beginning, end, or center.

Statom deliberately obfuscates his memories within the artwork, effectively inviting viewers to bring their own experiences and memories to the glass. Bachelard writes, "the daydream transports the dreamer outside the immediate world to a world that bears the mark of infinity."[53] Change is a condition of the universe, and even small things carry large opportunities for change. Statom, for example, has spent much of his life advocating for children through creative workshops at children's hospitals, Girl Scout troops, Omaha Public Schools' Native Indigenous Centered Education Program, and alternative schools in Nebraska. Through outreach, Statom fuses the values of skill, creativity, and collaboration. In a 2020 lecture, Statom exclaimed, "I love working with people. It's more fun in the world blowing glass with a team making something. You can change the world when you do that. You really do."[54] His life is a constellation of acts that move the imagination, from art to activism.

The incomprehensible, immense scale of the universe remains intimate because

CAT. 30 Howard Ben Tré,
Wrapped Light #3/2, 2008,
cast glass with gold leaf
and pigmented waxes
on metal base, overall:
22 ¾ × diam. 8 ¼ in.

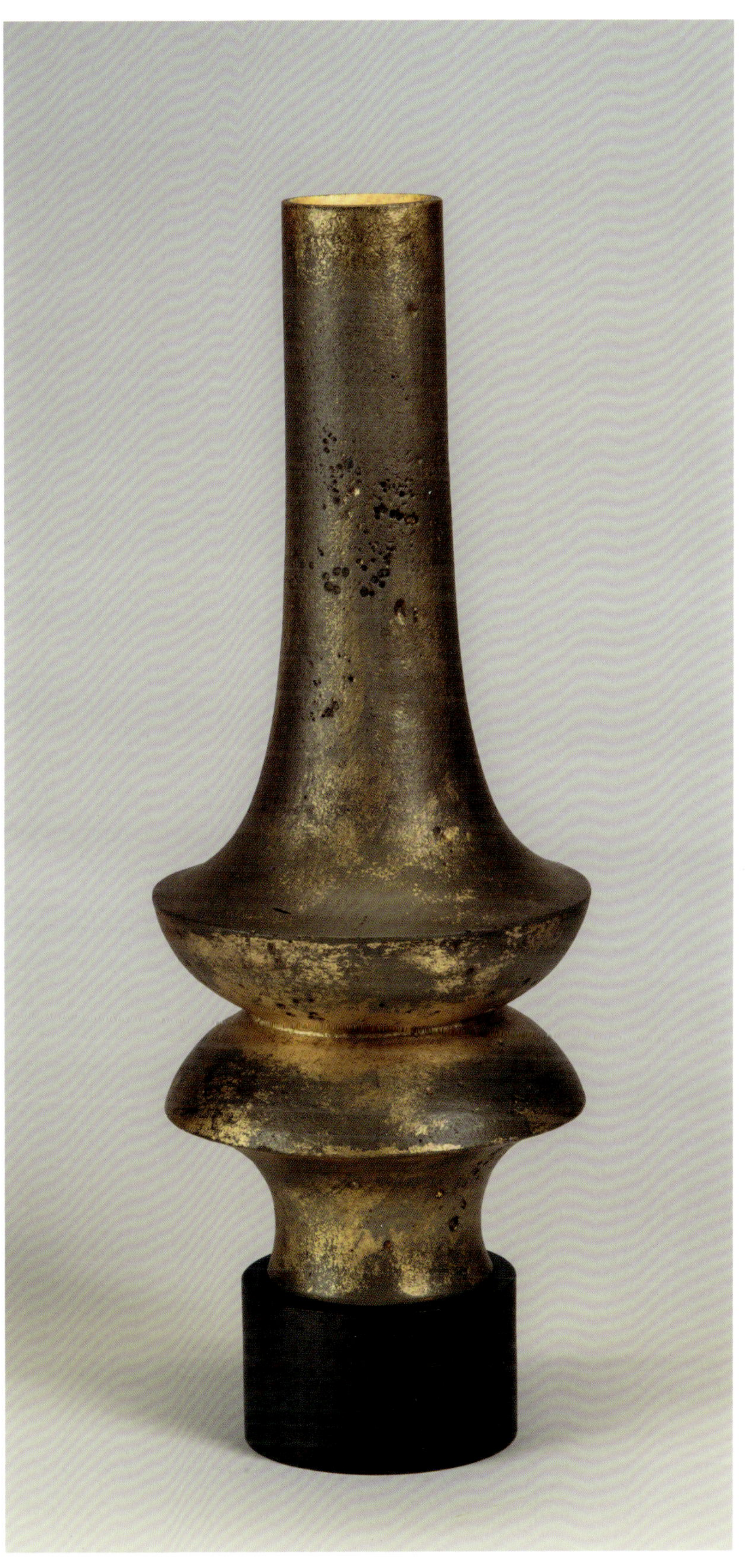

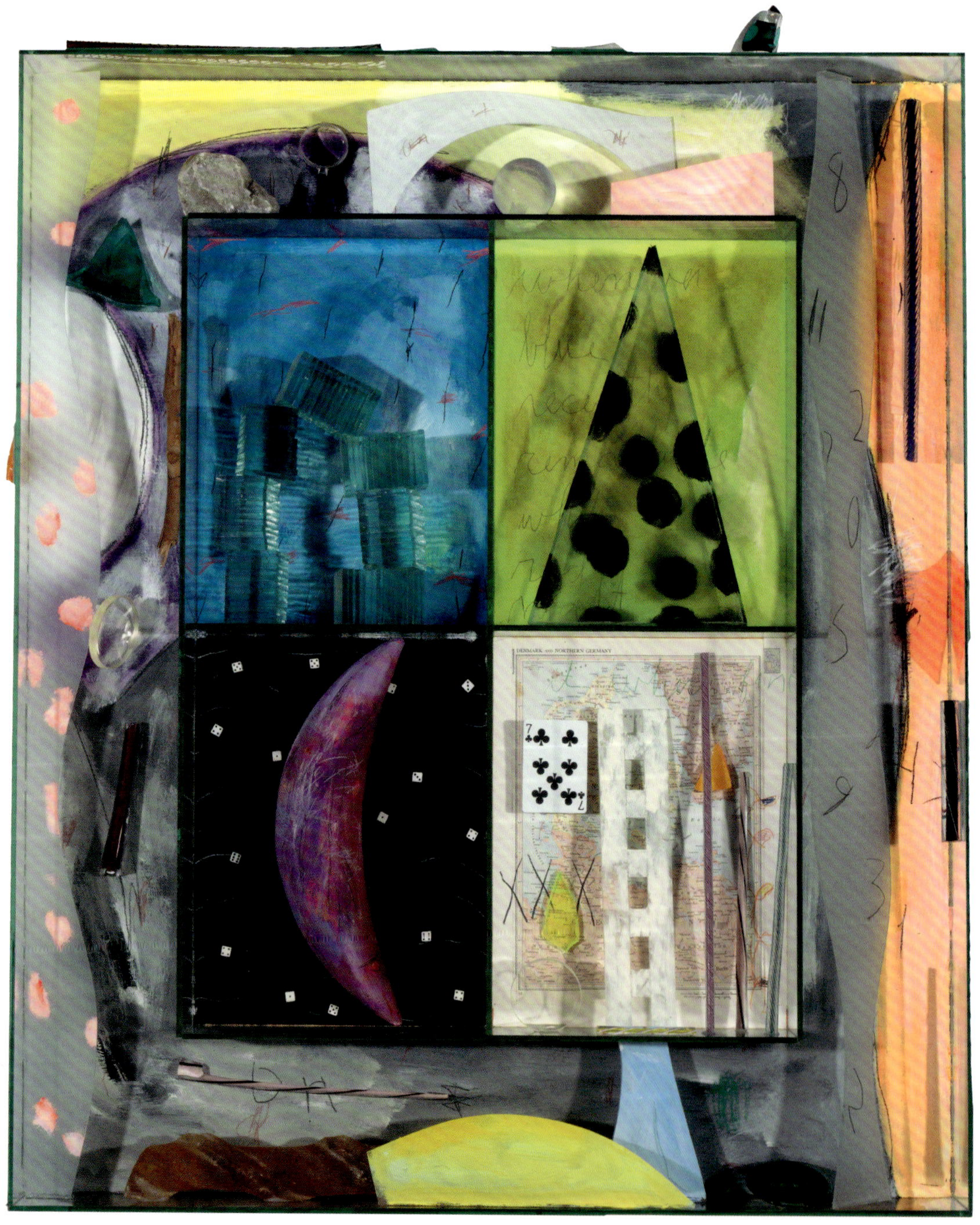

Fig. 17   Therman Statom, *Arabian Seasons*, 1994, glass with paint and found objects, 42 × 36 × 4 5/8 in., Gift of the James Renwick Alliance and museum purchase made possible by the Smithsonian Institution Collections Acquisition Program, 1995.5

CAT. 31 Rick Dillingham,
Large Silver Globe, 1978,
reassembled raku-
fired earthenware with
glaze and silver leaf,
12 ⅞ × diam. 15 ⅞ in.

everything on this planet is made from the same cosmic dust.[55] In this way, an egg is doing the same journeywork as a moon. Expressions of craft help us feel the world we presently inhabit and make possible new stories and paths for the next fifty years and beyond, or as long as people are here to dream and make. Perhaps this is the constant relevance of craft. In order to craft a better world, it must first be imagined. ✳

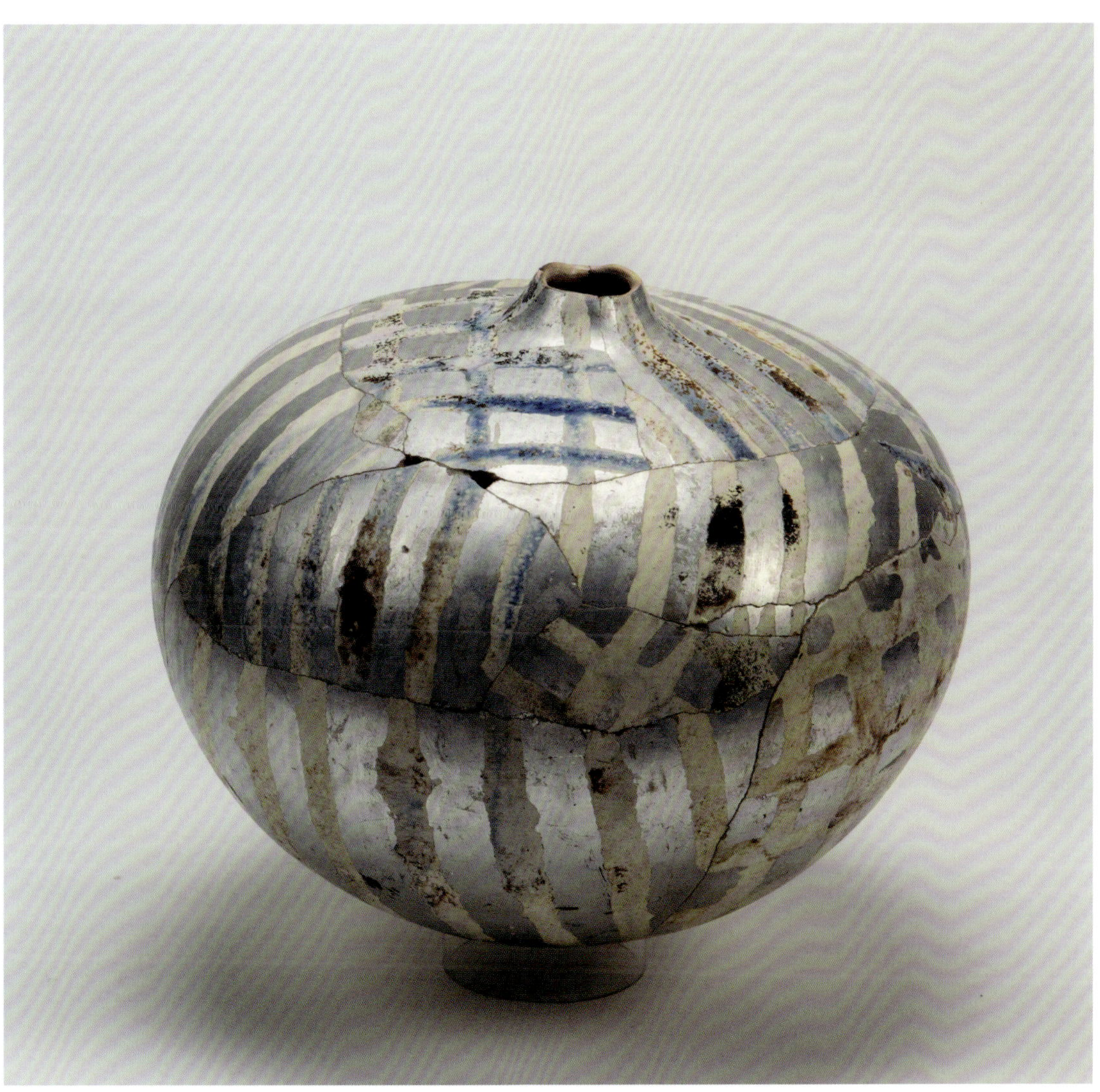

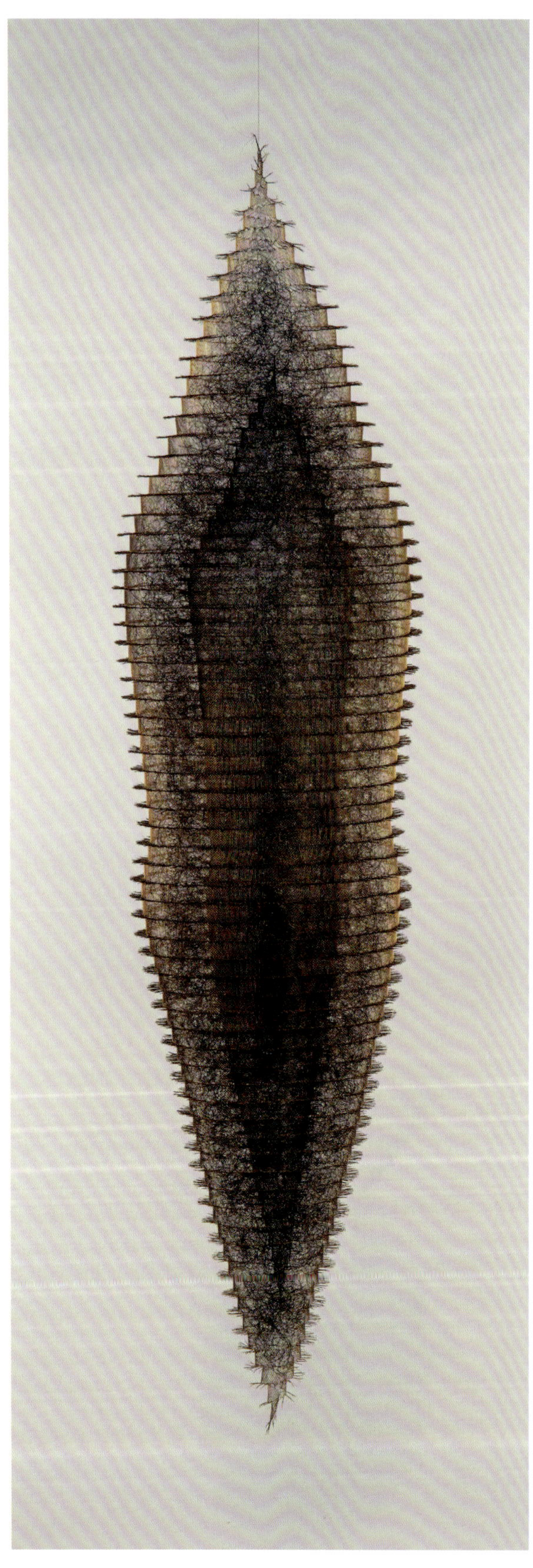

CAT. 32   Lanny Bergner, *Celestial Body*, 2005, bronze, brass, and aluminum, 63 × diam. 15 in.

CAT. 33   Ché Rhodes, *Untitled*, 2007, blown and cut glass, 4 pieces: 18 ½ × diam. 6 in., 23 ½ × diam. 6 in., 19 × diam. 9 in., and 22 × diam. 9 in.

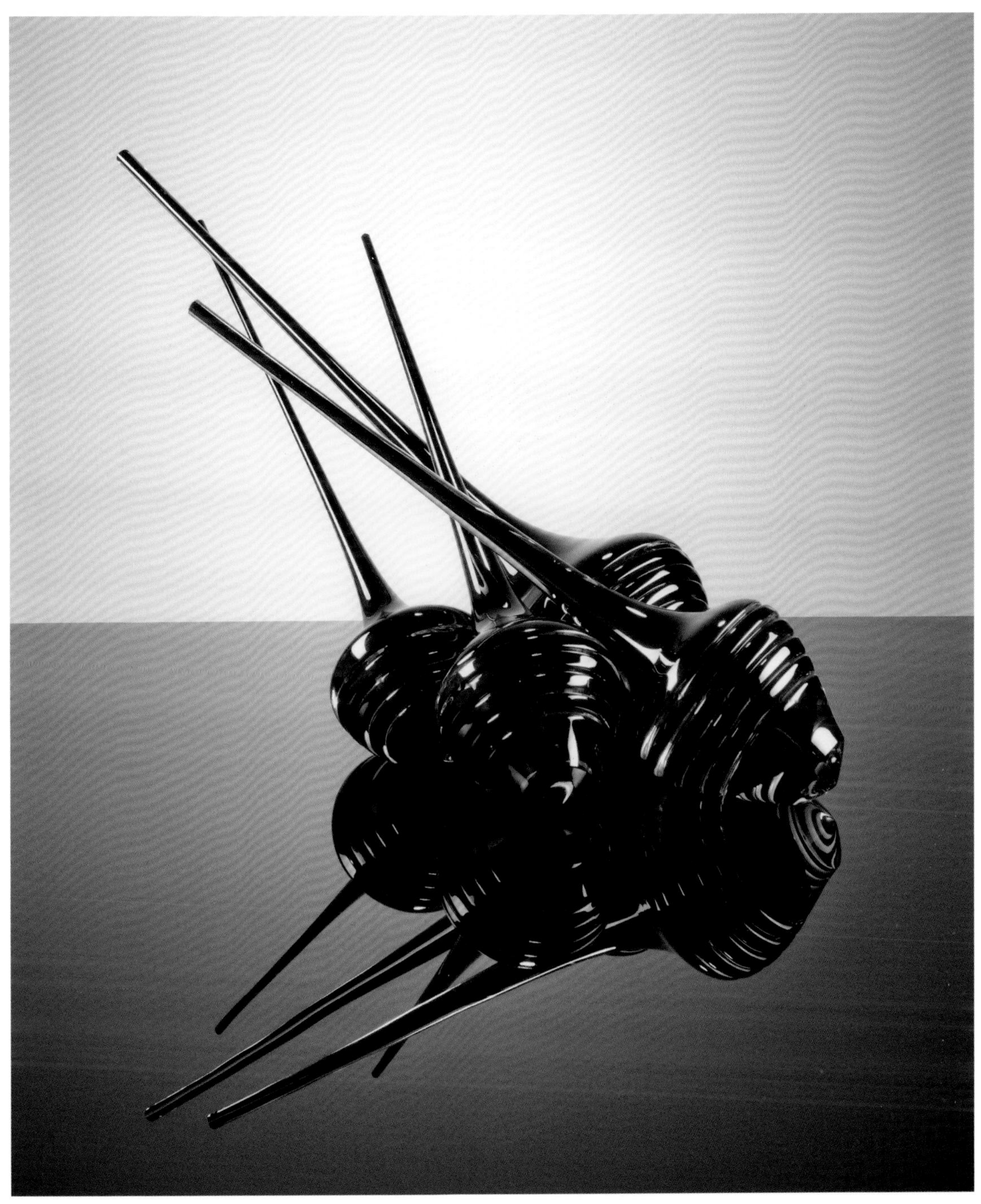

Fig. 18   Dale Chihuly,
*Niijima Floats: Garnet
Black and Mint Green
Float with Dimple*, *Snow
White and Gold Leaf*, and
*Mottled Blue Black Float
with Silver Leaf*, 1991, 1991,
and 1992, blown glass,
18 ¾ × 22 ¾ × 19 ½ in.,
21 ⅝ × 25 × 24 in., and
25 × 26 ¼ × 25 ¾ in., Gift
of Dale and Doug Anderson,
1993.46.1–.3

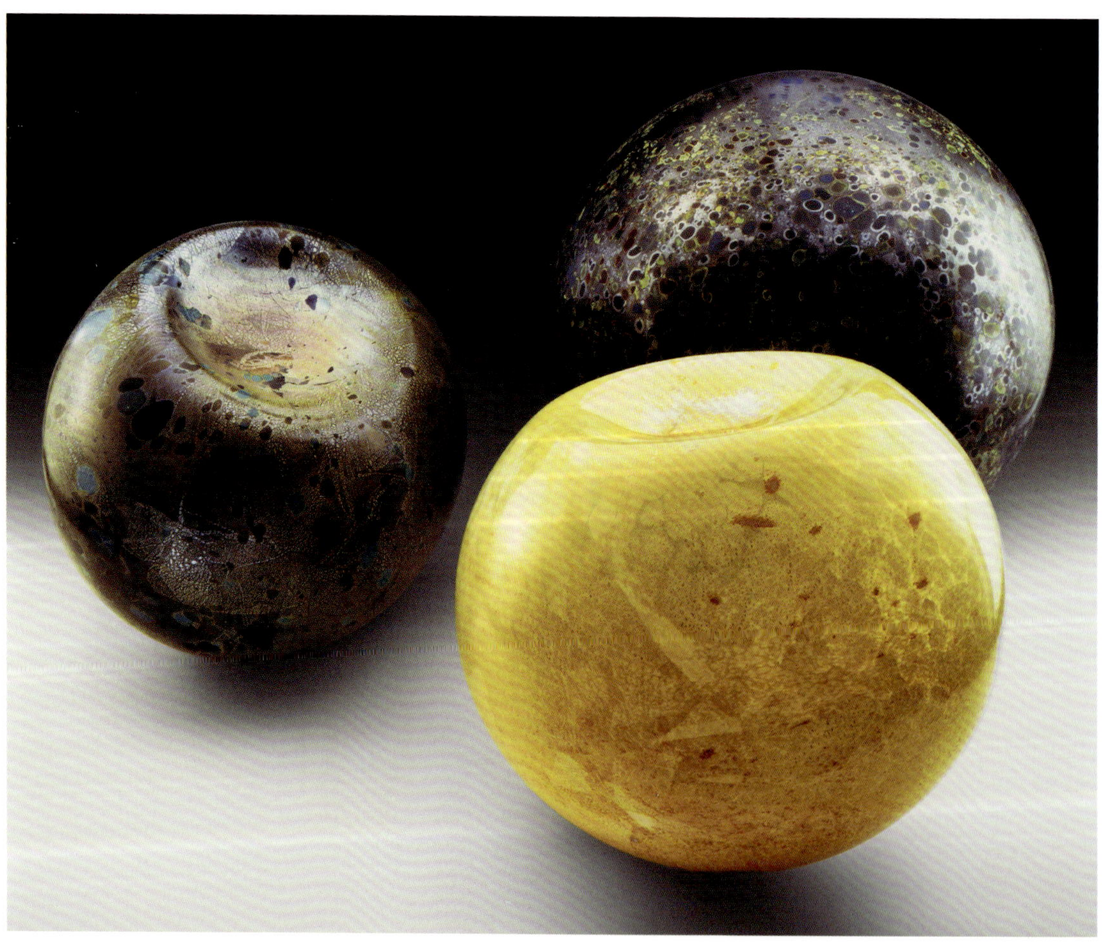

NOTES

1. brown, "this is the only moment (species love poetry)," *adrienne maree brown* (blog), July 27, 2021, http://adriennemareebrown.net/2021/07/27/this-is-the-only-moment-species-love-poetry.

2. Lonnie G. Bunch III, "Secretary Lonnie Bunch: Learning From Americans' Past Ordeals," *Smithsonian Magazine*, July 2020, https://www.smithsonianmag.com/smithsonian-institution/lonnie-bunch-secretary-learning-from-americans-past-ordeals-180975197/.

3. Oral History Interview with Lloyd E. Herman, September 21, 2010, Archives of American Art, Smithsonian Institution.

4. "Health Equity Considerations and Racial and Ethnic Minority Groups," Centers for Disease Control and Prevention, last updated April 19, 2021, accessed July 29, 2021, https://www.cdc.gov/coronavirus/2019-ncov/community/health-equity/race-ethnicity.html.

5. One of my peer reviewers observed that voter turnout for the 2020 election arguably proved that Black women saved democracy.

6. Sharon Kerry-Harlan, Artist Statement, email to the author, January 11, 2021.

7. See Elsa Barkley Brown, "African-American Women's Quilting," *Signs* 14, no. 4 (Summer 1989): 922.

8. Mazloomi, "Quiltmaking for Social Justice," in *We Are the Story: A Visual Response to Racism* (West Chester, OH: Paper Moon Publishing, 2021), 5.

9. Sara Ahmed, *What's the Use? On the Uses of Use* (Durham, NC: Duke University Press, 2019), 65.

10. Ibid., 7.

11. James Watkins, "Studio Visit: James Watkins, Lubbock, Texas," *Ceramics* 69, no. 7 (September 2021): 25.

12. Ahmed, *What's the Use?*, 24.

13. Katie Hudnall, email to the author, April 29, 2020.

14. Ibid.

15. David Harper Clemons, Artist Statement, email to the author, March 12, 2021.

16. I'm grateful to artist Annet Couwenberg for reminding me of *The Poetics of Space* during a virtual conversation with students at the Maryland Institute College of Art (MICA) in 2020.

17. Gaston Bachelard, *The Poetics of Space*, trans. Maria Jolas (Boston: Beacon Press, 1994), 4. Originally published Paris: Presses Univeristaires de France, 1958.

18. Ibid., 12.

19. Bachelard explains homes become imbued with "dream values" that remain after the house is gone. He states, "And we should not forget that these dream values communicate from soul to soul. To read poetry is essentially to daydream." Ibid., 17.

20. Ibid., 90.

21. Victor Hugo, *Notre-Dame de Paris*, trans. Isabel F. Hapgood (New York: Thomas Y. Crowell & Co., 1888), 1:161.

22. Mary Oliver, "With Thanks to the Field Sparrow, Whose Voice Is So Delicate and Humble," in *Devotions: The Selected Poems of Mary Oliver* (New York: Penguin Press, 2017), 74.

23. Toshiko Takaezu, Interview by Sinika Lane, April 14, 2000, transcript edited by Karen Boates, Toshiko Takaezu papers, 1937–2010, Archives of American Art, Smithsonian Institution.

24. Oral History Interview with Toshiko Takaezu, June 16, 2003, Archives of American Art, Smithsonian Institution.

25. Ezra Shales, "Throwing the Potter's Wheel (and Women) Back into Modernism: Reconsidering Edith Heath, Karen Karnes, and Toshiko Takaezu as Canonical Figures," in *Ceramics in America*, ed. Robert Hunter (Hanover, NH: Chipstone Foundation, 2016), 2–30, http://www.chipstone.org/article.php/739/Ceramics-in-America-2016/Throwing-the-Potter's-Wheel-(and-Women)-Back-into-Modernism:-Reconsidering-Edith-Heath,-Karen-Karnes,-and-Toshiko-Takaezu-as-Canonical-Figures.

26. Scott A. Shields, *Echoes of the Earth: Ceramics by Toshiko Takaezu* (Sacramento, CA: Crocker Art Museum, 2007), 11.

27. David Allen Sibley, *What It's Like to Be a Bird: From Flying to Nesting, Eating to Singing—What Birds are Doing, and Why* (New York: Knopf, 2020), 12.

28. Aimee Nezhukumatathil, *World of Wonders: In Praise of Fireflies, Whale Sharks, and Other Astonishments* (Minneapolis, MN: Milkweed Editions, 2020), 97.

29. Bachelard, *The Poetics of Space*, 92.

30. "Birds have evolved many different strategies and styles for building nests.... [some] are almost entirely dependent on human structures for their nest sites." Sibley, *What It's Like to Be a Bird*, 101.

31. See also David Pye, *The Nature and Aesthetics of Design* (London: Barrie and Jenkins, 1978), 16: "My motor car has at present, perhaps, the purpose of taking the children to school. But I think, perhaps, that the time has about come when its purpose should change to housing the chickens. Then the purpose of my car is housing chickens and that is all about it."

32. Nicholas Bell, notes from interview with Leona Waddell, Renwick Gallery curatorial files. See also Bell, *A Measure of the Earth: The Cole-Ware Collection of American Baskets* (Washington, DC: Smithsonian American Art Museum, 2013).

33. Polly Adams Sutton, Artist Statement, Mobilia Gallery, accessed March 18, 2021, https://www.mobilia-gallery.com/artists /polly-adams-sutton/.

34. Fath Davis Ruffins, "The Paradox of Preservation: Gullah Language, Culture, and Imagery," in *Grass Roots: African Origins of an American Art,* ed. Dale Rosengarten, Theodore Rosengarten, and Enid Schildkrout (New York: Museum for African Art, 2008), 231. See also Theodore Rosengarten, "Introduction," in *Grass Roots*, 13.

35. Gail Tremblay, Interview with Cathy Denny, September 2020, Froelick Gallery, accessed April 20, 2021, https://froelickgallery.com/usr/library /documents/main/artists/53/gail -tremblay-interview-final-092020.pdf.

36. Carmen Maria Machado, *In the Dream House* (Minneapolis, MN: Graywolf Press: 2019), Kindle edition.

37. Carolyn Mazloomi, *Spirits of the Cloth: Contemporary African American Quilts* (New York: Clarkson Potter, 1998), 44.

38. See ibid., 145–47. Mazloomi further states, "Contemporary black quiltmakers have made important statements about the nature of womanhood and have expressed both the joys and difficulties of what it means to be black and female. Their works express the poignancy of being devalued as human beings in a value-conscious society."

39. Chawne Kimber, "still not," *completely cauchy.* (blog), November 3, 2019, https:// cauchycomplete.wordpress.com/2019 /11/03/still-not/.

40. Ibid. "I am" emphasis by the artist.

41. Kimber uses vintage fabrics to ensure they were made under relatively humane labor conditions.

42. Kimber, "Brief Artist Statement," *completely cauchy.* (blog), accessed March 18, 2021, https://cauchycomplete .wordpress.com/about-2/.

43. Elizabeth Landau, "'I Can't Breathe': How One Black Quilter Channels Social Justice into Her Work," *Washington Post*, December 23, 2020, https://www .washingtonpost.com/lifestyle/home /social-justice-quilts-chawne-kimber /2020/12/22/0f517ab8-205f-11eb-b532 -05c751cd5dc2_story.html.

44. Kimber, "still not."

45. Ahmed, *What's the Use?*, 217.

46. Ahmed, Ibid., 7.

47. "*Queer Houses* honors queer, feminist and trans histories such as the Stonewall Uprising, activist movements such as ACT-UP and the collective grief and perseverance of the AIDS Quilt, which included thousands of participants from around the world. In a way that is meant to evoke both the formal and the radical, this work celebrates the existence of chosen and deliberate queer families built on a fierce spirit of love, sex, collective liberation, and gender, sexual, and self-determination." Roberts, Statement on *The Queer Houses of Brooklyn*, L. J. Roberts, accessed March 18, 2021, https:// www.ljroberts.net/the-queer-houses-of -brooklyn. See also L. J. Roberts, "Put Your Thing Down, Flip It, and Reverse It; Reimagining Craft Identities Using Tactics of Queer Theory," in *Extra/Ordinary: Craft and Contemporary Art*, ed. Maria Elena Buszek (Durham, NC: Duke University Press, 2011), 243–59.

48. Gloria Anzaldúa, *Borderlands/La Frontera: The New Mestiza* (San Francisco, CA: Aunt Lute Books, 1987), 2.

49. Jiménez Underwood's description of her work *C. Jane Run*, Consuelo Jiménez Underwood, accessed March 18, 2021, http://www.consuelojunderwood.com /c-jane-run.html.

50. adrienne maree brown, *Emergent Strategy: Shaping Change, Changing Worlds* (Chico, CA: AK Press, 2017).

51. Phone conversation between the artist and author, April 30, 2020.

52. Ursula K. Le Guin, *The Lathe of Heaven* (New York: Scribner, 2008), 82.

53. Bachelard, *The Poetics of Space*, 183.

54. Therman Statom, "GEEX Talks: Therman Statom," November 2, 2020, *Glass Education Exchange*, accessed March 18, 2021 (with subscription), https://geex.glass /programming/geextalks/thermanstatom/.

55. "Immensity is within ourselves.... As soon as we become motionless, we are elsewhere; we are dreaming in a world that is immense." Bachelard, *The Poetics of Space,* 184.

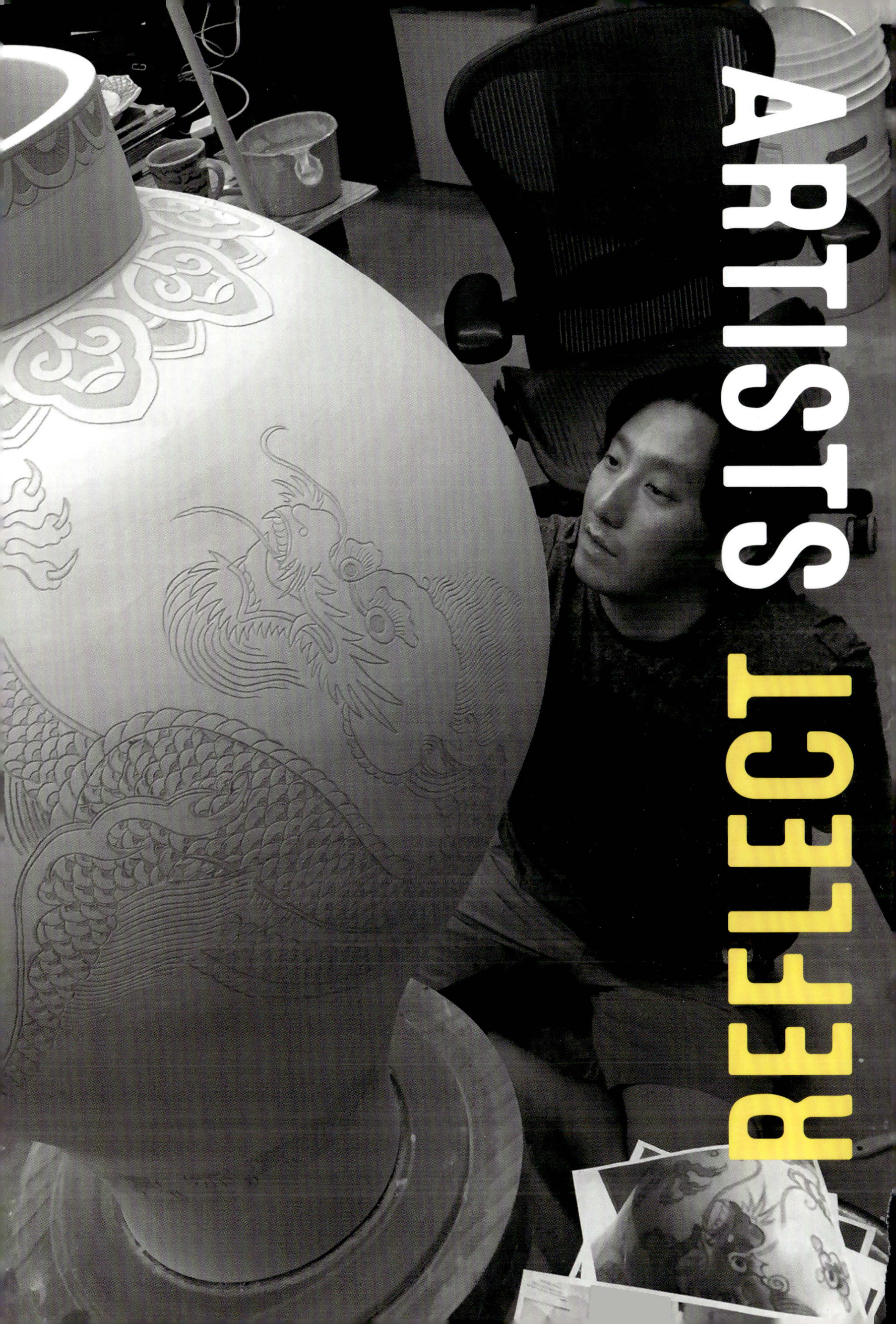
ARTISTS
REFLECT

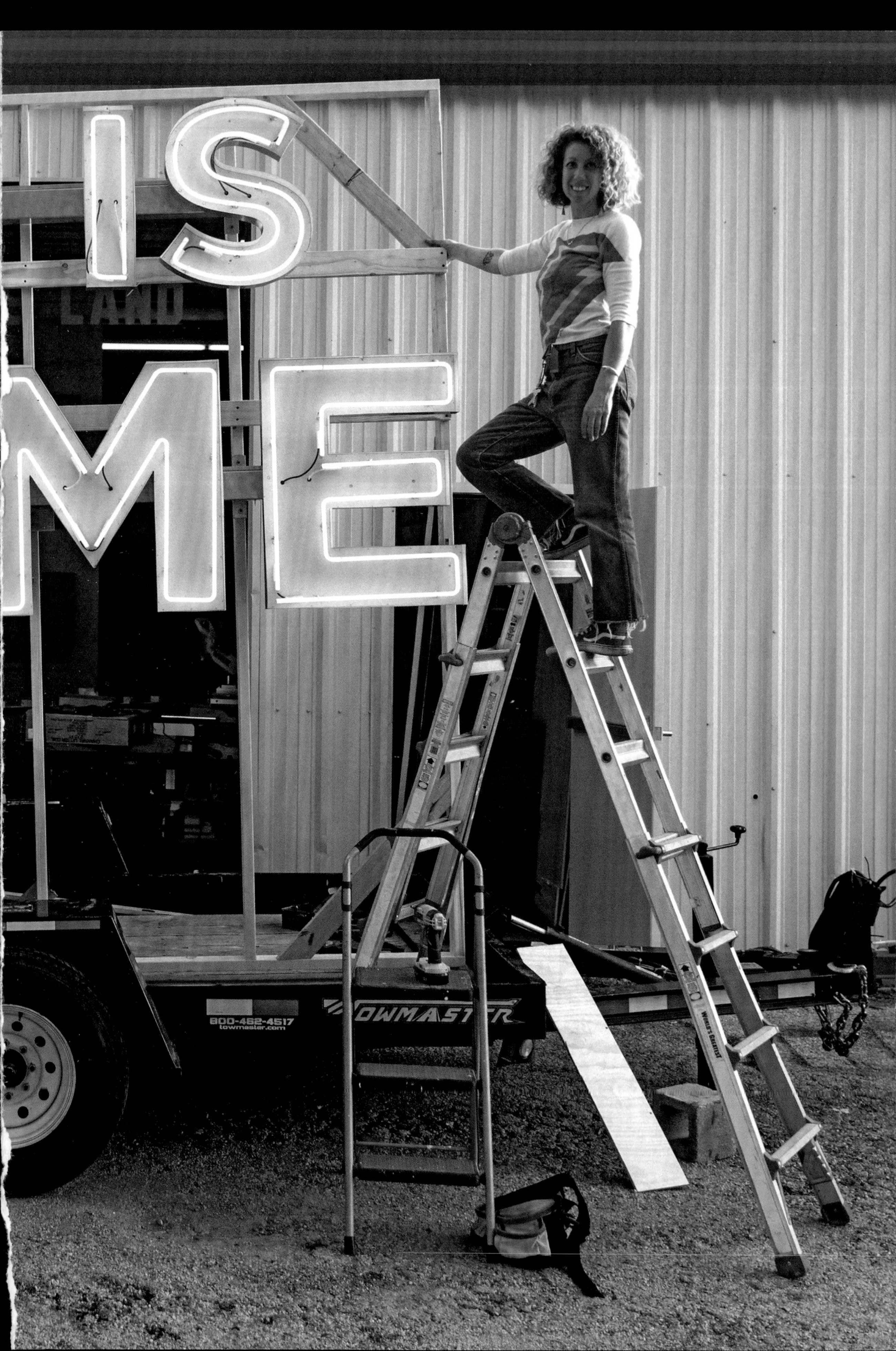
IS
LAND
ME
800-462-4517
towmaster.com
TOWMASTER

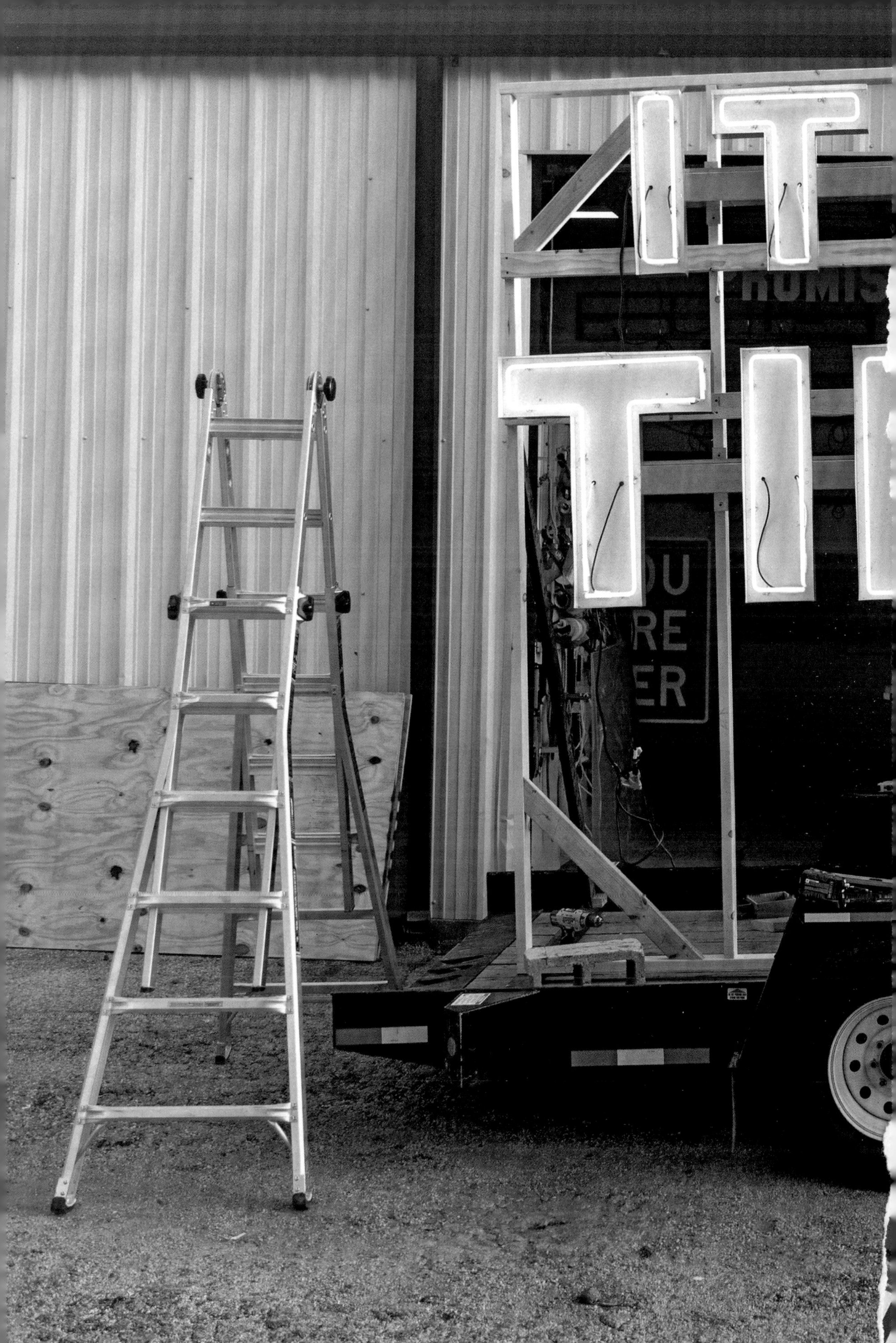
A T
T I
U
R E
E R

Several artists were asked to reflect on the past, present, and future in relationship to their work. They were given the following prompts:

* What is important about looking back?

* What is important about moving forward?

* What is most important to you in this present moment?

* What is the use of the past in your work?

* What is the use of imagining the future in your work?

* How do you want the future—ten, fifty, one hundred years from now—to understand your art in this present moment?

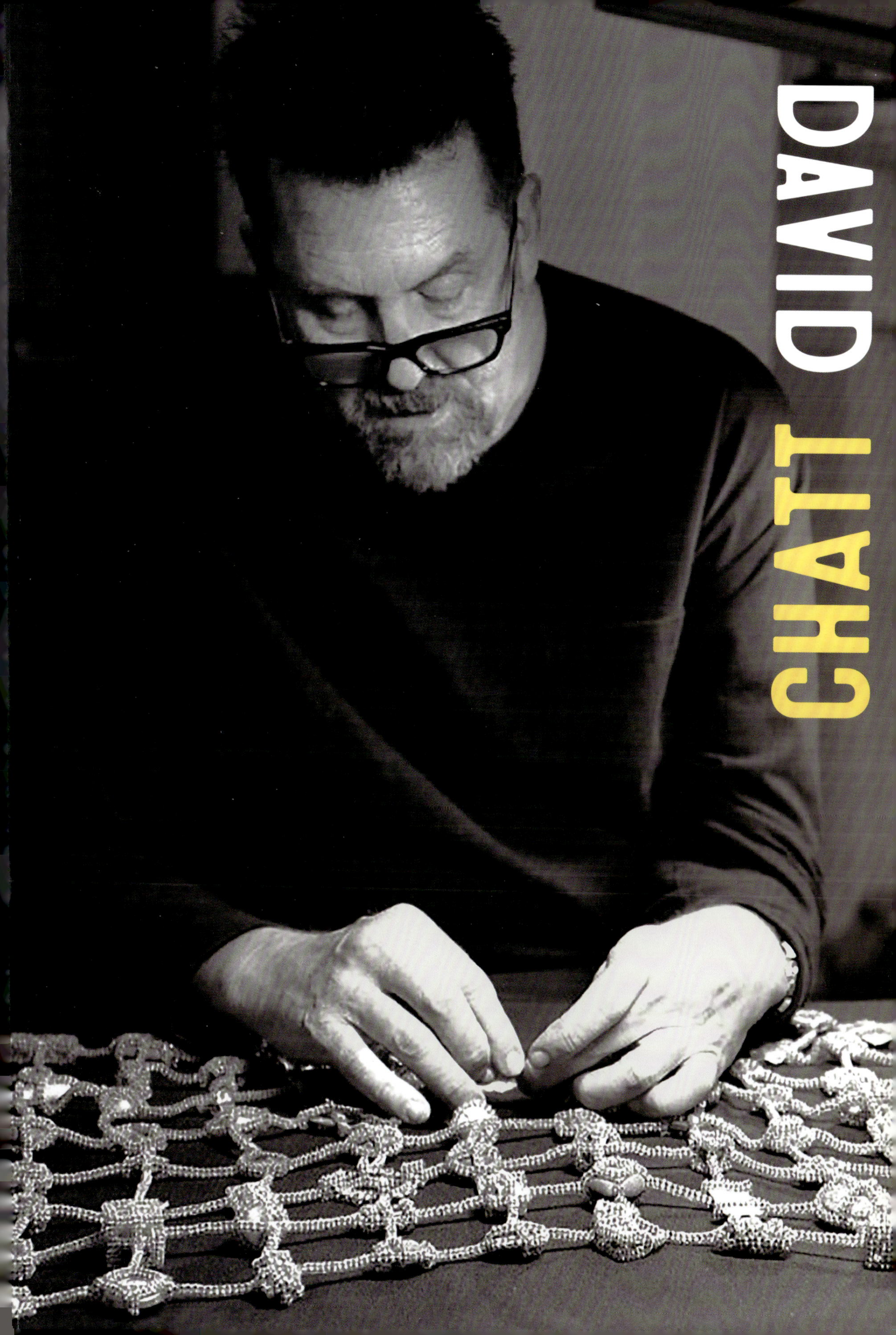

DAVID
CHATT

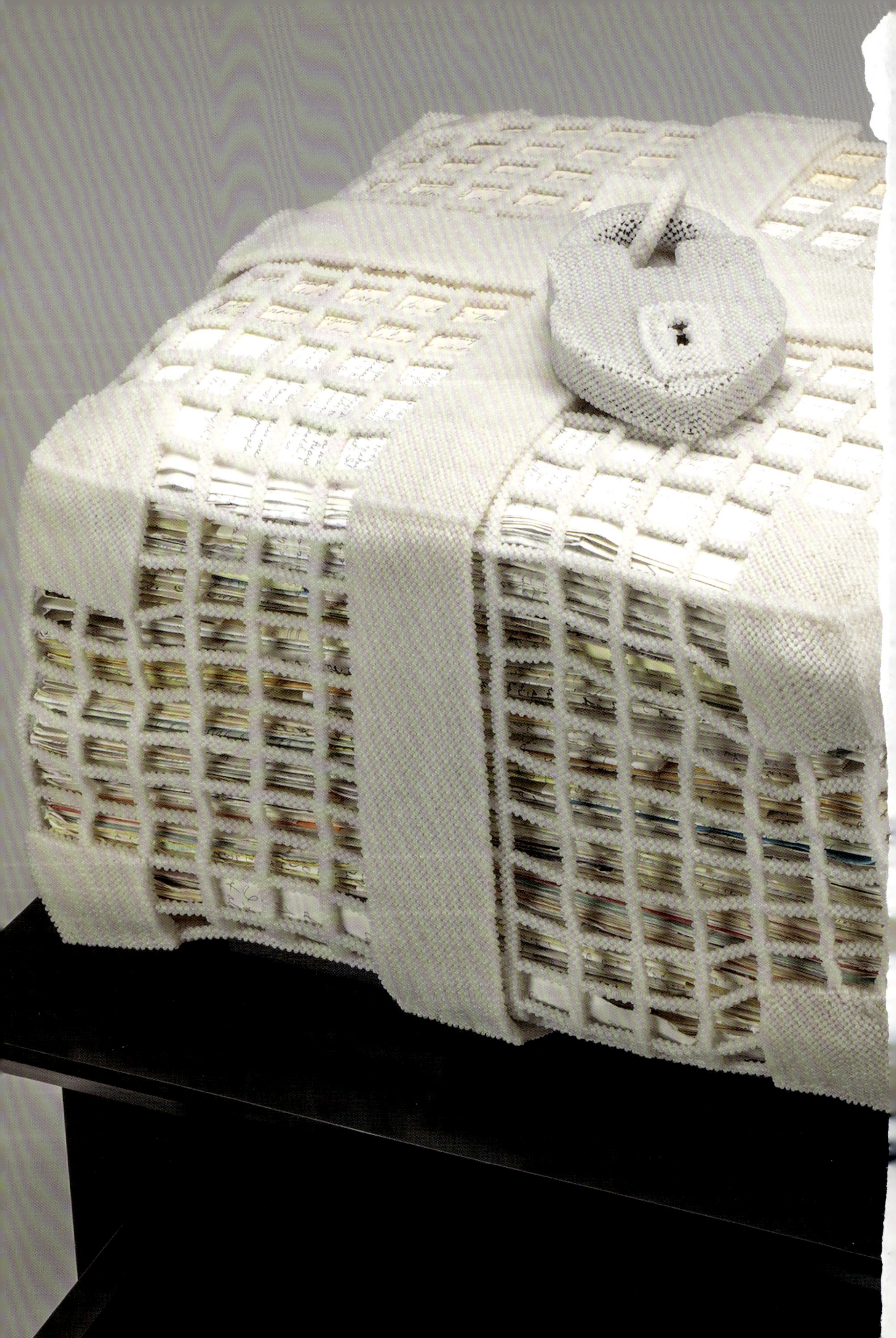

CAT. 34 David Chatt, *Love, Dad*, 2012–13, glass beads and thread with wooden table and thirty-year collection of letters from the artist's father, overall: 47 ½ × 16 ½ × 16 ½ in.

DAVID CHATT

I am a traveler. Wherever I go, I visit second-hand shops. This habit began at my father's side and continues. I don't need more of anything except time and resources, yet I spend a portion of each trawling these establishments for the occasional compelling curiosity. I sometimes chide myself for inviting clutter, but this is more than an opportunity to accumulate: this is research. These aisles—littered with cast-offs from the past, vying to find a place in the future—hold the history of the world. These chaotic collections tell me something about the community that created them. My regular exam-inations of detritus, both foreign and domestic, influence what I make and why I make. Like an archaeologist, I dig through layer upon layer of design from the recent past. Everything from the sublime to the misguided has taught me to see and to form opinions. These hunting trips remind me that an object can evoke something beyond utility. As a maker of evocative objects, I pay attention to that which causes me to feel. An antiquated key can transport me to the house my father grew up in; a home his older sisters shared and preserved, like a portal to another time. A dual cassette boom box reminds me of music I listened to when I was twenty-two and the friends I shared it with. I try to under-stand the power of an object and make work that reflects what I discover on these anthropo-logical excursions. Amongst the mass-produced, I sometimes find orphaned art. A lamp made from popsicle sticks, an original painting in a broken frame, or a wheel-thrown pot tells me something about the maker. Sometimes the artist leaves a signature, date, or the especially thrilling thumbprint found in the place where a ceramic piece is held while being glazed. I put my thumb where theirs once was and conjure the moment and the person that left this mark. Even something made with less-than skill can exhibit remnants of enthusiasm felt by the maker. It is good to remember that some of what we feel as we make lingers.

I sometimes imagine a future human finding my work on a fold-up table at a flea market. I would not mind. Will the finder of what remains wonder who, what, where, and how? What image will form as they try to imagine the hands that pursued this peculiar passion? Will they appreciate that an entire life was spent accumulating the skills required to make this thing they discovered for a few dollars amongst the bric-a-brac? Everything I make is a souvenir from an attempt to achieve perfection. I fail at this, as all humans must, but at times I have come, if not close, closer than I have been. This is a thrill worth all that was spent in pursuit of it. I hope some ghost of that thrill is felt by those who take our place and pause to consider the remnants of my life.

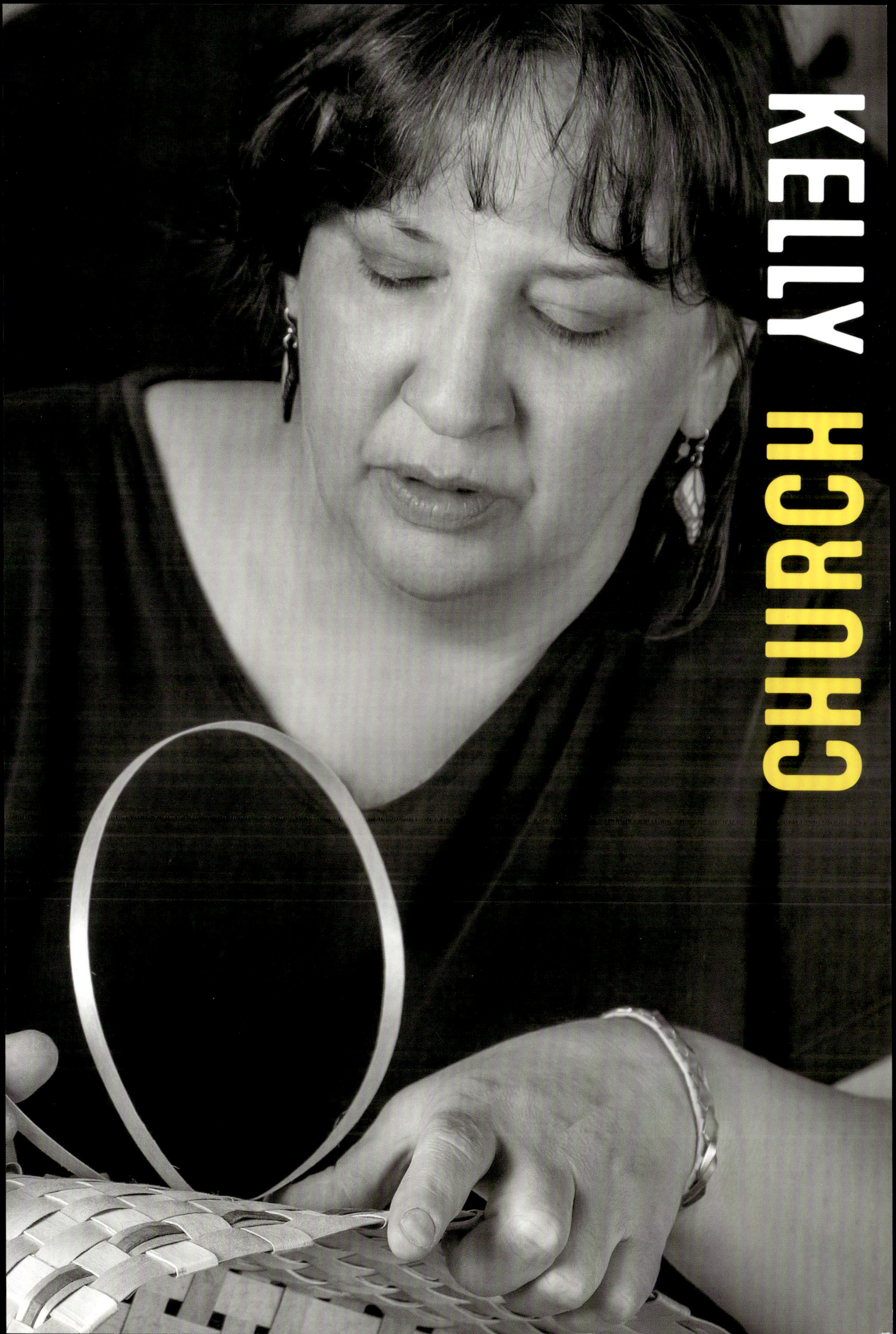
KELLY
CHURCH

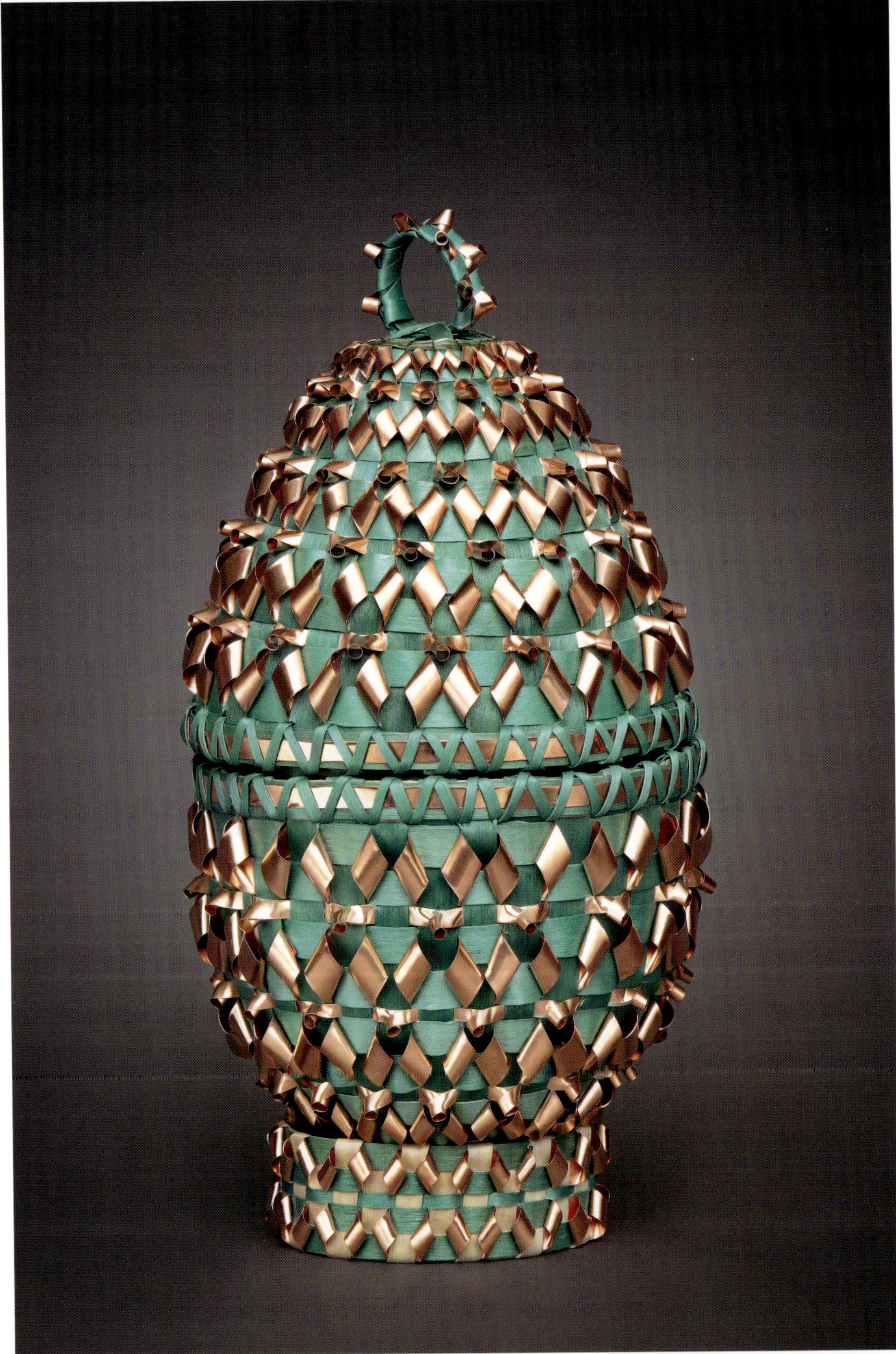

CAT. 35 Kelly Church, *Sustaining Traditions — Digital Memories* (closed and open), 2018, black ash and sweetgrass with Rit dye, copper, vial of EAB (emerald ash borer), and flash drive containing black ash teachings, overall: 9 ½ × diam. 4 ½ in.

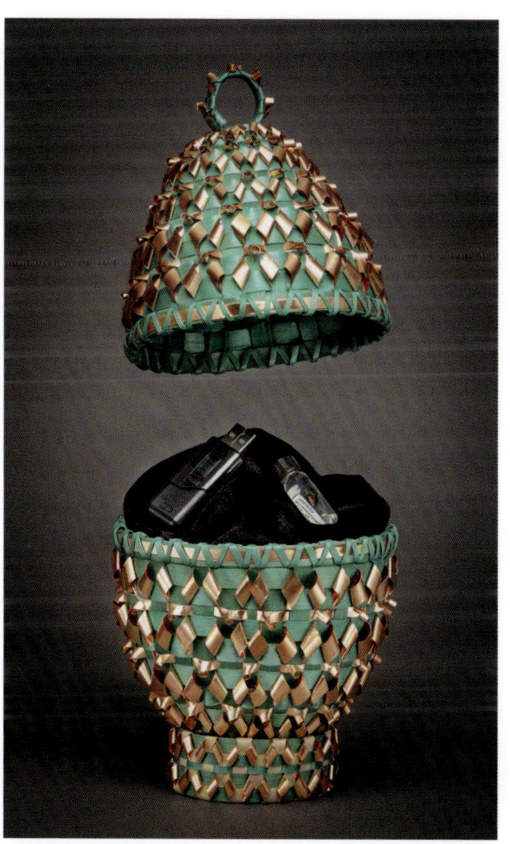

As an artist, you need to have a relationship with and knowledge of your materials, an understanding of how they can be used. I have this relationship with black ash and the metals I weave. I know by feel which splints can be used for embellishments, build up, or bottoms, and how to bend the metal to weave with it. It is all a learning process and it takes time, but it is what makes the finished weaving what it is meant to be.

The work I create comes from knowledge that has been passed down perpetually. Traditions of harvesting and preparing fibers are sustained through my vessels and creations, telling a story of my life today that will serve as a moment in history for future generations. The wonder and amazement I feel each time I begin to process a tree or fiber from the forest using this knowledge and these teachings is pure joy. As I use the words passed on orally for countless generations that allow me to recognize plants in nature and understand how these plants can be sustainably harvested and processed, I am aware of my part in this enduring equation as a tradition bearer, culture keeper, and mentor to the upcoming generations.

I combine these teachings of the past with the present by weaving in embellishments of copper and fine silver. These pieces remind us of the fragility of nature and the world we live in, as well as show the transition to nontraditional materials, which comes out of necessity but also adds expression. Technology, in the form of a flash drive in this work, captures these stories for future generations to remind them of where we started (our past), where we are (our present), and the direction we can choose to take to sustain what we have, while also making it stronger in the process (our future).

My weavings are records of moments in time. These records will serve as reminders of concerns we have today that need to be addressed for the benefit of future generations. They will mark the progress made, or not. When we can all one day see the true value and life sustenance in our water, trees, and all that nature provides without commercializing it for profit, we will have made progress.

As we forge our way into new destinies and what the future holds for us all, we must also retain our connection to the past and all that can be learned from it. These ancestral teachings are foundations that can be built upon and strengthened. We can sustain past knowledge while incorporating relational practices that we live with today for a better understanding of tomorrow. *

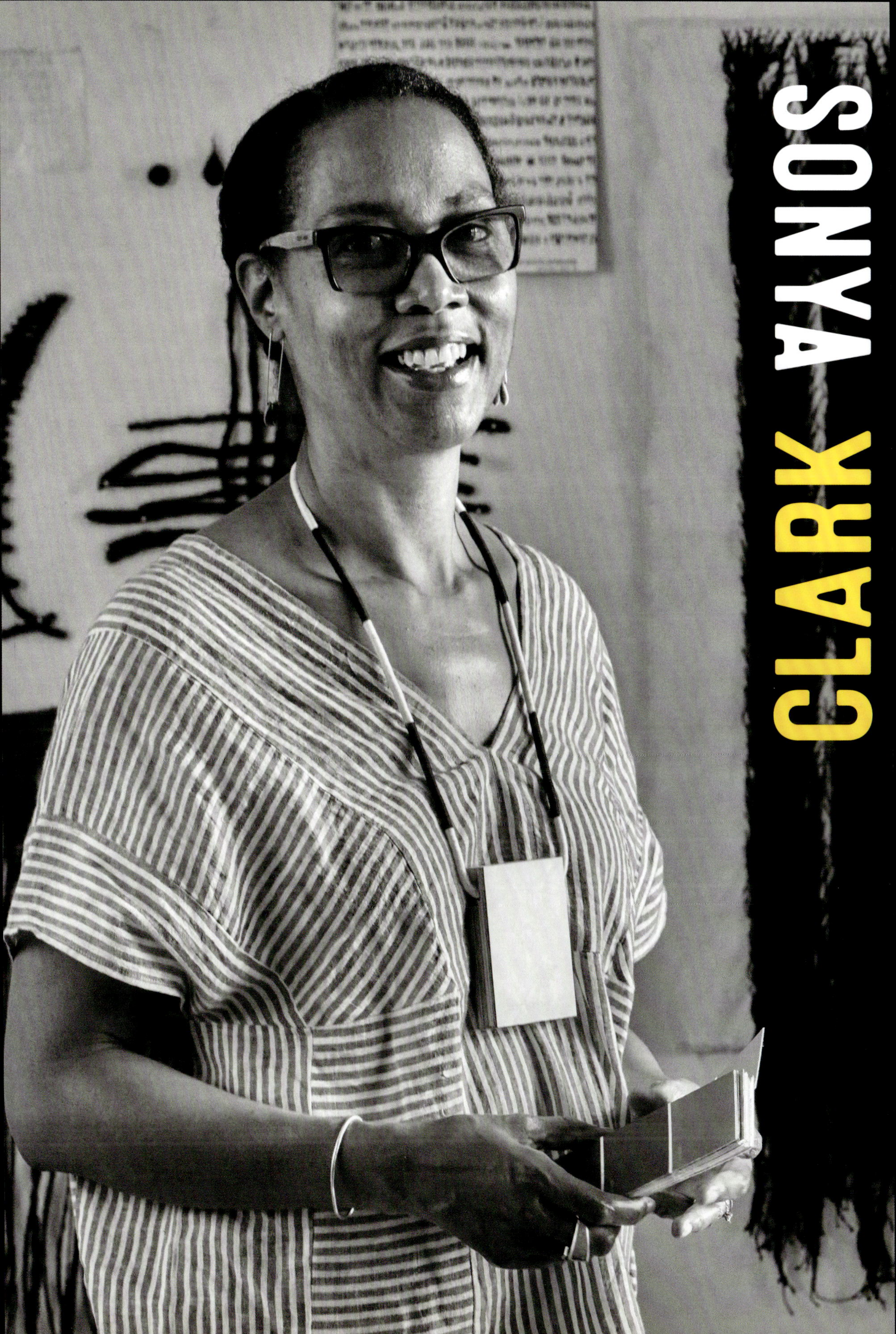

SONYA
CLARK

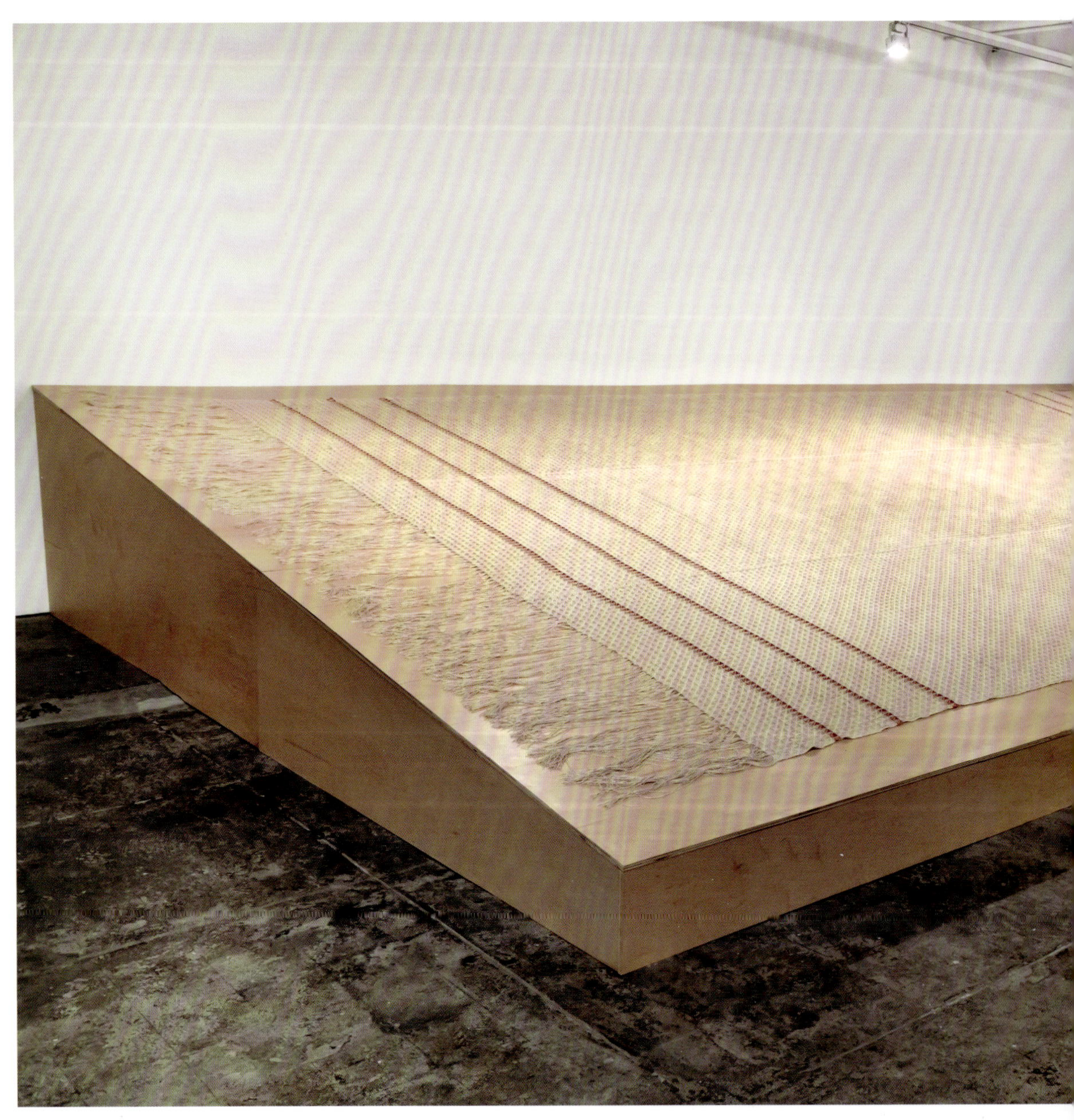

CAT. 36   Sonya Clark, in collaboration with The Fabric Workshop and Museum, Philadelphia, *Monumental*, 2019, woven linen with madder dye and tea stain, 180 × 360 in.

SONYA CLARK

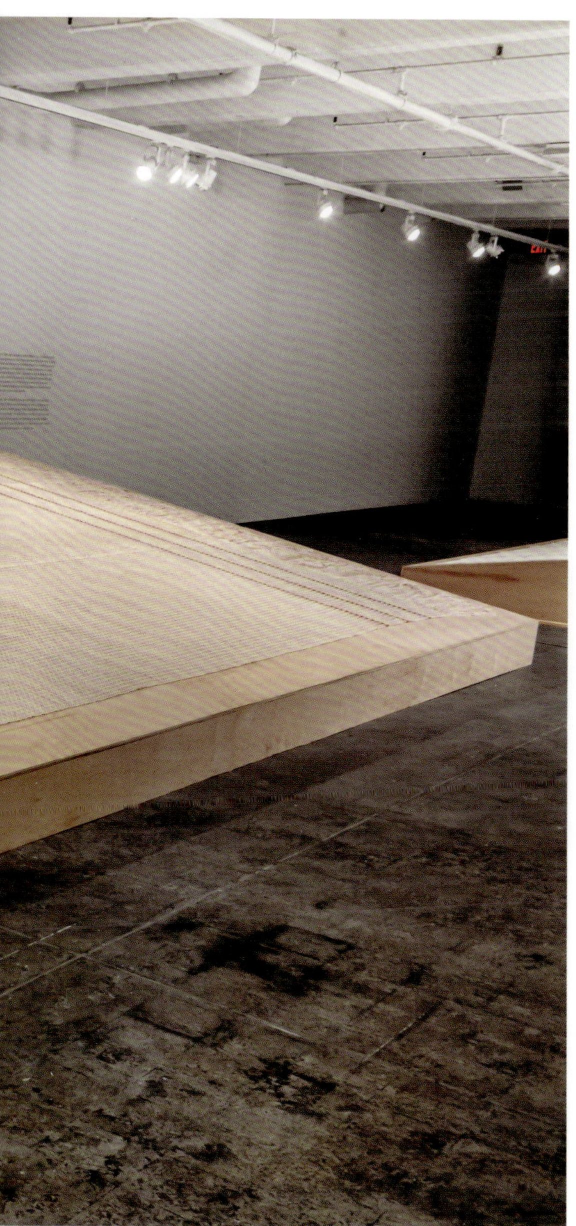

We do. We are. We make.

James Baldwin said, "History is literally present in all that we do." It is also present in all we are and all we make. We are texts, books written in the language of DNA. Each syllable articulates a trace of our ancestral archive. The same is true of crafted objects. Every designed, functional, aesthetic object is a collaboration with our ancestors across the slow arc of time. Who we are and what we make belong both to the past and the history of the future. The stories intertwine.

Crafted objects are slick surfaces and thirsty sponges that reflect and absorb us.

Imagine a mirror with a memory, one that retains fleeting moments like a chorus of ghostly whispers, a palimpsest. On April 9, 2017, shortly after my fiftieth birthday, I stared into the Voigtländer barrel lens of a camera from 1867. This antique object eyed my very existence with its glassy pupil. As my face reflected in its gaze, I wondered what the lens had witnessed in all those years from post–Civil War to the present. The light and shadow bounced between us as the bright tapestry, the *tapetum lucidum*, a nocturnal eye of cats and spiders, an eerie earthly sun. Or was it a moon, both source and reflection?

Recalling what Toni Morrison referred to as "desperately creative strategies of survival," I think of human eyes adjusting to the thick velvet of night, heads turned upward to distant suns, retinas tethered to pricks of light arranged as asterisms guiding paths to freedom. We are heavenly bound. The sparkling universe reminds us that we too are stardust, filled with tiny suns, more than we can see with the naked eye. We are universally free. Yet the *we* of then and now must continuously demand our earthly freedoms.

Now, imagine a textile, its complex structure taken for granted, endlessly drinking narratives large and small. What do we make of the particular dish towel that absorbed a pivotal moment of history? Its words muted over time. How do we wring out its stories so truth can be told? Bleached flax spun into linen, dressed on a loom, and structured as an absorbent waffle weave with red pinstripes for contrast. If it had taken the expected path, it would be a rag. But it was repurposed. An insurrectionist—not one from January 6, 2021, but one from April 9, 1865—knows his Confederate general will surrender and requires a white cloth for the task. Finding none, he settles on one with the three red lines on either side, knowing the predominance of white will do the work of surrender on the battlefield.

Imagine if each time we reached for the dishcloth by our sinks, we recalled the war waged by yesteryear's enemies of the country and their surrender. Would we ask what of that surrender held? What was reneged? As we reflect on the past held in everyday objects, are we mindful of Alice Walker's words? "Look closely at the present you are constructing: it should look like the future you are dreaming." Are we creating the future we desire through what we do, how we are, and what we make?

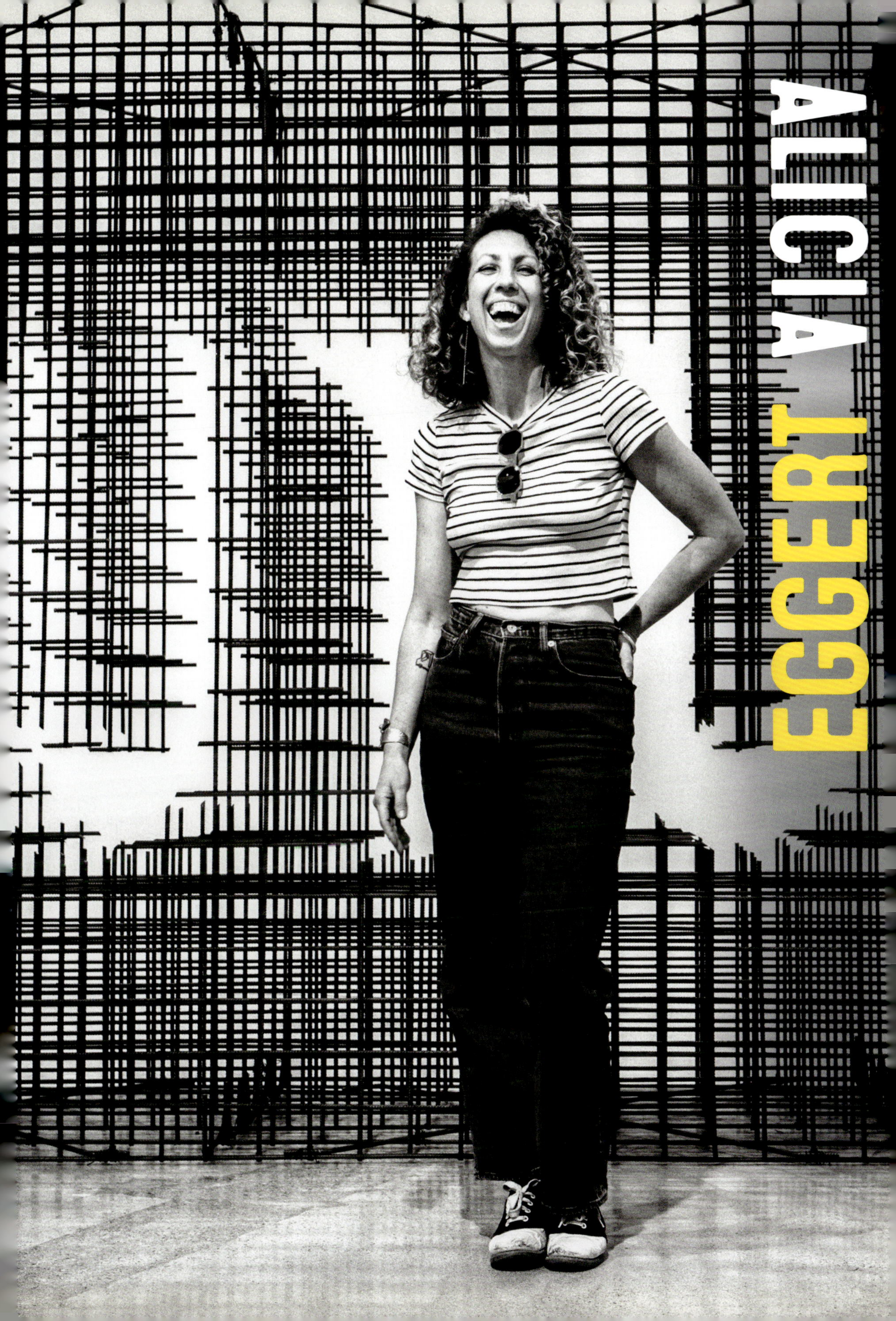

ALICIA
EGGERT

CAT. 37 Alicia Eggert,
This Present Moment (two
views), 2019–20, neon,
custom controller, and
steel, 144 × 180 × 48 in.

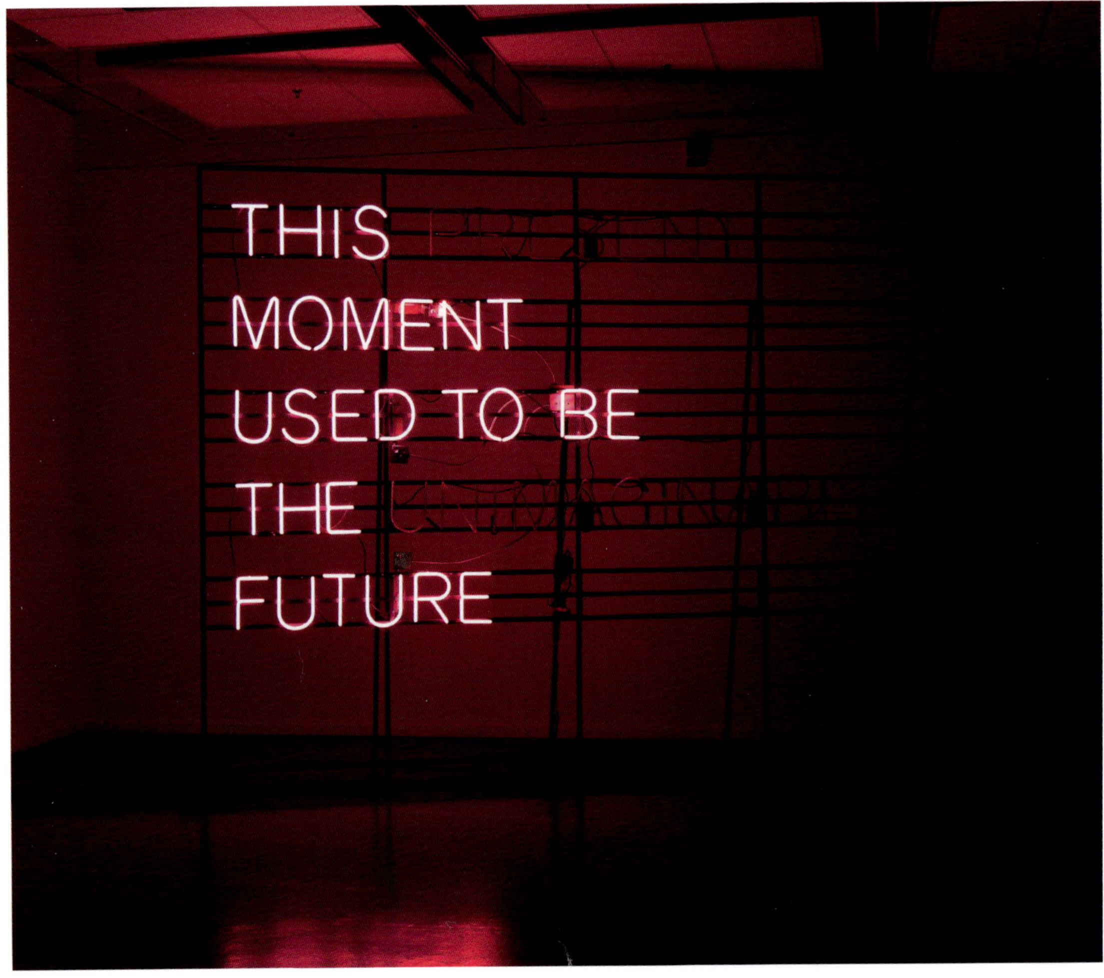
THIS
MOMENT
USED TO BE
THE
FUTURE

ALICIA
EGGERT

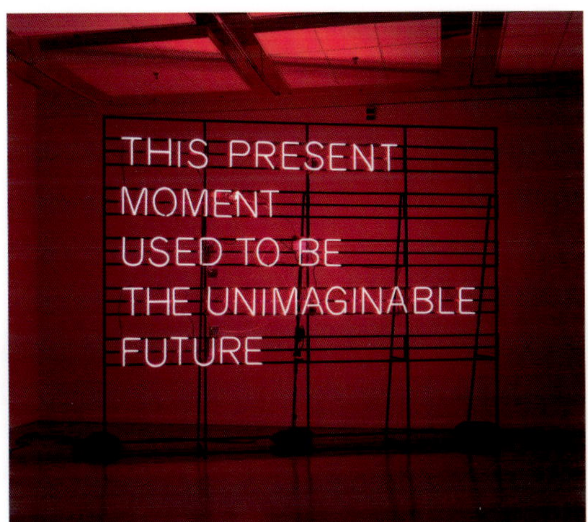

In the summer of 2019, I visited the site of Hutton's Unconformity at Siccar Point in Scotland. I hiked across a green pasture and down a steep hill to a rocky promontory that is considered the birthplace of modern geology. On that promontory in 1788, James Hutton noticed small ripple marks in the stone that represented a distant moment in history, when that spot was at the bottom of the sea. In Hutton's time, it was commonly believed that the earth was only thousands of years old, but his observation revolutionized our Western understanding of time. Scientists now believe the true age of the earth to be 4.54 billion years. All because one person looked closely at a rock, noticed the marks made by time, translated their form, and then told a new story.

My experience at Siccar Point continues to resonate with me. It has made me appreciate all the ways Time is made tangible. It's in the light that takes eight minutes to travel from the sun, whose warmth on my skin reminds me that everything I see in the present moment is technically an image of the past. It's in the rocks beneath my feet, some of which retain the visible footprints of dinosaurs in a riverbed not far from my home in Texas. And it's in the leaves that collect in my gutters, which I should clean out more often than I do.

I consider myself a conceptual artist, but I don't think ideas alone are ever enough. I like to give language physical, material forms, because I believe we might be able to understand something more fully if we can experience it physically. I like to think of time as a sculptural medium. Time binds individual moments and actions together to create new forms, in the same way that oil binds particles of pigment together to create paint. Time itself cannot be made, but if time is a medium, what can be made present with it? Can it be stretched and compressed like clay? Can it be turned like wood, carved like stone, bent like glass, or woven like twine? If we use time to make new forms, perhaps those forms can help us tell stories that have previously gone untold.

In our daily lives, we tend to think in short terms and see the present moment as narrow and small. But the same laws of nature that formed the ripples in those rocks at Siccar Point millions of years ago are still in operation right now. And it seems like our collective future might depend on our ability to conceive of "this present moment" as much longer and wider than our narrow field of vision can contain. Perhaps, like Hutton, we just have to look more closely at what we already have the ability to perceive. I wonder, what have we yet to notice? And with time as a medium, I wonder what previously unimaginable futures we can make present. ✳

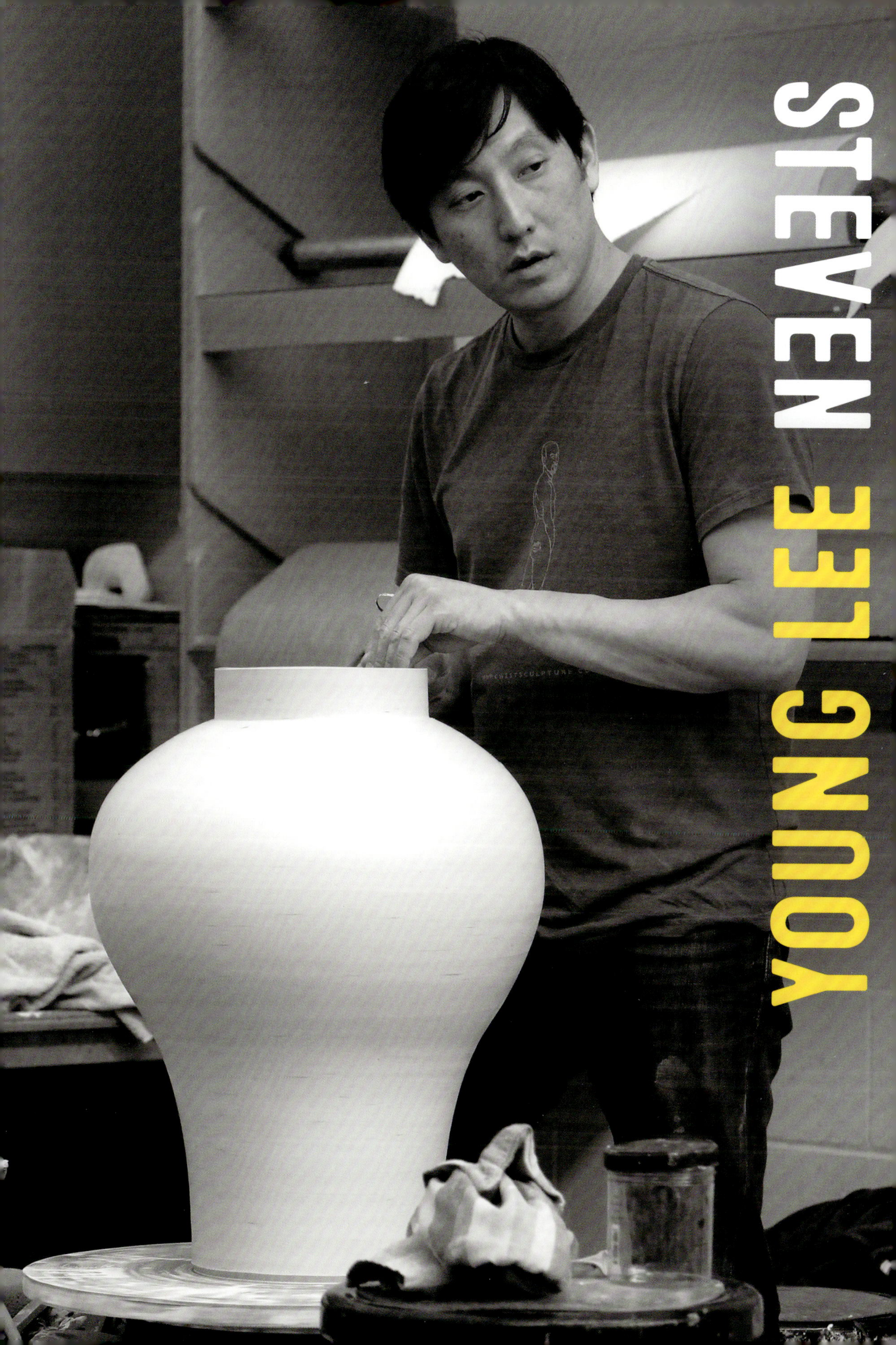

STEVEN
LEE
YOUNG LEE

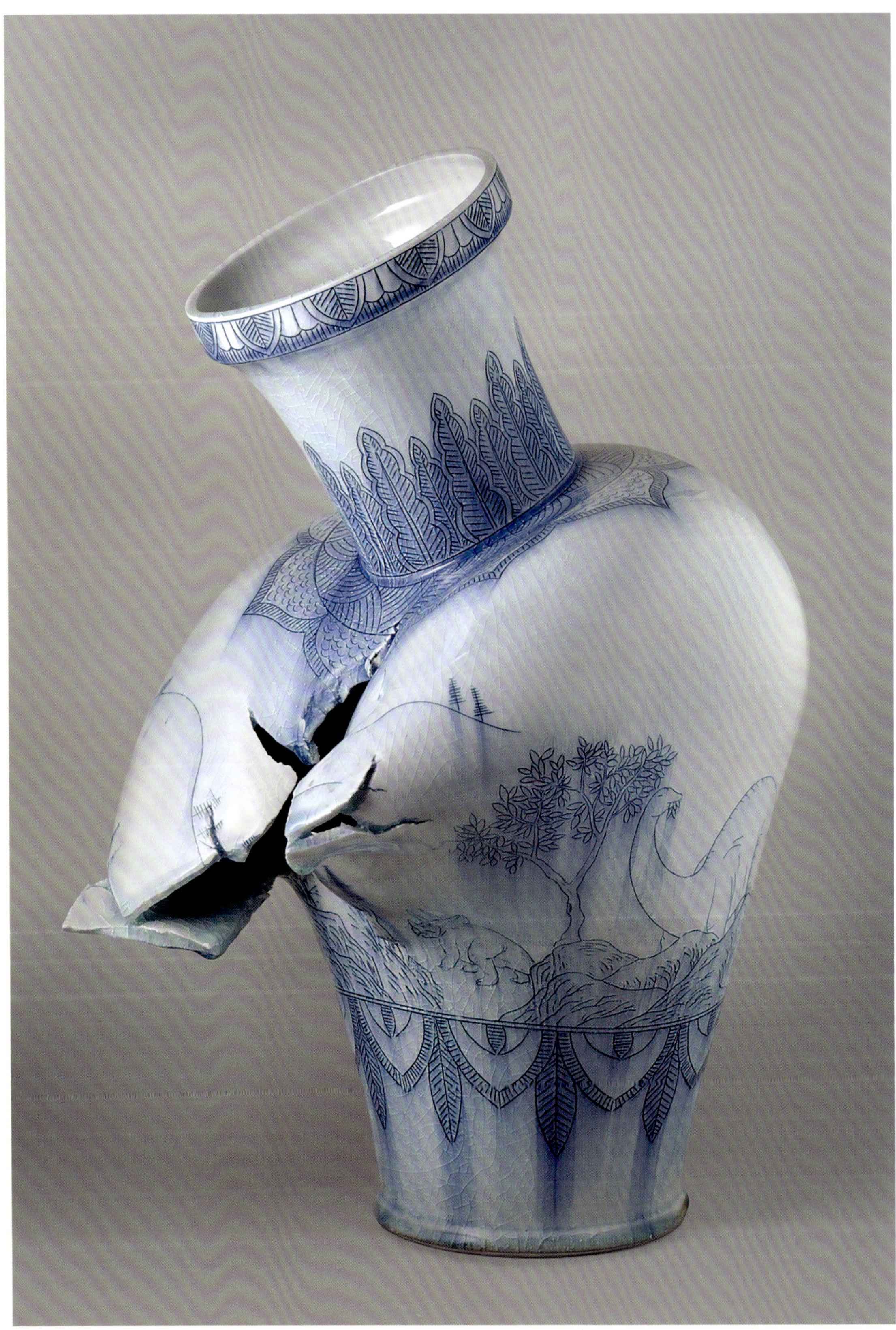

Fig. 19 Steven Young Lee, *Vase with Landscape and Dinosaurs*, 2014, porcelain with pigment and glaze, 20 ½ × 13 ½ × 12 ¾ in., Gift of Richard Fryklund, Giselle and Ben Huberman, David and Clemmer Montague, and museum purchase through the Howard Kottler Endowment for Ceramic Art, 2015.17

STEVEN YOUNG LEE

In 2017 I was asked to curate an exhibition that eventually became *Within the Margins* at the Penland Gallery in Penland, North Carolina. The exhibition did not prioritize aesthetic congruity, but rather focused on a common ethos among artists who otherwise might be perceived as having disparate viewpoints and backgrounds. It included artists such as Zemer Peled, Roberto Lugo, Sanam Emami, Kathy King, Brooks Oliver, and others who, while residing within one set of perceived margins or another, were working from within to expand or redefine those boundaries, ultimately shifting the lines of ethnicity, race, gender, sexuality, cultural identity, or material association. This exhibition felt appropriate at the time and feels especially relevant today, but the jury may still be out on how much progress has been made in blurring these boundaries, or perhaps that exhibition's moment reveals how the perception of progress has changed in that short time.

A margin can be defined as the edge or border of some concrete, or even abstract, category. In and of itself, a margin is innocuous and used to establish a boundary or guideline. We are taught to stay between the margins on a sheet of notebook paper when learning penmanship, or to remain inside a margin of error for an intended result. However, establishing these boundaries can naturally promote a sense of where you or others think you should be, creating a dynamic of being either inside or outside, included or excluded. Being on the appropriate side of the margin is considered safe and acceptable, and is often encouraged.

Marginalization is driven by the perception of those living and operating well inside the margins. The result is a projected sense of insignificance to the "other"—that those living outside of the center exist apart from the whole. A natural human response is to feel comfortable with what is familiar or similar to oneself, but, when that response is the result of a limited worldview, the consequence is the alienation of others in an attempt to feel safe. Commonly, this is seen in categories of race, ethnicity, gender, class, and/or sexual orientation, but the desire to marginalize can also take place in perceptions of art versus craft, high art versus low art, or in the use of certain materials, processes, or concepts. Often these acts of marginalization are an attempt to make one side feel smarter or stronger and the other powerless or unimportant.

As artists, our role is to observe, question, and articulate the moment. An important aspect of this work is the sincerity of the investigation and the willingness to engage in difficult conversations. Recognizing that there is a space "within the margins" confronts the idea that while boundaries do exist, the mere fact of their existence invites—if not demands—that they be confronted, challenged, and reshaped. *

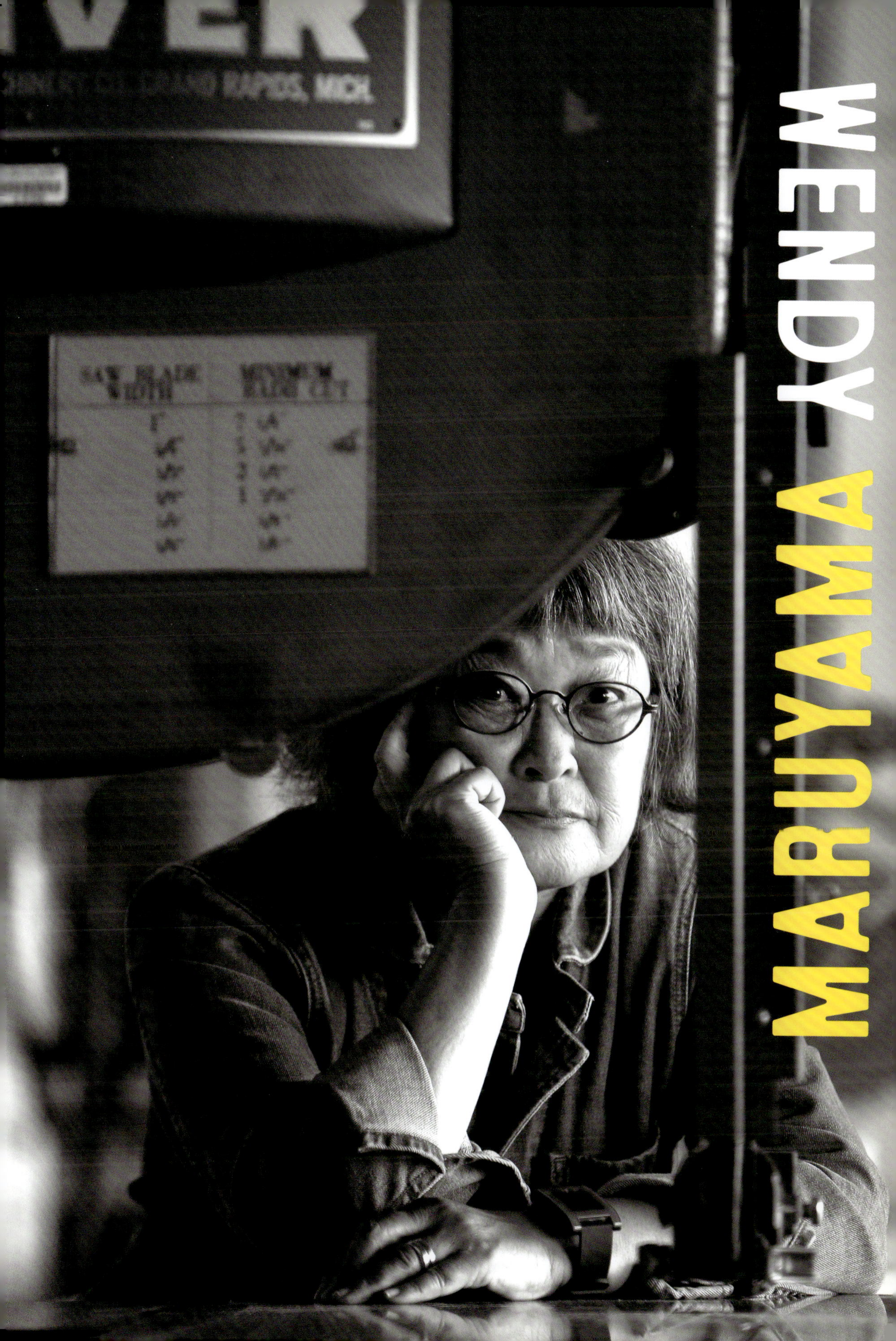
WENDY
MARUYAMA

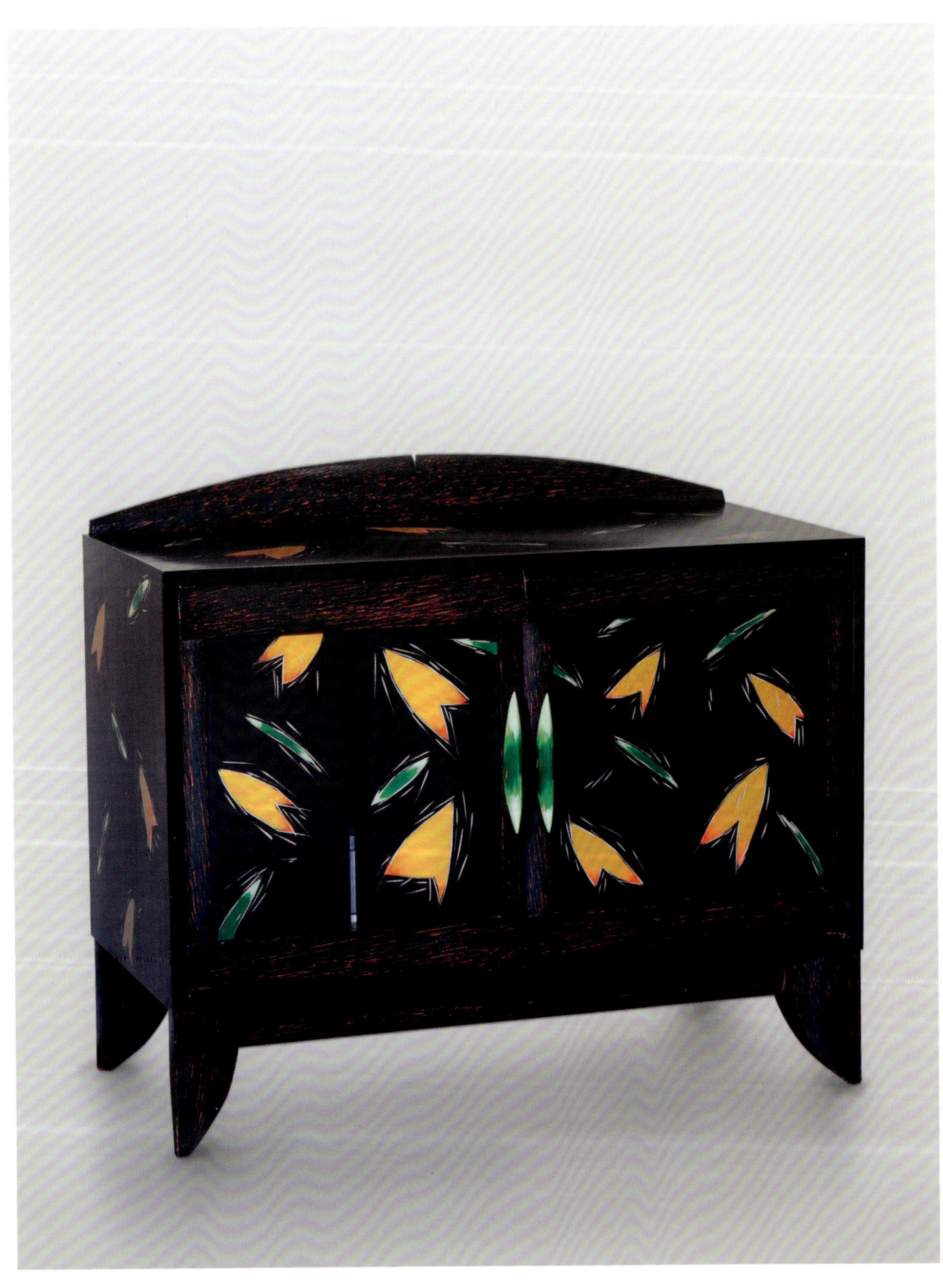

CAT. 38 Wendy Maruyama,
Patterned Credenza,
1990, painted poplar,
36 ½ × 42 × 20 in.

WENDY MARUYAMA

After living a "sheltered" life in California, I moved from San Diego to Richmond to begin my serious foray into craft as a grad student at Virginia Commonwealth University. I was scared, having never lived farther than twenty minutes from family. I did not partake in any major cultural experiences growing up. Between living on a farm in the early part of my life and then in a lower-middle-class suburb, these experiences were not part of our family routine and the public school system did not consider field trips part of the curriculum. (Except for that one time, when I was elected to be an animal control officer during "city governance" day, and I spent an entire day with the dog catcher, mostly just driving around, picking up roadkill and rounding up a stray dog or two.)

Struggling with disability was probably the reason I gravitated to the arts in school—while we did not go to museums, we did have a lot of art materials at our disposal, and I would just light up when it was "art time." I was quiet and had difficulties expressing myself in school, but in art class I could be the best, at least in my mind. The societal norms of sewing/cooking classes only being for the girls, and woodshop and car maintenance being just for boys, went unquestioned in high school. I was happy enough because I loved to sew, and it was a form of making. The opportunity to take a wood class in college was really a game changer for me. Maybe it was a good thing I waited until college, because in high school, all that those boys were ever taught to make were baseball lamps and checkerboard sets. As an undergraduate student at San Diego State, our assignments were based on themes unrelated to techniques: we based our designs on nature, or location, or habits and rituals that we loved. (One guy in my class made a fancy pot pipe.) Most of my work then was stack laminated, and I guess there was some benefit to being a little naive at the time—it was a carefree time for me there.

I had hoped to pursue graduate school at VCU to study with Alphonse Mattia, who would be one of my mentors, but I quickly discovered that there was a lot I did not know about woodworking. I did not know what a dovetail or mortise and tenon were, I had never used a hand plane before, nor did I own a set of chisels. I realized I needed to "go back to school" and study the basics before I embarked on graduate studies. It was a hard pill to swallow. It also seemed that ability was judged by different criteria than I was used to. Because the field has been largely patriarchal, the emphasis on skill has been based entirely on virtuosity: how well that joint is cut, or how complex the techniques used are—i.e., who can do it bigger and better? So, I decided that I better hop to it. I cut my dovetails and made some mortise and tenons, threw in a bit of veneer work, used a hand plane, and bought a set of chisels. I emerged with some basic knowledge of "traditional" woodworking.

It took a few years to be able to meld my newly found skill set with the ideas I wanted to pursue, and sometimes it was like trying to fit a square peg into a round hole. It frustrated me at times, but once I had graduated and was able to work away from the eyes of my teachers, I felt more freedom to break some rules. To borrow a quote from Glenn Adamson, he described my earlier work as "A liberating disruption in studio furniture…and sheer sense of occasion."

My observations of the woodworking and furniture field over the past several decades are in some ways shaped by my early background—a balance of the earlier naivete that I spoke of and my eventual acquisition of skill. I also think that the direction(s) I have taken with my own work are profoundly impacted by my own lived experiences as a Deaf woman in a male-dominated field, with my own insecurities, personal history, ethnic background, and personal passions. There were moments when my work was "out there"—loud brash colors, weird shapes, which then veered into embracing my heritage in a historical context, as told by my mother. And my lifelong love of animals also came into play.

It also pleases me greatly that there are many more women in this field now than ever before. The environment in regard to gender dynamics has improved, but only in the secure bubble of academia: all of that wishful thinking goes out the window when one goes out in the "real world." When I say the real world, in this instance, I mean places like Home Depot or the local hardware store, where you must convince the guy behind the counter that you really do know what you are talking about. But as we have seen most recently, we are a long way from equality on all fronts. And we are seeing powerful works emerging on all levels in response. ✳

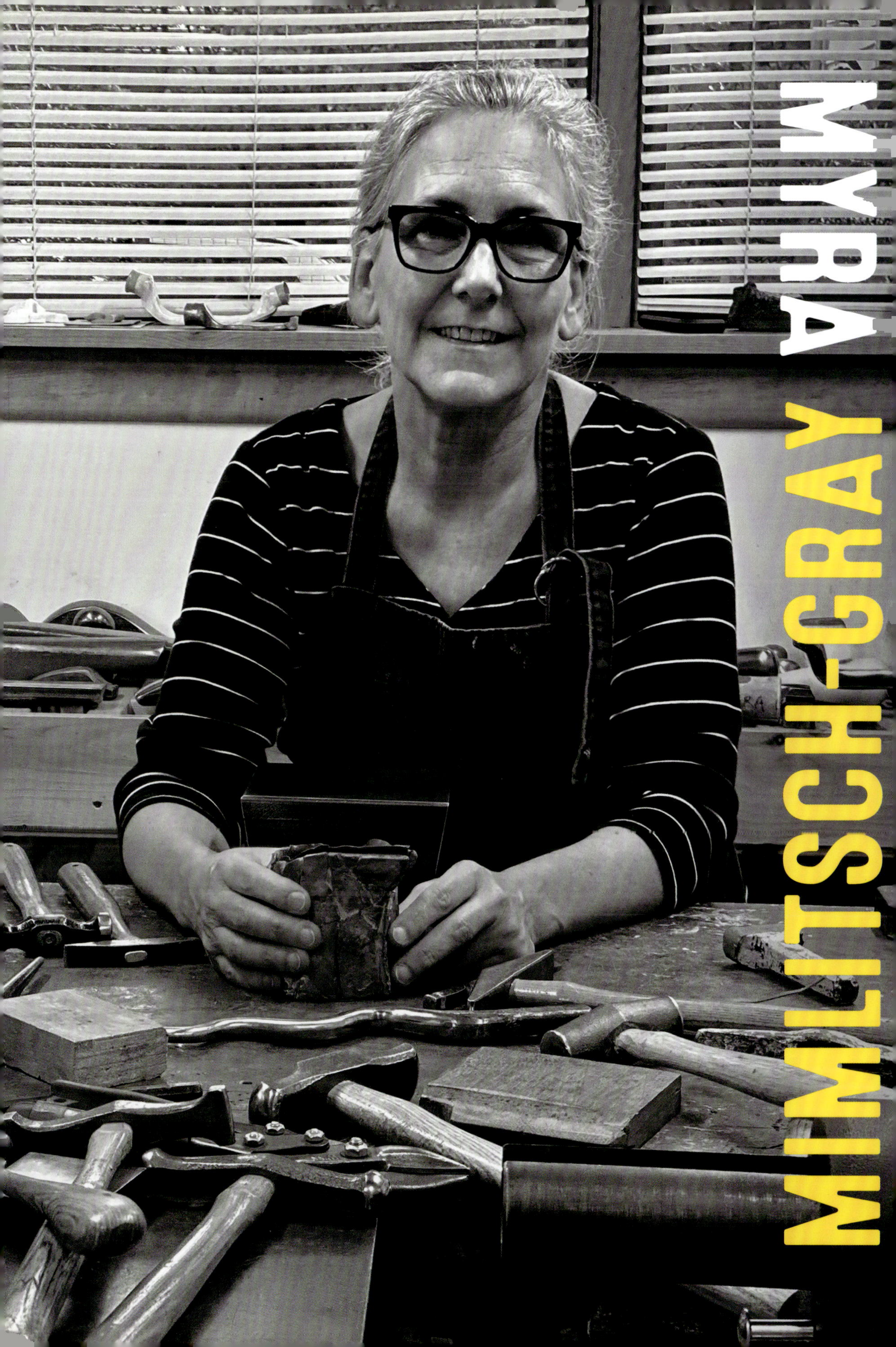
MYRA
MIMLITSCH-GRAY

Fig. 20 Myra Mimlitsch-Gray,
Sugar Bowl and Creamer III,
1996, copper, sugar bowl:
10 ⅞ × 6 ⅞ × 5 ⅛ in., creamer:
10 ⅞ × 9 ⅞ × 4 ¼ in., Gift of the
James Renwick Alliance on the
occasion of the 25th anniversary of
the Renwick Gallery, 1997.56A–B

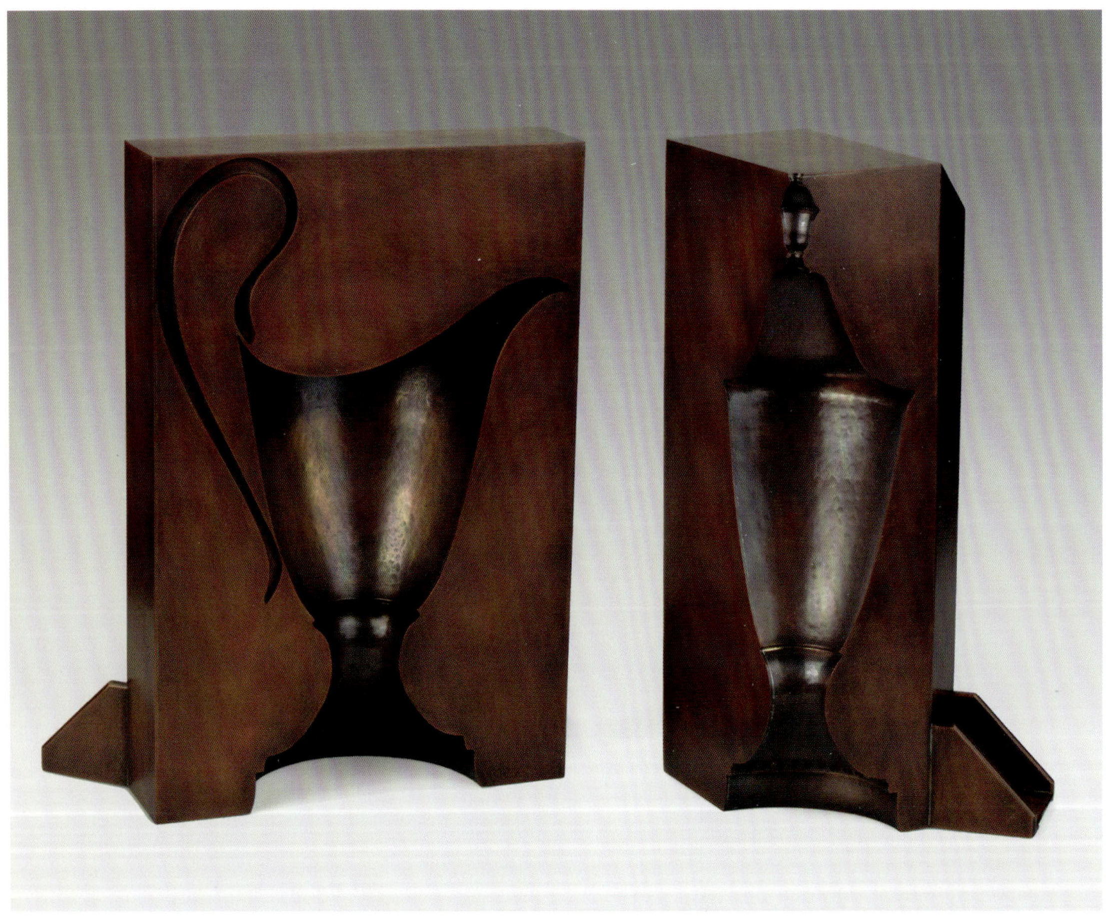

Fig. 21   Marcel Duchamp, *50 cc of Paris Air*, 1919, glass ampoule (broken and later restored), 5 ¼ × 2 ½ in., Philadelphia Museum of Art, The Louise and Walter Arensberg Collection, 1950

MYRA MIMLITSCH-GRAY

This writing began at a resonant moment — the breach of our Capitol Dome. On January 6, 2021, swirls of smoke and gas, banners and bodies amassed into a forceful ball that smashed glass and broke through barriers. As the terrorists cut through the dust, they paused, their maniacal pace halted by the aesthetics of the site: architecture, art, craft, décor — the spectacle of grandeur. They drew in the awe and solemnity of the curated, crafted experience while the world gasped in disbelief, watching it all unfold.

What is it to concretize a thought, a notion, a moment? A century ago Marcel Duchamp captured a moment of air as a souvenir. Gathered in a delicate glass vial, *50 cc of Paris Air*'s fragility complicated its preservation (Fig. 21). A year

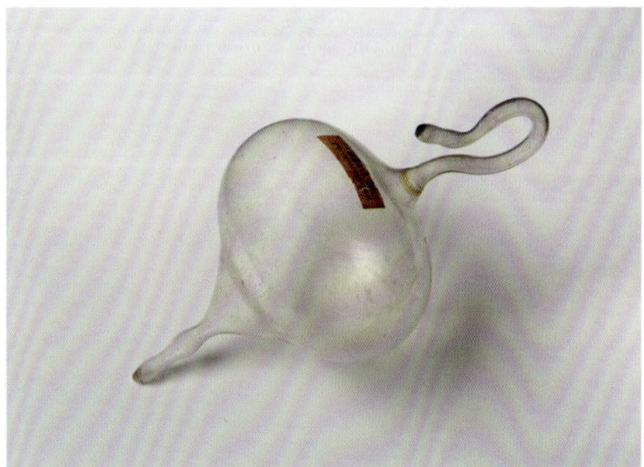

later he joined with Man Ray to document *Dust Breeding* — the ultimate slacker art, made with the most persistent yet evanescent of all media: dust. As a student, I was infuriated by Duchamp's work — its arrogance, feigned indifference, and, frankly, its superb genius. It won me over, even while he offended my feminist sensibilities. The readymade concept was a tough pill for this silversmith, who was striving to transform ore into *objet*. At this same time, I became aware of Toshiko Takeazu's work: the potter threw a vessel that grew in size equal to her own, then drew the form in completely to contain the sense/essence of self inside. Physicality, materiality, and intentionality combined in Takeazu's defining work (see p. 54), conversant with Duchamp's *Paris Air*, in my mind.

We declare a moment as "defining," knowing it will be overwritten by the next. My formative research occurred at the juncture of modernist and postmodernist theories, between the avant-garde ideal and critical deconstruction. Each was *the* definitive ideology, and difficult terrain to navigate. Asserting myself as a journey(wo)man, I built precise work that explored and reified these philosophies. The craft object would become the subject, staged to assert a critical dialogue. And while I secured a love for the rigor, the haptic knowledge and satisfaction of achievement that craftwork can embody, I also saw how mastery, in essence, reinforces hierarchies that privilege and oppress. You can achieve so-called mastery, but it's what you do with it that counts.

I am motivated by craft's agency, whether asserted by the maker or instrumental through use; by its potential to cultivate community, and its symbolic resonance garnered across generations. Craft is power. Choice is power. This is a modern luxury. Taking craft to its essential function, I can choose to make a tool: knife, spoon, bowl. I can enhance the form, nuance its utility: bottle, beer stein, butter dish. I can combine all of these things into a conglomerated sculptural work, but to what purpose? This is my creative prerogative, and also my conundrum: where is the audience for it, and who can nurture that engagement? Oh, hello, museum!

My teacher Bill Daley once told me that *craft* simply means that "someone went and did something intelligently," and by this I understood him to mean that a decision was made. Not necessarily about the best way to do it, or with the highest level of expertise, but that a considered choice was made in how to make, and how to own it: intent. Directed, intentional non-crafting is as creatively important as mastering the medium, and withholding skill is as much a part of excellence in craft as virtuosity. Choice is not an aside. *Craft* the verb is assertive, establishing new priorities for an expanding audience, and its progressive evolution is very much a part of this present moment. Thank you for including me in this project. ✳

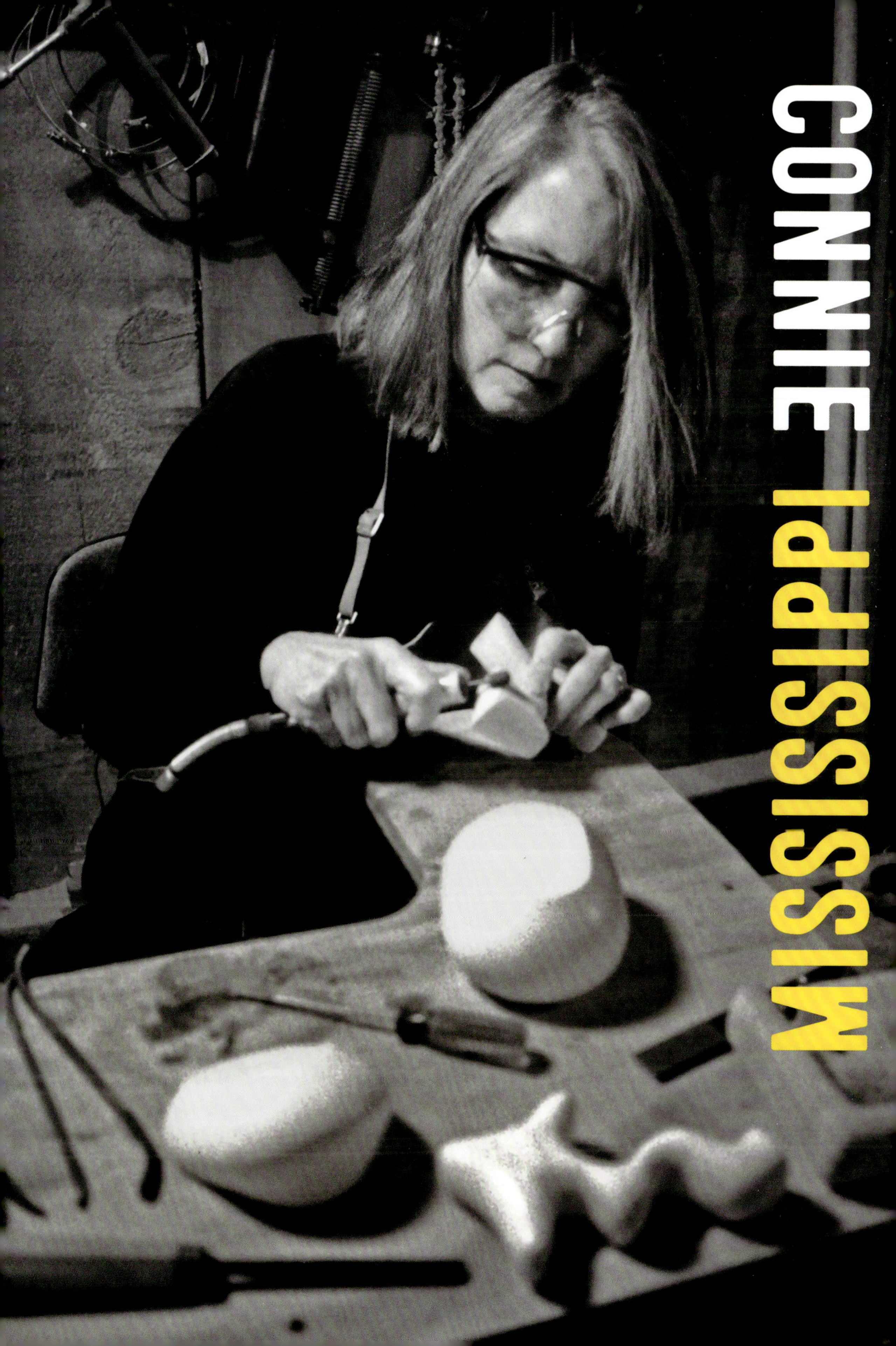
CONNIE
MISSISSIPPI

CAT. 39   Connie Mississippi,
Midnight Mountain (two views),
2001–4, Baltic birch plywood,
6 ½ × diam. 22 in.

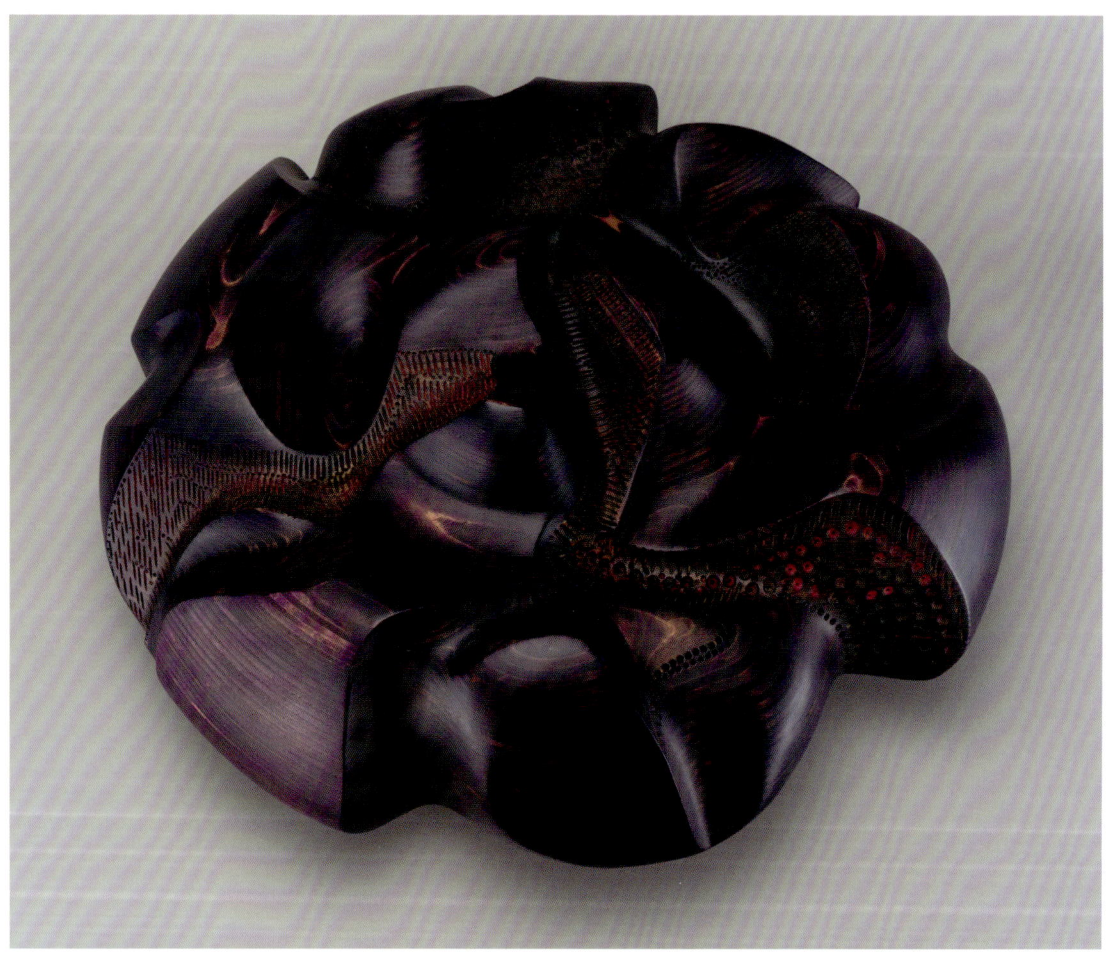

CONNIE MISSISSIPPI

We exist today in a completely new reality. The last several years have so shaken and changed us that we feel we have passed through a period of great darkness and into a new beginning. How could it not change our creative lives as well? The woodturned and carved sculpture that I executed in 2001, and which is part of this Renwick exhibition in 2022, has become such a distant offering that I barely recognize it.

However, there is an opportunity in this new global moment to use the lessons we have learned and create a social discourse between the maker and the viewer. This may be done in a search for understanding in an American culture entering a portal filled with the serious problems of climate change, racism, poverty, and homelessness.

Thinking of craft as it relates to the home, what about homelessness? How does this change our discourse about the field? Thinking

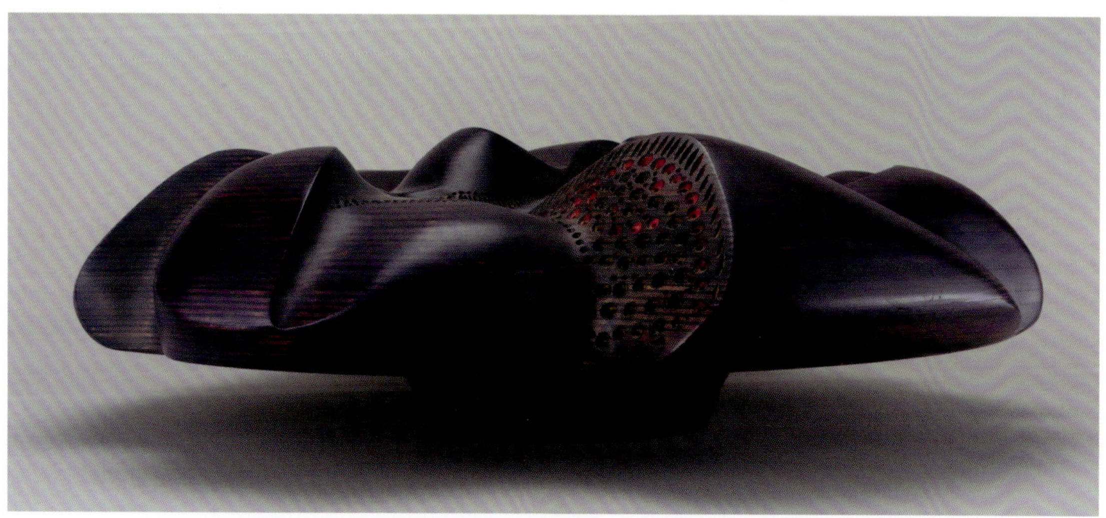

about where the home is in the physical environment, what about the effects of climate change? Fire, desertification, drought? Recognizing that time as we have experienced it in the distant past is not the same as the time we have lived through in the ongoing pandemic and unstable political environment, we look to the future for new beginnings and explorations. Craft becomes more of an embrace, a comfort, a gift to be explored and a new way of knowing and giving, a tender offering between the maker and the viewer.

Looking forward from the present moment, there are so many possibilities available to us in this new time of exploration. Baskets floating from the ceiling become dust and storm clouds, ceramic plates become murals suspended on the walls and ceilings, glass is transformed into standing monoliths and molded into exquisite mysteries, fiber is made from recycled detritus and cigar wrappers. Wood turning is no longer limited to the size of the tree it derives from but may be laminated into large blanks that soar into monuments of unexpected origin. The lathe itself, an industrial and seemingly unromantic tool, has taken on new possibilities as a source for creative explorations. The artist is no longer limited to the lathe of the past, turning spindles and bowls, but has discovered an untapped reference to a universe yet to be explored.

As we imagine how craft, as a living thing in a changed world, can impact and change lives, we allow for new responses to objects from the viewer as well as from the artists who make them. This exhibition is in part about surviving an unimagined darkness and dreaming ourselves into a new and powerful reality. It is a time filled with hope and new beginnings. I am honored to have my work be a part of it.

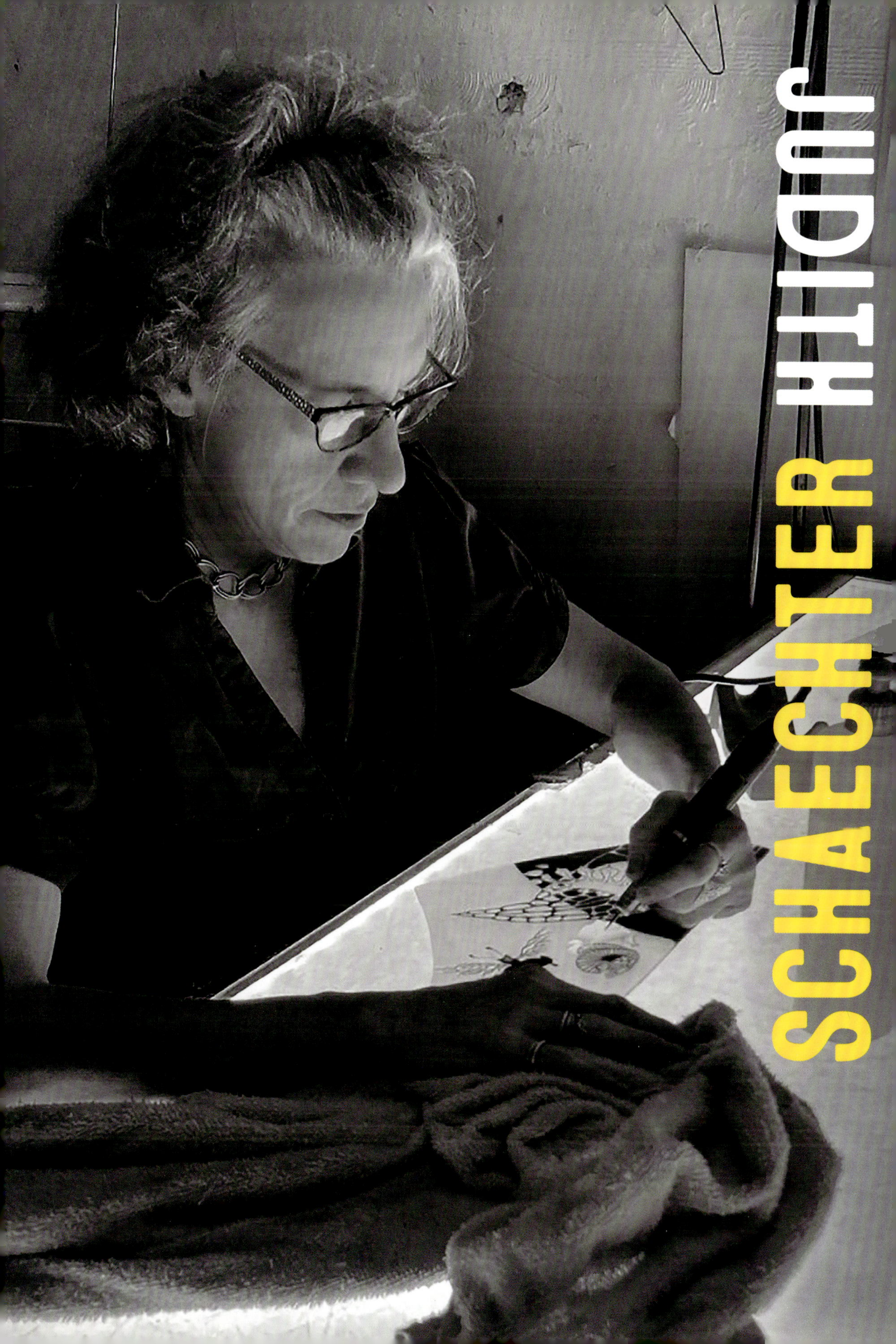

JUDITH
SCHAECHTER

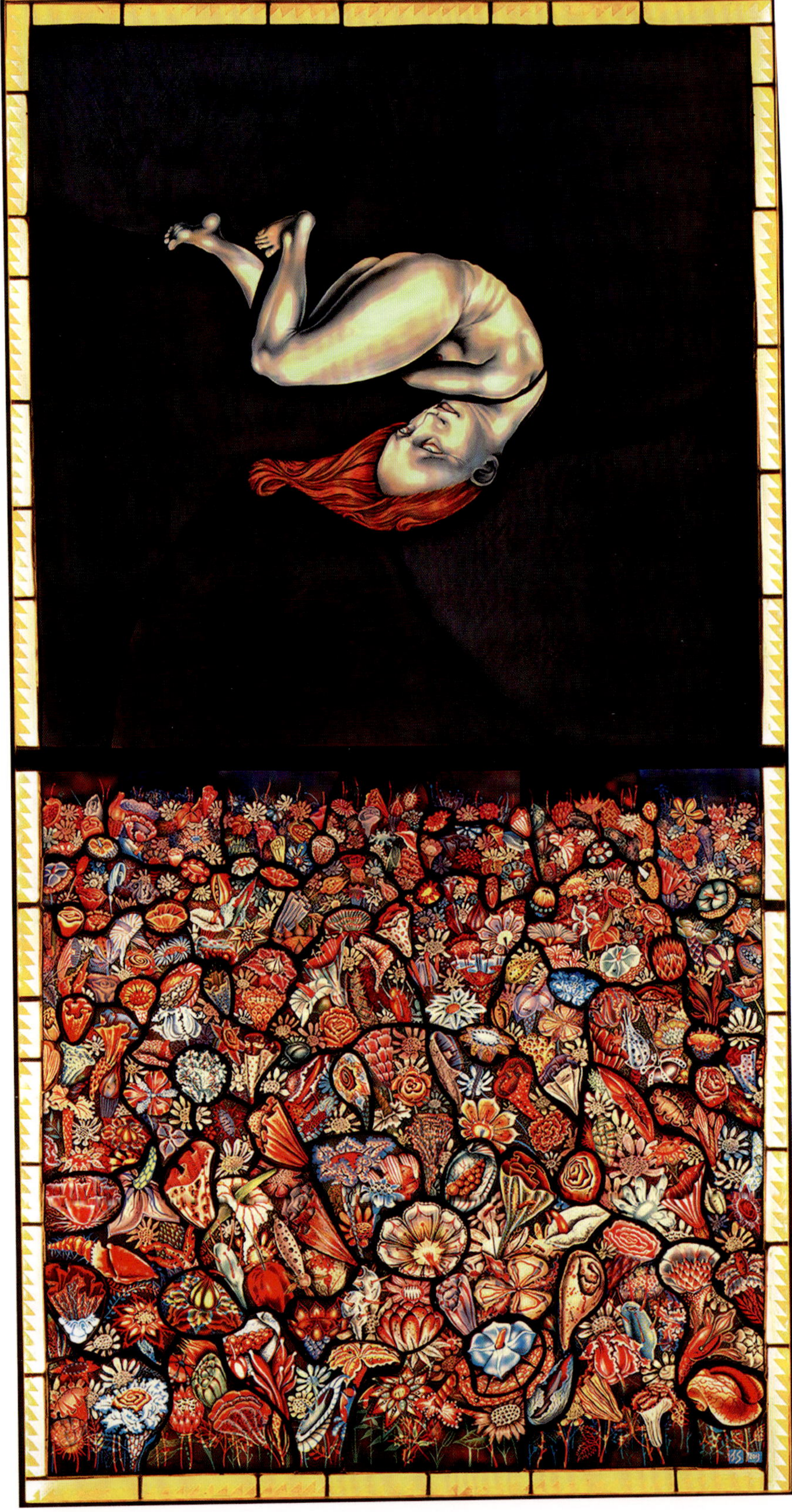

Fig. 22   Judith Schaechter, *The Birth of Eve*, 2013, flash glass with vitreous paint, silver stain, and copper foil, 57 × 31 × 2 in., Gift of the James Renwick Alliance, 2015.12

JUDITH SCHAECHTER

As a single human being with the task of being an "artist," I feel it is at least part of my job to put my own consciousness forward in my work—not as some vainglorious monument to my own puny ego (or maybe it is, but I hope it's more than just that!), but as an example of the struggle to balance between a past one cannot return to and a future one can barely imagine. Either way, both past and future are narrative (and I am a narrative artist) — not realities. To look back is to create a story about where we come from, and to look ahead is to create a story about where we are going.

I recognize that, as a living person, the only real choice is to live in the present moment, but I find that close to impossible! Artwork for me is a way of creating an instance, an isolated singularity, as record of the moment's own the-oretical existence—like a cross section or a core sample of a single immediate "now," flash frozen for contemplation at another time. In my work, there is narrative, but one that I hope defies any sense of past or present — it is a narrative in which those possibilities are impossible and time exists as a sort of eternal present. When I work with the image of the human figure, I imagine it to have arisen spontaneously as it is seen in the image and to remain there unchang-ing for eternity, suspended in whatever context I imagined for it at the time. I don't see a story with a beginning or an end, although I think it is possible for others to see a more temporal linear story. I work hard to eradicate clues of history in my work — even the most neutral clothing or minute detail can identify the time in which the piece was created. My characters don't have a biography. Like dolls, they are there to adapt to the immediate needs of the player.

Why all this insistence on the here and now? Because infinity, the eternal, if it can be experienced at all, must be felt in the subdivisions of the present. And really, visual art is a great way to create that singular moment as it exists more obviously in space and not time.

In 1990, Renwick Gallery curator Michael Monroe took a big chance on me and featured my work in the *Glassworks* exhibition. It was my "big break." I will never stop being grateful for the opportunity. *

THE BERNSTEIN-CHERNOFF COLLECTION OF SCULPTURAL WOOD ART

BY MARY SAVIG

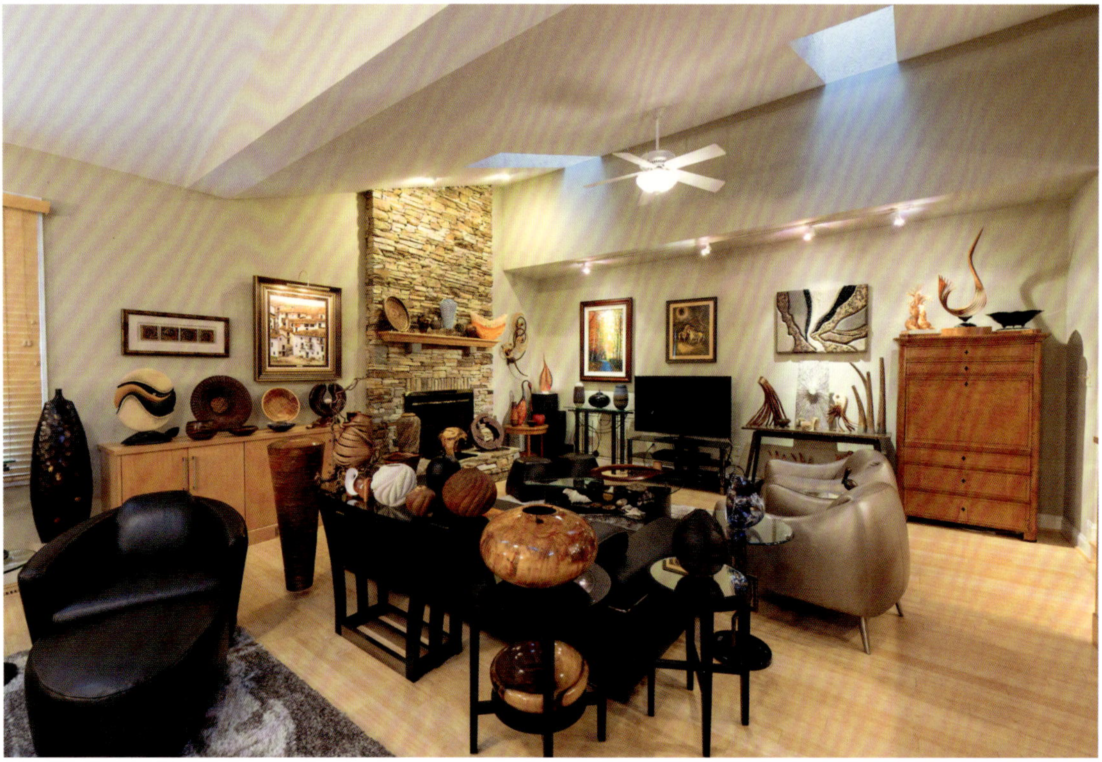

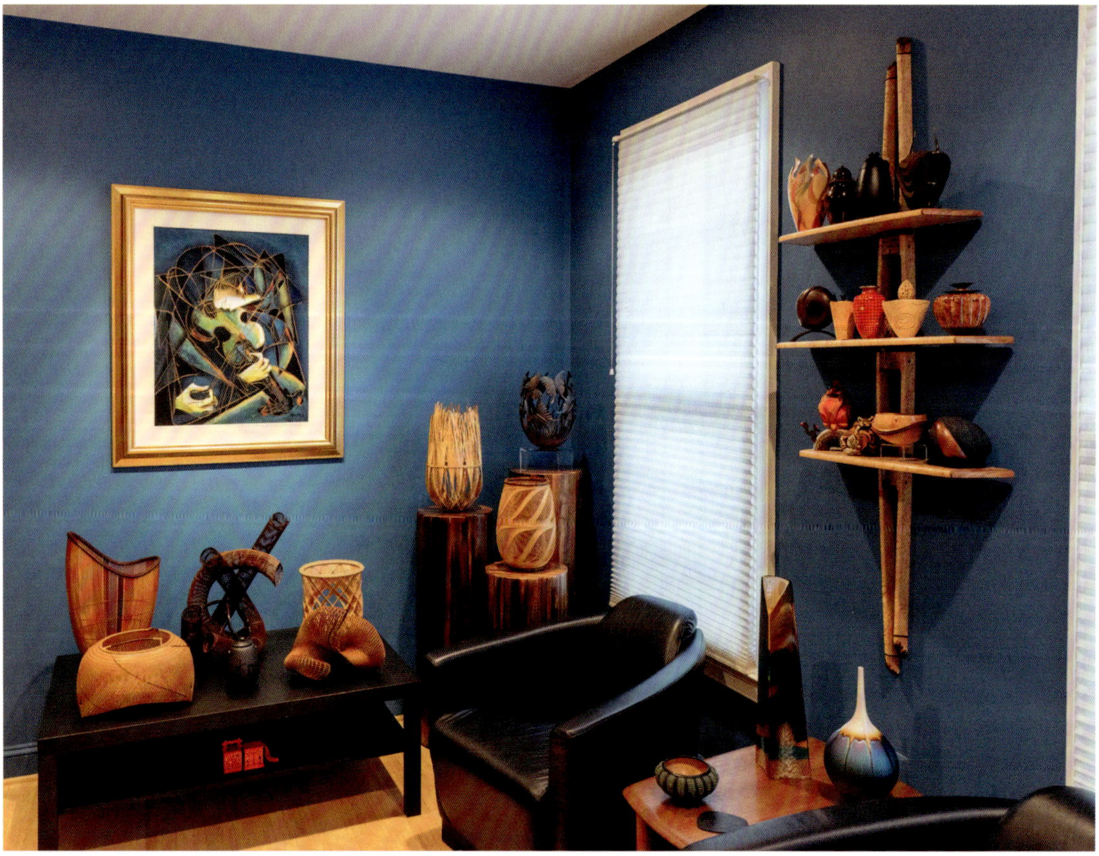

In 2021 collectors Judith Chernoff and Jeffrey Bernstein donated forty-three sculptural wood artworks to the Renwick Gallery. Bernstein and Chernoff, both trained as physicians, collected their first artwork—that just happened to be made of wood—in 1994. At the time, their home revolved around the activities of their growing children. The family began to imagine how they might slowly replace toys and storybooks with art. They did not begin with a focus on wood, but they soon made it their niche.

In 2002 they acquired *Fusion* by Mark Nantz (CAT. 40), an otherworldly burl vessel suspended within an ebony exoskeleton. An important accomplishment in the artist's career, this acquisition marked the shift in the collectors' journey from curious seekers to informed advocates. Their evolving collection expresses their commitment to education, culminating with this transformative gift to the Renwick. It builds on a previous gift to the museum by Fleur and Charles Bresler, the Bresler Collection of Turned and Carved Wood. Another deeply personal collection of the finest examples, it established the Renwick Gallery as one of the preeminent public collections of contemporary wood art in the United States. The Bernstein–Chernoff gift will energize scholarship on this field for many generations to come.

The Bernstein–Chernoff home in Laurel, Maryland, realizes French philosopher Gaston Bachelard's notion of inhabiting a space with intensity, one of the prevailing themes tying together *This Present Moment: Crafting a Better World*. With thoughtful care, they assembled not merely a collection, but a constellation of rooms and nooks, each with its own personality (Figs. 23 and 24). When they acquired a new work, they took time to harmonize it with existing displays. As the collection grew, the works rotated and fostered new emotions, memories, and experiences in their daily lives. In an interview, Chernoff recalled that while they read books, listened to their children play piano, or enjoyed lively dinners, the artworks listened and offered moments of reflection. The artworks index the family's memory of the artist and help create new memories within the home. The feeling of the collection even changes with the season, invoking the very memory of the trees.

Collecting has been a social and educational pursuit for the couple. Each work is carefully selected after they meet the artist and learn firsthand about their practice. The couple never stop learning about the craft from a variety of perspectives. Bernstein emphasizes the importance of skill and technical ingenuity, or how the artists mediate the language of the wood. Chernoff notes that the intangible resonance of an artwork, or how it makes them feel, is also an important criterion. Given Bernstein and Chernoff's commitment to the individual artist's vision, the collection is dynamic and of the moment, introducing a new group of woodturners to the Renwick's holdings. Chernoff would know—since 2015 she has volunteered as a docent at the museum.

Many artists, notably Pat Kramer (CAT. 41), Dixie Biggs (CATS. 42–44), and John Beaver (CATS. 45 and 46), capture the ephemerality of nature in the forms of a night-blooming flower, autumn foliage, or ocean waves. Others are showy performances of skill. Cindy Drozda's signature finials are so thin, they toe the line between beauty and anguish (CAT. 48). Likewise, the spherical sculptures by J. Paul Fennell (CATS. 49–51) have a quiet wonder to them, each an artful feat of engineering. Works by Hunt Clark (CAT. 52), Betty Scarpino (CAT. 53), and Connie Mississippi (CAT. 39; see pp. 130–31) are voluminous and sensual, inviting viewers to rethink the very parameters of the medium. John Mascoll (CATS. 54–56) and Avelino Samuel and Harvey Fein (CATS. 57–59) continue the tradition of turning to reveal the poetry of distinct species of trees.

On the occasion of the fiftieth anniversary of the Renwick Gallery, the Bernstein–Chernoff collection arrives amid changes in the field. In their leadership positions with the Collectors of Wood Art (both are past presidents of the organization), they have helped support an expanding community, to include more women, artists of color, and second-career artists than do current Renwick holdings. As Bernstein and Chernoff intend, the artworks will continue to inspire others to discover the intricacies of knots, burls, and grain, to learn more about process and skills, and then perhaps to cherish wood art in their own homes. ✳

The history and description of the collection were taken largely from the author's interview with Judith Chernoff and Jeffrey Bernstein on November 30 and December 28, 2020.

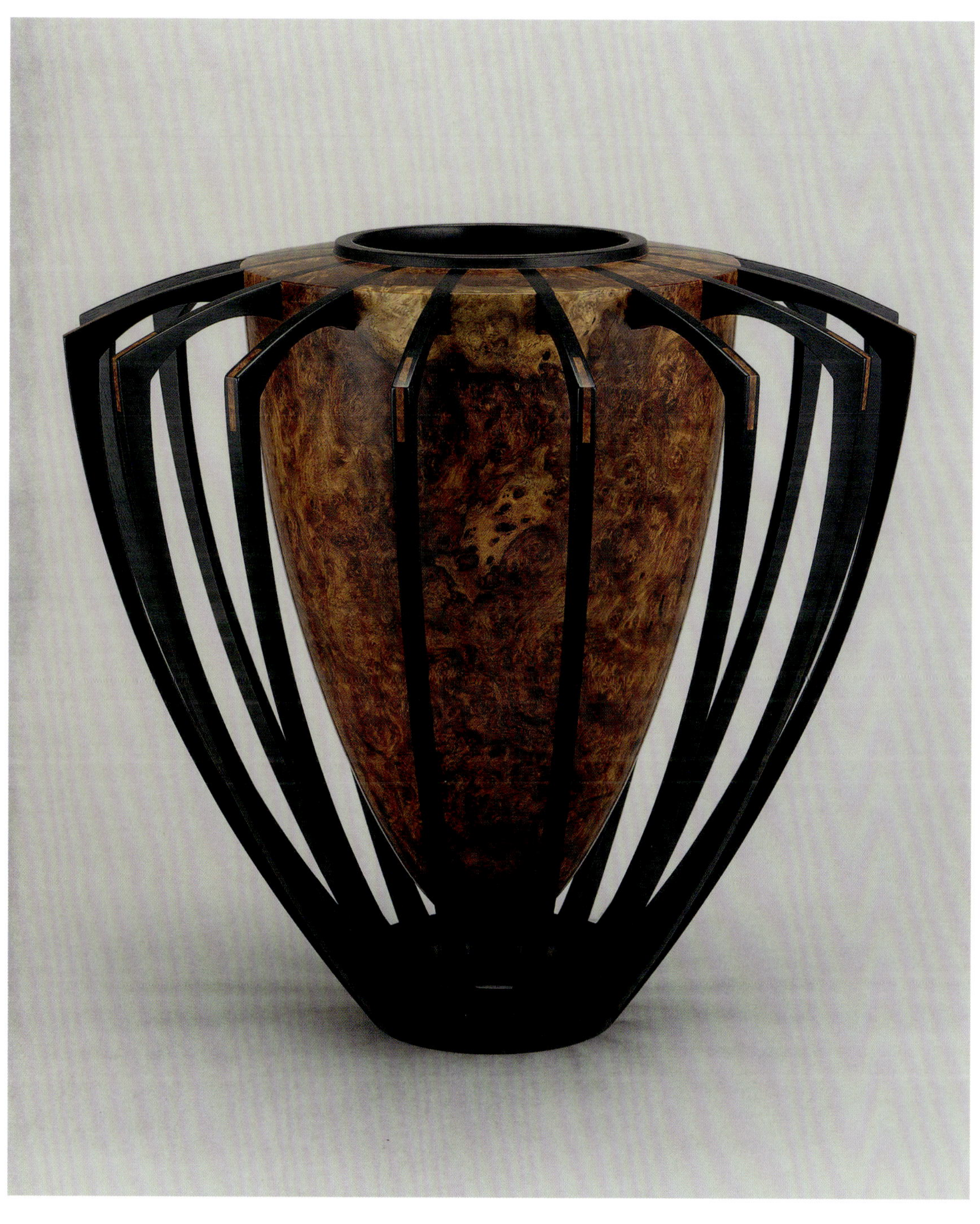

CAT. 41 Pat Kramer,
Night Blooming Serious,
2003, Norfolk Island pine,
5 × diam. 15 ½ in.

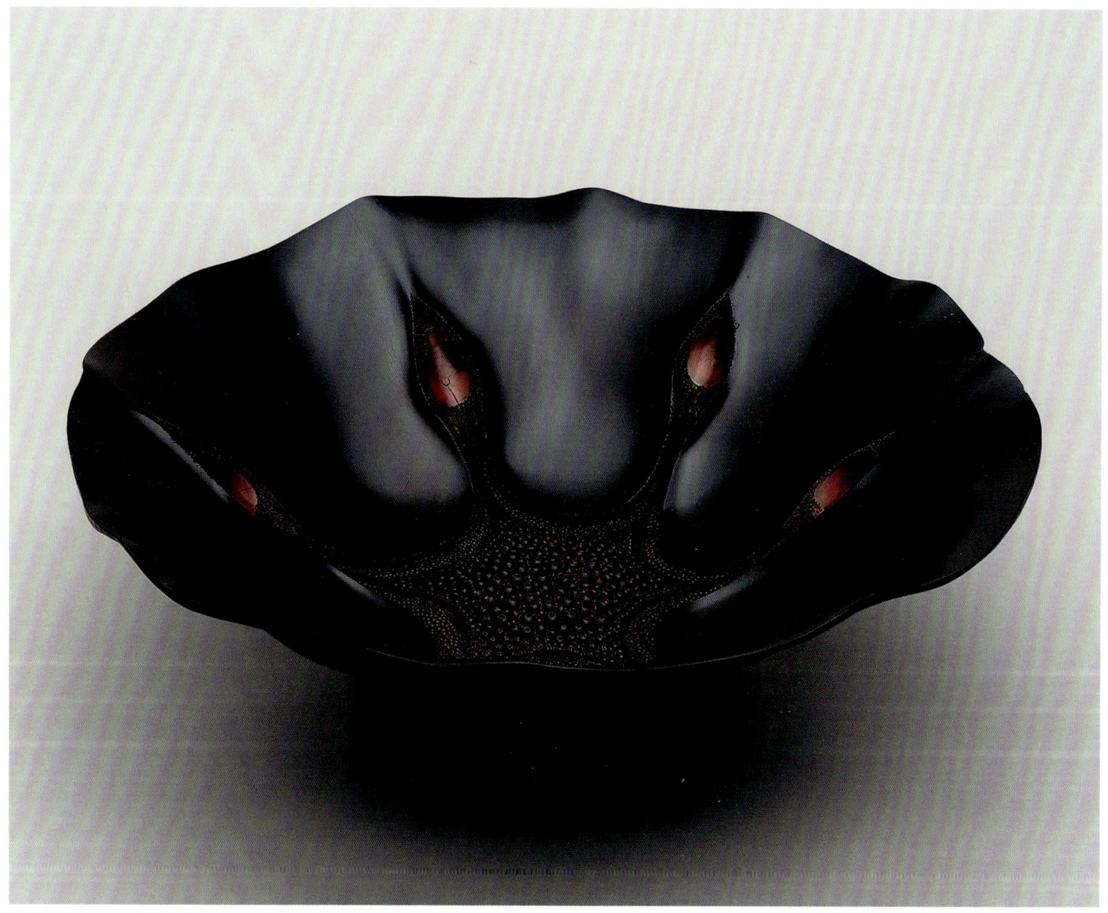

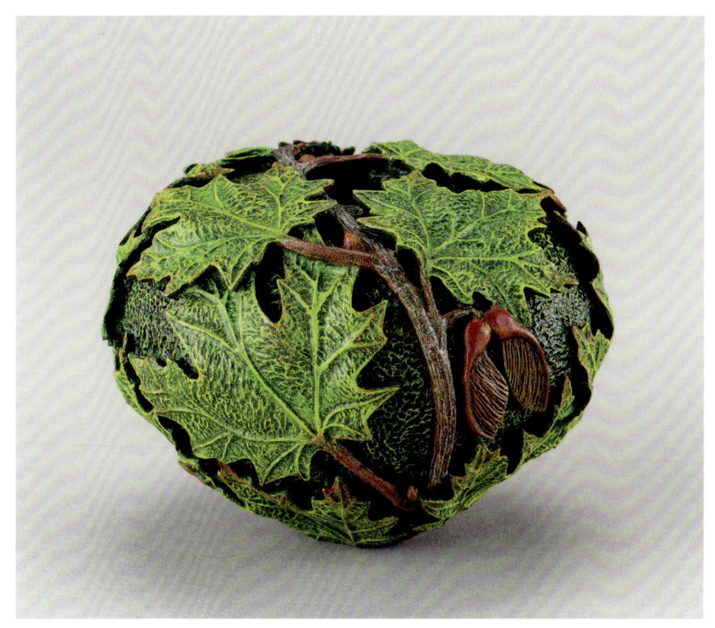

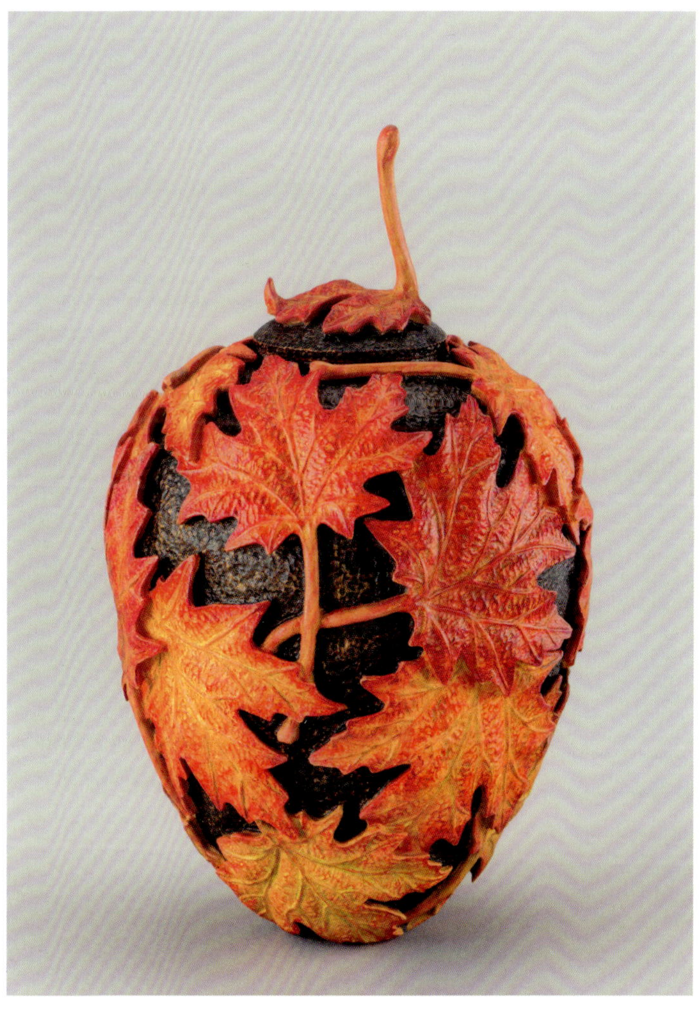

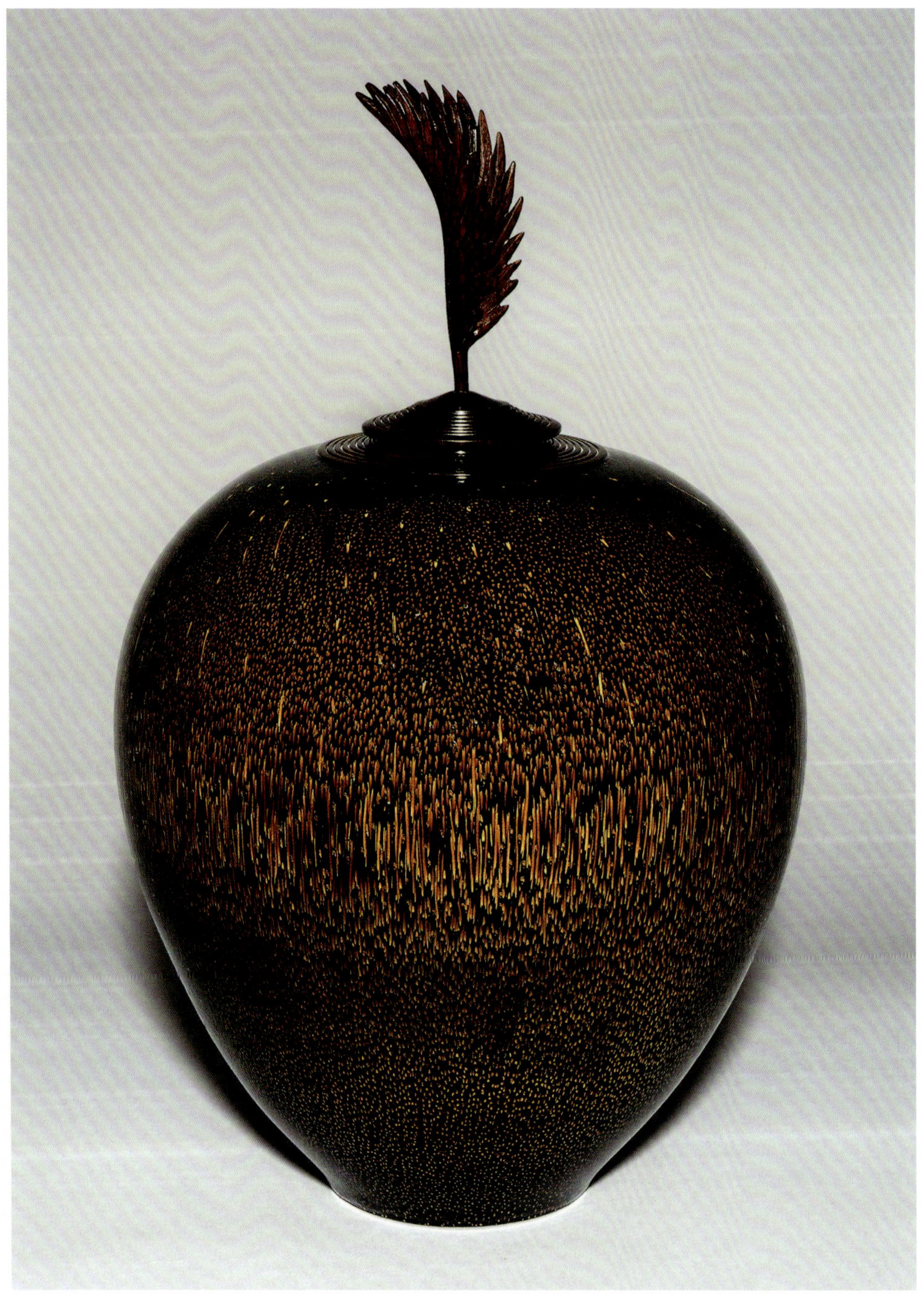

CAT. 44   Dixie Biggs, *Dated Material*, 2003, dyed palm and ziricote, 18 × diam. 11 ¼ in.

CAT. 45 John Beaver,
3 Protruding Wave Bowl,
2011, alder and padauk,
3 × diam. 5 in.

CAT. 46 John Beaver,
Intersecting Waves,
2016, walnut and maple,
6 × diam. 8 in.

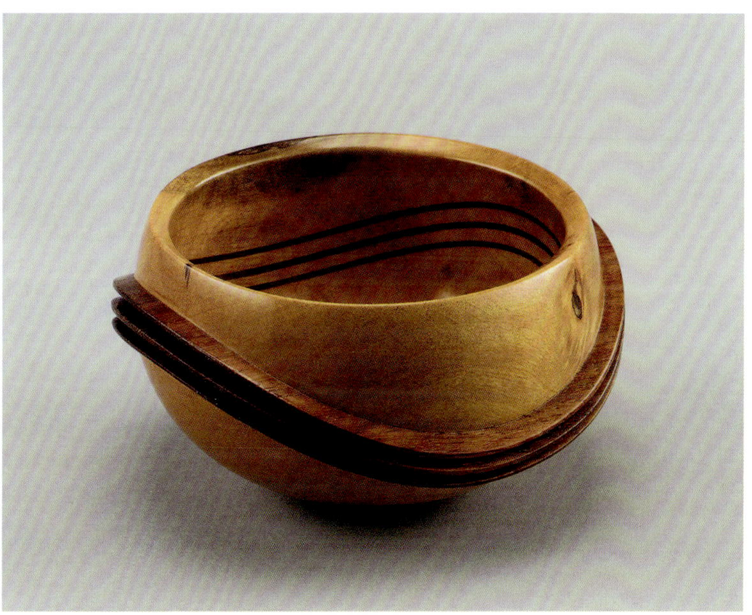

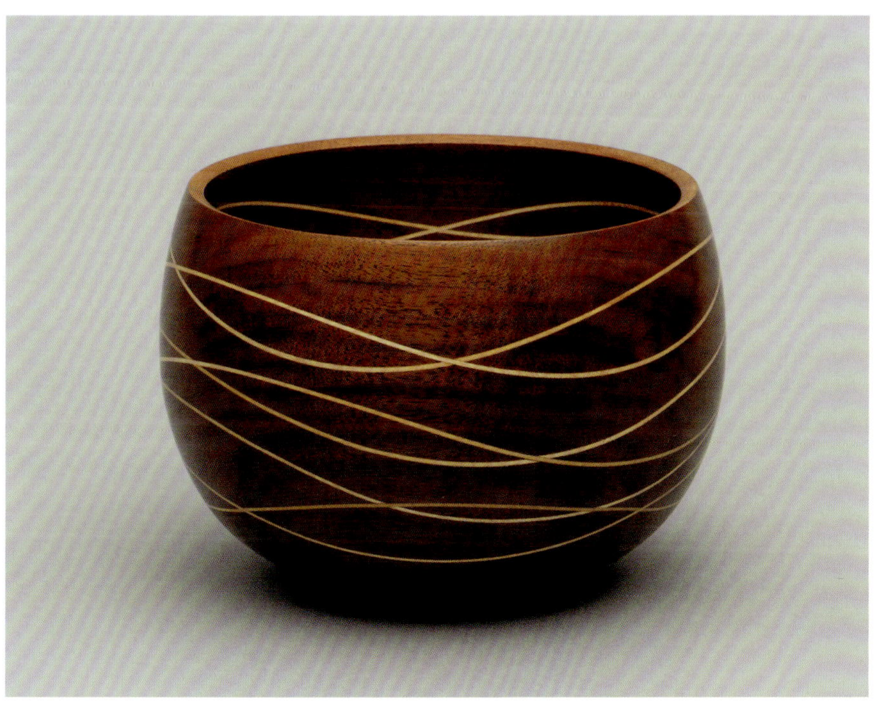

CAT. 47 Cindy Drozda,
Wooden Bowl #157, n.d.,
eucalyptus gum burl
and desert ironwood
with 23-karat gold leaf,
3 × diam. 6 ½ in.

CAT. 48 Cindy Drozda,
*Pele (Hawaiian Goddess of
Fire)*, n.d., Australian red
mallee burl and blackwood
with garnet in 14-karat gold,
15 4/5 × diam. 9 in.

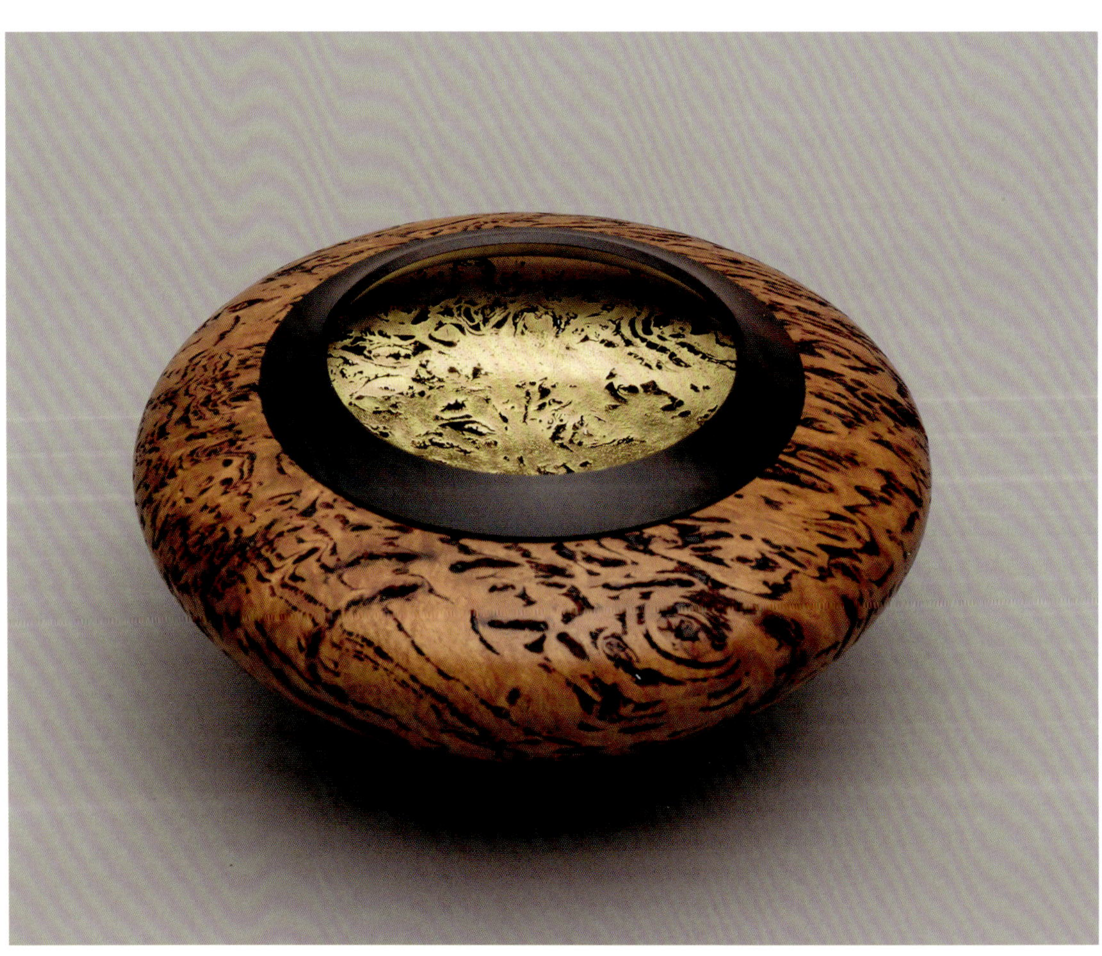

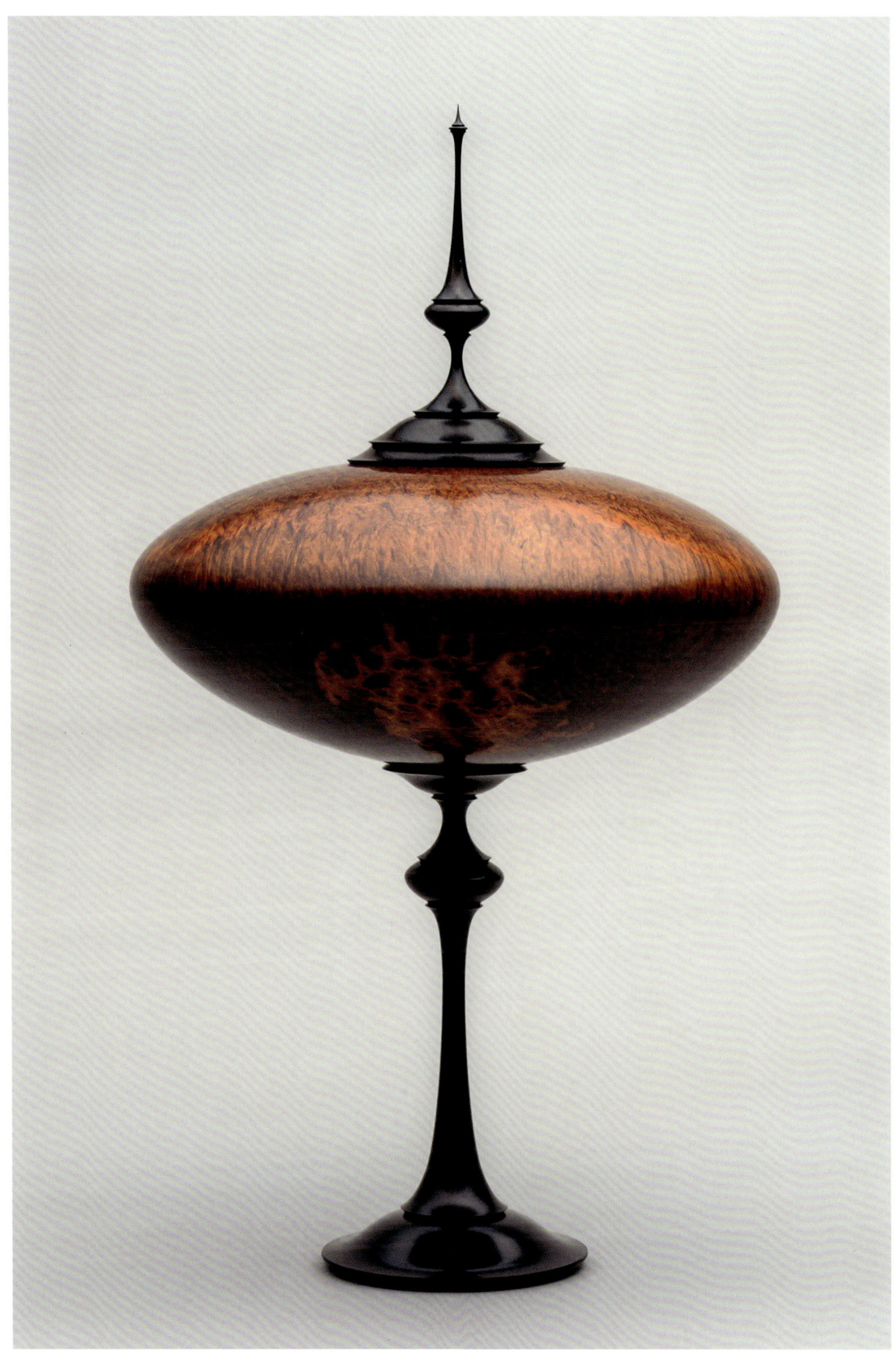

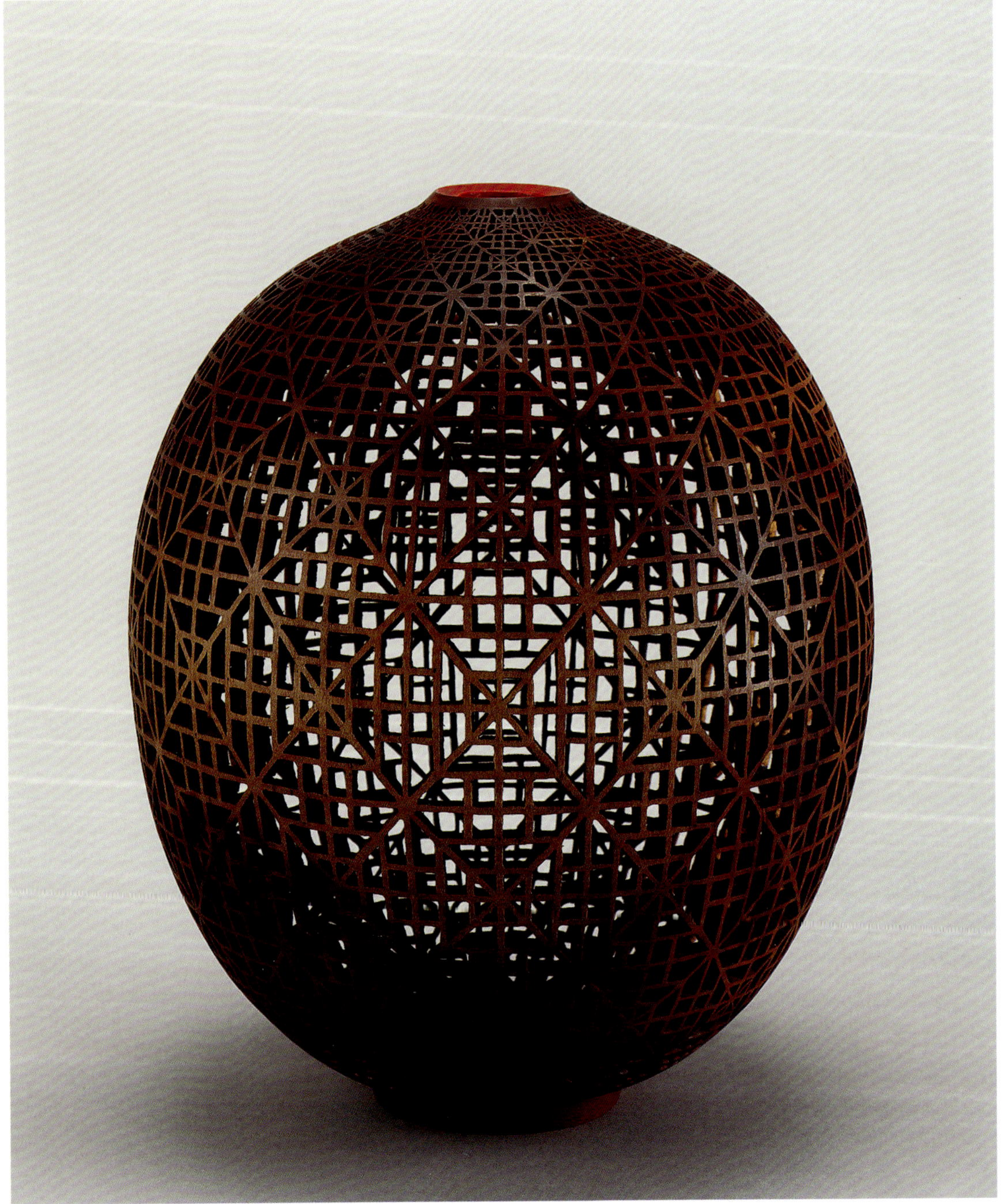

CAT. 50 J. Paul Fennell,
Untitled Vessel, 2004,
carob, 5 × diam. 6 in.

CAT. 51 J. Paul Fennell,
Offering Vessel, 2015, ficus,
10 ½ × diam. 9 in.

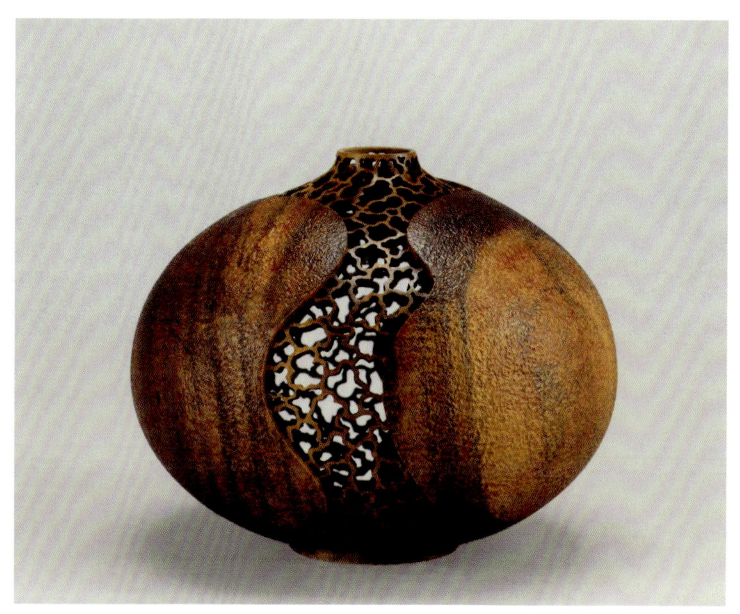

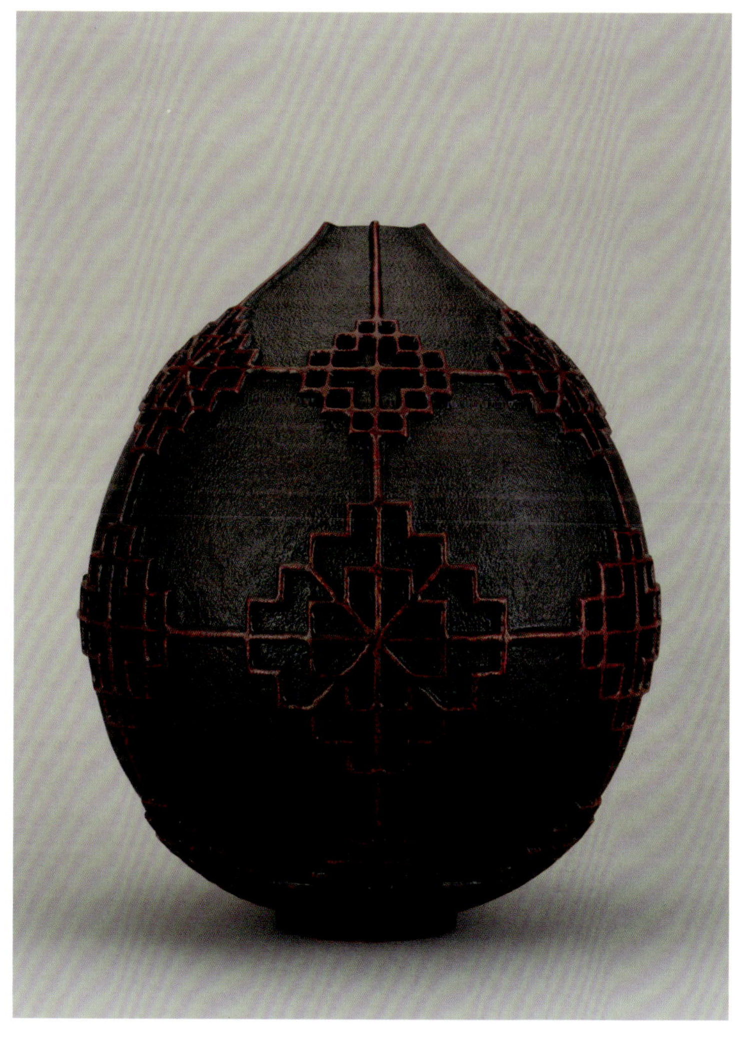

CAT. 52 Hunt
Clark, *Untitled Wood
Sculpture*, 2011, maple,
15 ½ × 20 × 20 in.

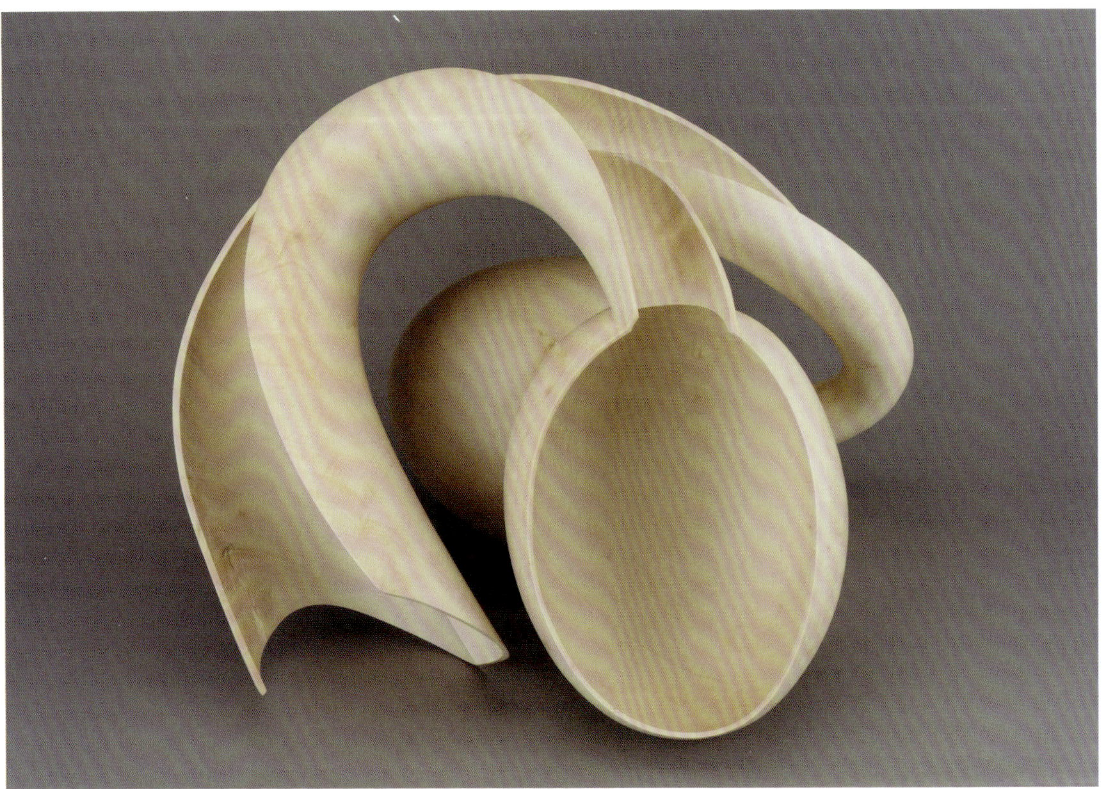

CAT. 53 Betty Scarpino,
Inviolate Portal, 2007,
ash, oak, and walnut,
16 × 14 × 3 ½ in.

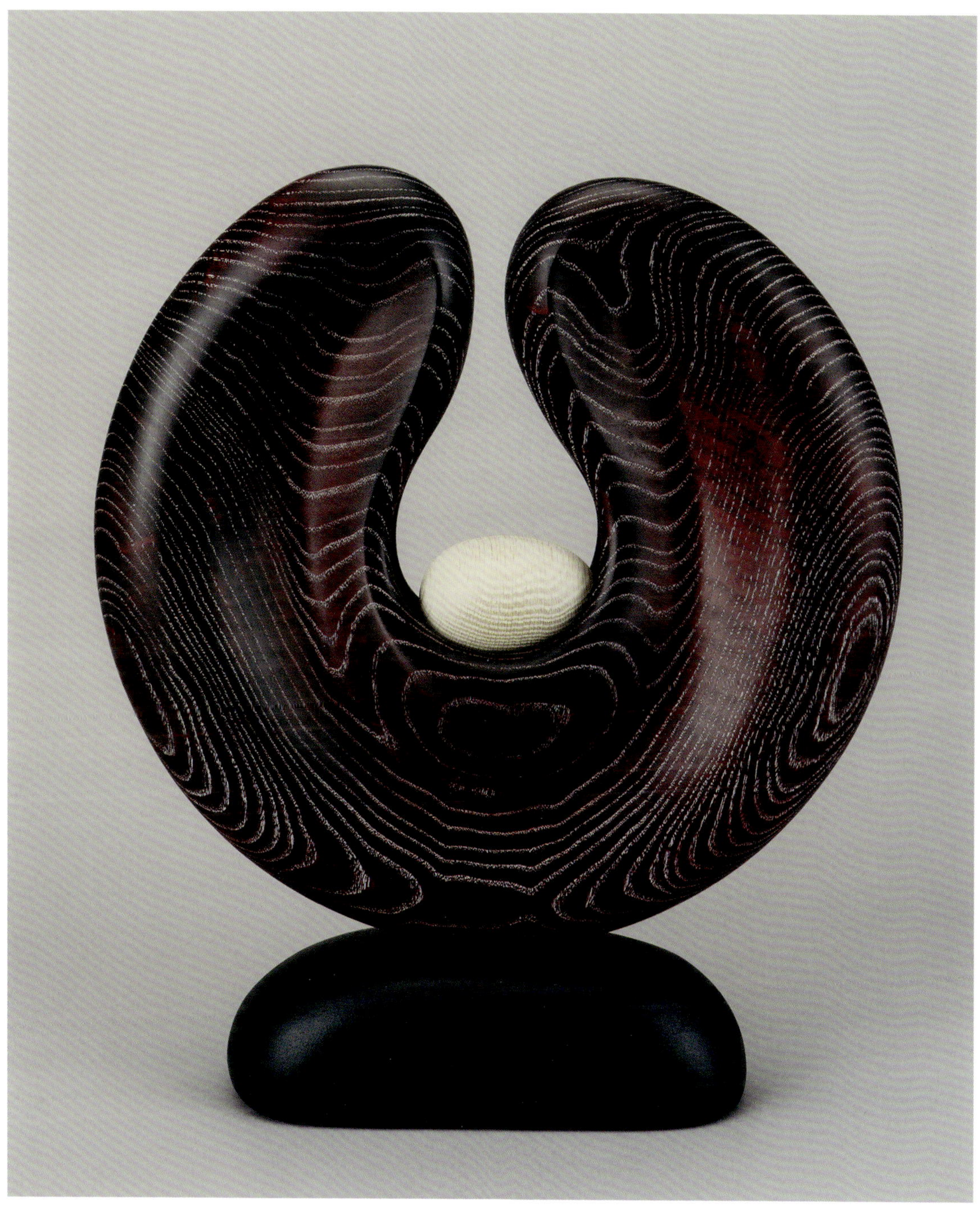

CAT. 54 John Mascoll,
Untitled Lidded Vessel,
n.d., royal palm and
cocobolo, overall:
17 ¼ × diam. 8 ¾ in.

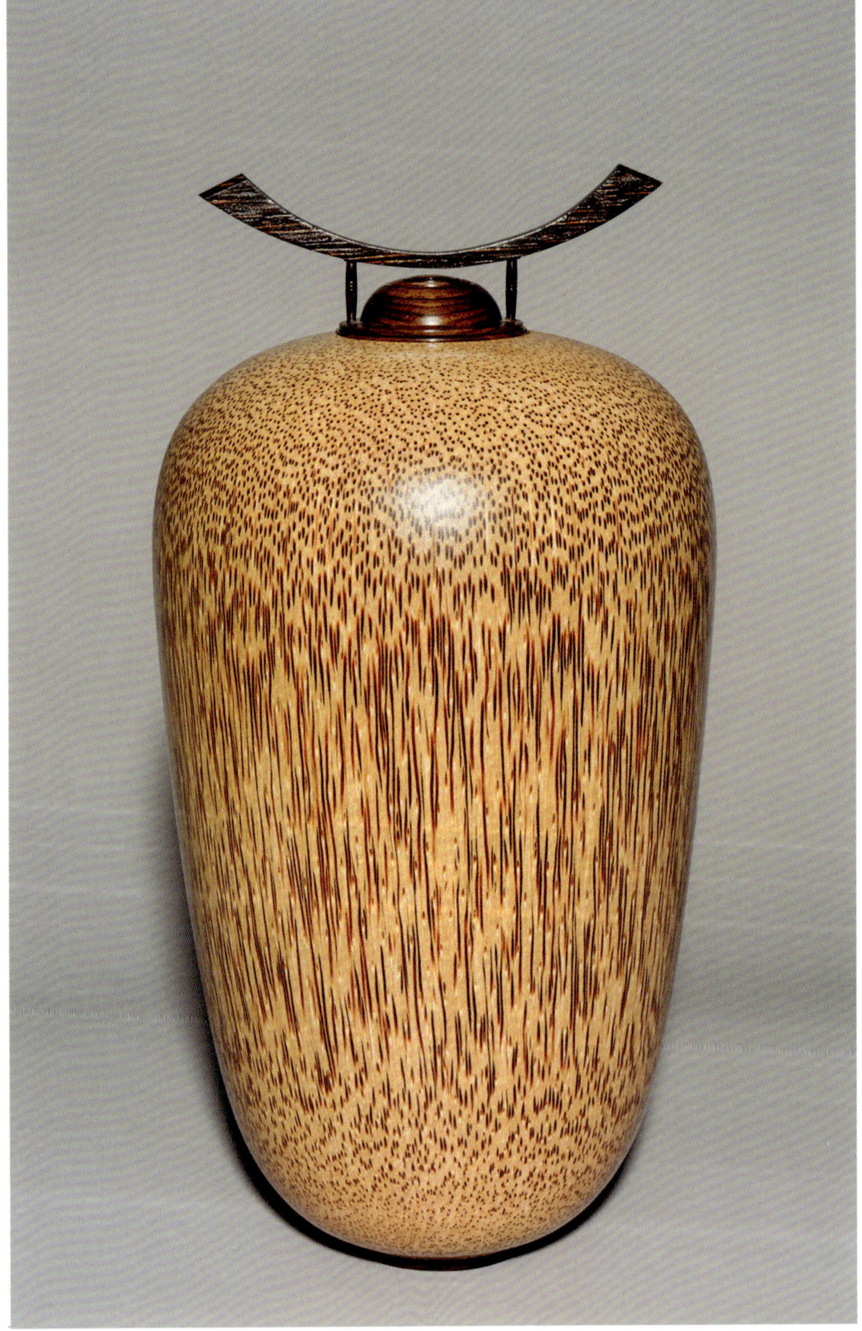

CAT. 55   John Mascoll, *Untitled Lidded Vessel*, 2016, citrus, overall: 11 × diam. 4 ¾ in.

CAT. 56   John Mascoll, *Untitled Lidded Vessel*, 2016, bleached chinaberry, overall: 12 ¾ × 7 ¼ × 7 in.

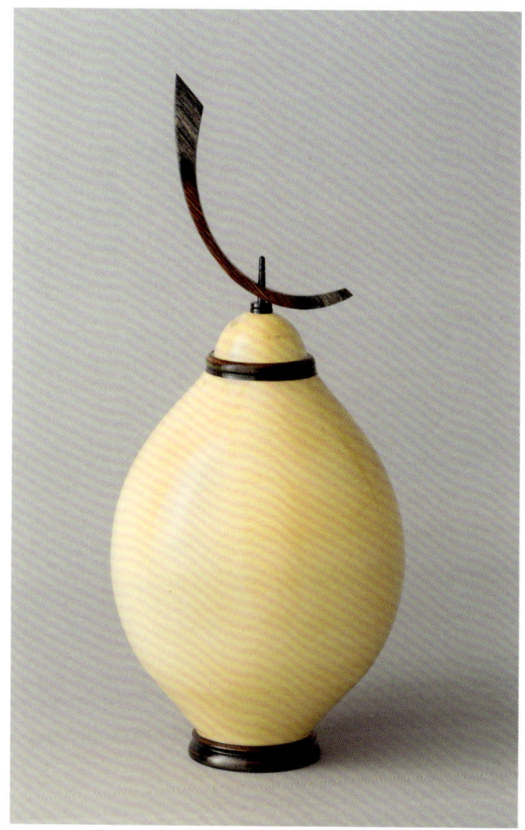

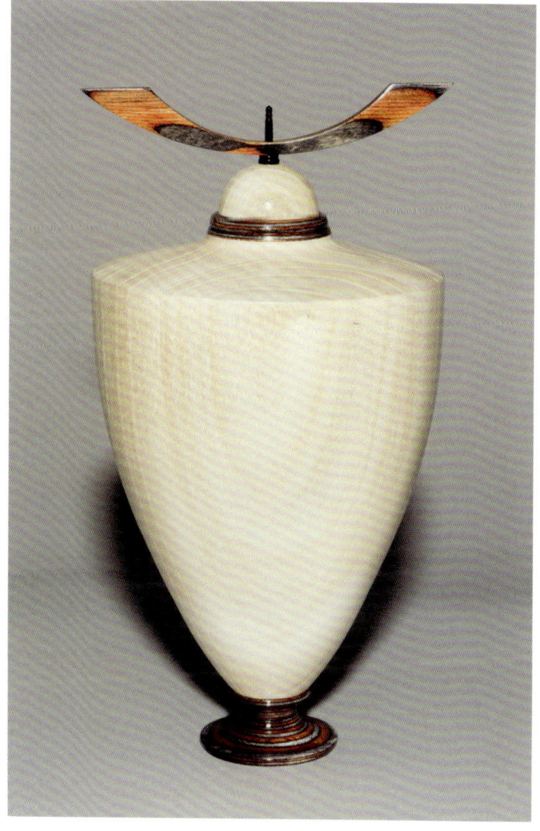

CAT. 57 Avelino Samuel, *Spiral Carved Vessel*, n.d., black olive, 8 ¾ × diam. 5 in.

CAT. 58 Harvey Fein and Avelino Samuel, *Untitled*, 2011, cocobolo, 10 × diam. 6 ¾ in.

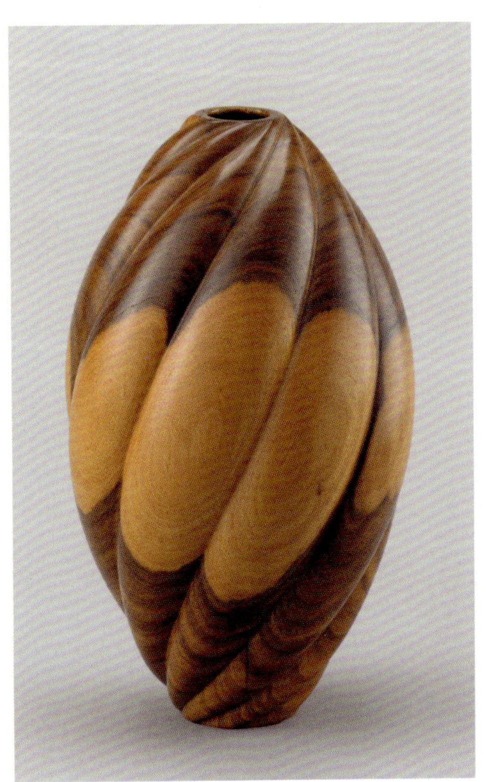

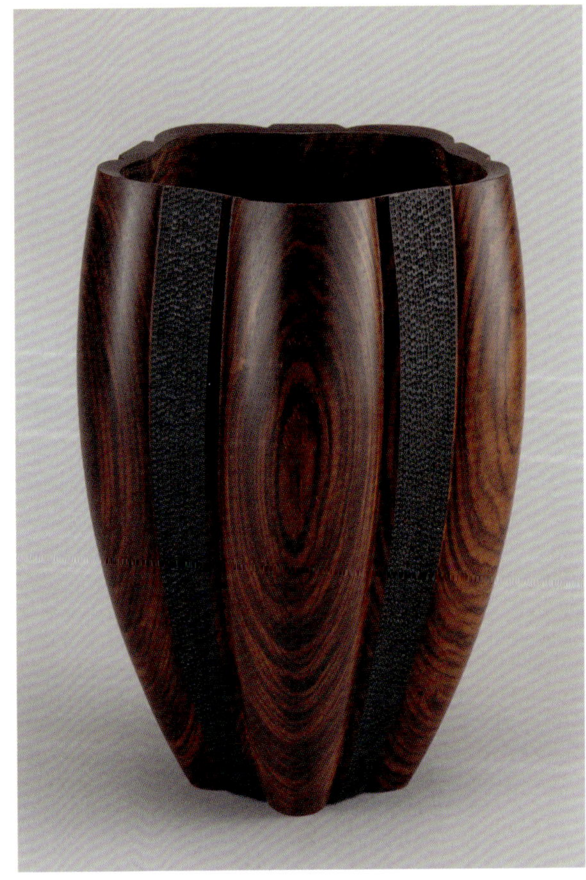

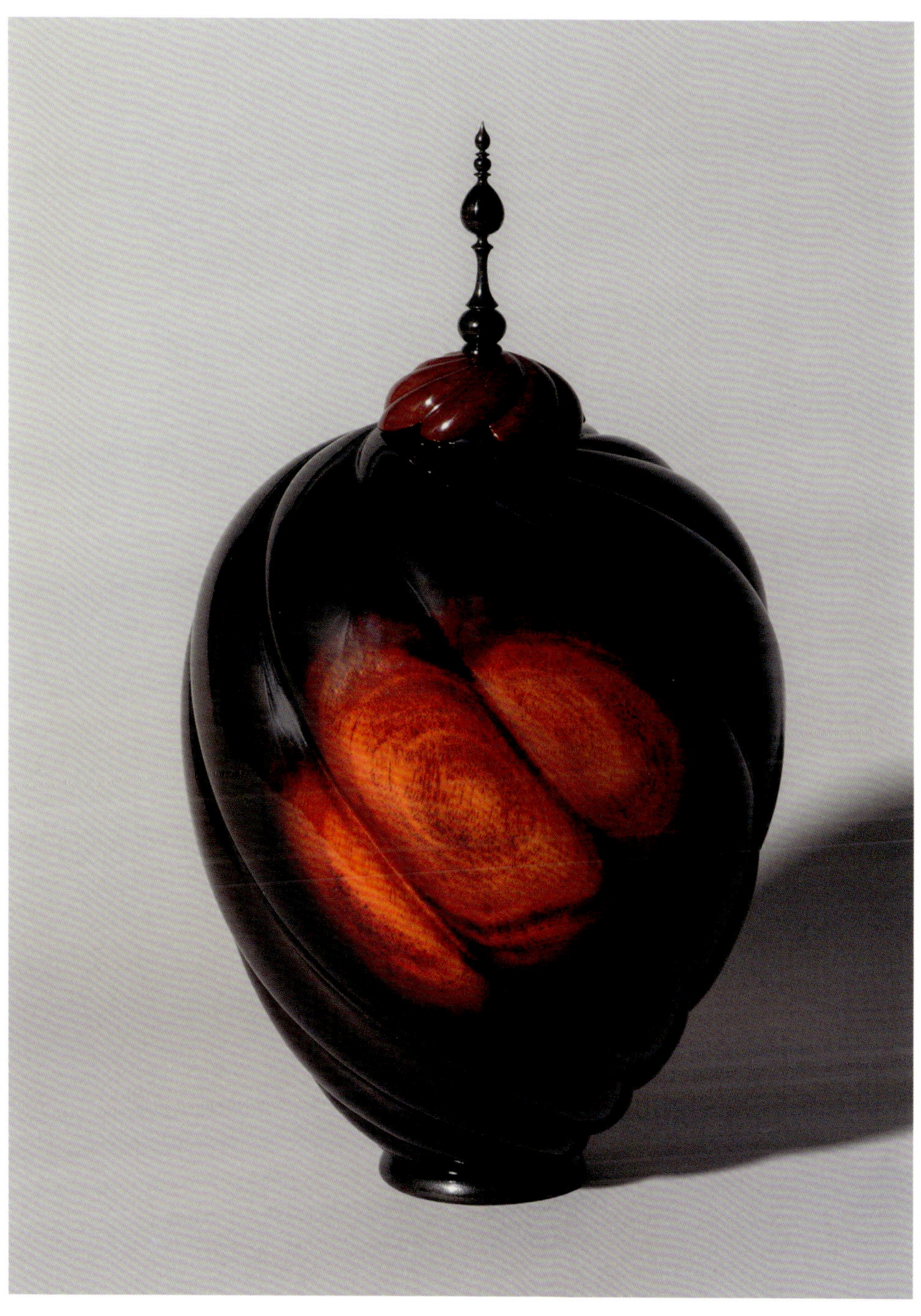

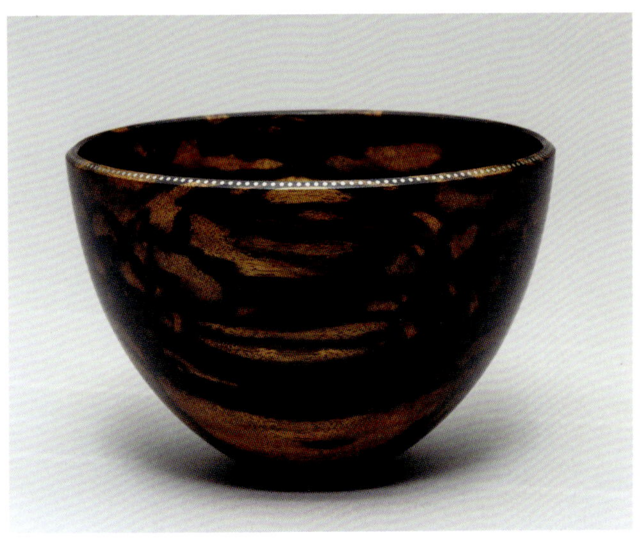

CAT. 60 Mark Nantz,
*Mottled Ebony Bowl
with Silver Inlay*, 2013,
ebony with silver,
3 ½ × diam. 5 ¼ in.

CAT. 61 Mark Nantz,
Artifact Series, 2007,
stabilized, dyed blue maple
burl and ebony with silver,
14-karat gold, steel, and
solvent-based aniline dye
suspended in liquid acrylic,
10 × 6 ¼ × 5 ⅝ in.

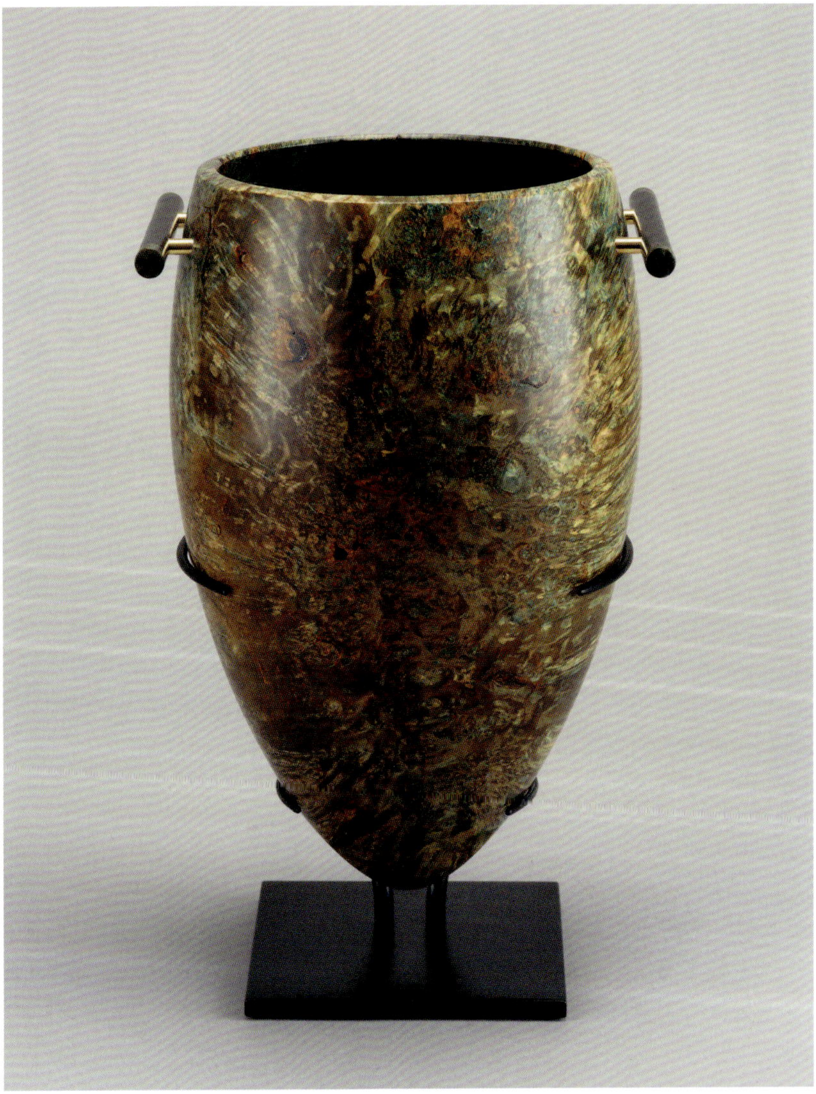

CAT. 62 Andi Wolfe, *When I Let Go of What I Am, I Can Become What I Might Be— Lao Tzu (Carved Sphere, No. 2)*, 2008, redwood burl, diam. 4 in.

CAT. 63 Michael Hampel, *It's Not a House, It's a Home*, 2007, English walnut, 11 × 13 × 12 in.

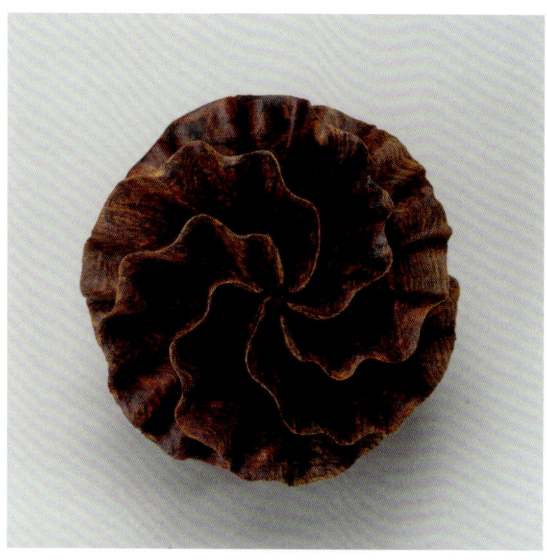

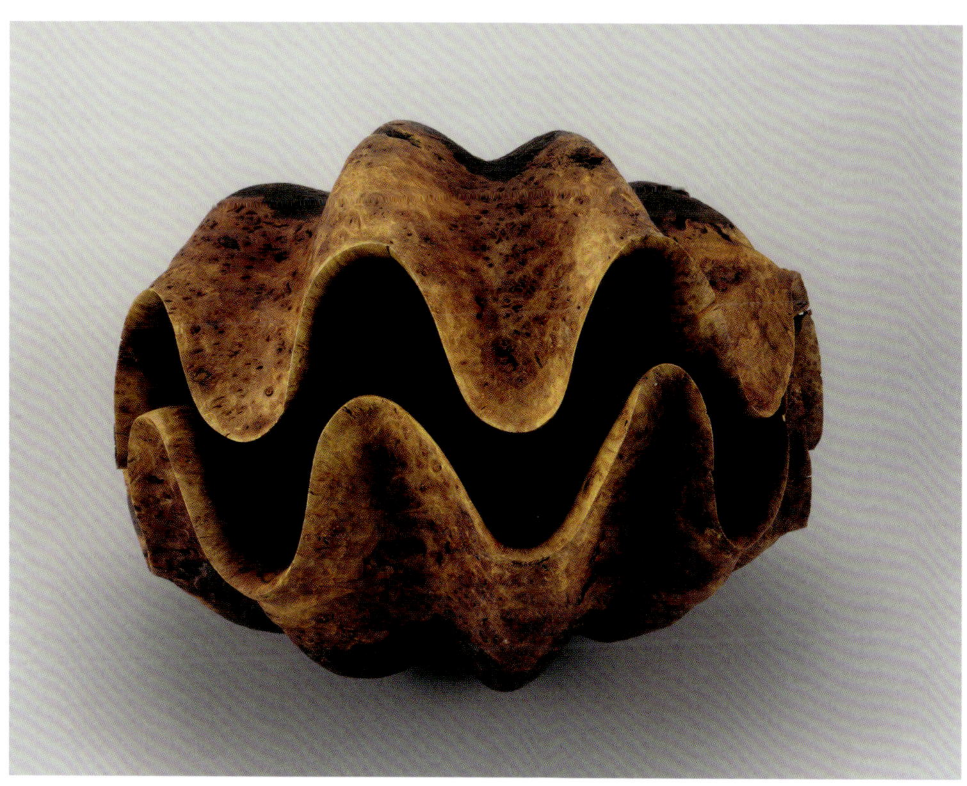

CAT. 64   Jerry Kermode,
Untitled Bowl, 2007,
redwood lace burl,
5 ¼ × diam. 18 ¾ in.

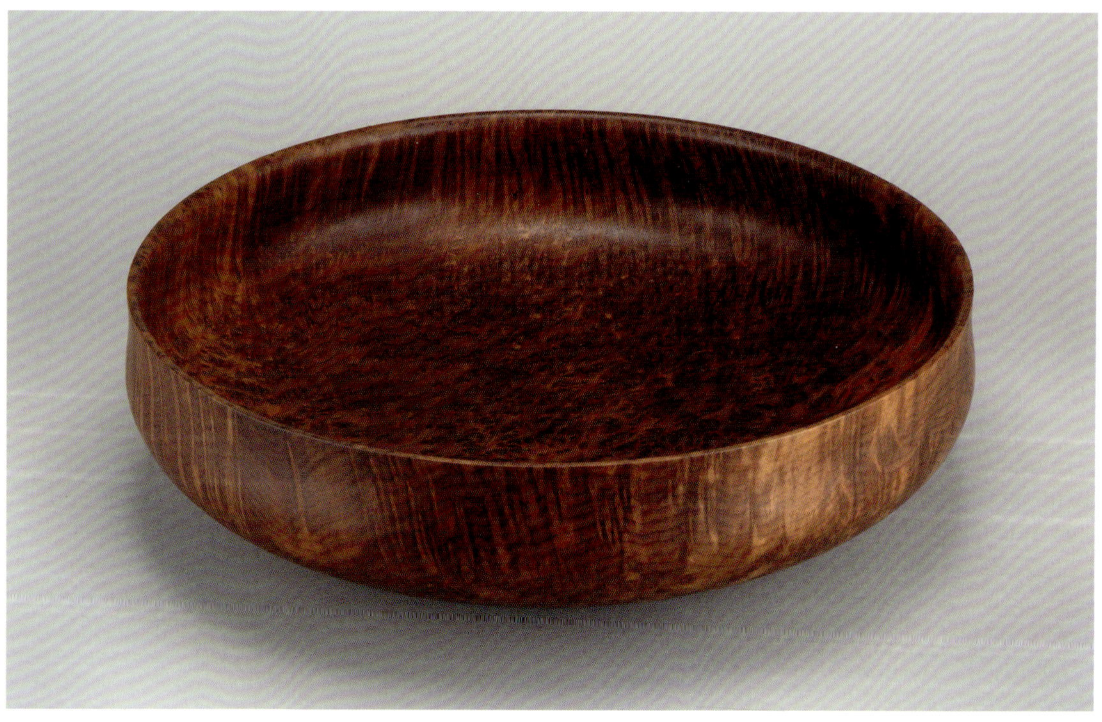

CAT. 65 Andy Cole,
Hawaiian Six Pack
(full set and detail),
2015, macadamia,
6 pieces: ranging from
7 3/8 × 12 1/4 × 10 5/8
to 1 3/8 × diam. 1 7/8 in.

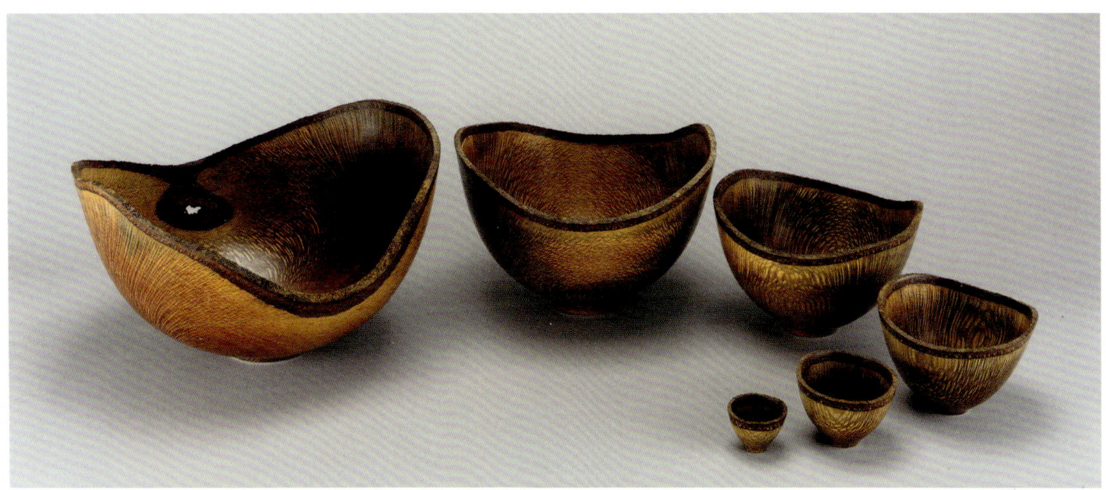

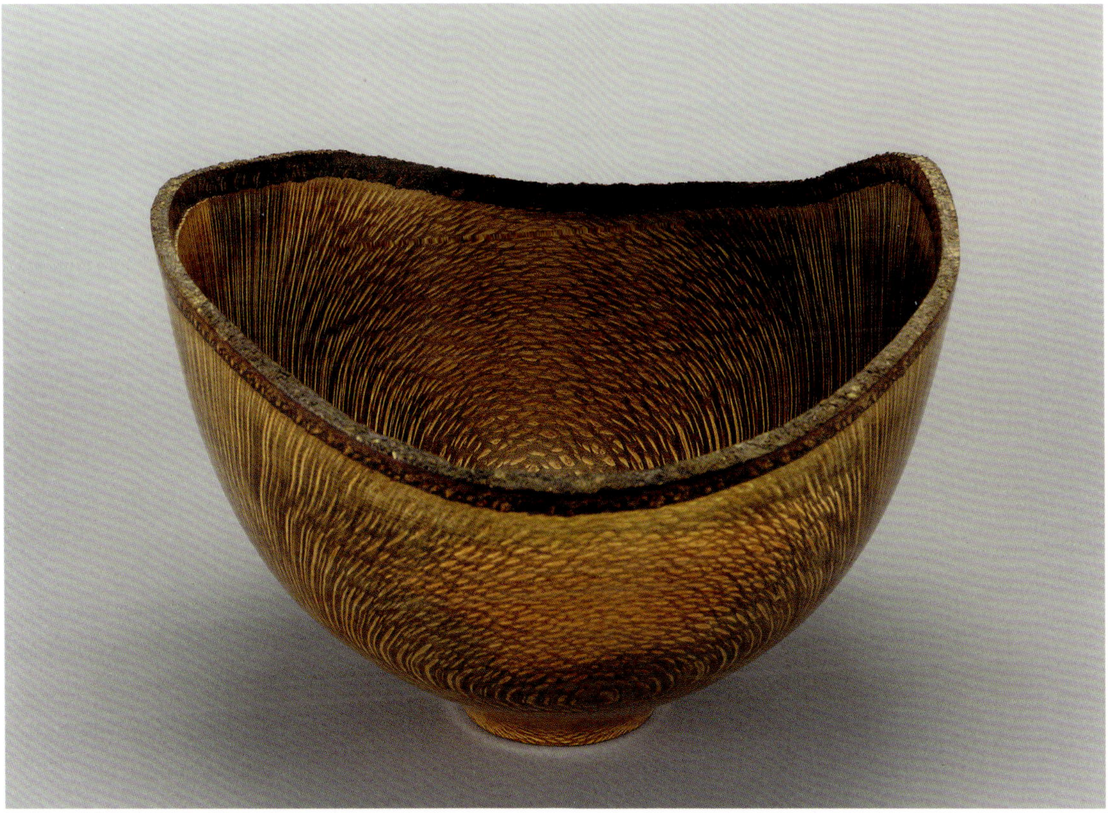

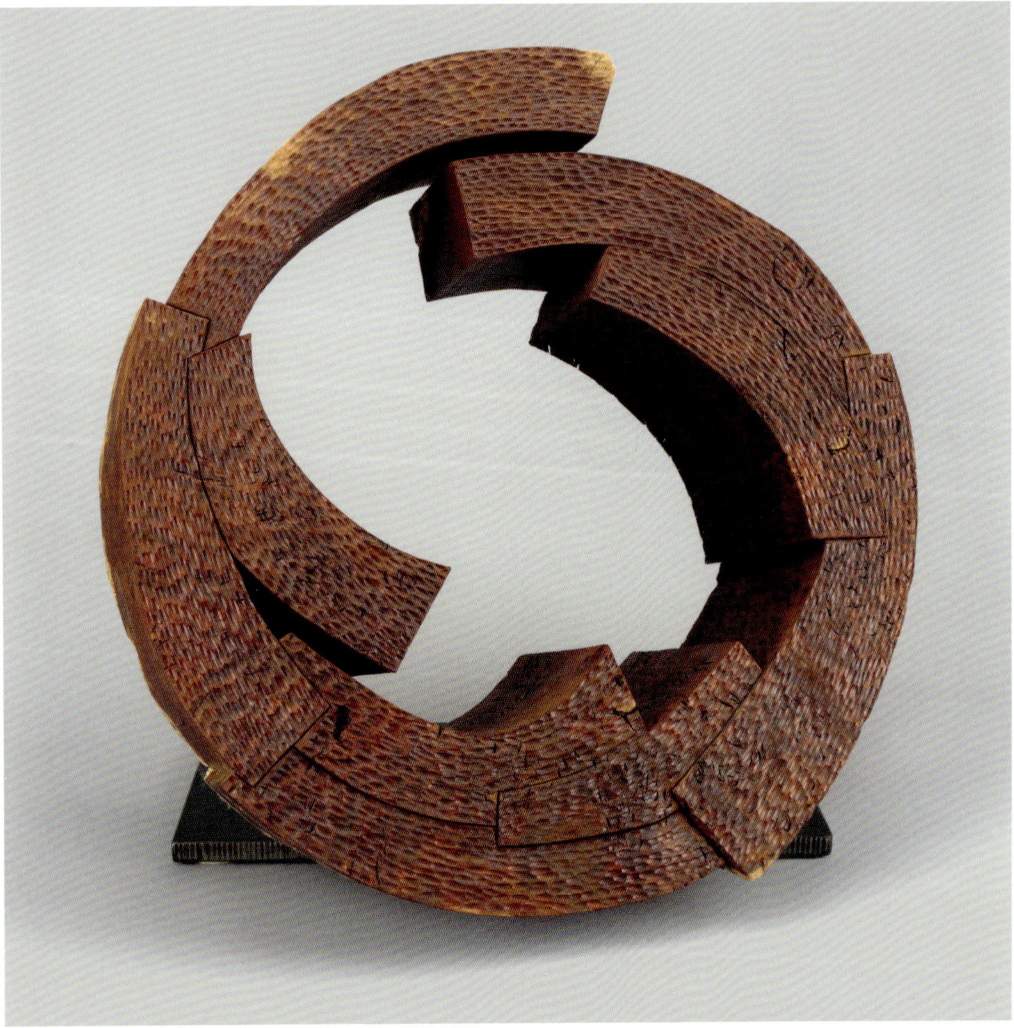

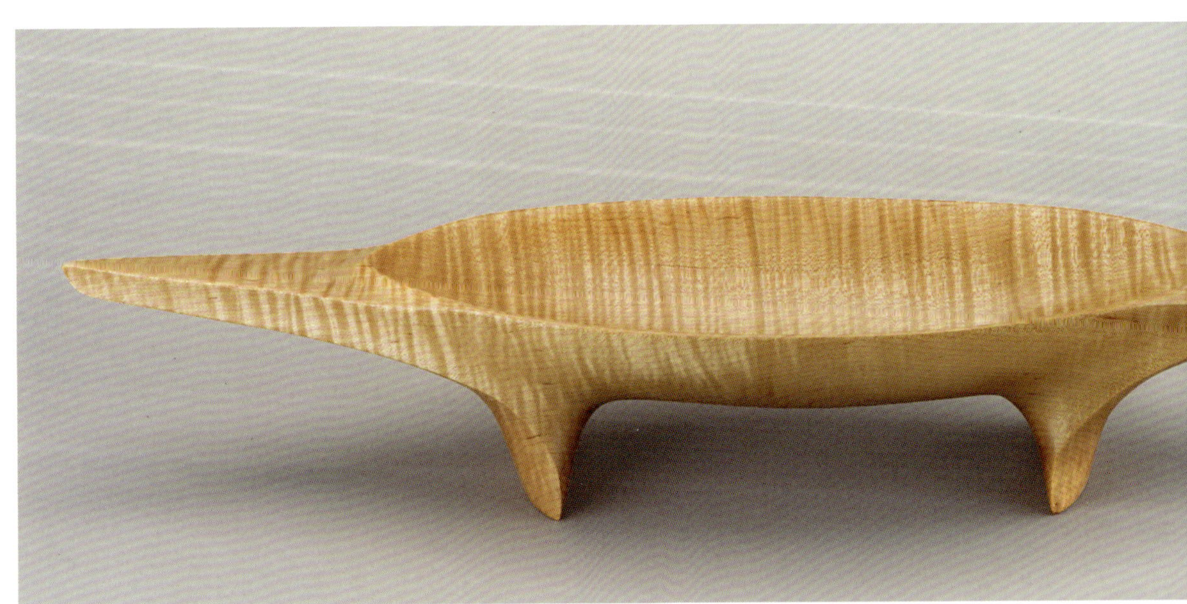

CAT. 66 Robyn Horn, *Stone Circle*, 2006, jarrah burl on steel base, 18 ¼ × 19 ⅛ × 14 in.

CAT. 67 Holly Tornheim, *Vessel II*, n.d., curly maple, 3 ¾ × 24 ⅜ × 5 ⅜ in.

CAT. 68 Stephen Hatcher, *Falling Blossoms*, 2016, big-leaf maple, Gabon ebony, and fiber veneer with mineral crystal inlay, rare-earth magnets, resin, dyes, and lacquer, 6 ½ × 7 ¾ × 6 ½ in.

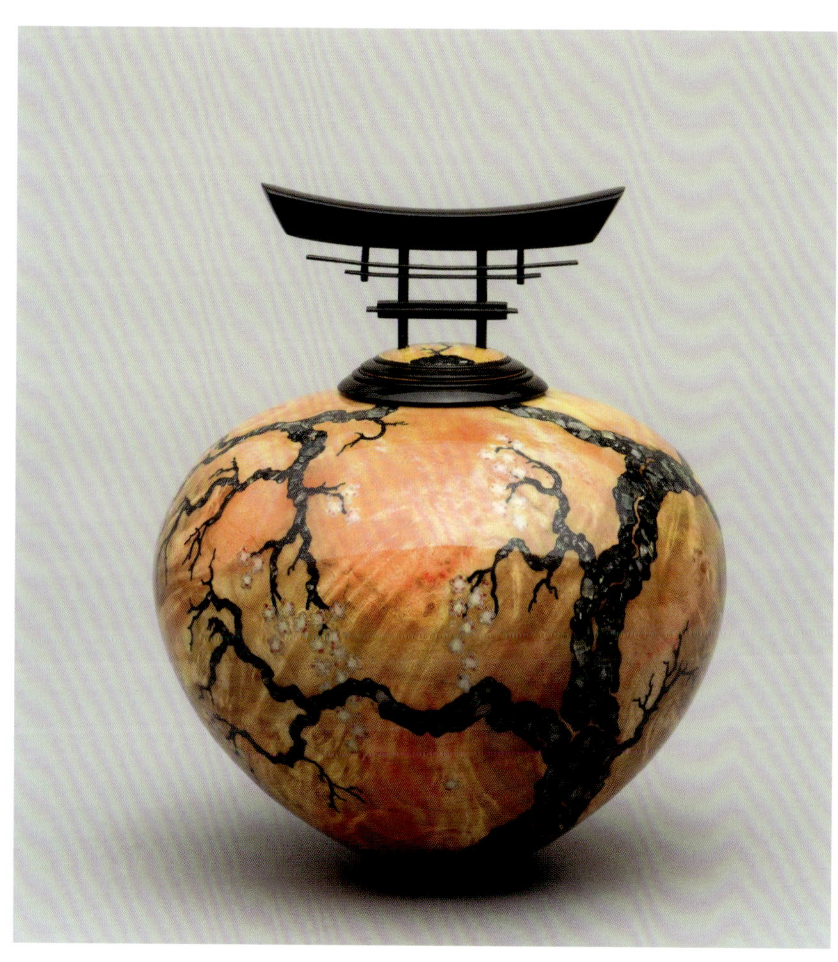

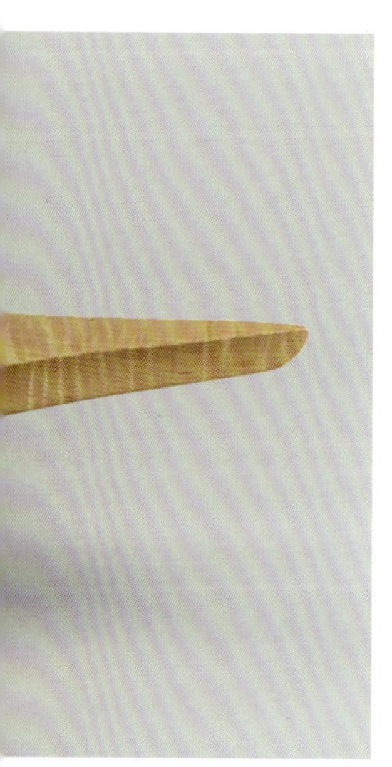

CAT. 69   Ray Feltz, *Ribbon Bowl II*, n.d., bloodwood, holly, and pink ivory, 1 ⅛ × diam. 3 ½ in.

CAT. 70   Curt Theobald, *Eye of the Storm*, 2013, butternut, maple, and bubinga, 3 ½ × diam. 15 in.

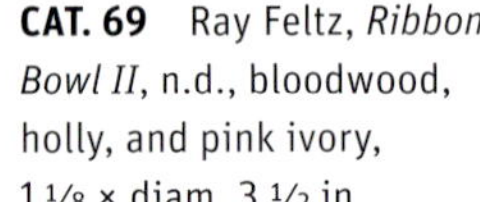

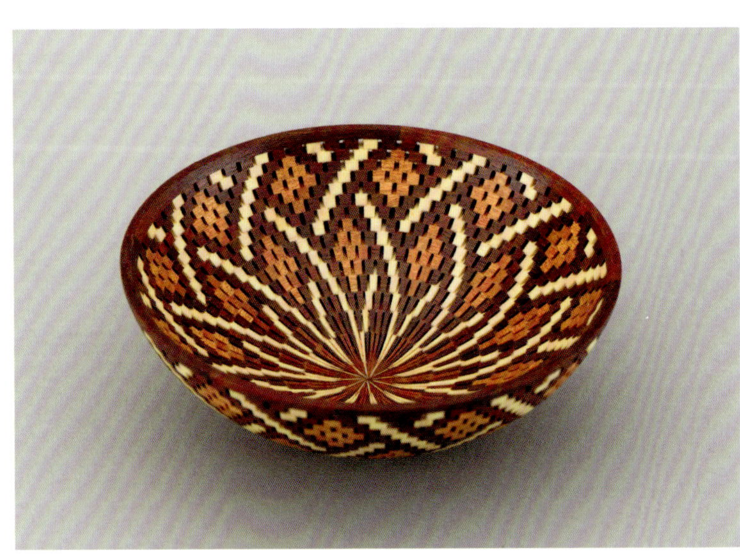

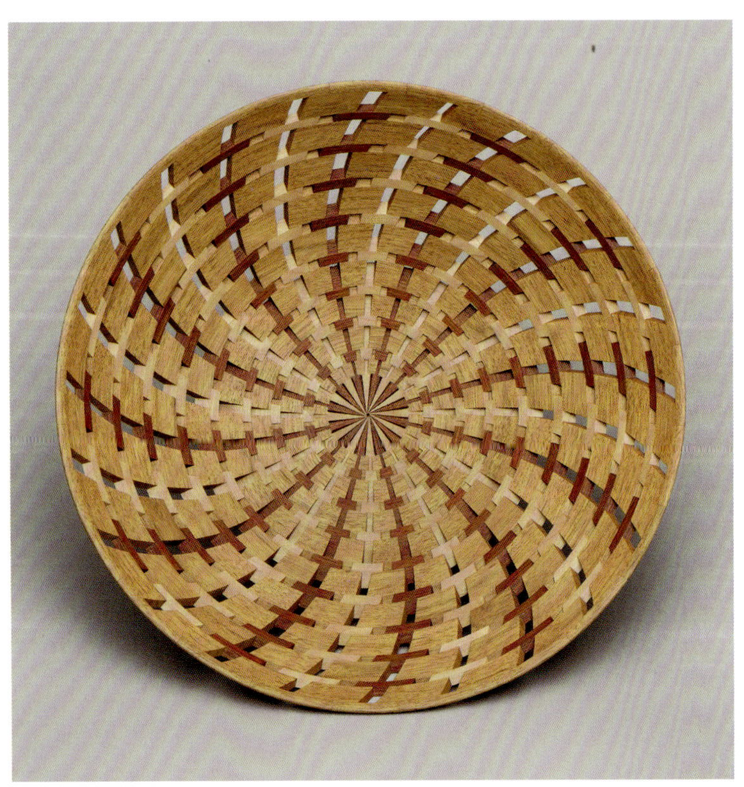

CAT. 71   Hal Metlitzky, *Cyclone*, 2012, yellowheart, Gabon ebony, holly, imbuia, black walnut, satiné, and old-growth East Indian rosewood, 15 × diam. 21 in.

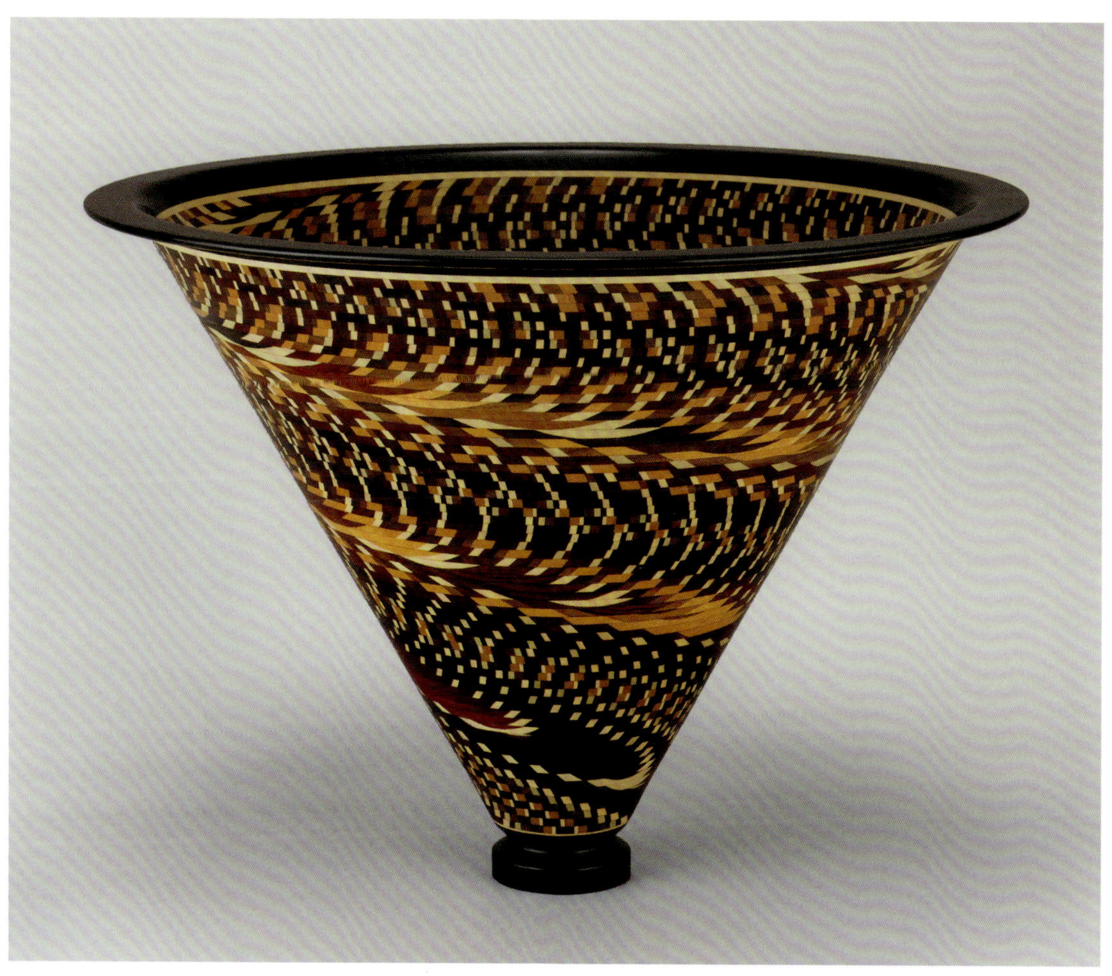

CAT. 72   Sharon Doughtie, *Four Winds, Two Poles*, 2005, Norfolk Island pine, 3 × diam. 9 in.

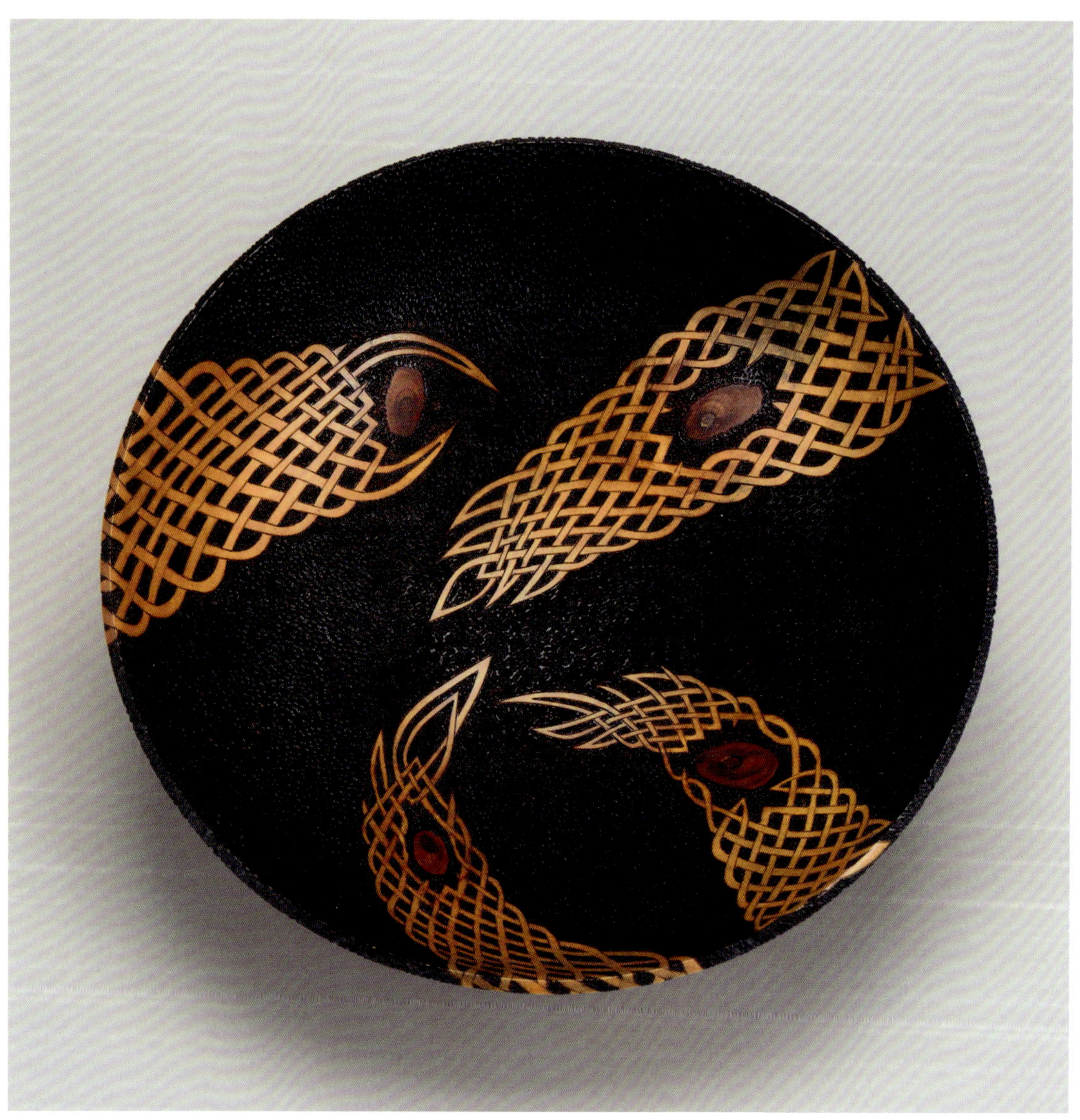

CAT. 73   David Sengel,
*Round Lidded Container with
Legs*, n.d., Bing cherry with
rose, blackberry, and locust
thorns, 4 × diam. 3 ¼ in.

CAT. 74   Ron Fleming,
Echo, n.d., spalted
hackberry, 8 × 15 × 9 in.

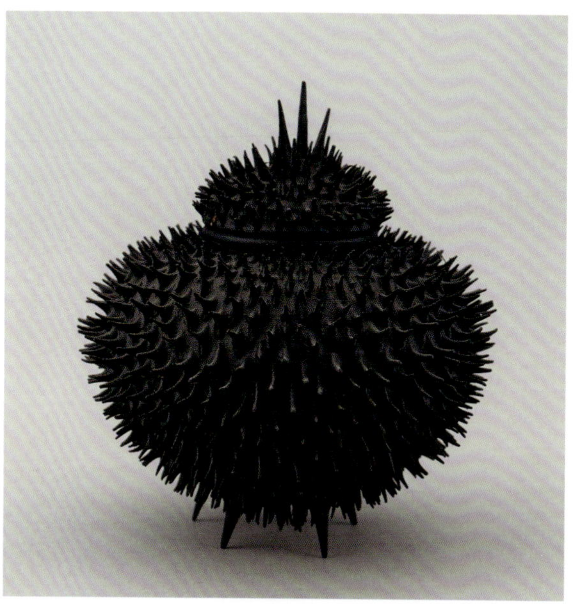

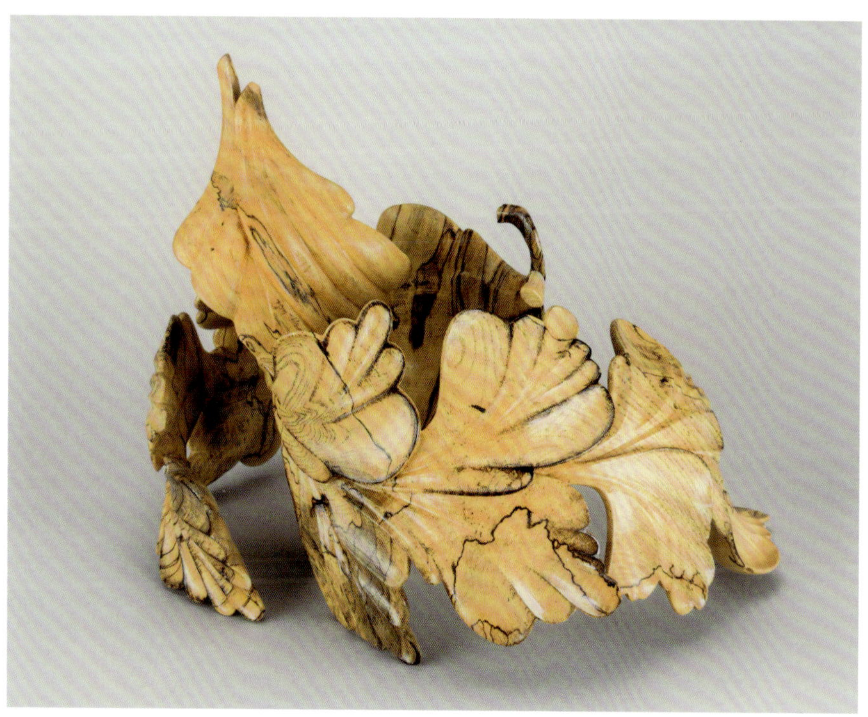

CAT. 75 Jacques Vesery, *Makana Ka Na Hoku (Gift of the Stars)* (two views), 2006–7, cherry with 23-karat gold leaf and acrylic paint, 2 ½ × diam. 5 in.

CAT. 76 Koji Tanaka, *Uragaeshi (Inside Out)*, 2013, African mahogany, 6 ⅛ × 29 × 2 ⅞ in.

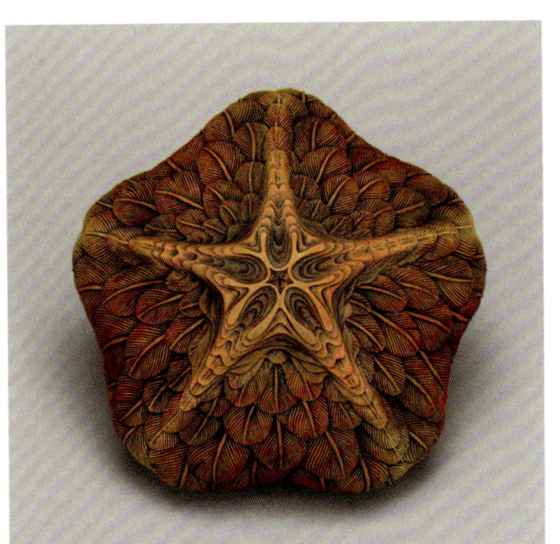

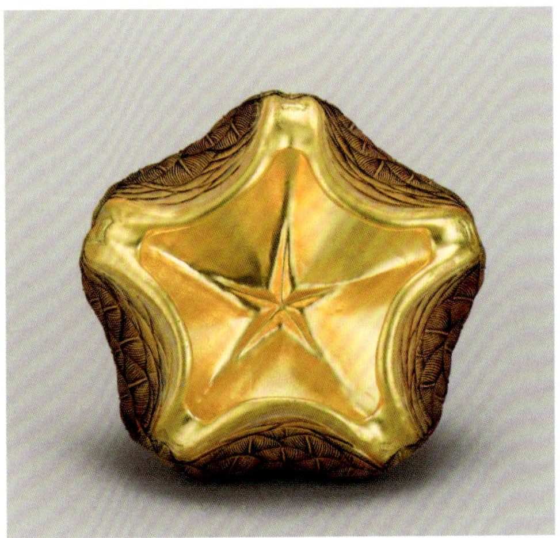

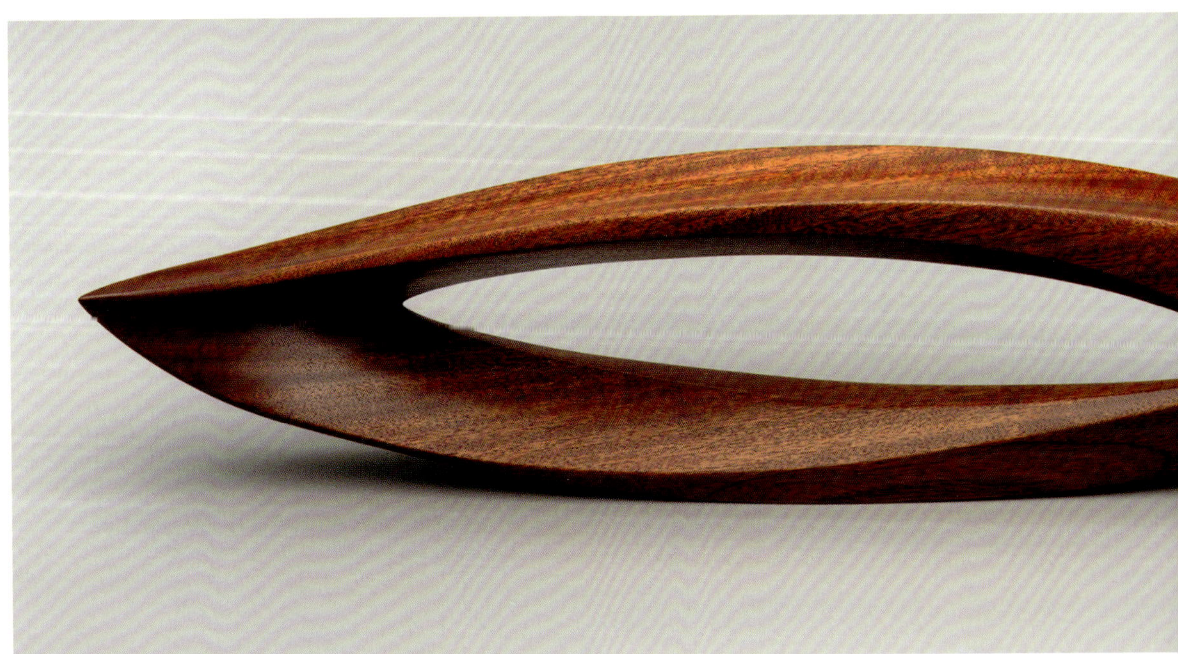

CAT. 77 Koji Tanaka,
Nagamé, 2013,
African mahogany,
5 ¾ × 27 ⅞ × 2 ¾ in.

CAT. 78 Philip Moulthrop,
Mixed Mosaic, n.d., pine,
mimosa, oak, pear, and
cherry, 9 × diam. 13 in.

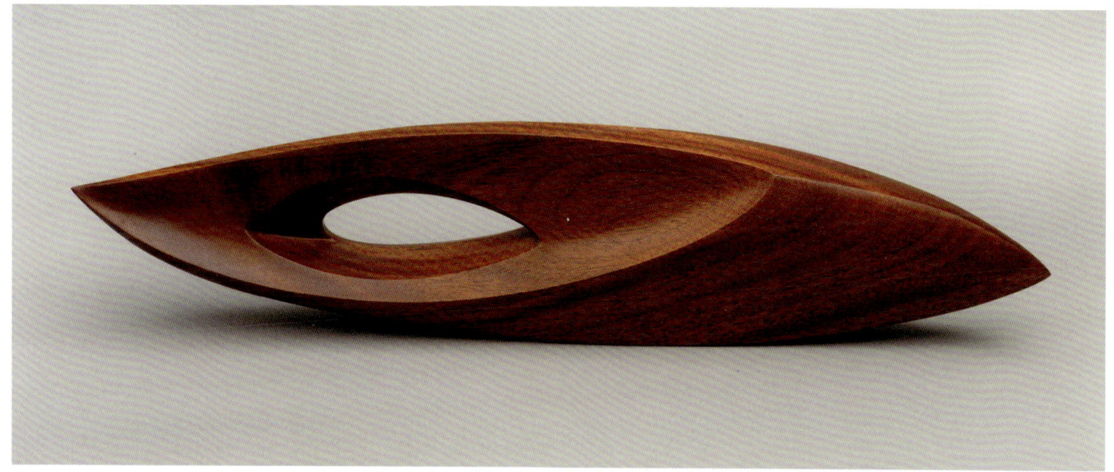

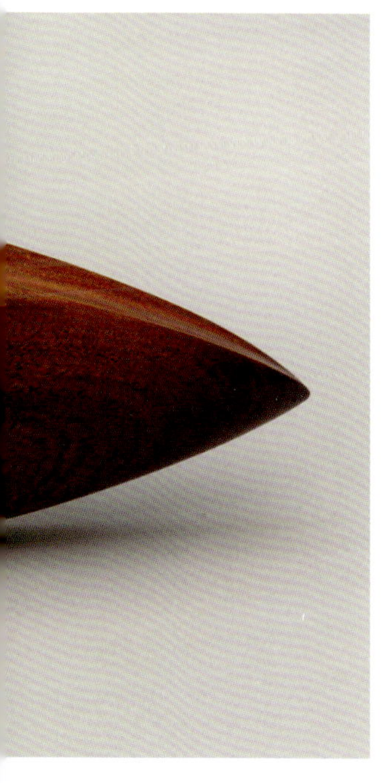

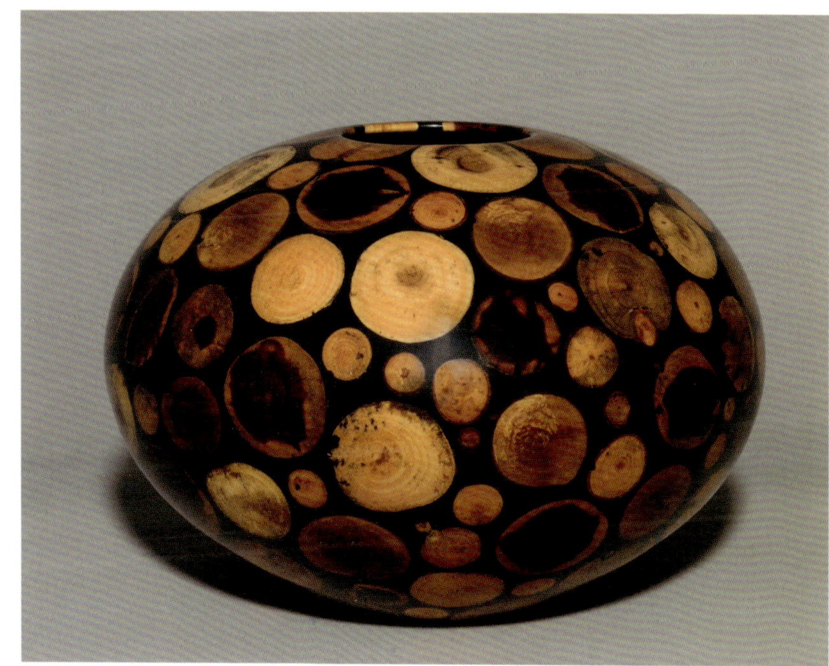

CAT. 79 Louise Hibbert, *Radiolarian Vessel VII*, 2004, English sycamore with silver, texture paste, and acrylic ink, 2 ½ × 6 × 6 in.

CAT. 80 Louise Hibbert, *Cinachyra Box*, 2000, sycamore and boxwood with polyester resin and acrylic ink, diam. 4 ¼ in.

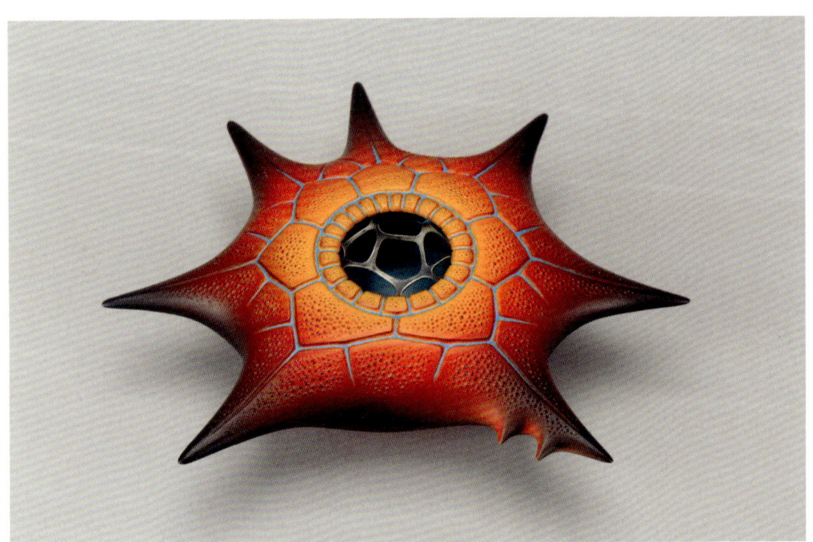

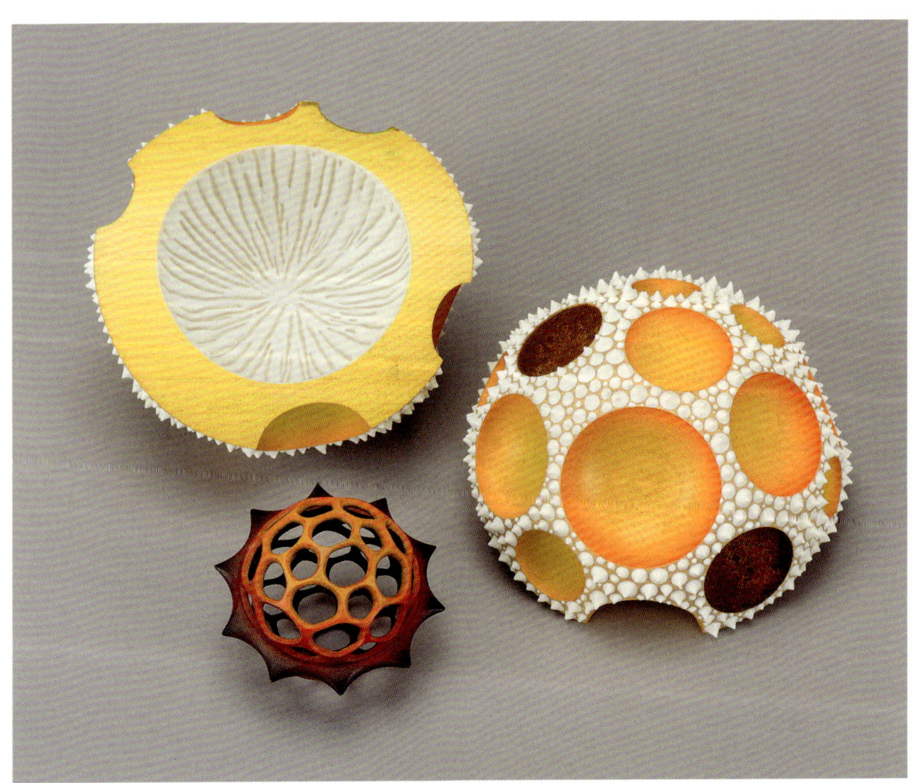

CAT. 81 Graeme Priddle,
Reflection, 2006, macrocarpa
with acrylic paint, 2 pieces:
14 ¼ × 4 ¼ × 4 in. each

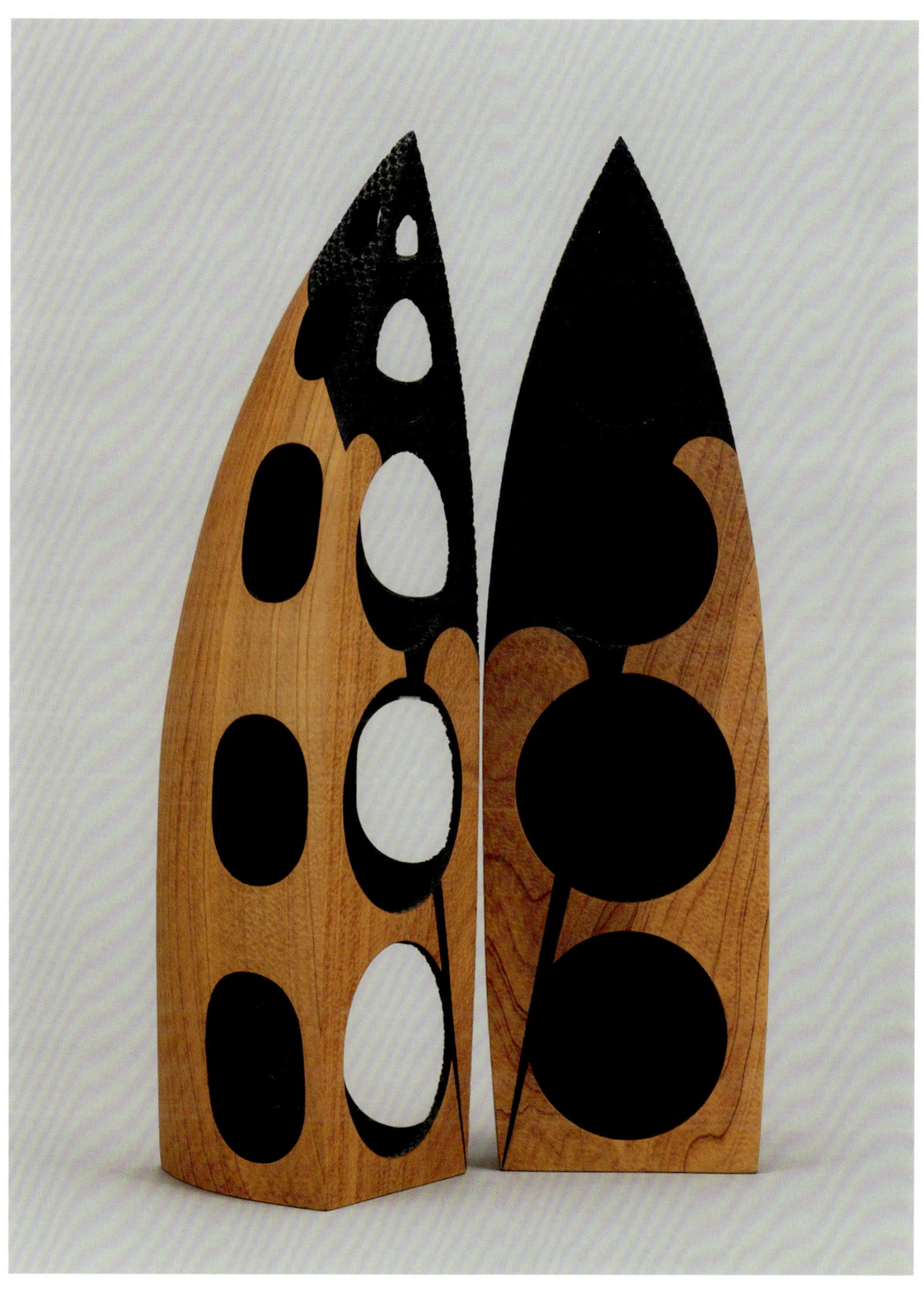

RESPECT, REC[...] AND RE[...]

BY ANYA MONTIEL

It's such an uncertain time right now. But what are people creating? What are we going to see out of the women even now? I guarantee you it's going to be nothing but beauty.

— Carla Hemlock

Artist Carla Hemlock offered this premonition of the art being created during the COVID-19 pandemic — especially art by Indigenous women — in October 2020 during a curator and artist conversation organized by the Smithsonian American Art Museum for the *Hearts of Our People: Native Women Artists* exhibition, then on view at the Renwick Gallery.[1] Hemlock, a textile and multimedia artist from the Kahnawake Mohawk territory along the St. Lawrence River, explained that many artworks in the exhibition were created during terrible hardships, such as forced removal from homelands, massacres, denial of religious freedoms, and catastrophic epidemics. Despite repeated widespread trauma, Indigenous artists made works of beauty with absolute care, resolve, and fearlessness. Now, as I write this essay in the spring of 2021, the coronavirus pandemic continues to bring sickness and death, while nationwide protests have reignited calls for social justice and equity as systemic racism and structural violence have been made more and more apparent. How will artists move forward in this current difficult moment and shape the future?

Living in a melancholic and unpredictable time makes the future seem almost impossible to imagine. One aspiration is for people to emerge from this present moment creating spaces and

IPROCITY, SPONSIBILITY

A WAY FORWARD

works that are therapeutic and synergistic and kinder. If so, what will American craft look like in the future? More importantly, what *should* guide the future of craft? American craft and art have their origin stories and locales, but *this land has memory*, and this continent holds ancient, interconnected knowledge systems from Indigenous observations of the flora, fauna, and cosmos.[2] Indigenous scholars have articulated Indigenous knowledges, worldviews, and methodologies to counter dominant "Western" paradigms and advance other ways of knowing. Scholars Cora Weber-Pillwax (Métis/Woodland Cree) and Shawn Wilson (Opaskwayak Cree), in particular, have proposed three principles essential to Indigenous research and learning: Respect, Reciprocity, and Responsibility.[3] Known as the three R's, they "are key features of any healthy relationship," Wilson notes, and are valuable for non-Indigenous people as well.[4] Respect, reciprocity, and responsibility

are principles that will provide a restorative framework for American craft moving forward.

There are artists and craftspeople who already follow these ways of knowing throughout their practice and with others, and by examining the principles along with examples of their work, each principle's purpose becomes clear. The first principle, respect, extends beyond humans to all living beings and life-forms. Weber-Pillwax explains, "All forms of living things are to be respected as being related and interconnected....It means believing and living that relationship with all forms of life and conducting all interactions in a spirit of kindness and honesty."[5] Respect acknowledges this connectedness between all beings and life-forms. Artists Kevin and Valerie Pourier (Oglala Lakota) live and work on the Pine Ridge Reservation in South Dakota and create works of art from buffalo horn, a material used by their Lakota ancestors for countless

CAT. 82   Vicki Lee Soboleff, *Yellow Cedar Face Mask*, 2020, yellow cedar and sinew, overall: 4 × 5 5/8 × 3/4 in.

CAT. 83   Marlana Thompson, *Ononkwashon:a (Medicine Plants)*, 2020, black velveteen with red flannel, Czech seed beads, sweetgrass, sage, and leather, overall: 5 × 51 3/4 × 1 7/8 in.

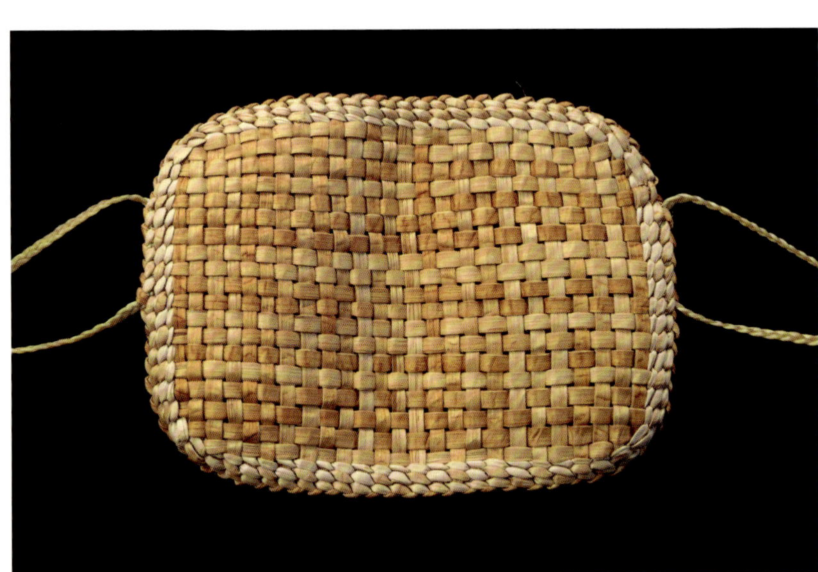

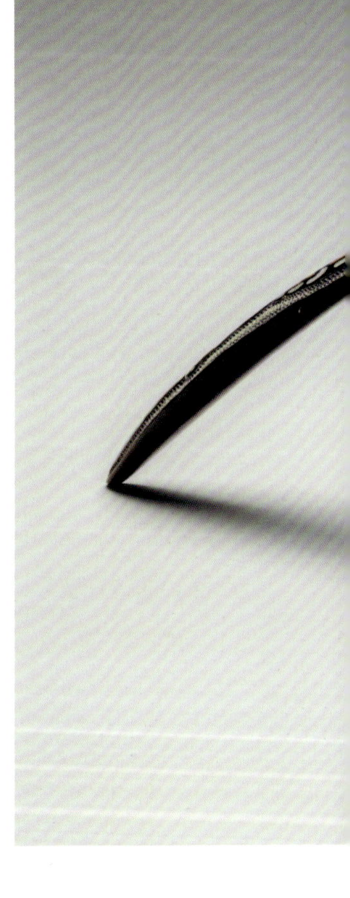

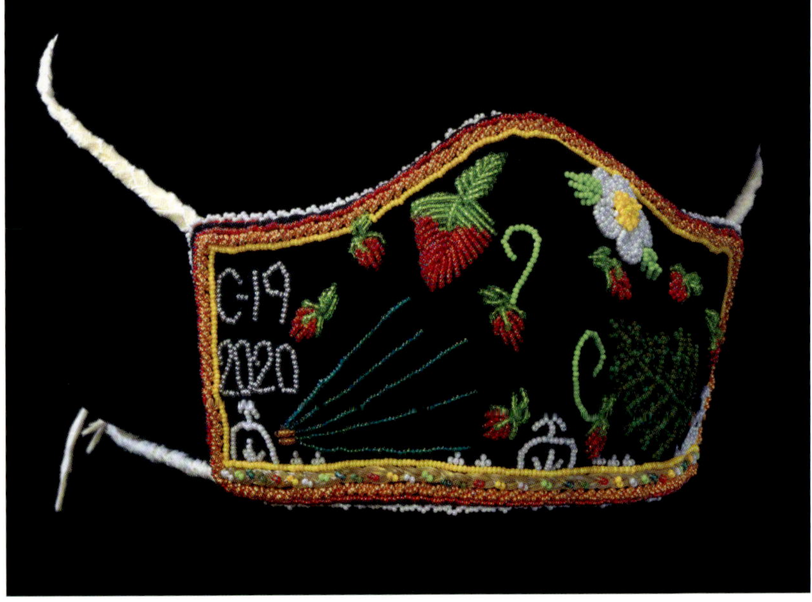

CAT. 84   Kevin and Valerie Pourier, *Monarch Nation*, 2019, carved bison horn with inlaid orange sandstone and white mother of pearl, 3 ¾ × 3 × 11 ¾ in.

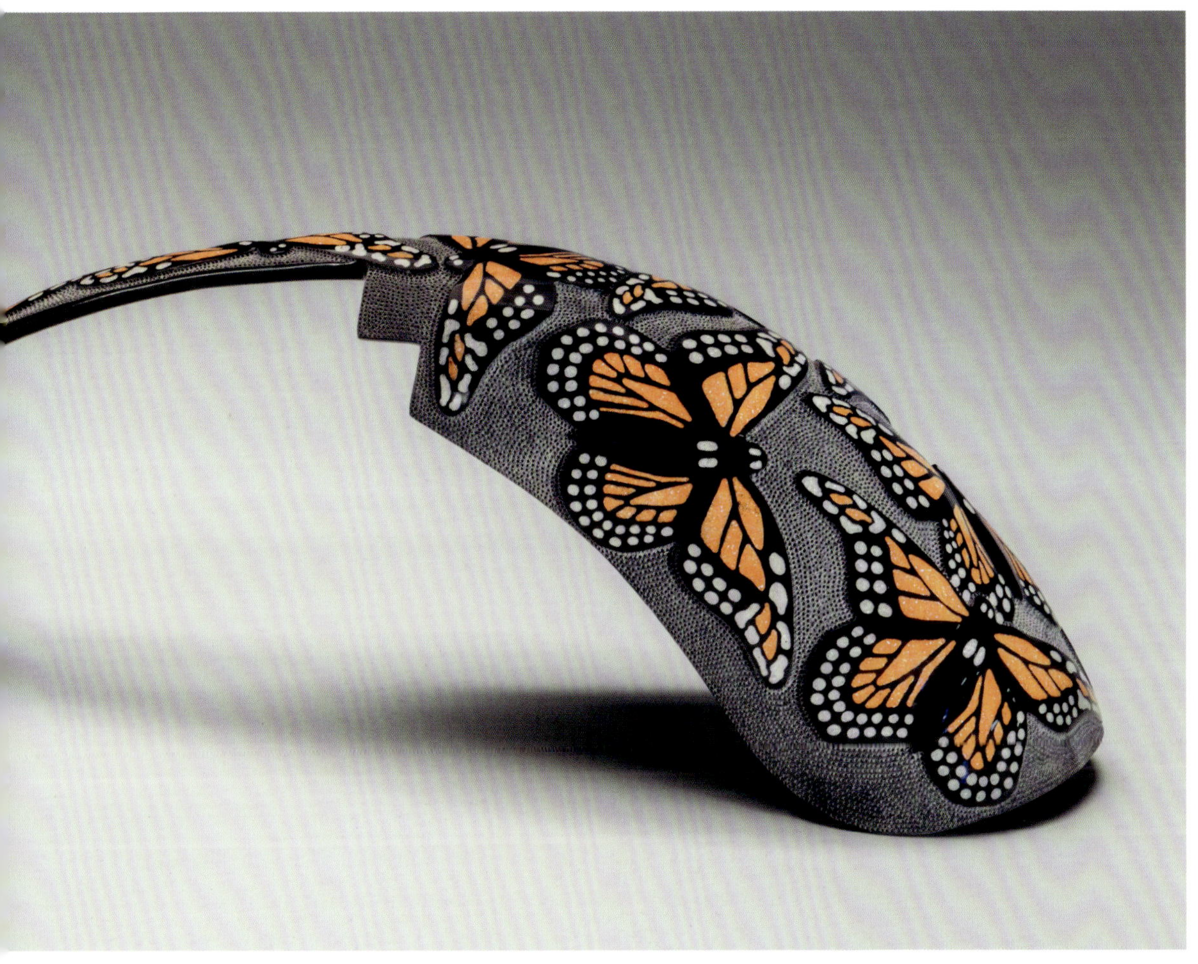

generations.[6] The Lakota name for themselves, Pte Oyate, translates as "buffalo people," and the buffalo is a respected relative integrated into everyday and ceremonial life. *Monarch Nation* (CAT. 84), the Pouriers' buffalo-horn spoon with inlaid orange sandstone and mother of pearl, continues a long-ago artform and ensures that little of the buffalo is wasted. Likewise, the overlapping pattern of monarch butterflies on the spoon's surface pays tribute to the "small ones" (the insects) and to the annual migration of monarch butterflies from Canada to Mexico. All forms of connection are acknowledged with respect and care.

Respect also centers on being a good relative *and* descendant. Ancestors struggled and endured so that the succeeding kin might thrive. Saint Louis–based artist Basil Kincaid comes from seven generations of quilters and creates quilted paintings that reflect ancestral connections, collective memory, and healing. He feels his art is "a way to honor my predecessors while addressing the questions and concerns of where I am — we are — today. It's a way towards restoring and reconstructing with the resourcefulness born within us."[7] For *Riverside Revival: Lift Every Voice and Sing* (CAT. 85), Kincaid collected old choir robes from local Black churches to construct the central figures with arms extending upward in praise. He then assembled the multichromatic background from pieces of vintage quilts, donated clothing, and Ghanaian fabric and embroidery. The work offers both personal and collective connections. Kincaid's

paternal grandparents met at a church revival, and the power of spirituality and song was ever-present in their lives. The subtitle, *Lift Every Voice and Sing,* pays tribute to the poem-turned-song by brothers James Weldon Johnson and John Rosamond Johnson that became the canonical song of the National Association for the Advancement of Colored People and is often referred to as the Black national anthem. Written more than 120 years ago, *Lift Every Voice and Sing* contains lyrics of hope and strength in the face of injustice. Kincaid's work, likewise, provides another story of ancestral resilience and respect carried forward.

The second principle to guide American craft is reciprocity. Michael Anthony Hart (Fisher River Cree), whose work focuses on Indigenous knowledges and social work, defines reciprocity as "the belief that as we receive from others, we must also offer to others," and further states that, "Since all life is considered equal, albeit different, all life must be respected as we are in reciprocal relations with them."[8] Reciprocity centers around a mutually beneficial exchange while incorporating the first principle of respect. Aram Han Sifuentes is a Chicago-based artist who practices reciprocity through her art and social action. She learned to sew at a young age to assist her mother's work as a seamstress. Through sewing, Sifuentes, who identifies as an immigrant of color, challenges notions of "identity politics, immigration and immigrant labor, possession and dispossession, citizenship and belonging,

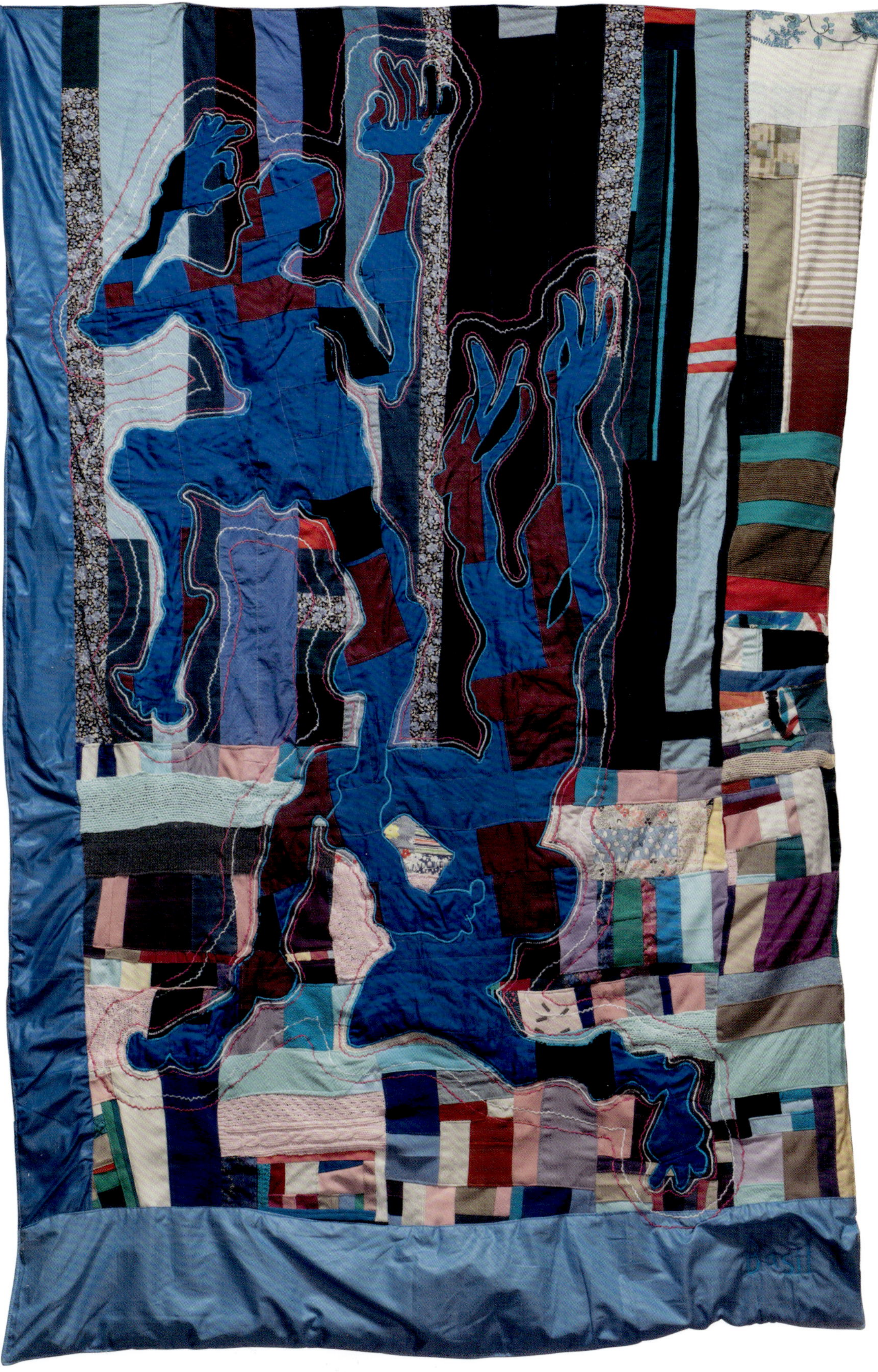

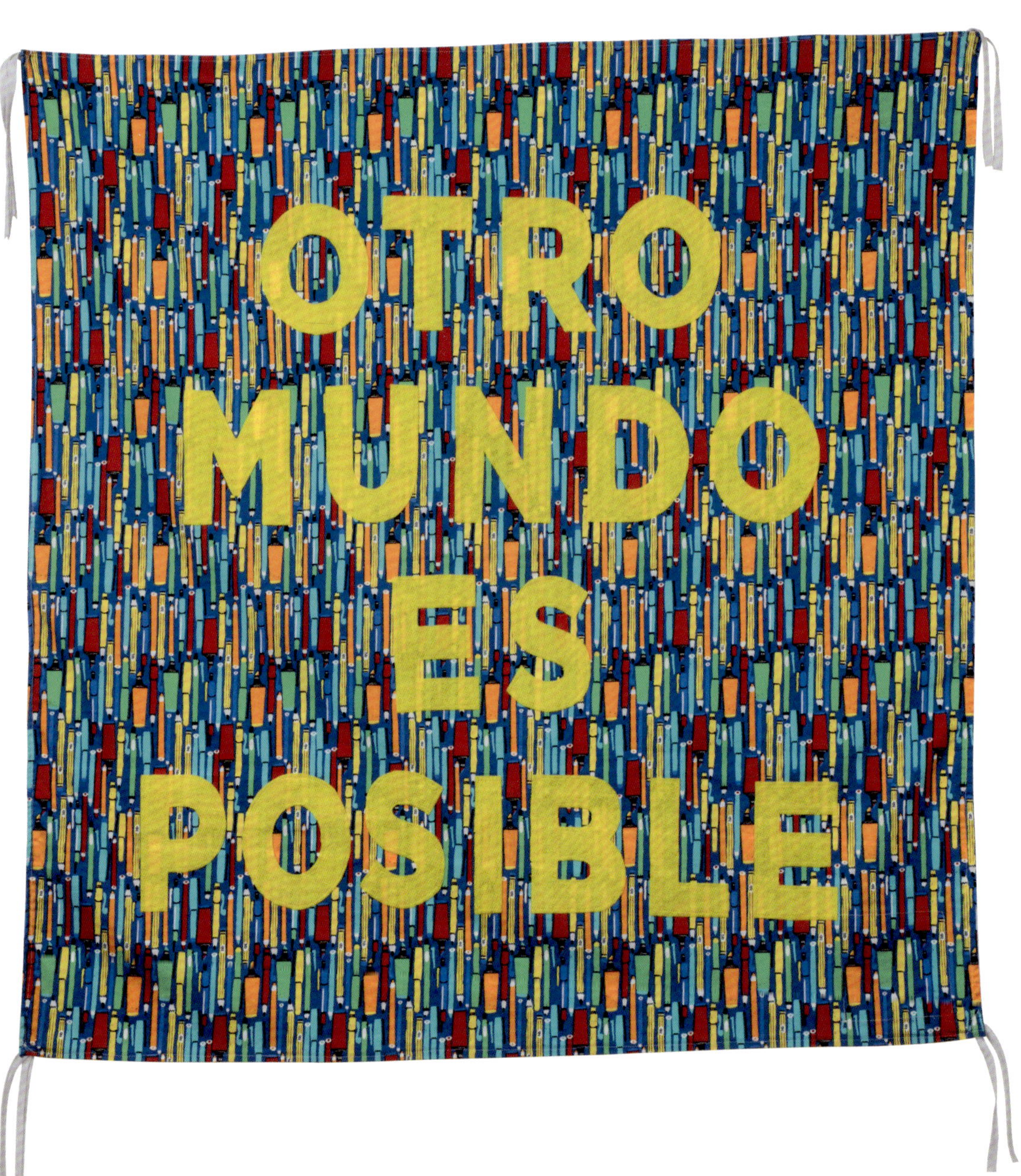

CAT. 86　Aram Han Sifuentes, *Otro Mundo Es Posible*, 2017, felt and fusible web on cotton; checkout card, banner: 42 ⅞ × 42 ½ in., card: 4 × 6 in.

dissent and protest, and race politics in the United States."[9] Discontent with the 2016 US presidential election results, Sifuentes used her medium to protest and build community. She established the Protest Banner Lending Library as a space for people to meet in a sewing circle, make their own banners, and "check out" banners to borrow (CAT. 86). The banners, carrying different messages and phrases—some elaborate, others purely textual—are taken to

protests, returned, and then used by someone else. The library allows the works to circulate and travel, thereby offering their messages far and wide. By prioritizing reciprocity, Sifuentes's artistic practice is a generative offering, benefitting everyone.

Quilt artist Carolyn Mazloomi also manifests reciprocity with socially engaged practices and community building. In 1985, she founded the Women of Color Quilters Network to support and preserve quiltmaking among women of color. Mazloomi, with a career spanning forty years, explained her purpose as an artist: "to

create work, to educate people, and to take the viewer to another place in the hope that they'll be educated and learn."[10] During the COVID-19 pandemic, many quilt and textile artists, like Mazloomi and her Quilters Network members, shifted to making face masks to protect family, friends, and health care workers from the virus. Mazloomi then sponsored an "Unmask Your Creativity Contest" so quilters could create artful masks as creative expressions for fun and reprieve. Entries came in from around the world, including from Houston-based artist Carolyn Crump, who submitted several masks, like *BLM-4* (CAT. 87). Crump, who is known for her three-dimensional quilts, made this figurative mask, stitched of multiple pieces of fabrics, with a Black woman emerging from it. The woman wears a BLM (Black Lives Matter) mask and holds several signs, including "STOP Killing Us" and "I Can't Breathe." Crump uses quilts to tell stories that often speak to current events. While the Quilters Network educates others about the history and traditions of quilt making, another essential feature of the organization is the socio-economic empowerment of its members through workshops on marketing, pricing, and selling. It is not surprising then, that when Mazloomi received a United States Artists Fellowship in early 2021 with a $50,000 cash prize, she donated the award money to the Quilters Network to expand their work and outreach.[11]

The final principle, responsibility, works in concert with respect and reciprocity. Scholar

CAT. 87   Carolyn Crump,
BLM-4, 2020, machine-
quilted cotton with
cotton thread and paint,
12 × 7 × 6 ½ in.

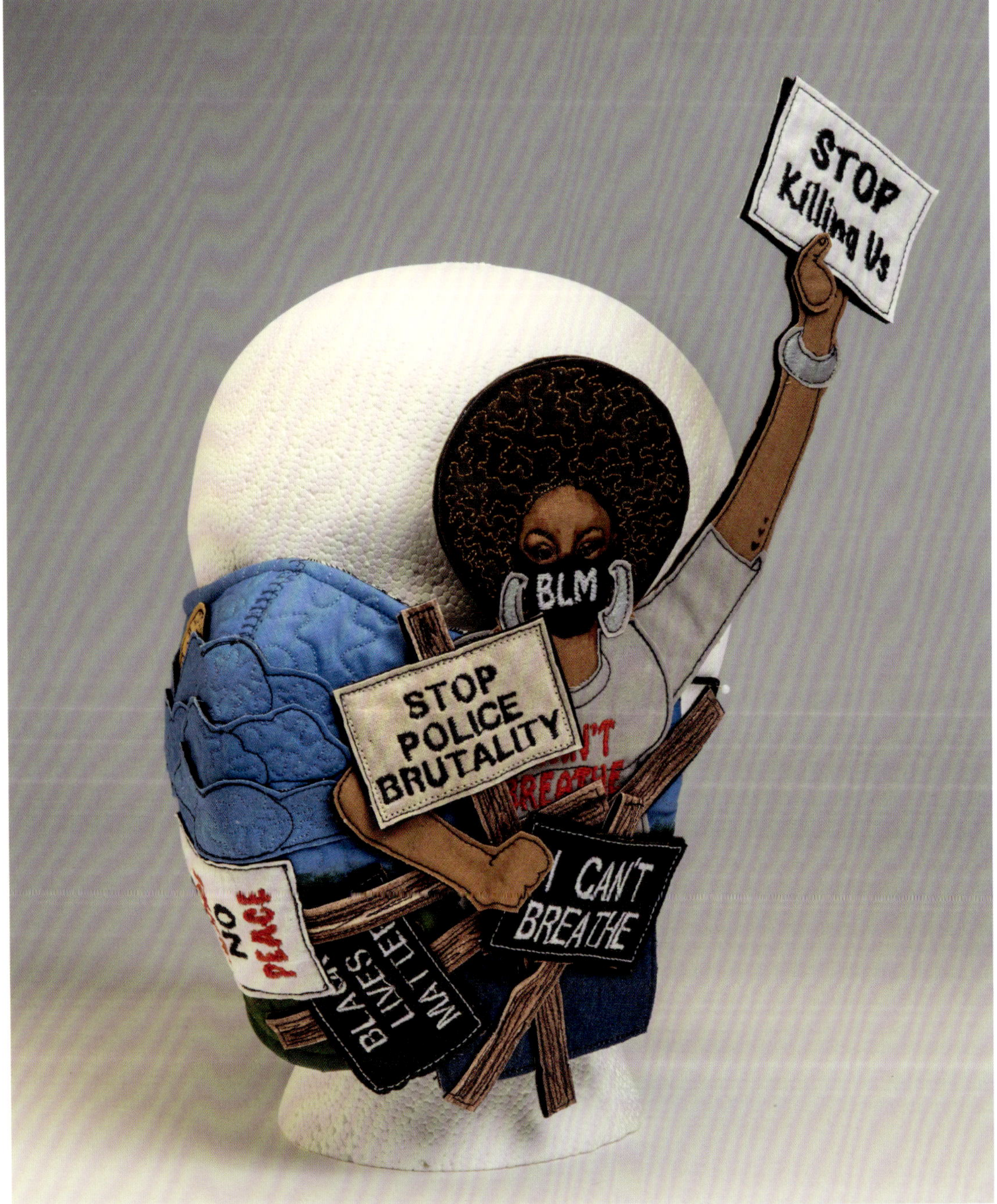
STOP
Killing Us
BLM
STOP
POLICE
BRUTALITY
I CAN'T
BREATHE
NO PEACE
BLACK LIVES MATTER

Leanne Betasamosake Simpson (Michi Saagiig Nishnaabeg) best explains how the three intertwine:

> **Our nationhood is based on the idea that the earth gives and sustains all life, that "natural resources" are not "natural resources" at all, but gifts from Aki, the land. Our nationhood is based on the foundational concept that we should give up what we can to support the integrity of our homelands for the coming generations. We should give more than we take. It is a nationhood based on a series of radiating responsibilities.[12]**

Simpson adds that the radiating responsibilities reach inward as well as outward. A person cannot practice respect and reciprocity without a healthy body, spirit, and mind. Responsibility is a reminder that all principles are equally important in building and sustaining relationships.

Hemlock, the artist who provided a premonition for artmaking during the current moment, created a work that exposes a deterioration in responsibility. Entitled *Our Destruction* (CAT. 88), the textile work is a hand-appliqué quilt on black and red wool. On the left, top, and right sides of the border are the words, "Our Heart — Our Home — Our Soul." Inside the border is a vibrant scene of beaded flowers, vines, birds, and dragonflies in the raised Mohawk beadwork style. The very center holds a pair of sequined ruby-red slippers identical to the ones worn by Dorothy in the Wizard of Oz. The toe of one slipper reads "tic" and the other "toc." The "tic toc" warning repeats, echoing in each corner of the quilt. Despite its outward beauty, *Our Destruction* speaks to the current state of the planet and global climate change. On the reverse of the quilt, Hemlock writes, "Our Destruction. Our Natural world is an environmental ticking time bomb on the eve of destruction. Time is running out. Our inaction will soon redefine those Ruby Red Slippers to symbolize 'No Place to Call Home.'" The quilt is a shrouded harbinger of what humans cannot lose — Our Heart, Our Home, Our Soul. But we can look toward a daily practice that engages body, spirit, and mind to acknowledge the interconnectedness of all beings (respect), create mutually beneficial offerings (reciprocity), and be accountable to these intertwining relationships (responsibility).

By centering and prioritizing these Indigenous worldviews and ways of knowing, American craft has a framework to imagine a future that benefits the artist, the community, and every being — one with respect, reciprocity, and responsibility joined together in a network that sustains and nurtures at each step. Simpson proposes that, "to survive and flourish the next four hundred years, we need to join together in a rebellion of love, persistence, commitment, and profound caring and create constellations of coresistance."[13] Such a path ahead connects all beings and holds up the world. ✳

CAT. 88   Carla Hemlock,
Our Destruction, 2019, wool
stroud cloth with wool,
glass beads, Swarovski
crystals, and sequins,
34 1/8 × 30 5/8 × 7/8 in.

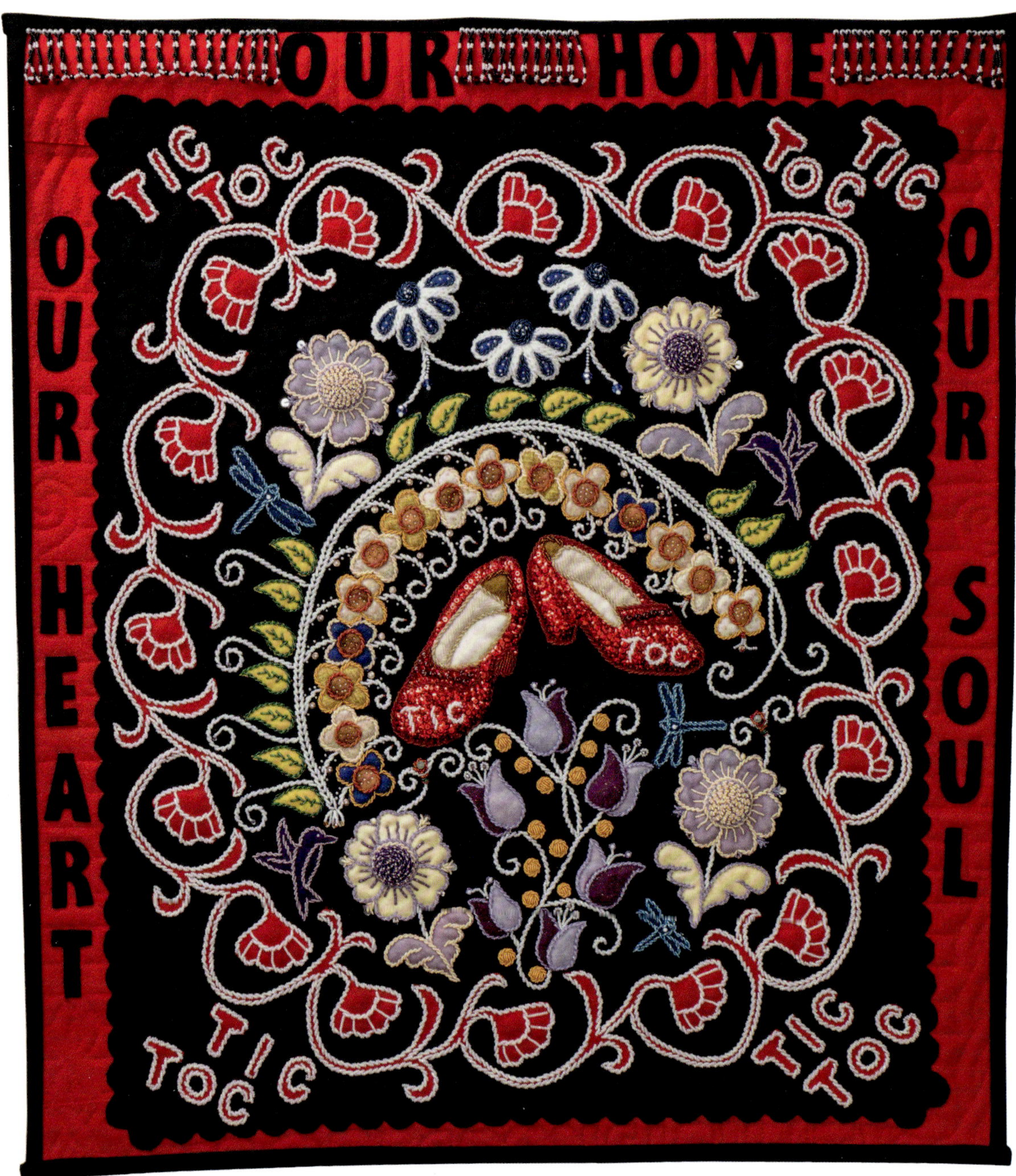
OUR HOME
OUR
OUR
OUR HEART
OUR SOUL
TIC TOC
TIC TOC
TIC TOC
TIC TOC
TIC TOC

NOTES

1. Carla Hemlock, "*Hearts of Our People* Curator and Artist Conversation," Smithsonian American Art Museum, YouTube video 48:28, October 1, 2020, https://youtu.be /D2drTA_6u6Q.

2. Phrase taken from Duane Blue Spruce and Tanya Thrasher, eds., *The Land Has Memory: Indigenous Knowledge, Native Landscapes, and the National Museum of the American Indian* (Chapel Hill: University of North Carolina Press, 2008).

3. Cora Weber-Pillwax, "Identity Formation and Consciousness with Reference to Northern Alberta Cree and Metis Indigenous Peoples" (PhD diss., University of Alberta, 2003), 42; Shawn Wilson, *Research Is Ceremony: Indigenous Research Methods* (Halifax: Fernwood Publishing, 2008), 77.

4. Wilson, *Research Is Ceremony*, 77, 59.

5. Cora Weber-Pillwax, "Indigenous Research Methodology: Exploratory Discussion of an Elusive Subject," *Journal of Educational Thought (JET)/Revue de la Pensée Éducative* 33, no. 1 (April 1999): 41.

6. While *bison* is the scientific term used for the animal found in North America, *buffalo* is the colloquial usage and best translation in this context.

7. Basil Kincaid, "Artist Statement," *Basil Kincaid*, accessed October 2021, https://basilkincaid.art/about.

8. Michael Anthony Hart, "Indigenous Worldviews, Knowledge, and Research: The Development of an Indigenous Research Paradigm," *Journal of Indigenous Voices in Social Work* 1, no. 1 (February 2010): 7–8.

9. Aram Han Sifuentes, "Artist Statement," *Aram Han Sifuentes*, accessed spring 2021, https://www.aramhansifuentes.com /artist-s-statement.

10. Emily Buhrow Rogers, "Stories to Tell: Carolyn Mazloomi and the Women of Color Quilters Network in 2020," *Folklife*, January 15, 2021, https://folklife.si.edu /magazine/crisis-carolyn-mazloomi-women -of-color-quilters-network-2020.

11. Janelle Gelfand, "Quilting Artist Mazloomi Wins $50,000, Gives It Away," *Cincinnati Business Courier*, February 18, 2021, https://www.bizjournals.com /cincinnati/news/2021/02/18/mazloomi -wins-50-000-gives-it-away.html.

12. Leanne Betasamosake Simpson, *As We Have Always Done: Indigenous Freedom Through Radical Resistance* (Minneapolis: University of Minnesota Press, 2017), 8–9.

13. Ibid., 9.

SELECTED ACC

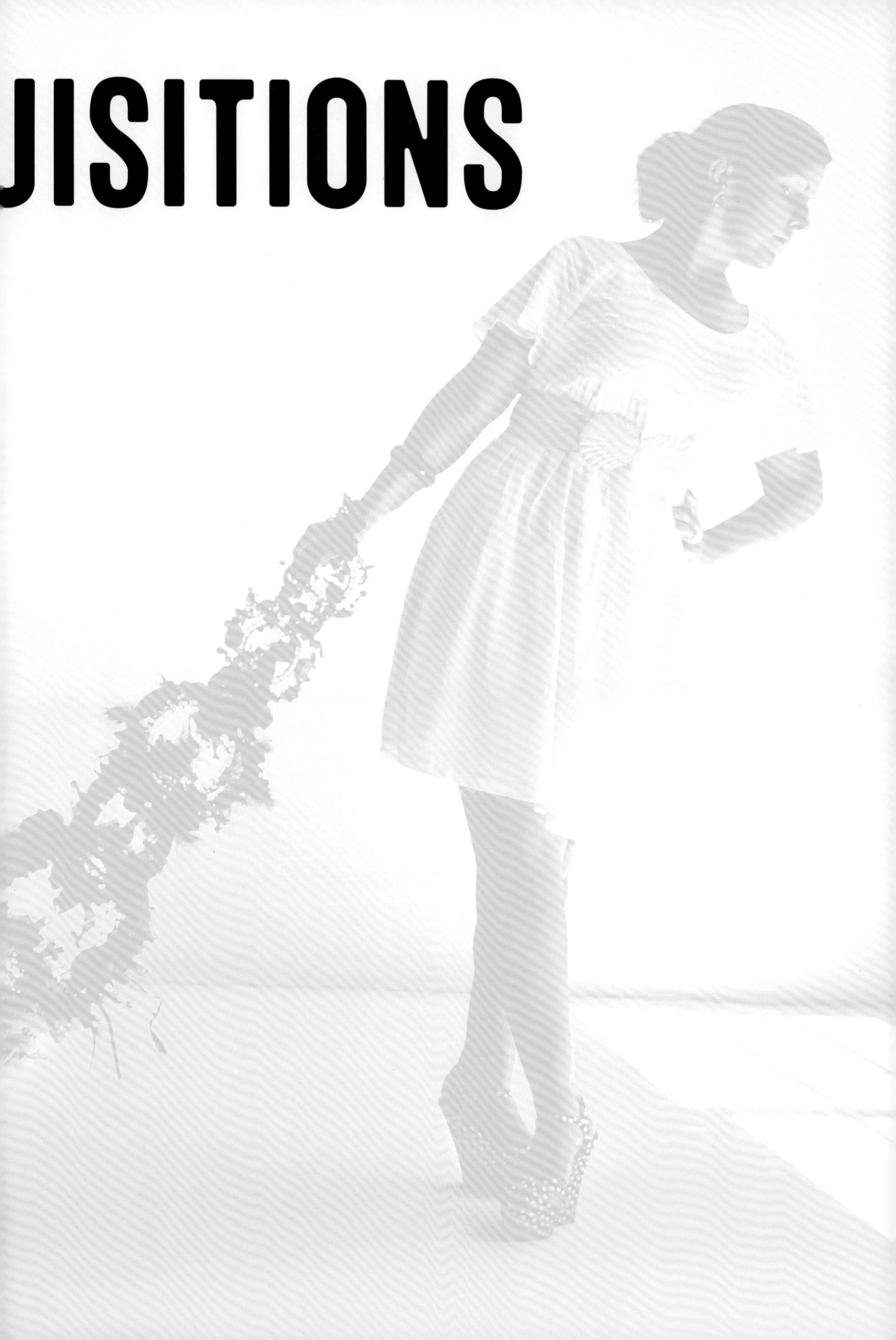
JISITIONS

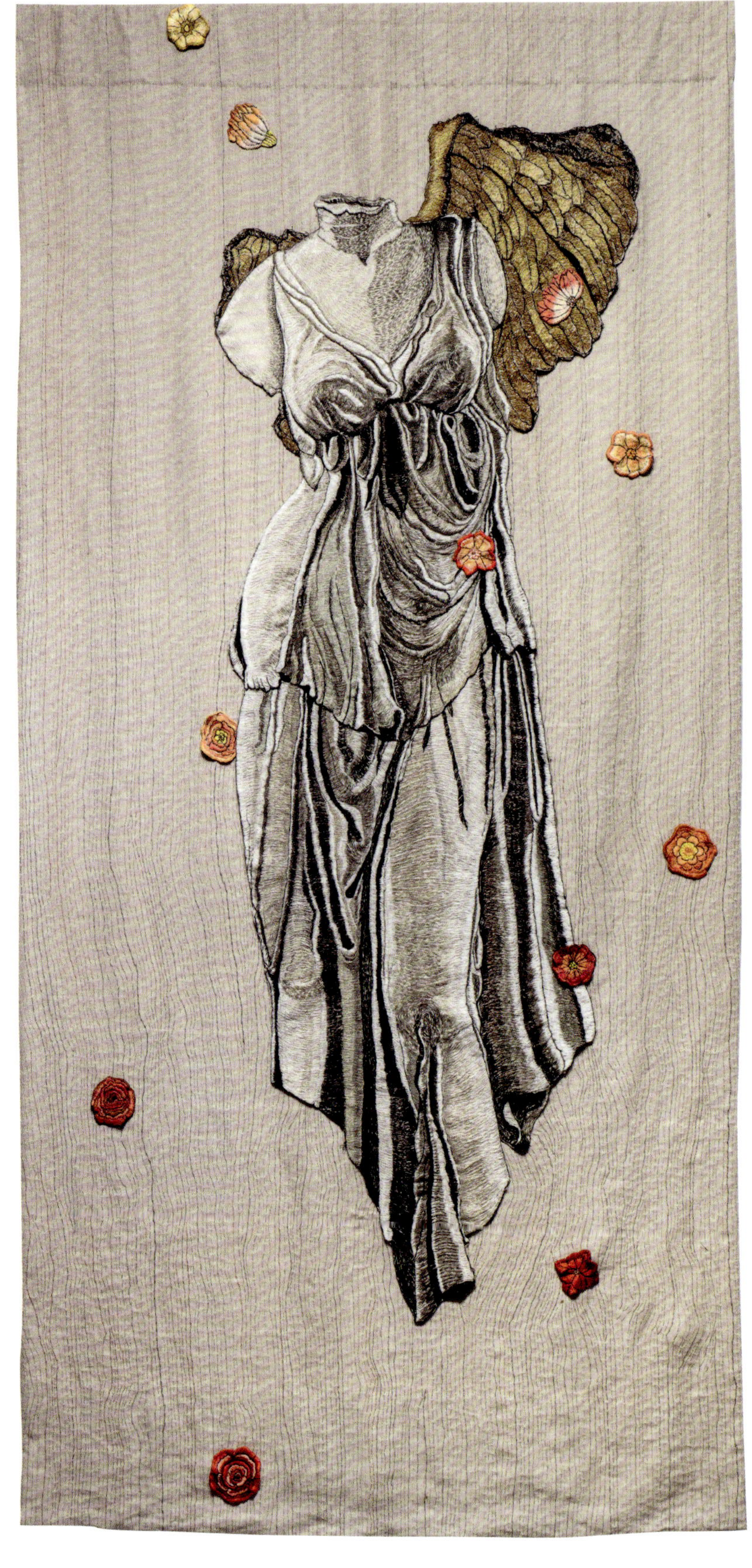

CAT. 89 Marilyn Pappas, *Nike with Broken Wings*, 2002–8, cotton and linen with gold thread, 66 ½ × 33 ½ in.

CAT. 90 Virgil Ortiz, *Pueblo Revolt 2180*, 2018–19, coil-built white bentonite clay with bee-weed (spinach) paint, 14 ⅝ × diam. 12 ⅞ in.

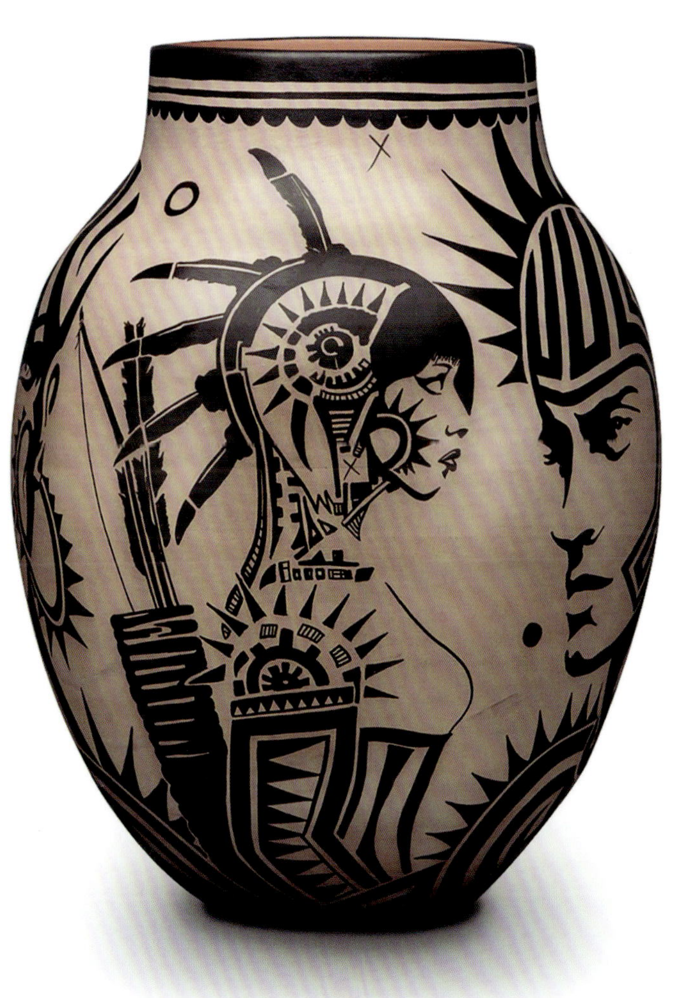

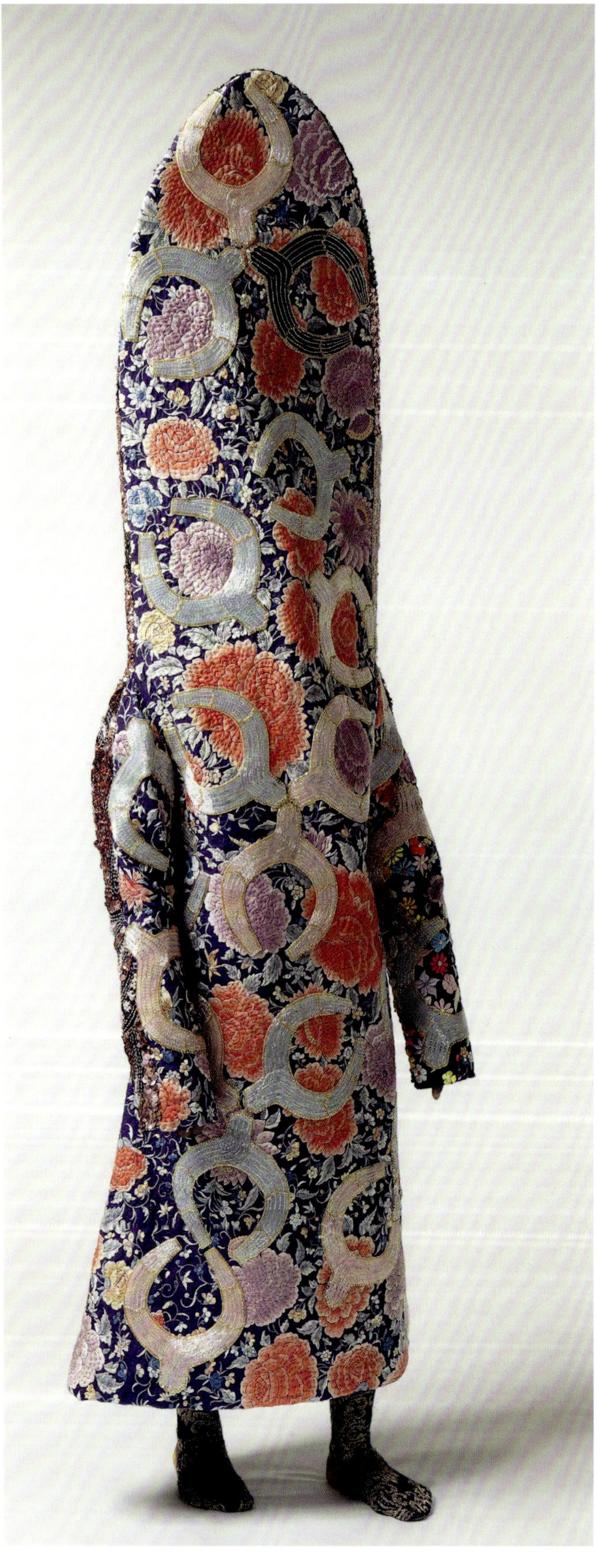

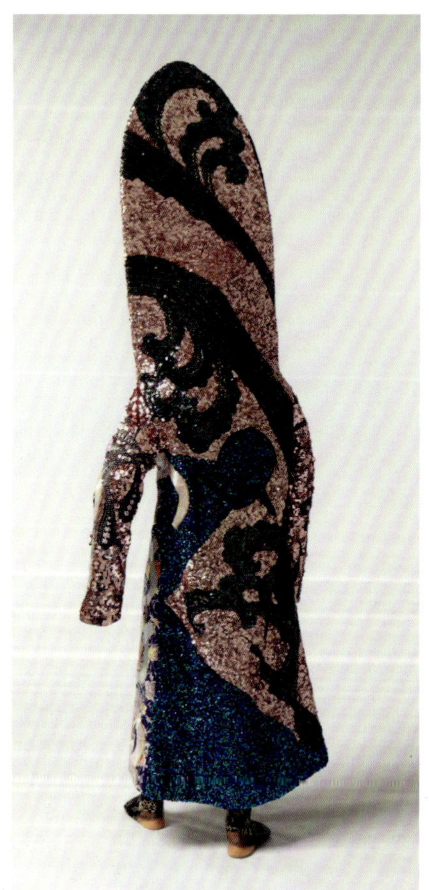

CAT. 91 Nick Cave,
Soundsuit (front and
reverse), 2010, fabric
with beads and sequins,
95 × 28 × 12 in.

CAT. 92 Lia Cook,
*Presence/Absence:
Touches II*, 1998, digital
jacquard–woven cotton
and rayon, 58 × 40 in.

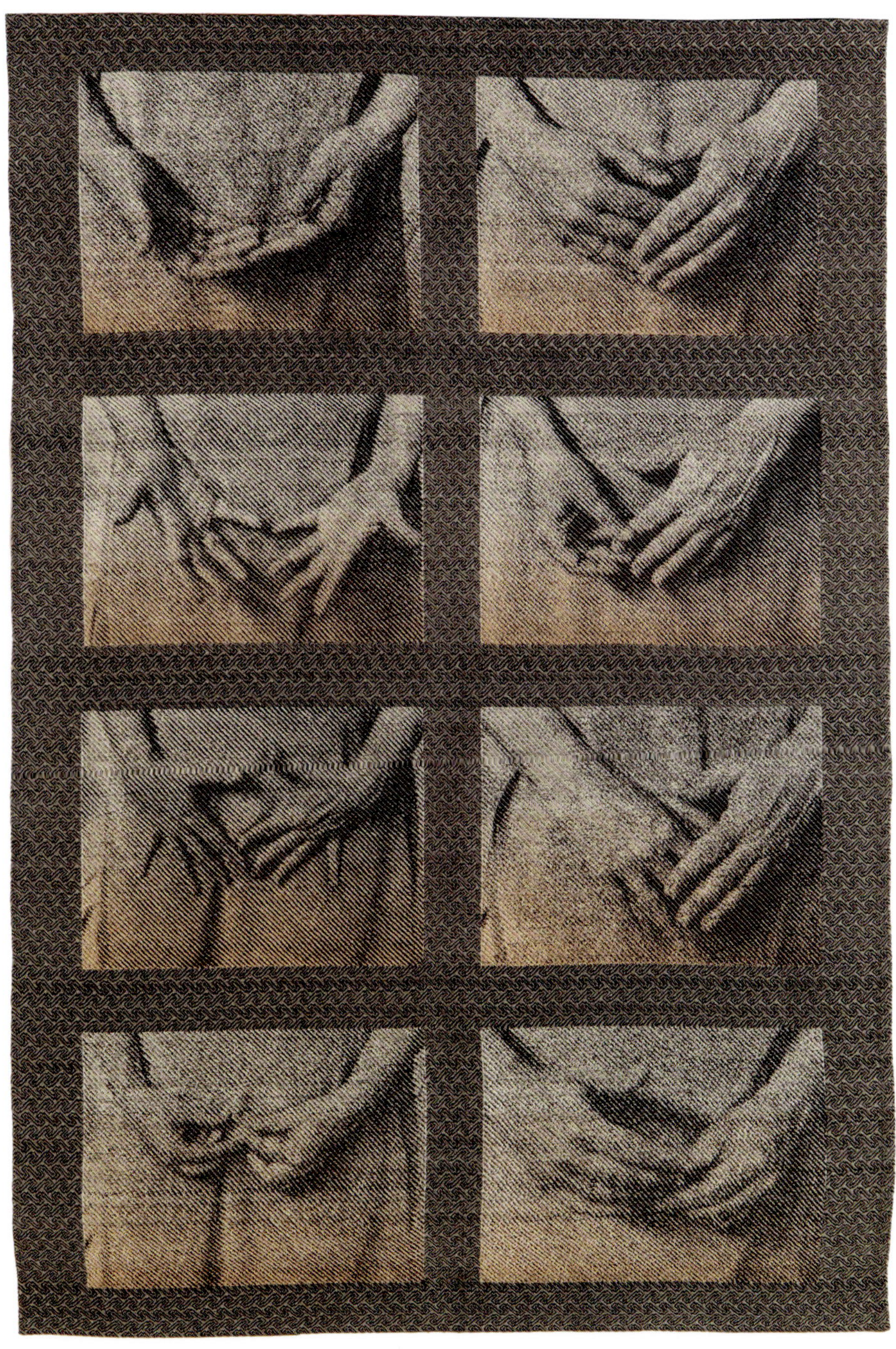

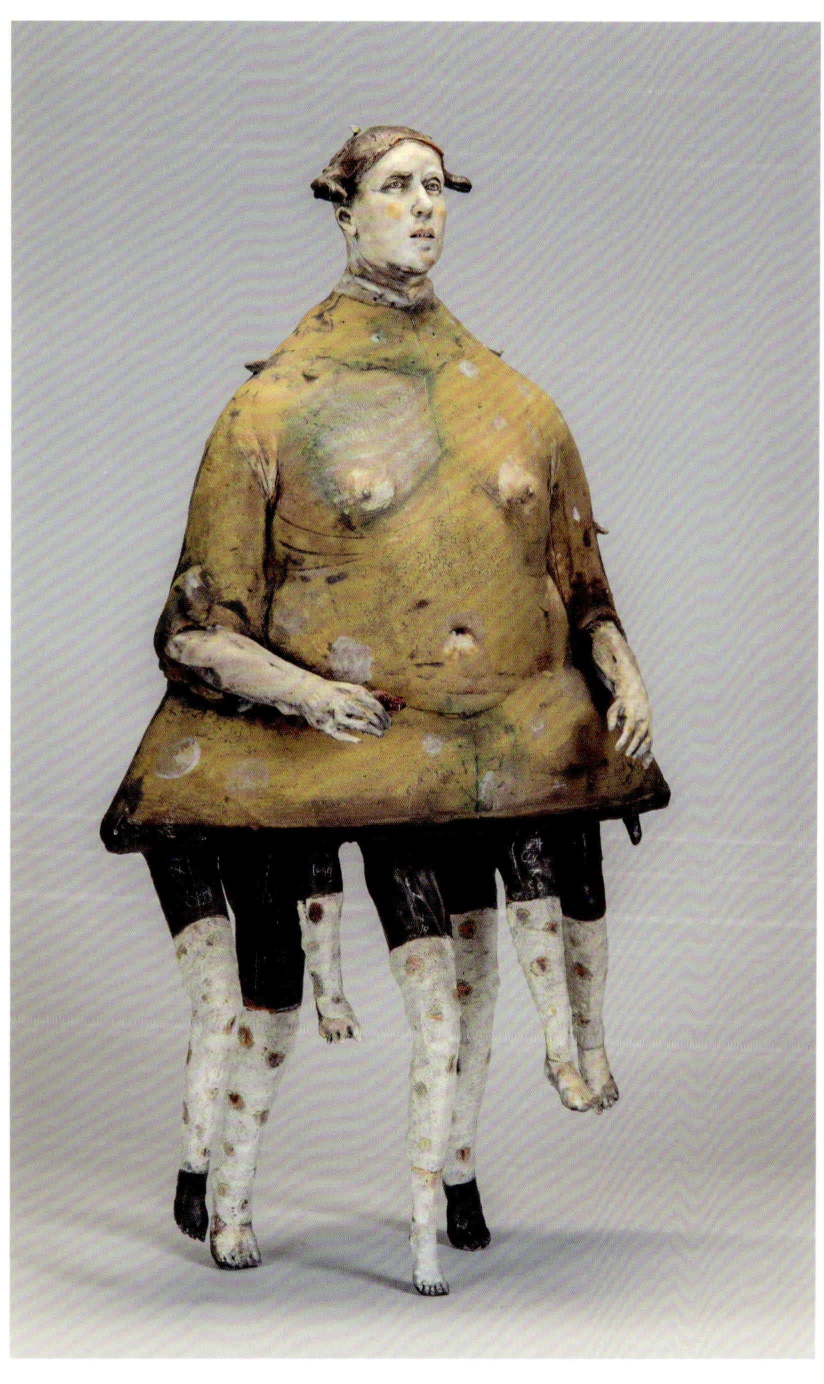

CAT. 93 Cristina Córdova, *Araña*, 2004, handbuilt ceramic with glaze and stain, 27 ¼ × 15 ⅛ × 9 ⅜ in.

CAT. 94   Richard Cleaver, *Head and Shoulders* (two views), 2007, handbuilt ceramic with freshwater pearls, garnets, Swarovski crystals, carnelian sapphires, bronze wire, metal, gold leaf, and oil paint, 11 ¼ × 7 ½ × 4 ⅝ in.

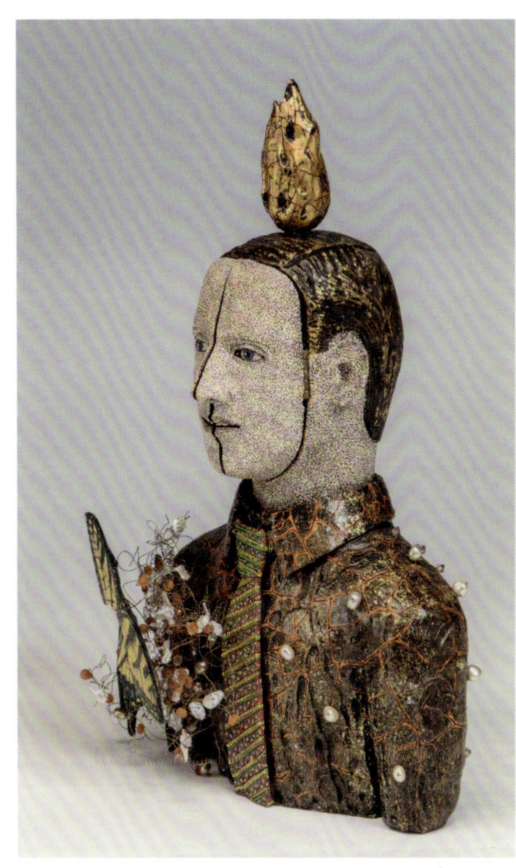

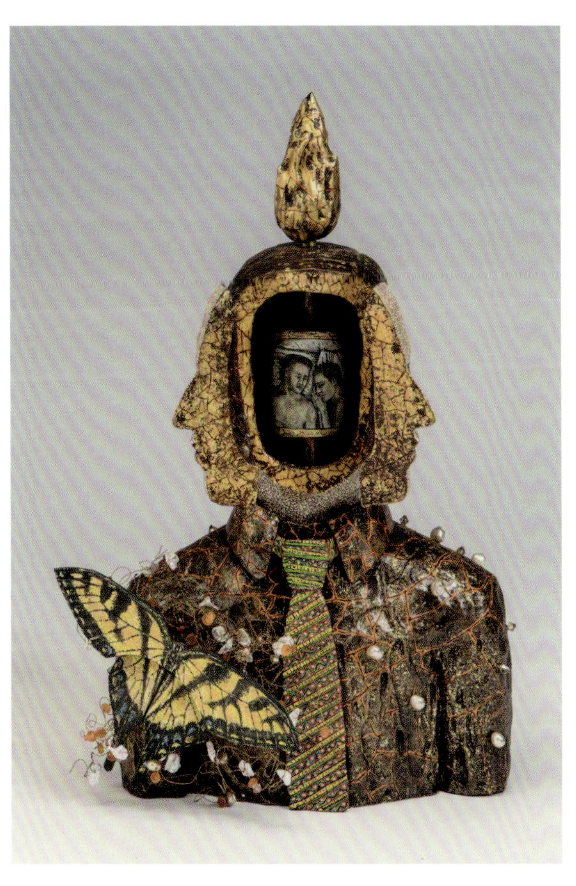

CAT. 95   Olga de Amaral, *Montaña #13*, 2001, handwoven linen with gold leaf and gesso, 60 × 77 × 1 in.

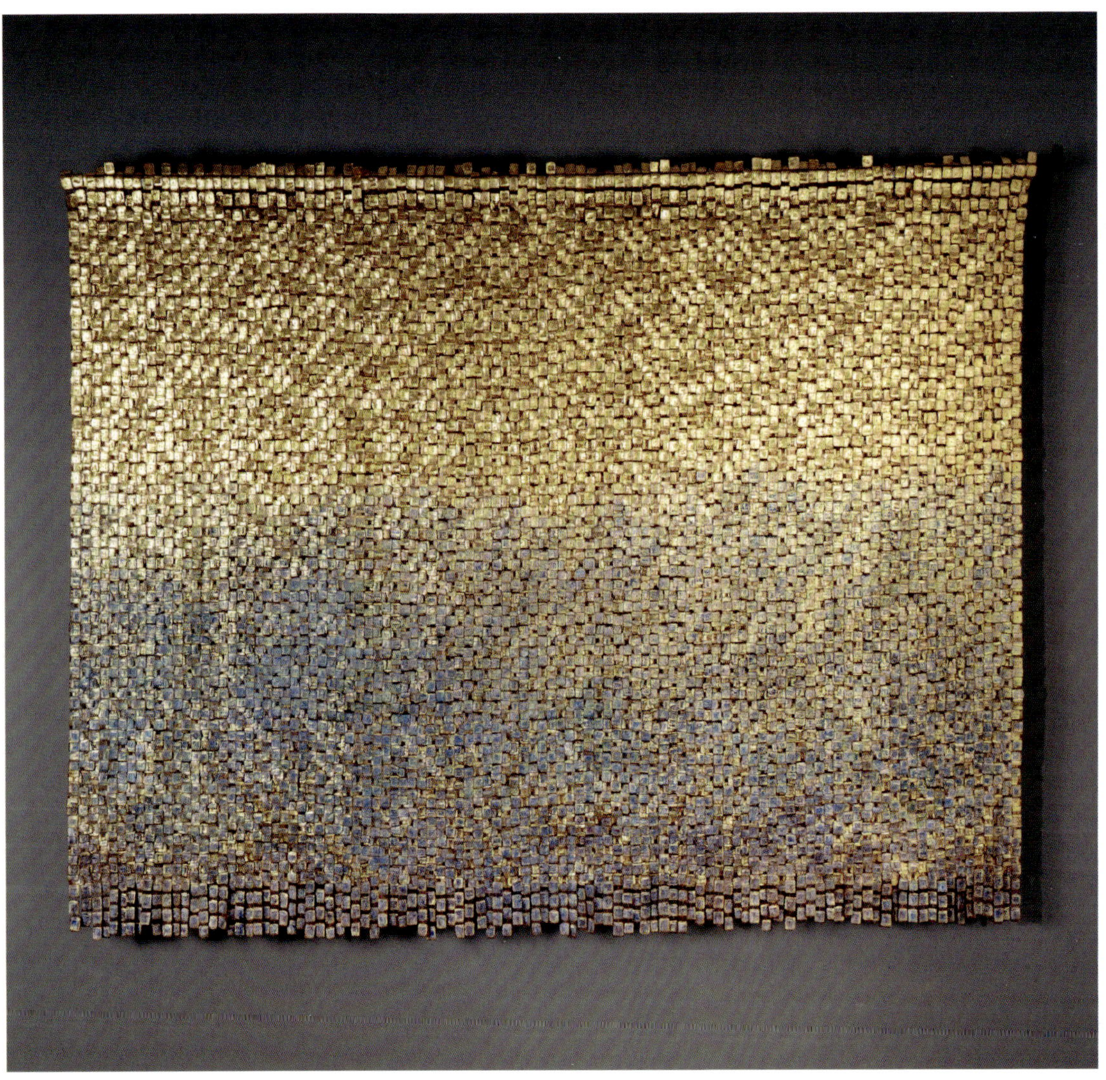

CAT. 96 Daniel Brush,
Diamond Egg (#90) (closed
and open), 1991–93,
24-karat gold and steel
with diamonds, overall:
2 × 1 ½ × 1 ½ in.

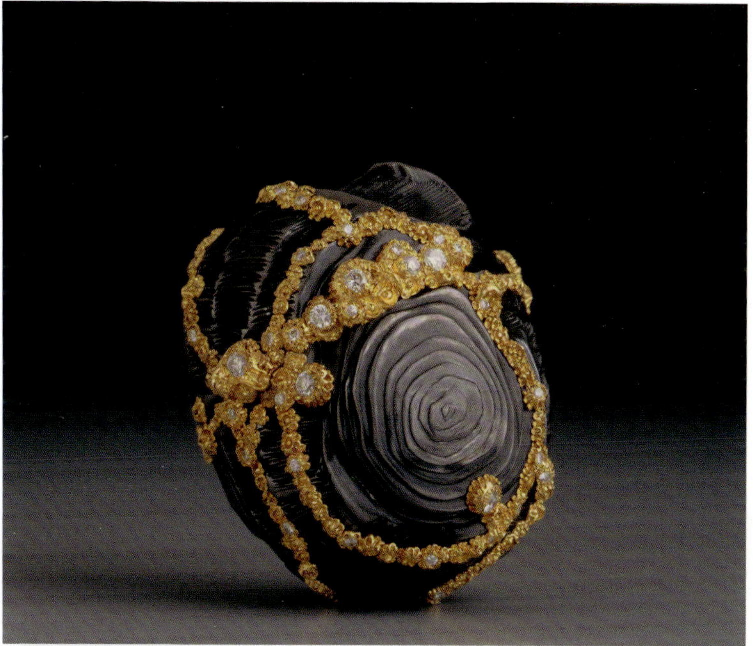

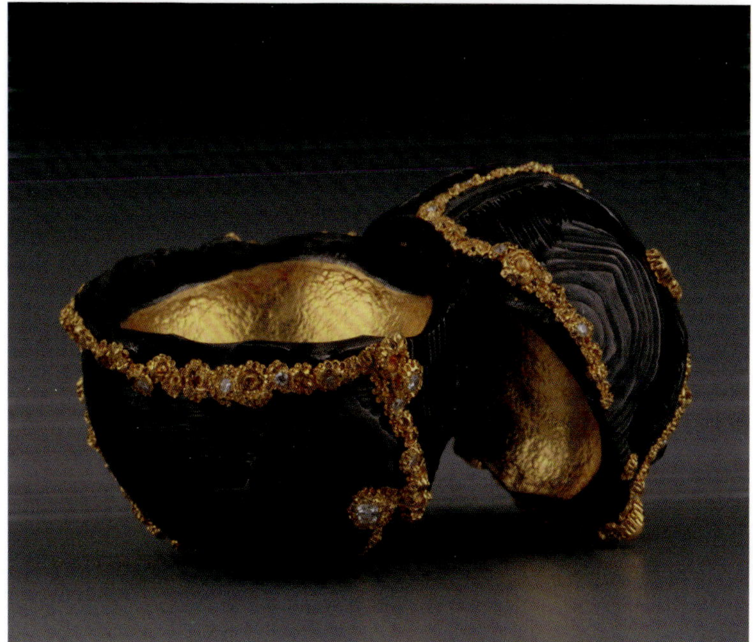

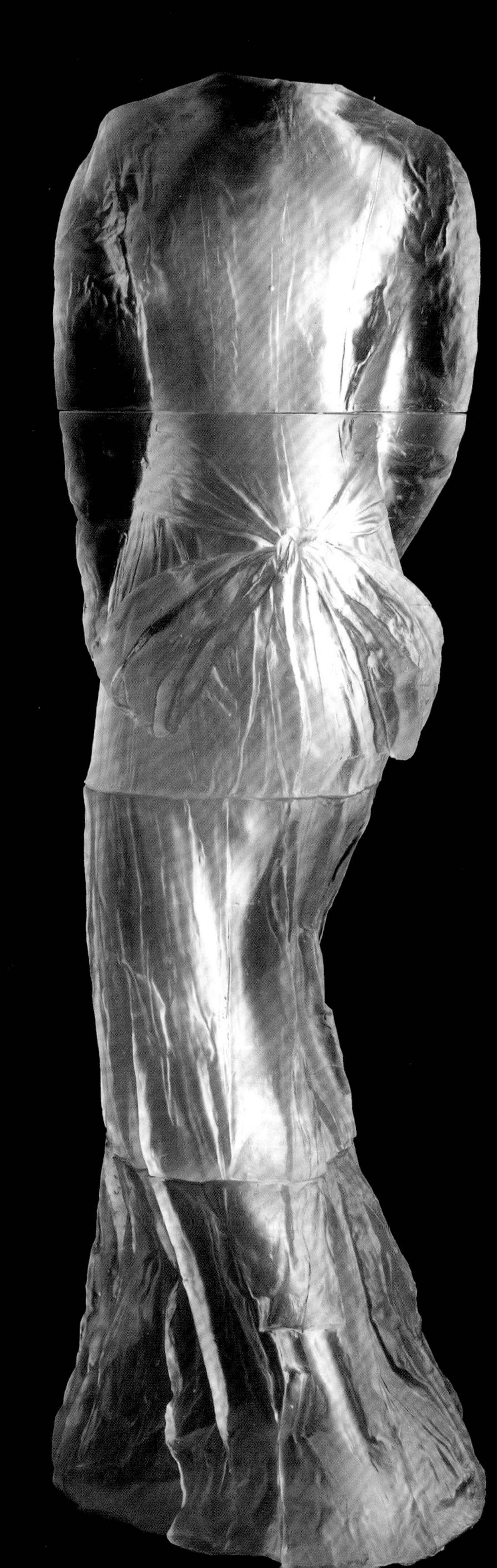

CAT. 97   Karen LaMonte,
Vestige (Pleated Dress),
2000, cast glass,
58 × 16 × 18 in.

CAT. 98   Shari Mendelson,
Animal with Caged Vessel,
2019, repurposed plastic
with hot glue, resin, acrylic
polymer, mica, glass frit,
and monofilament,
13 3/8 × 8 5/8 × 6 5/8 in.

CAT. 99   Jeannine Marchand,
FOLDS CLXVIII, 2019, clay,
steel, and wood with
painted wooden frame,
24 × 12 × 6 in.

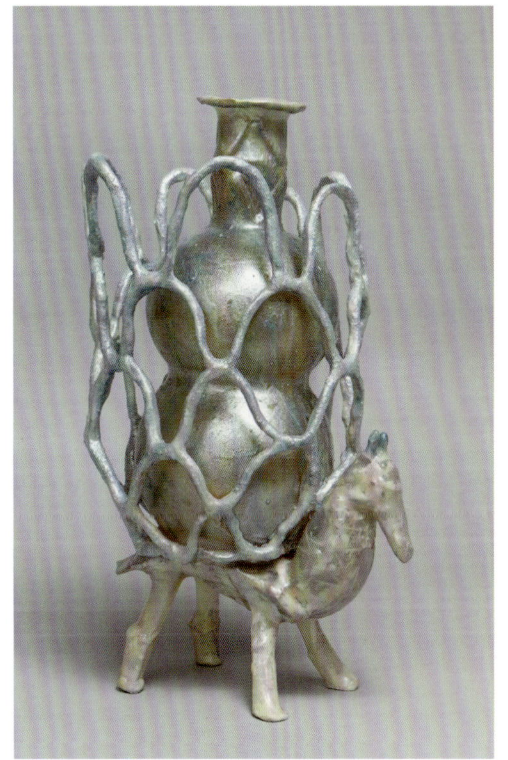

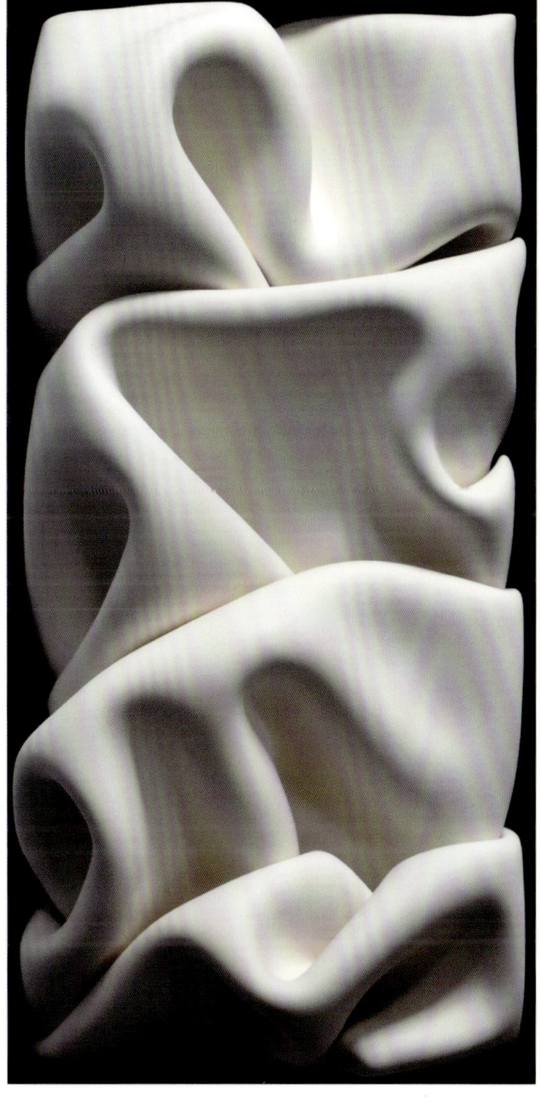

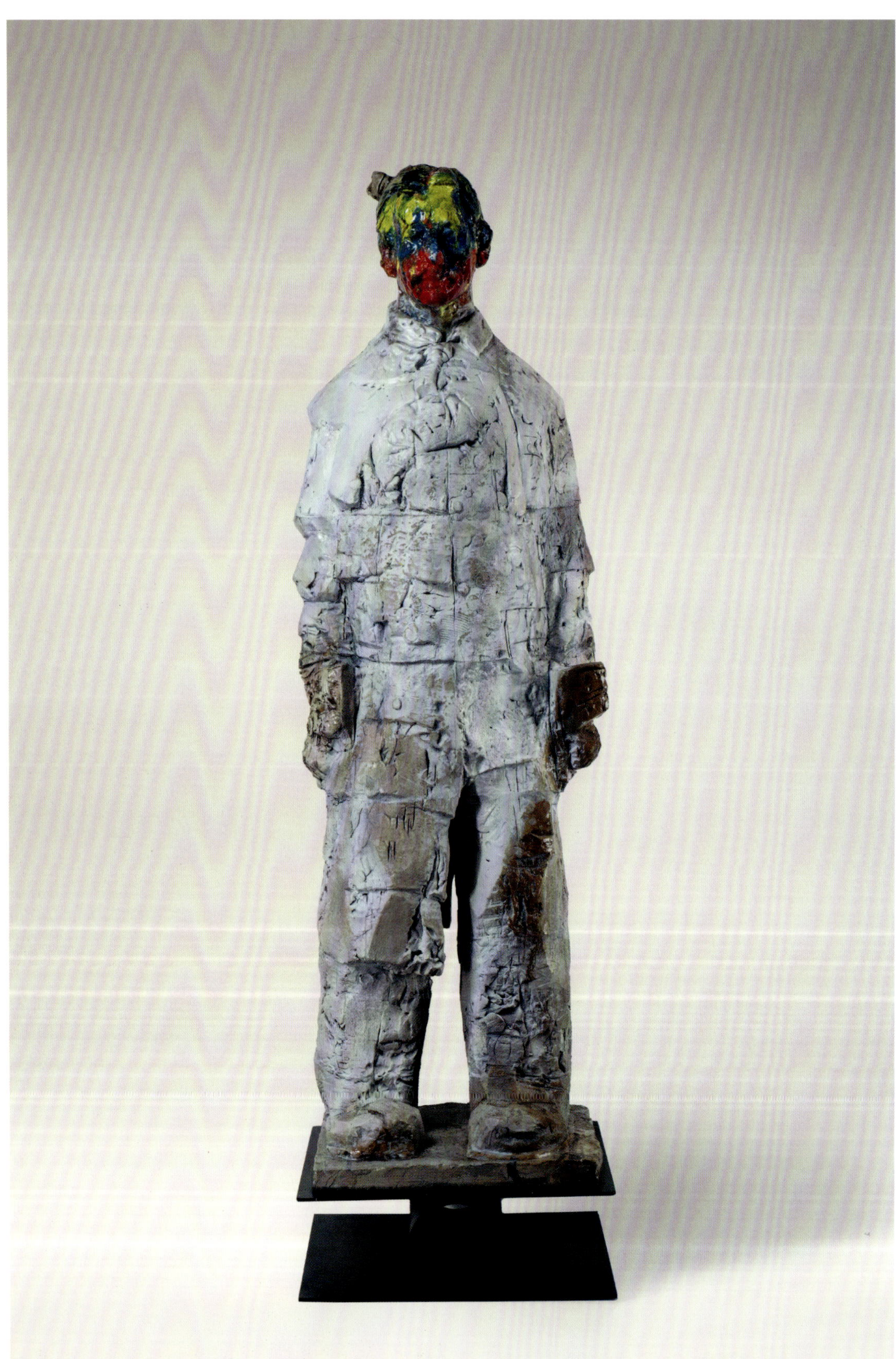

CAT. 100 Wanxin Zhang, *Warrior with Color Face*, 2009, high-fired stoneware with glaze, 77 ¾ × 23 × 24 in.

CAT. 101 Woody de Othello, *Covering Face*, 2021, stoneware with glaze on tiled base, overall: 47 × 21 ¼ × 21 ⅜ in.

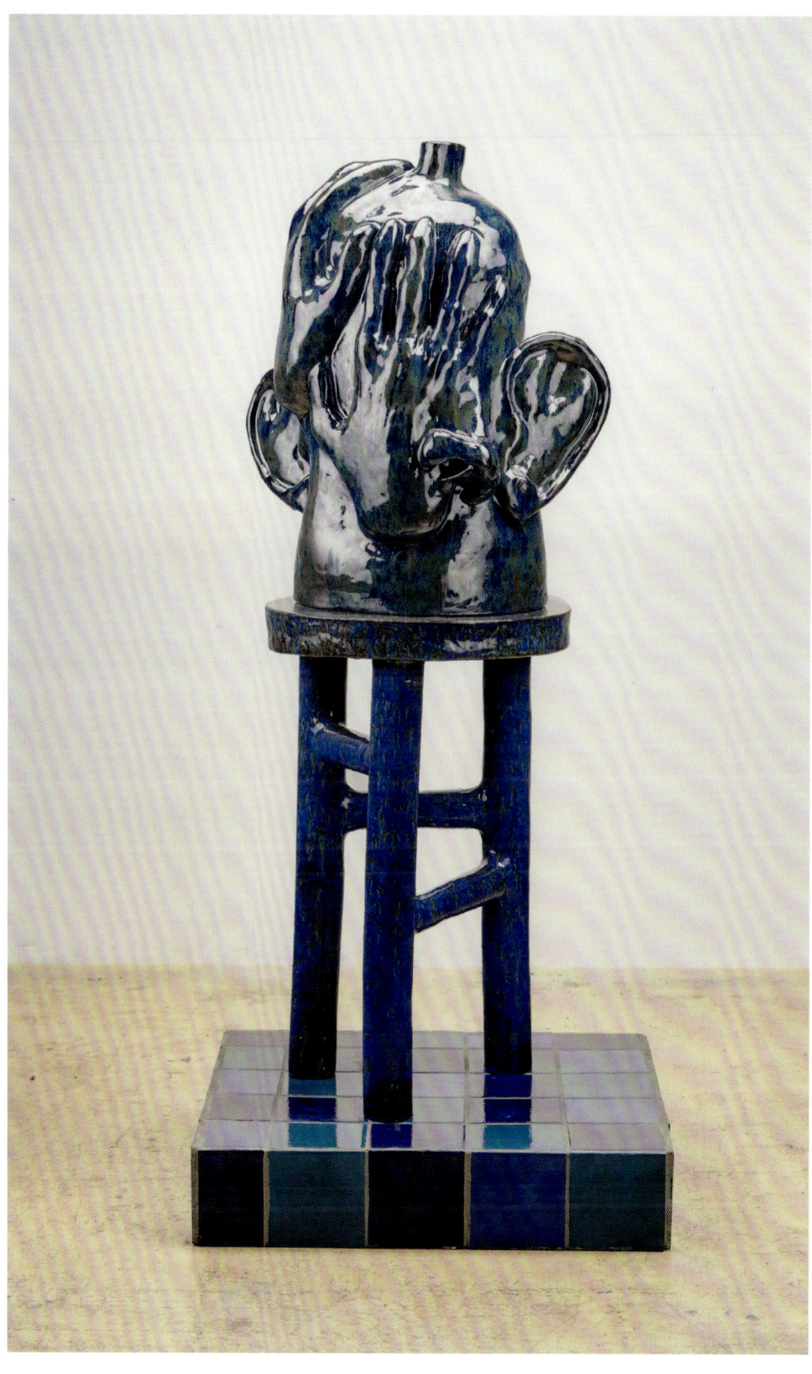

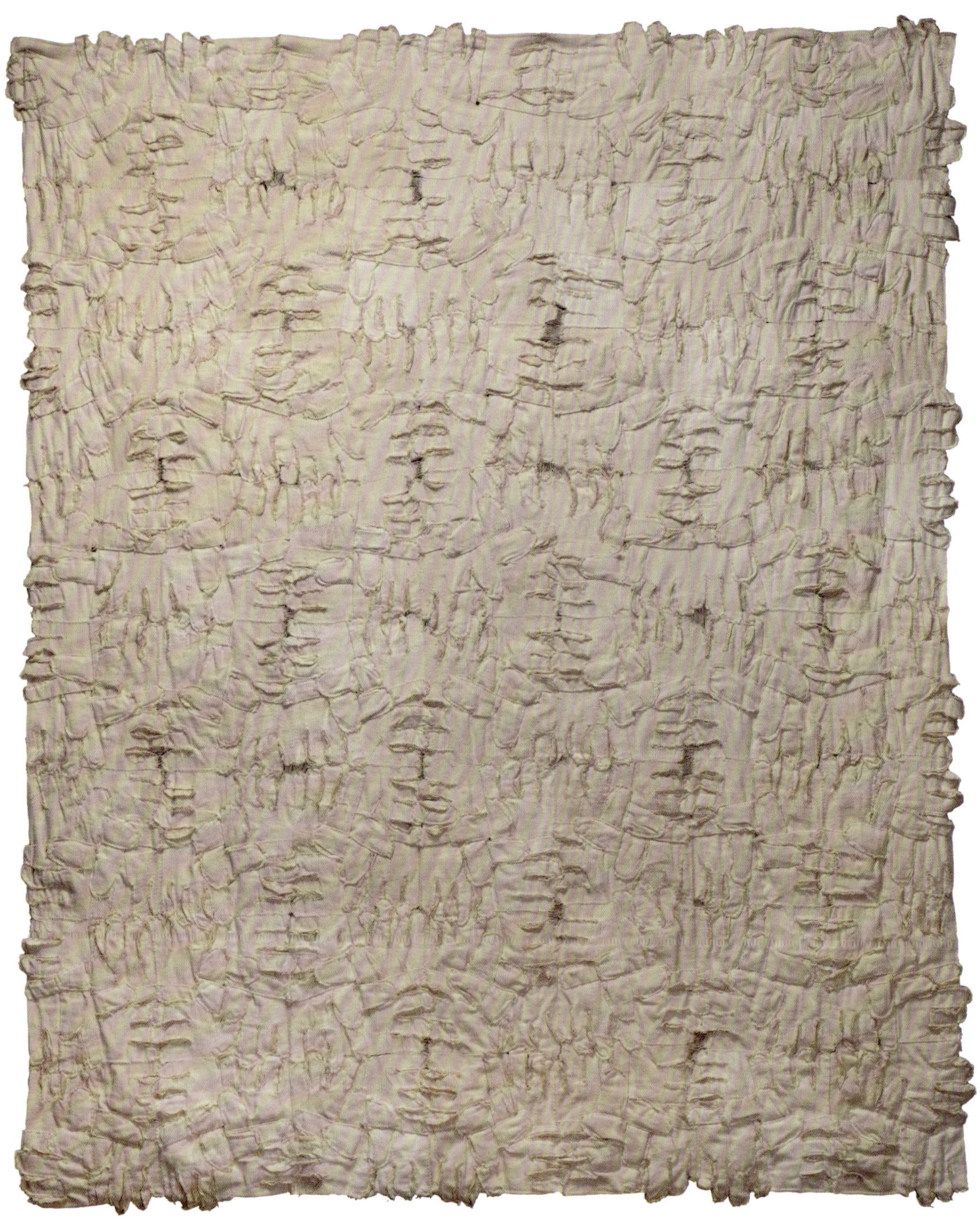

CAT. 103 Nancy Lee Worden, *Sexual Harassment in the Workplace*, 2018, silver, found gloves, found purses, and plastic flowers, 25 × 18 × 7 ½ in.

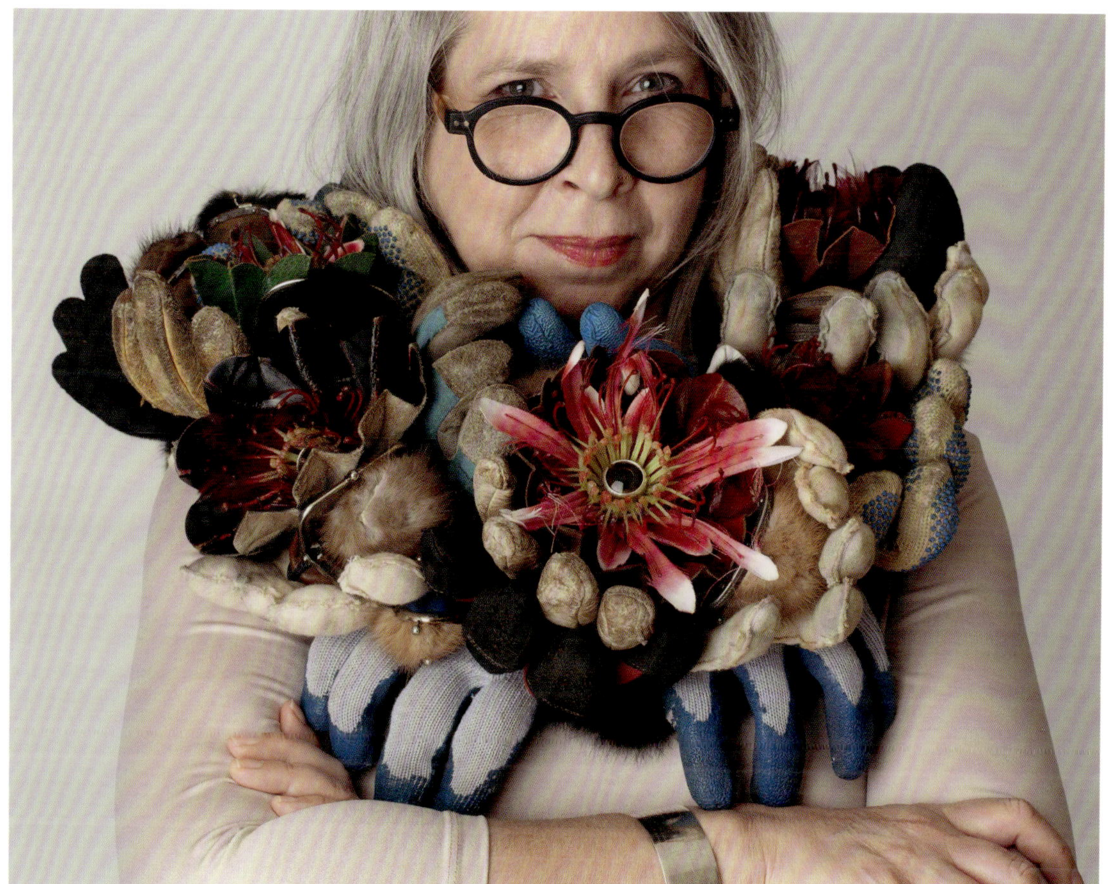

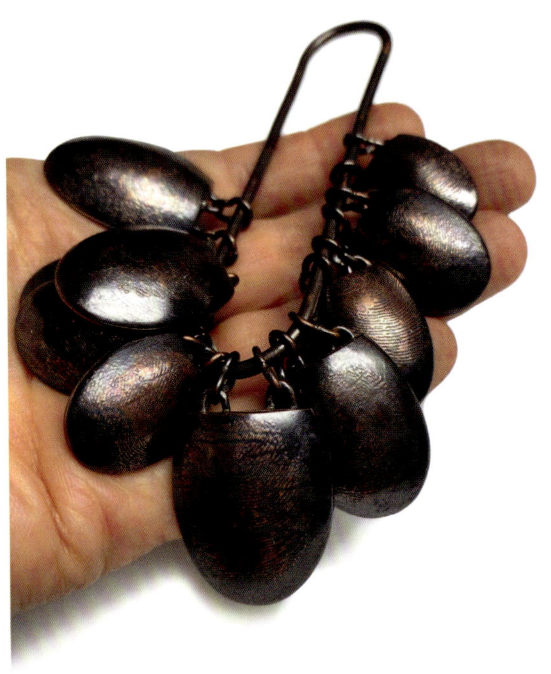

CAT. 104   Sharon Massey, *Touch (in the time of corona)*, 2020, copper, 3 ¼ × 6 ½ × ⅜ in.

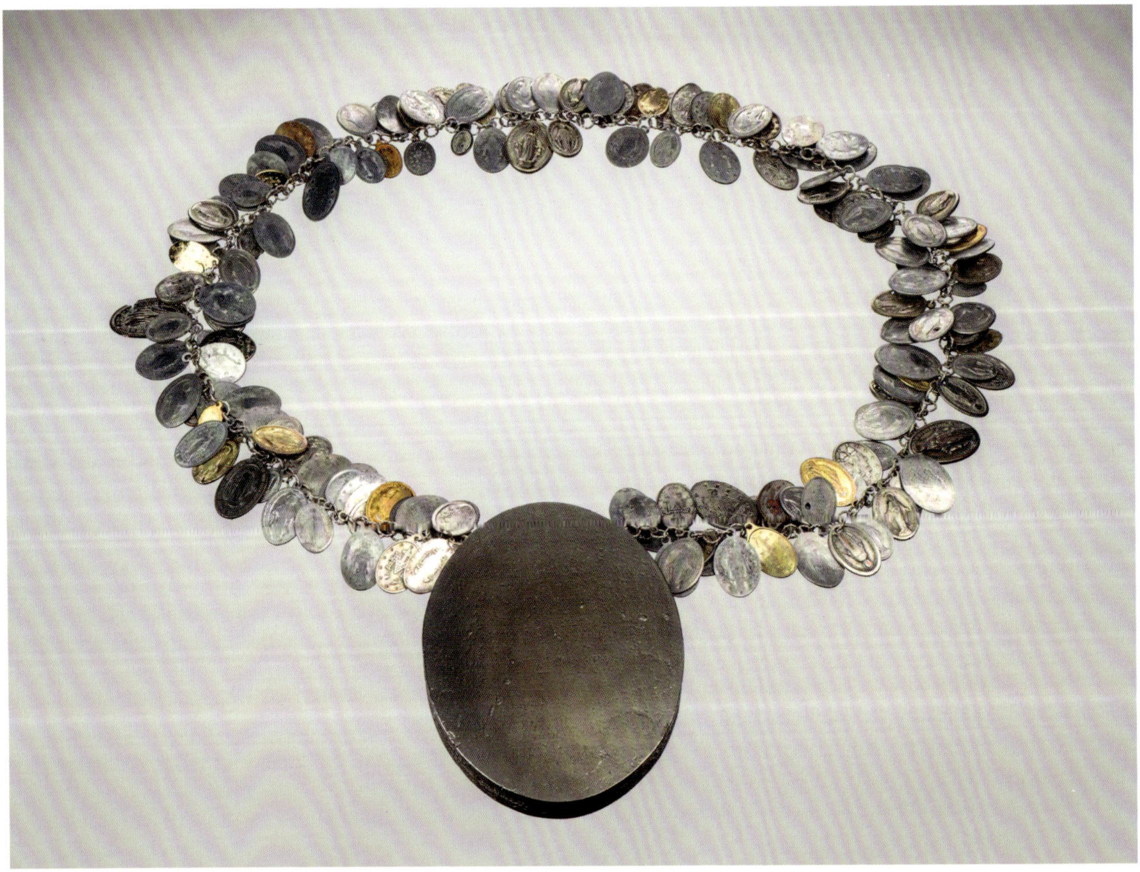

CAT. 105   M. J. Tyson, *Popular Devotion*, 2020, devotional medals with sterling silver and cast pewter, 19 ⅛ × 10 ½ × ½ in.

CAT. 106 Donté K. Hayes, *Initiate*, 2020, handbuilt black stoneware, overall: 19 ⅛ × 16 ⅝ × 17 ¼ in.

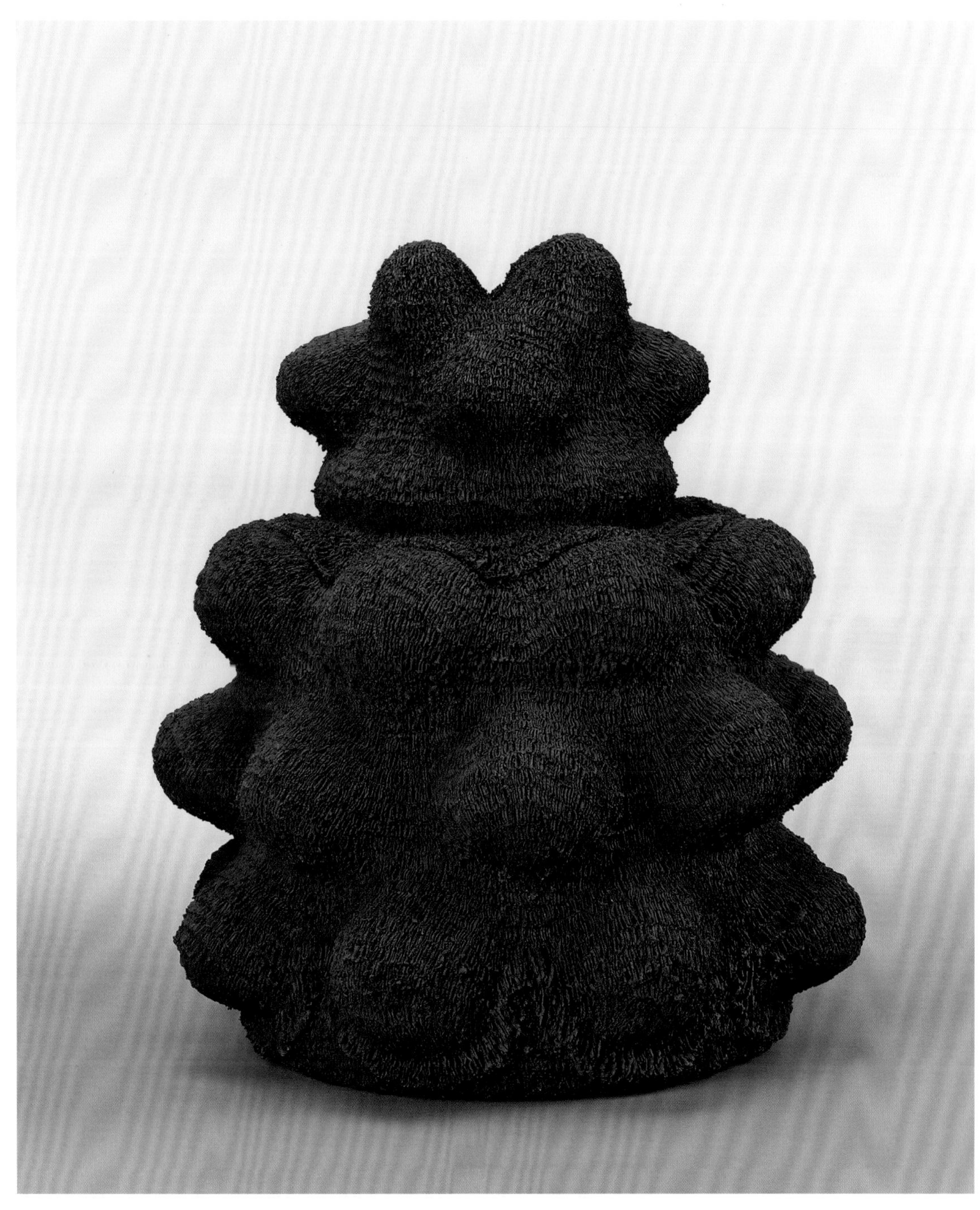

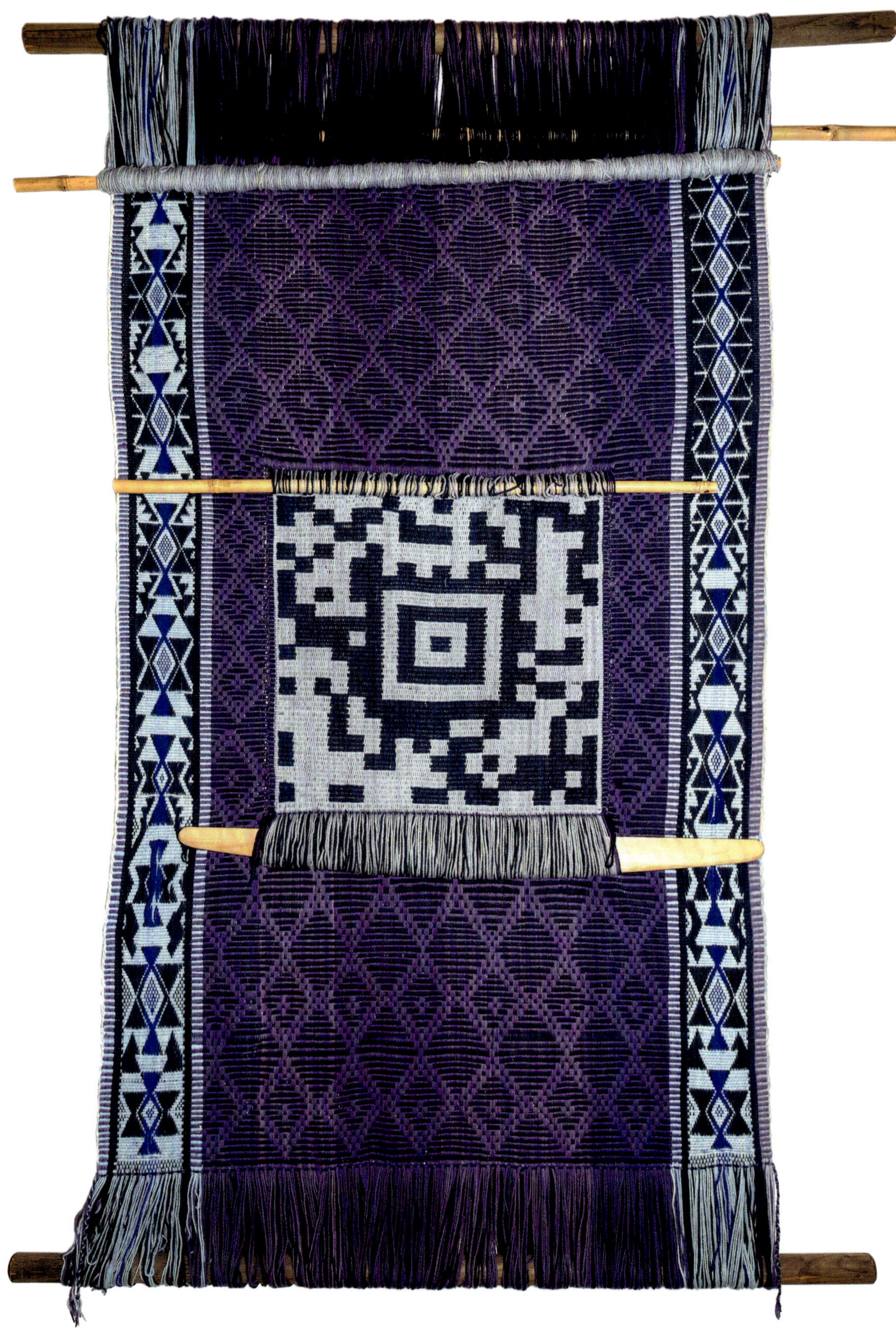

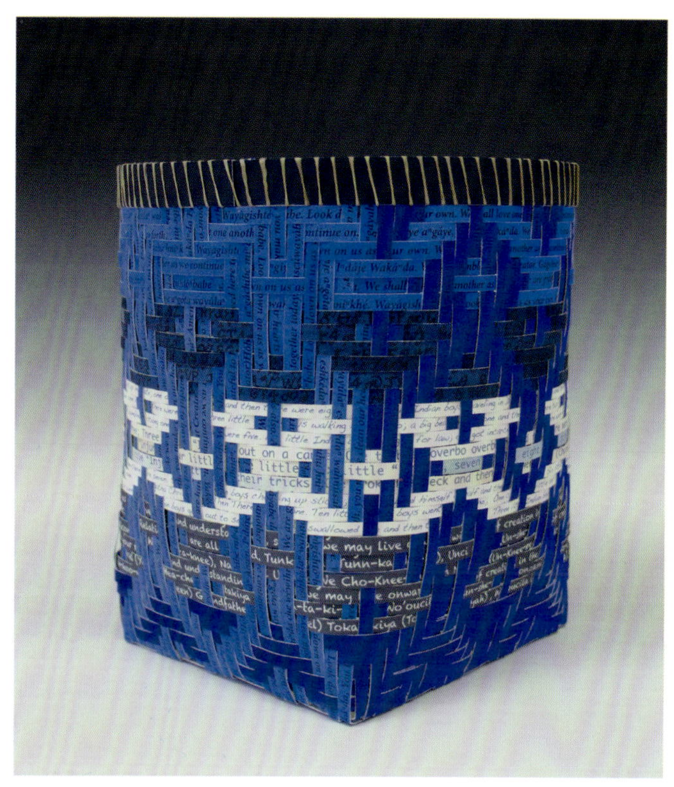

CAT. 107   Guillermo Bert, *Mapuche Portal #3*, from the series *Encoded Textiles*, 2014, wool with natural dyes; QR code to digital audio files of Mapuche Traditional Stories narrated by poet Graciala Huinao, 80 ½ × 58 ¼ × 2 ¼ in.

CAT. 108   Shan Goshorn, *Song of Sorrow*, 2015, watercolor paper splints with ink and acrylic paint, overall: 9 × diam. 8 ½ in.

CAT. 109   Roy Superior, *Peace Missile*, 1985, oak, walnut, laurel, and hardwoods with brass and music box, closed: 7 × 20 × 12 in.

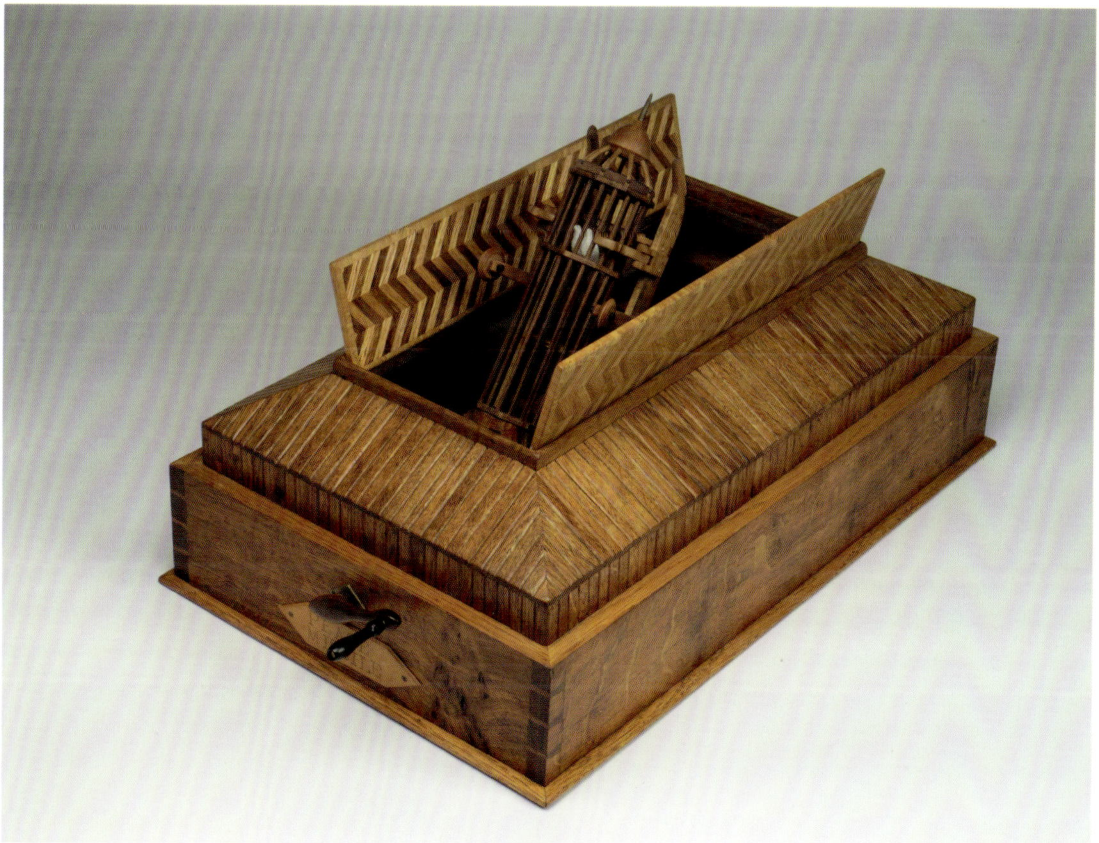

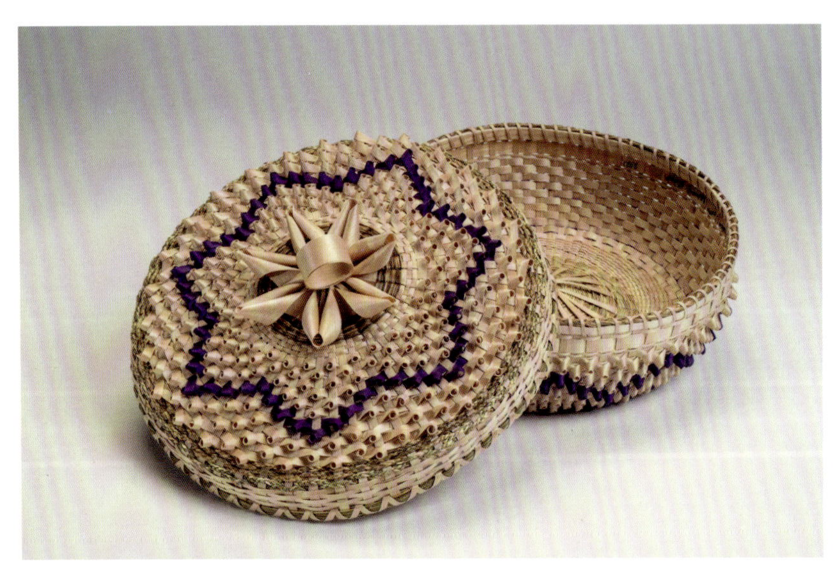

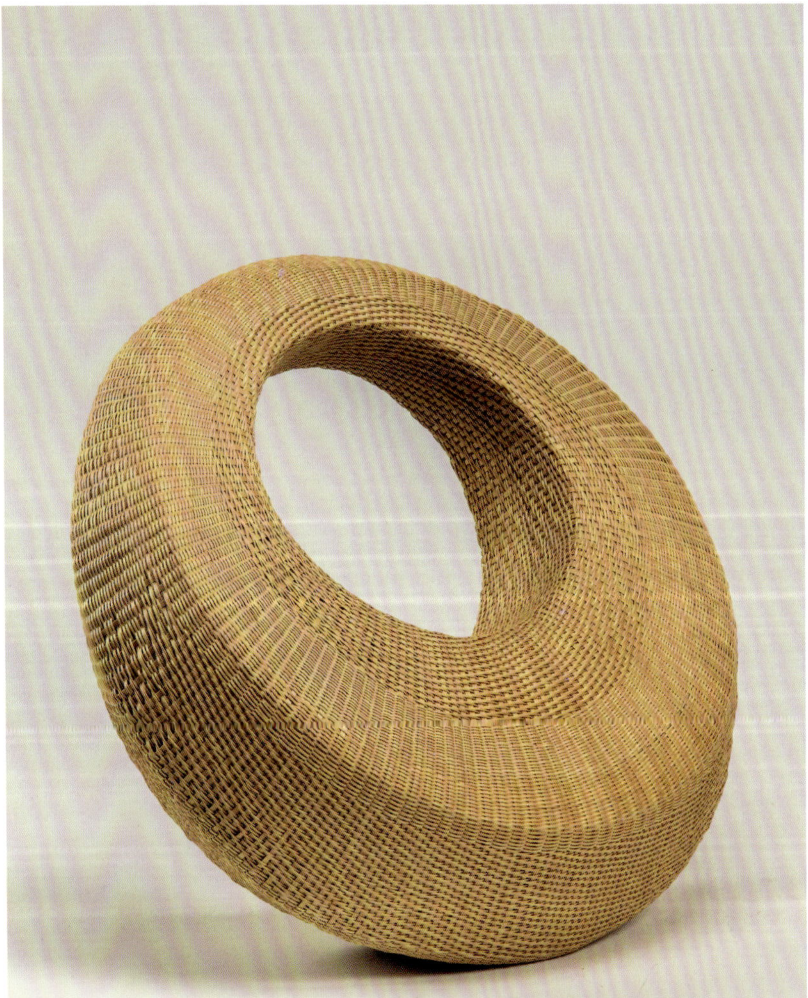

CAT. 110 Sheila Kanieson Ransom, *Pope Basket*, 2021, sweetgrass and black ash splints with commercial dye, overall: 6 × diam. 10 5/8 in.

CAT. 111 Susan Kavicky, *Sitting*, 2004, brown ash, fiberboard, and oak, 15 3/4 × 19 × 12 3/8 in.

CAT. 112 Micah Evans, *Raphine*, 2015, lampworked borosilicate glass, 11 3/4 × 7 3/4 × 9 3/4 in.

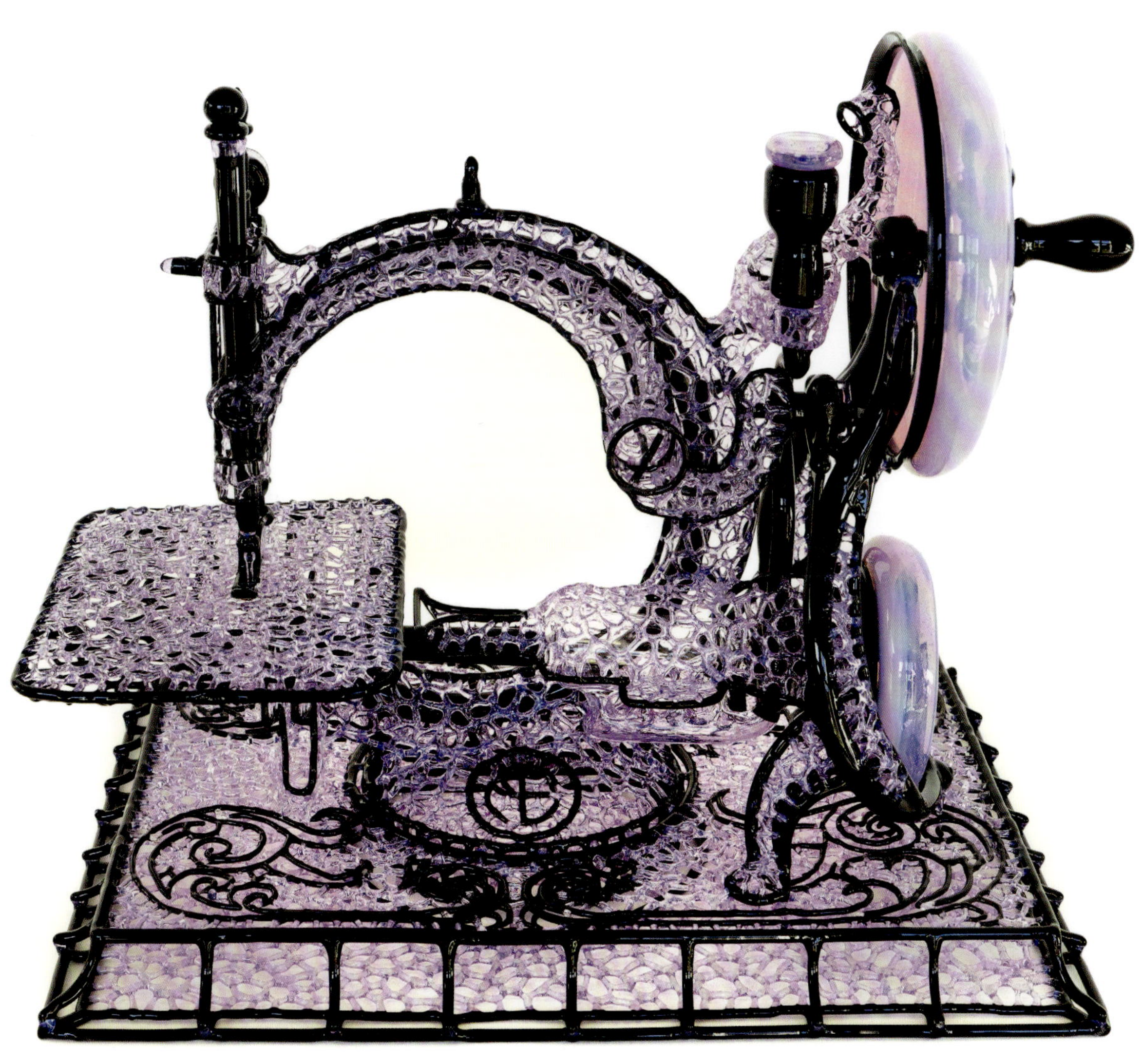

CAT. 113 Thomas Loeser,
With You in a Moment,
(detail and overall),
2016, honey locust and
found shovel handles,
120 × 35 × 21 in.

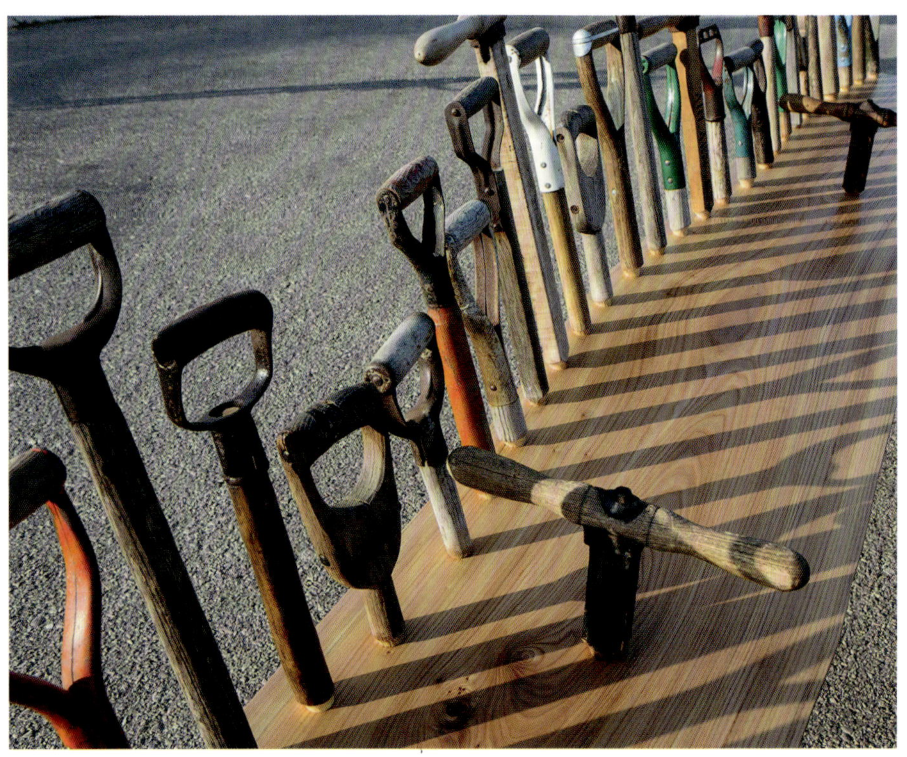

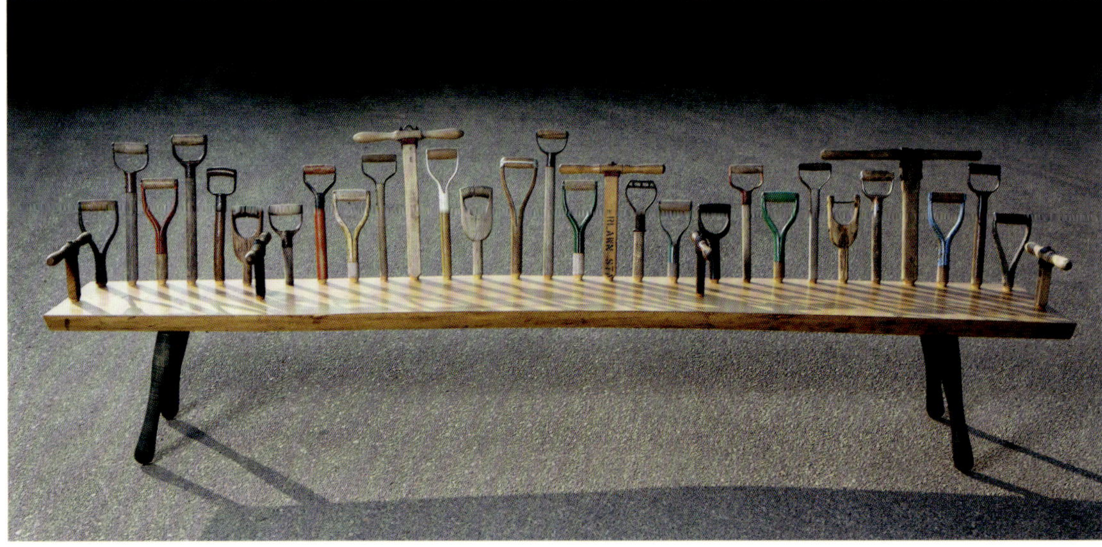

CAT. 114 Michael Cooper, *Modified*, 2010, painted hard maple, steel, aluminum, pneumatic system, engine, and mechanics, 33 × 48 × 67 in.

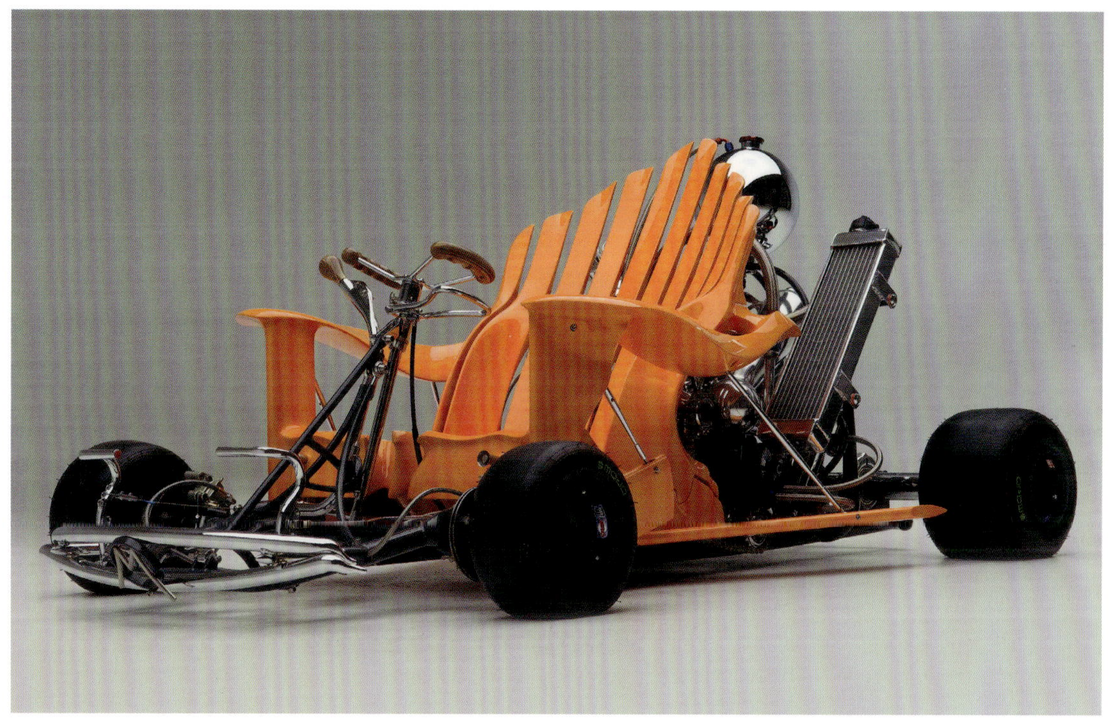

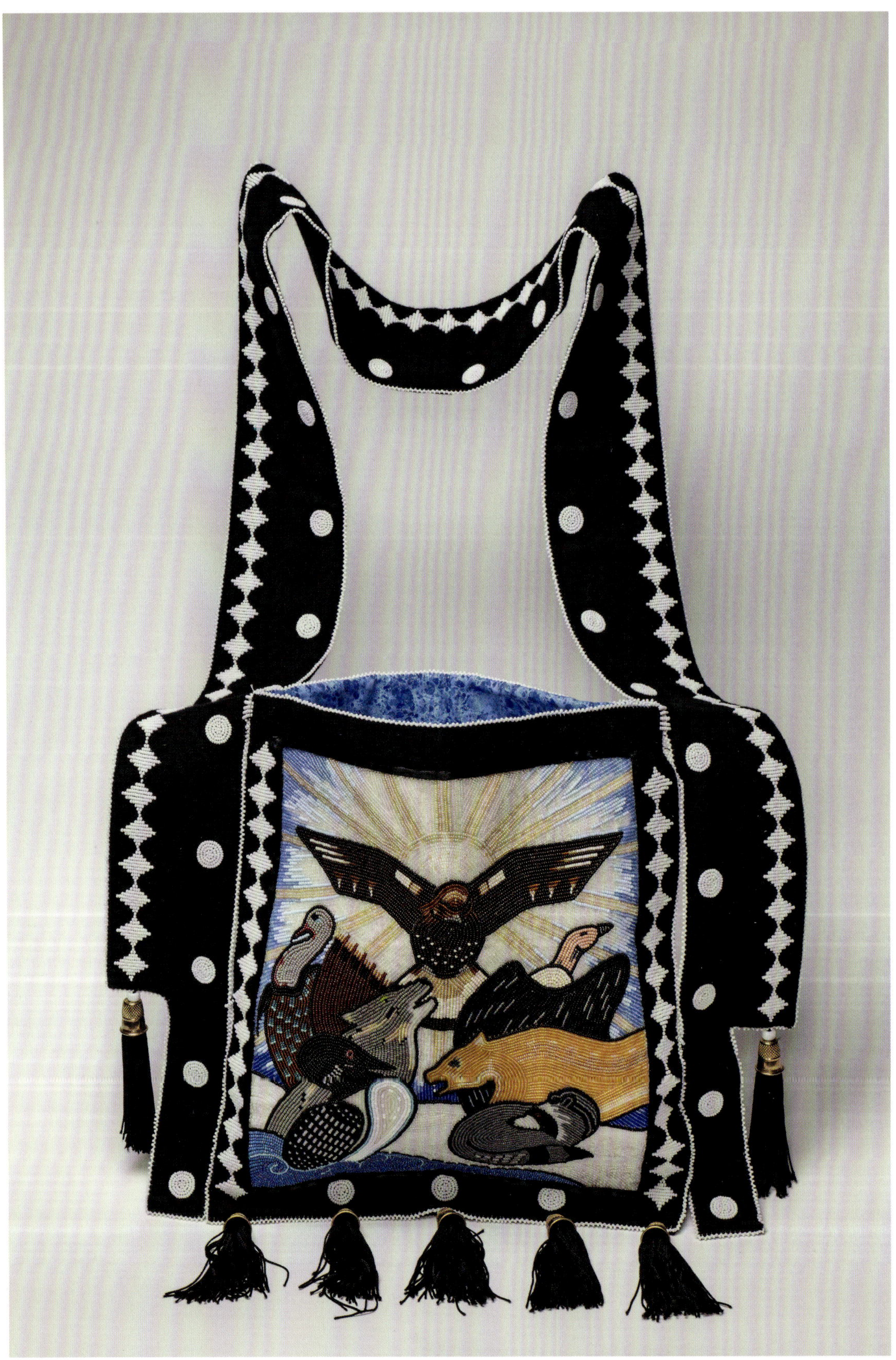

CAT. 115 Katrina Mitten,
*Ten Original Clans of the
Myaamia*, 2016, wool felt
with Czech seed beads,
pony beads, brass thimbles,
polyester tassels, satin
ribbon, and cotton liner,
41 ¾ × 22 × 3 ½ in.

CAT. 116 Joe Feddersen,
Horses and Deer, 2020,
blown and sand-carved glass,
13 ½ × 11 ¾ × 10 ⅜ in.

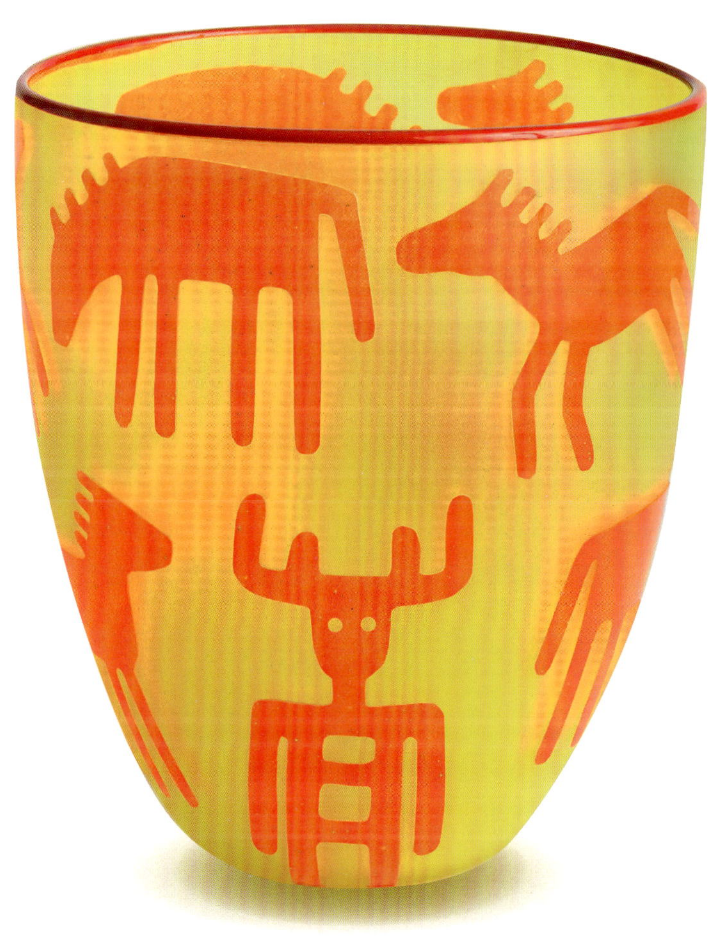

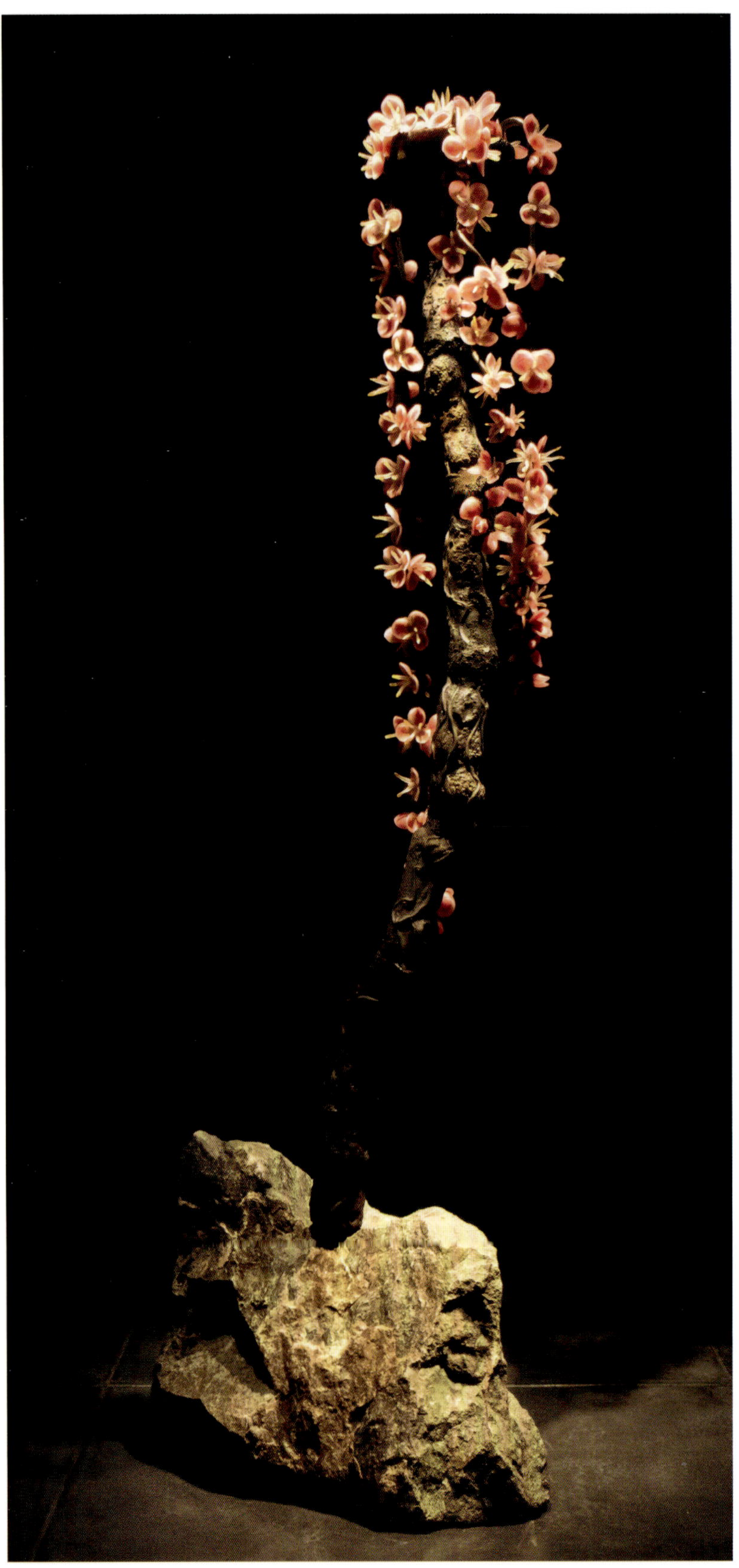

CAT. 117 Debora Moore, *Cherry*, from the series *Arboria*, blown and sculpted glass with natural boulder, approx. 90 × 28 × 20 in.

CAT. 118   Sharon Church, *Oh No!*, 2007, carved Castello boxwood with enamel paints, lacquer, 14-karat yellow gold, old European–cut diamonds, and epoxy, 6 ¼ × 3 ¼ × 2 in.

CAT. 119   Kurt Weiser, *Many, Many*, 2005, cast porcelain with glaze and china paint on bronze base, overall: 20 ³⁄₈ × 19 ½ × 17 ½ in.

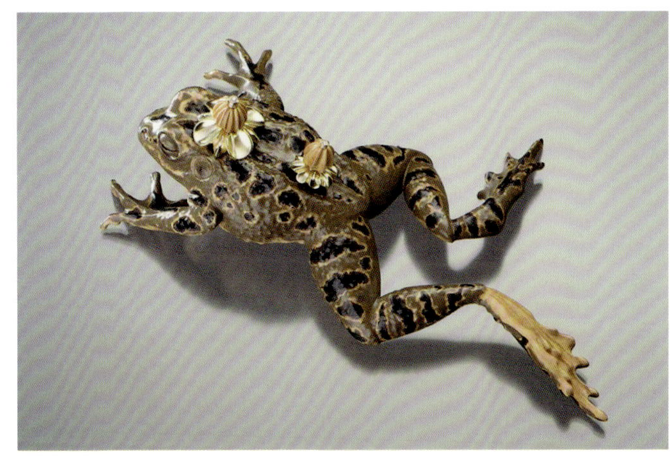

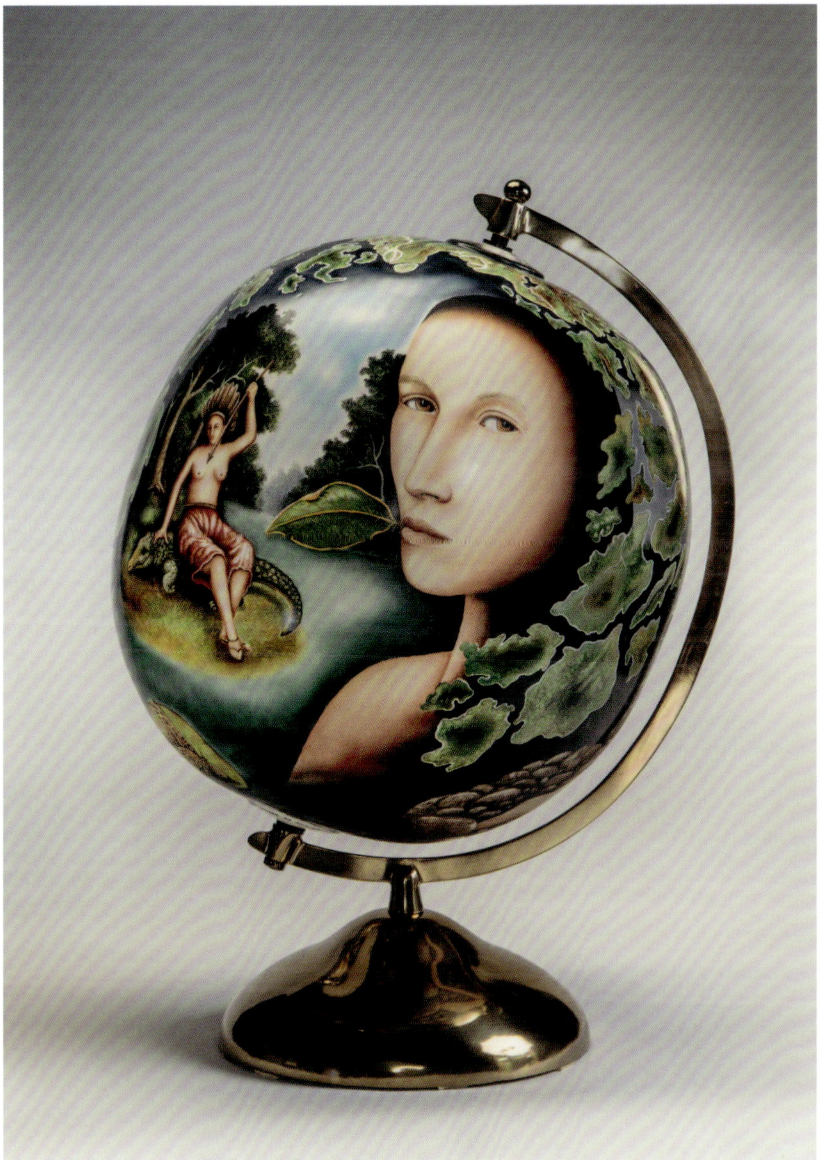

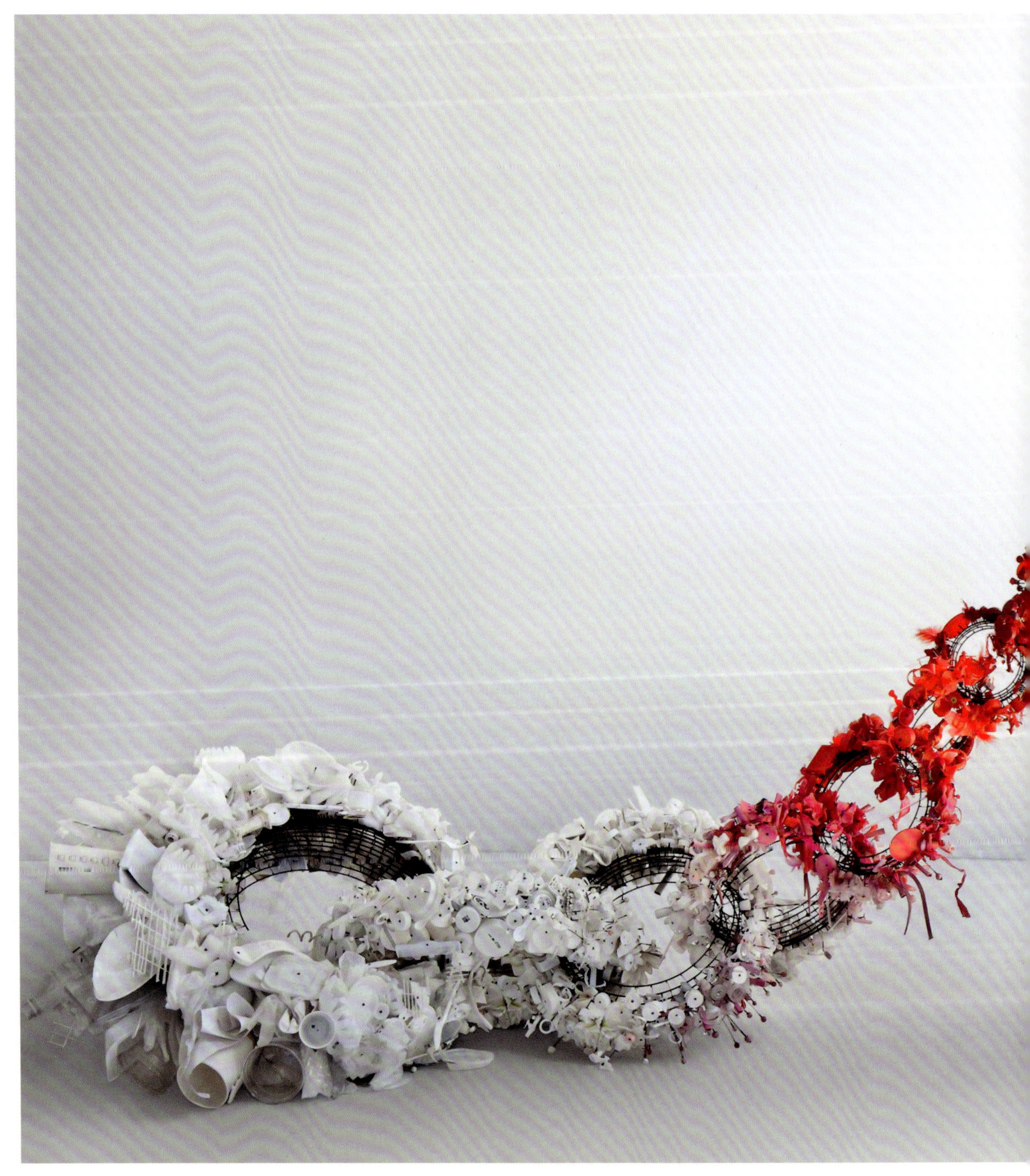

CAT. 120 Susie Ganch, *Drag*, 2012–13, collected detritus and steel, 32 × 32 × 132 in.

CAT. 121 Ron Ho, *Necklace Made for Patti Warashina*, n.d., silver, leather, and Plexiglas with two wood carvings by Julie Harrison and one carved wooden Japanese mask, 10 ½ × 7 ½ × 1 ¼ in. (irreg.)

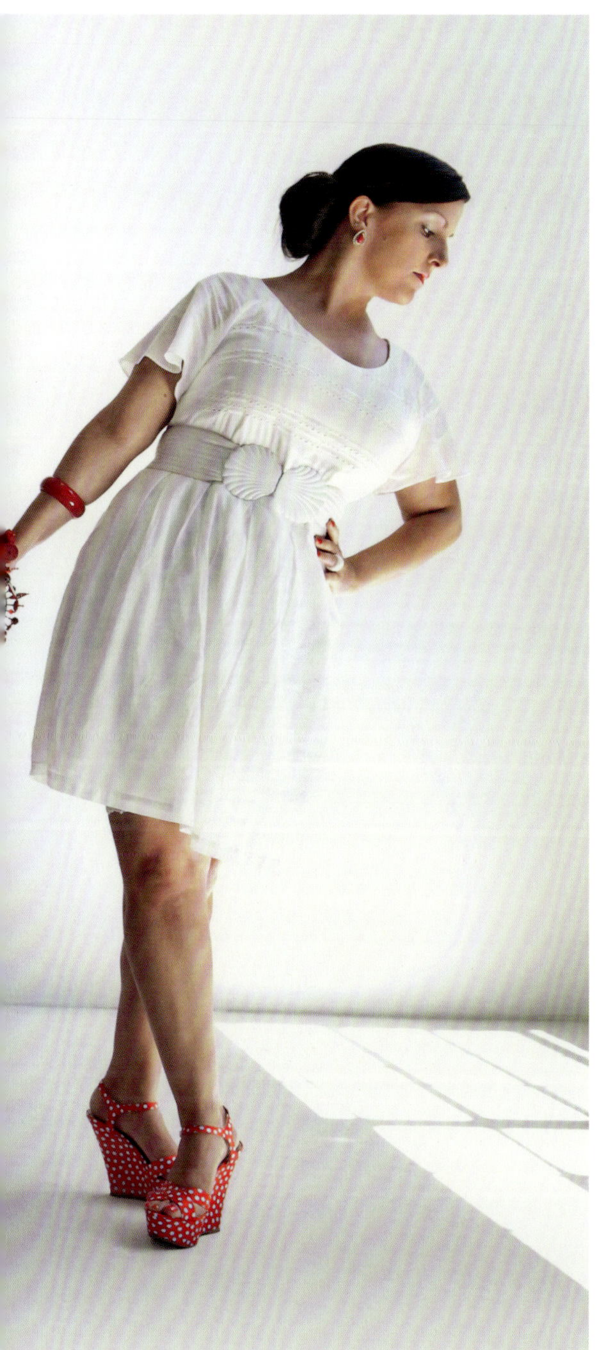

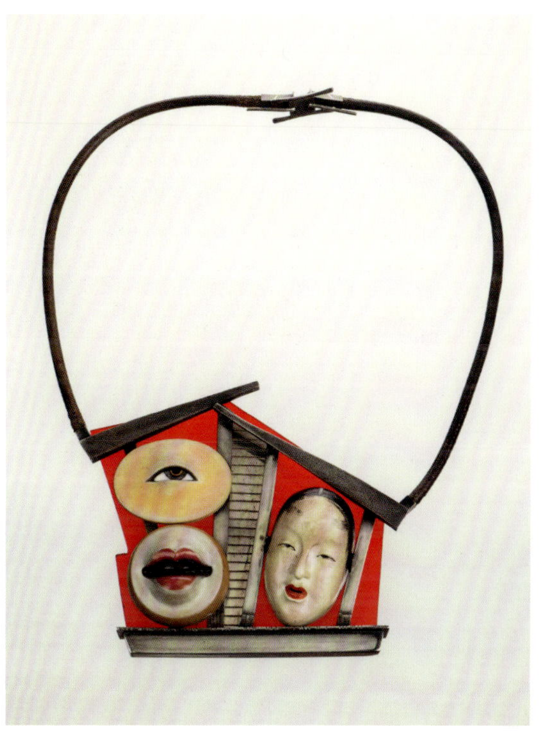

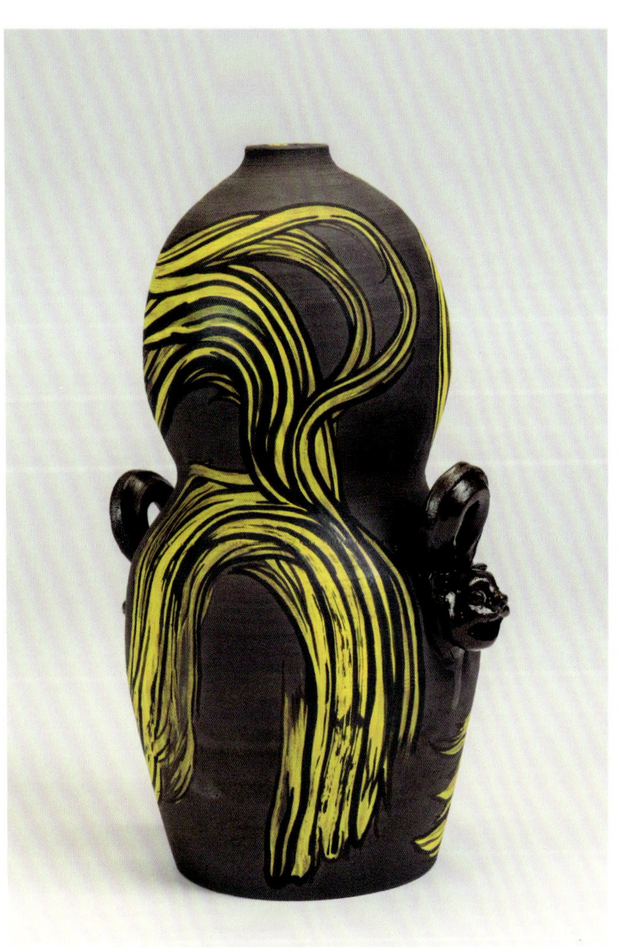

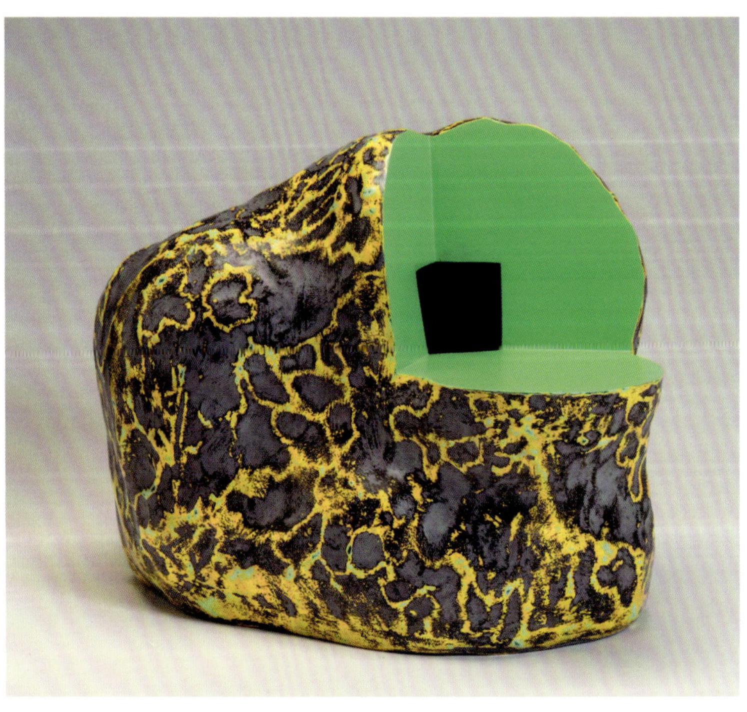

CAT. 122   Jiha Moon,
Yellowave (black) 1, 2020,
black stoneware with
underglaze and glaze,
11 1/8 × 7 1/2 × 5 3/4 in.

CAT. 123   Ken Price,
Nounless, 1989, fired
earthenware with acrylic
paint, 10 1/2 × 14 3/8 ×
10 5/8 in.

CAT. 124 Lauren Mabry,
Glazescape (Green Shade),
2021, earthenware
with slip and glaze,
20 ⅛ × 15 ⅞ × 6 ¾ in.

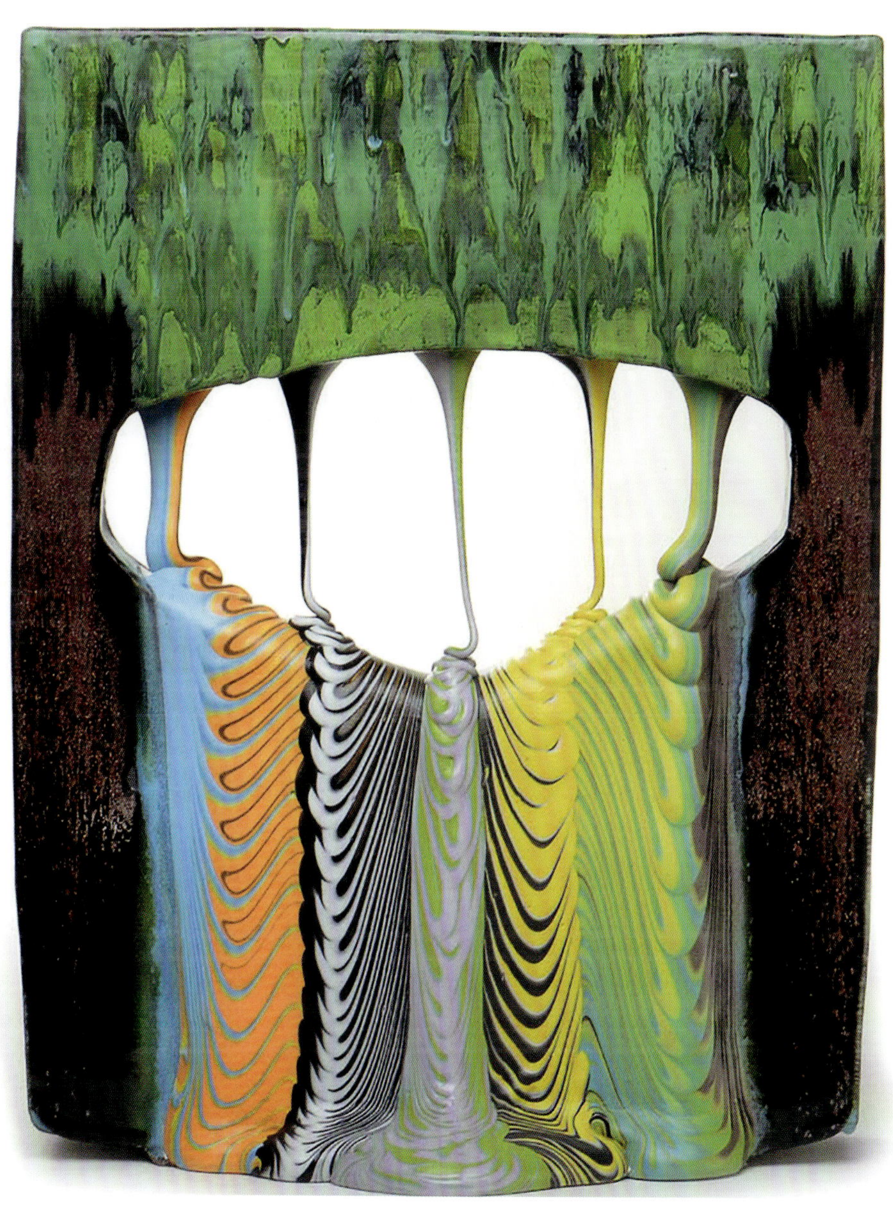

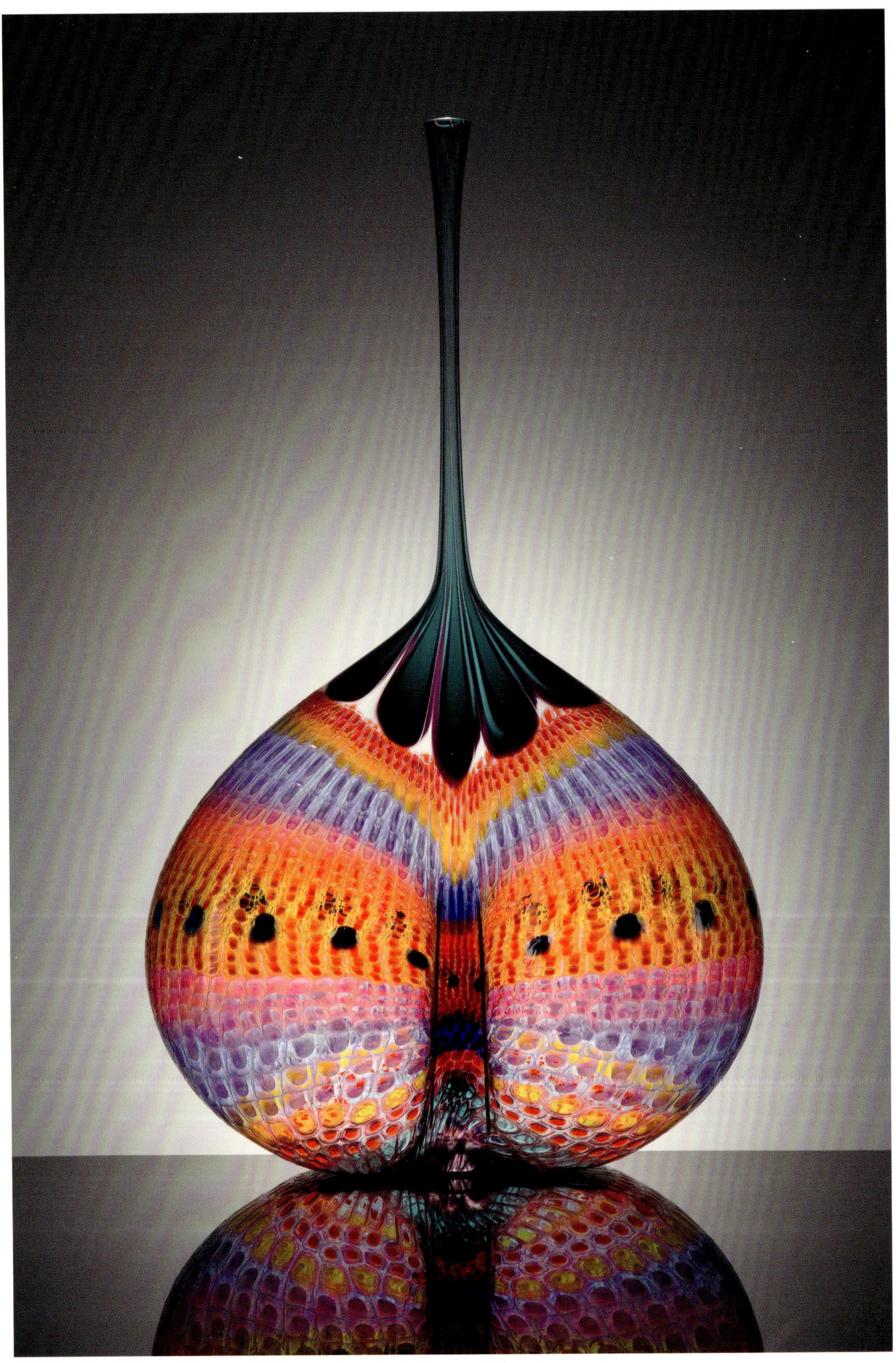

CAT. 125 Stephen Rolfe Powell, *Lascivious Torrid Cleavage*, 2003, blown glass, 41 ¼ × 25 ¼ × 14 ½ in.

CAT. 126 Linda Lopez, *Blue/Purple Ombré with Rocks*, 2018, handbuilt colored porcelain, 8 ¾ × 13 ½ × 5 ½ in.

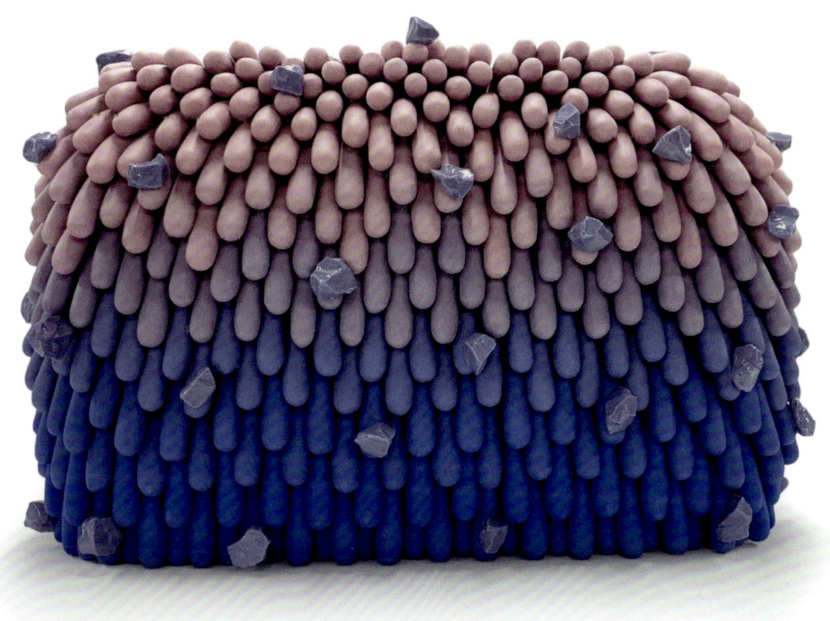

CAT. 127 George Rodriguez, *Mexican American Gothic*, 2019, stoneware with glaze and underglaze, 84 × 60 × 30 in.

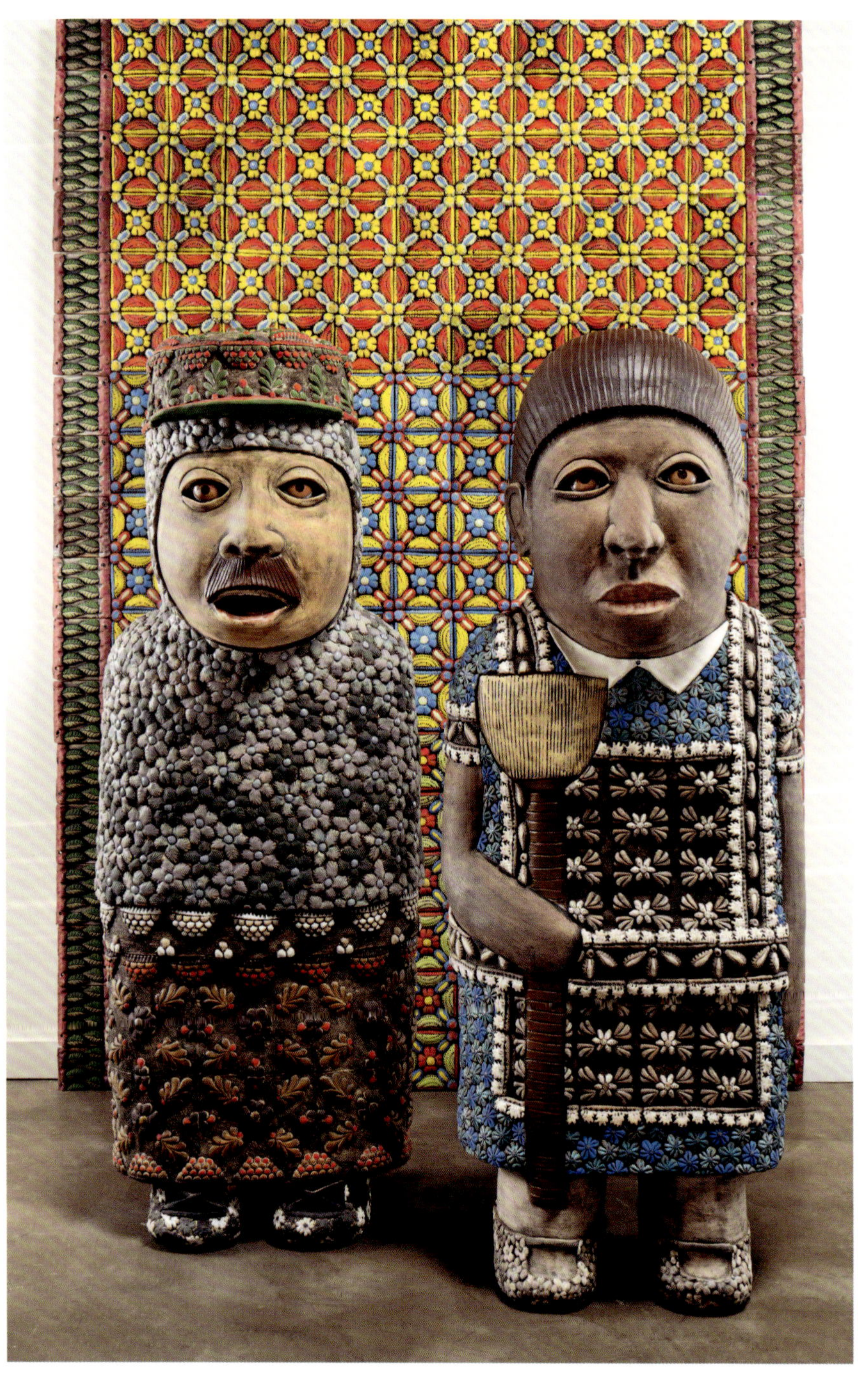

CAT. 128 Dora de Larios,
Opera Singer, ca. 1960,
stoneware with glaze,
18 ⅞ × 15 ⅞ × 8 ⅝ in.

CAT. 129 Akio Takamori,
Alice with Rose, from
the series *Alice/Venus*,
stoneware with underglaze,
approx. 45 × 26 × 22 in.

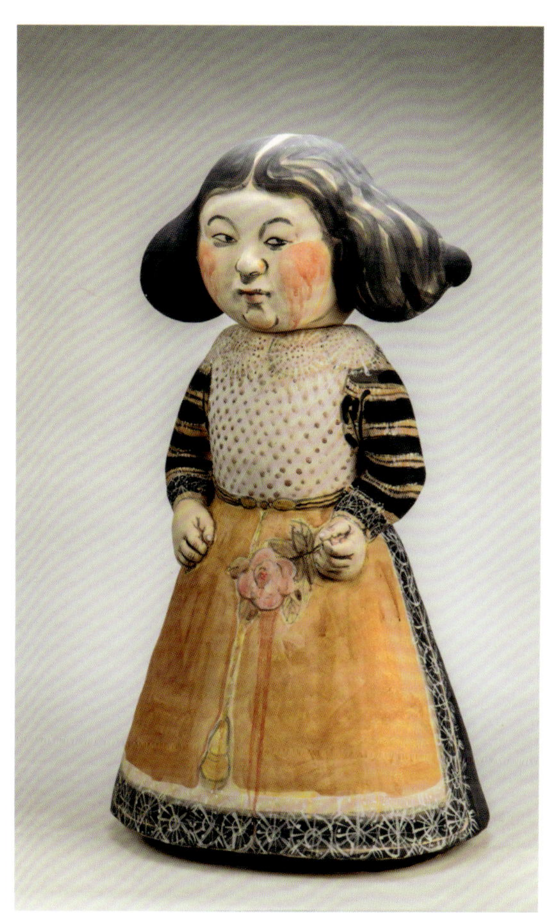

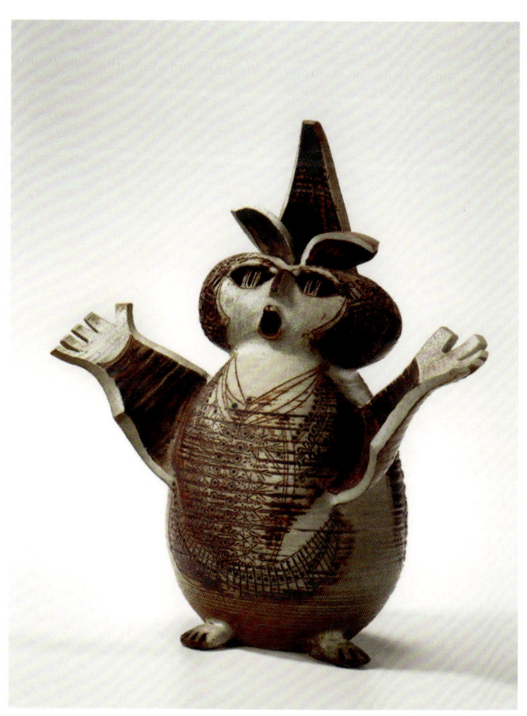

CAT. 130 Jon Eric Riis,
*Heart of Gold, Female
#2* (two views), 2002,
tapestry-woven silk
with metallic thread;
custom mount, tapestry:
29 × 66 ⅝ × 2 ½ in.

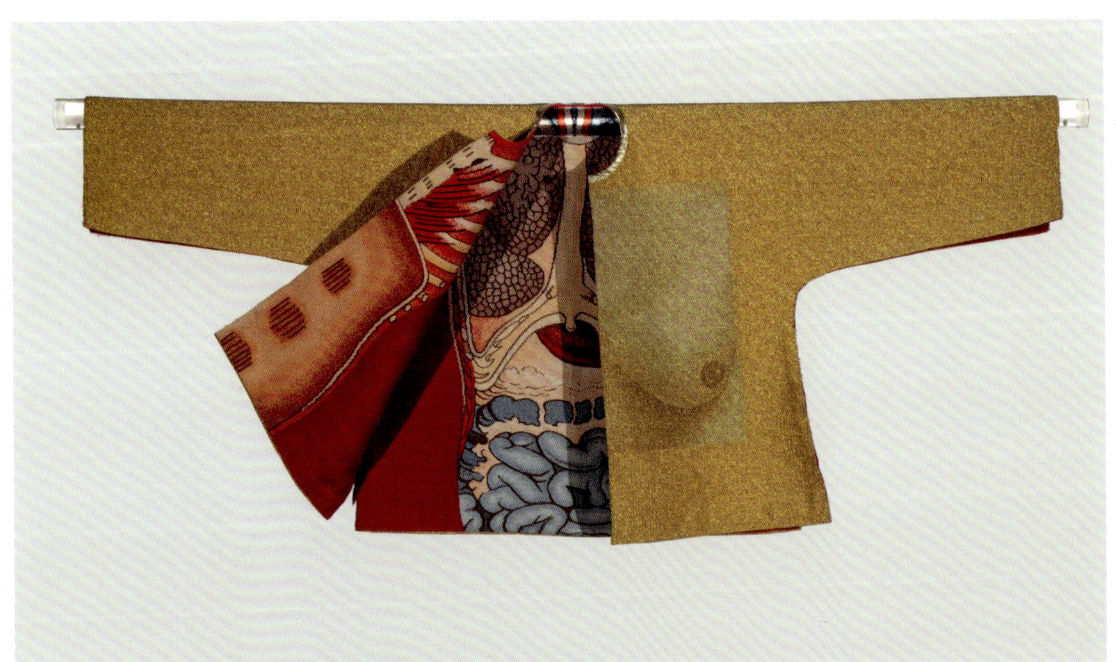

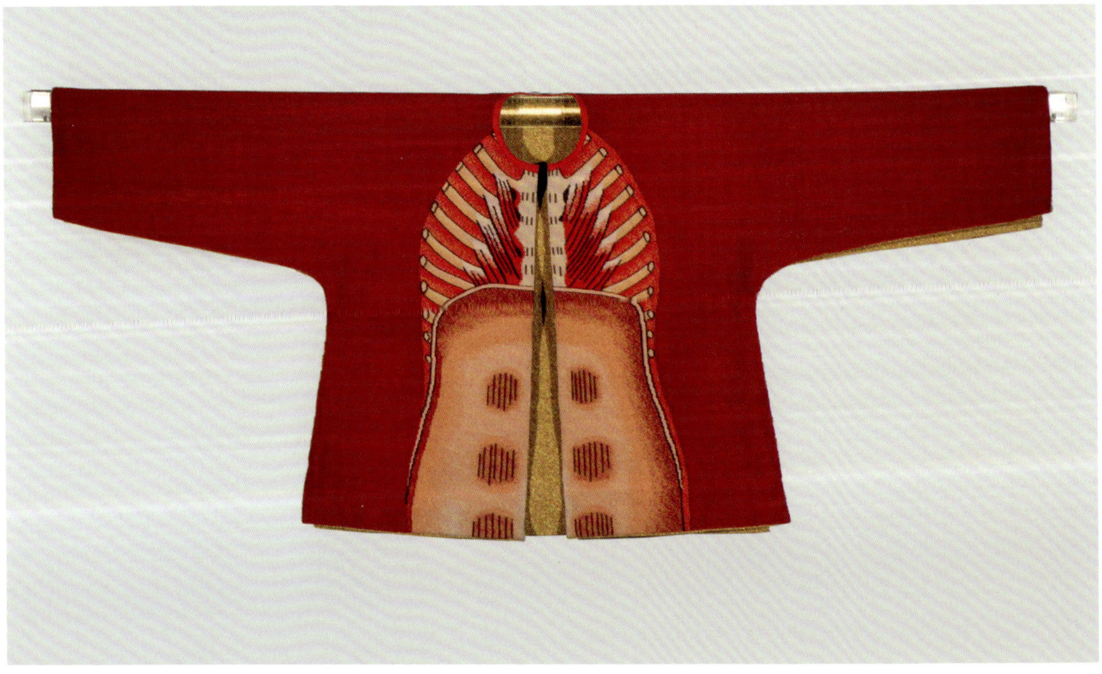

CAT. 131 Kukuli Velarde, *Santa Chingada: The Perfect Little Woman*, 1999–2000, slip-cast ceramic and mixed media, 25 × 18 × 11 ½ in.

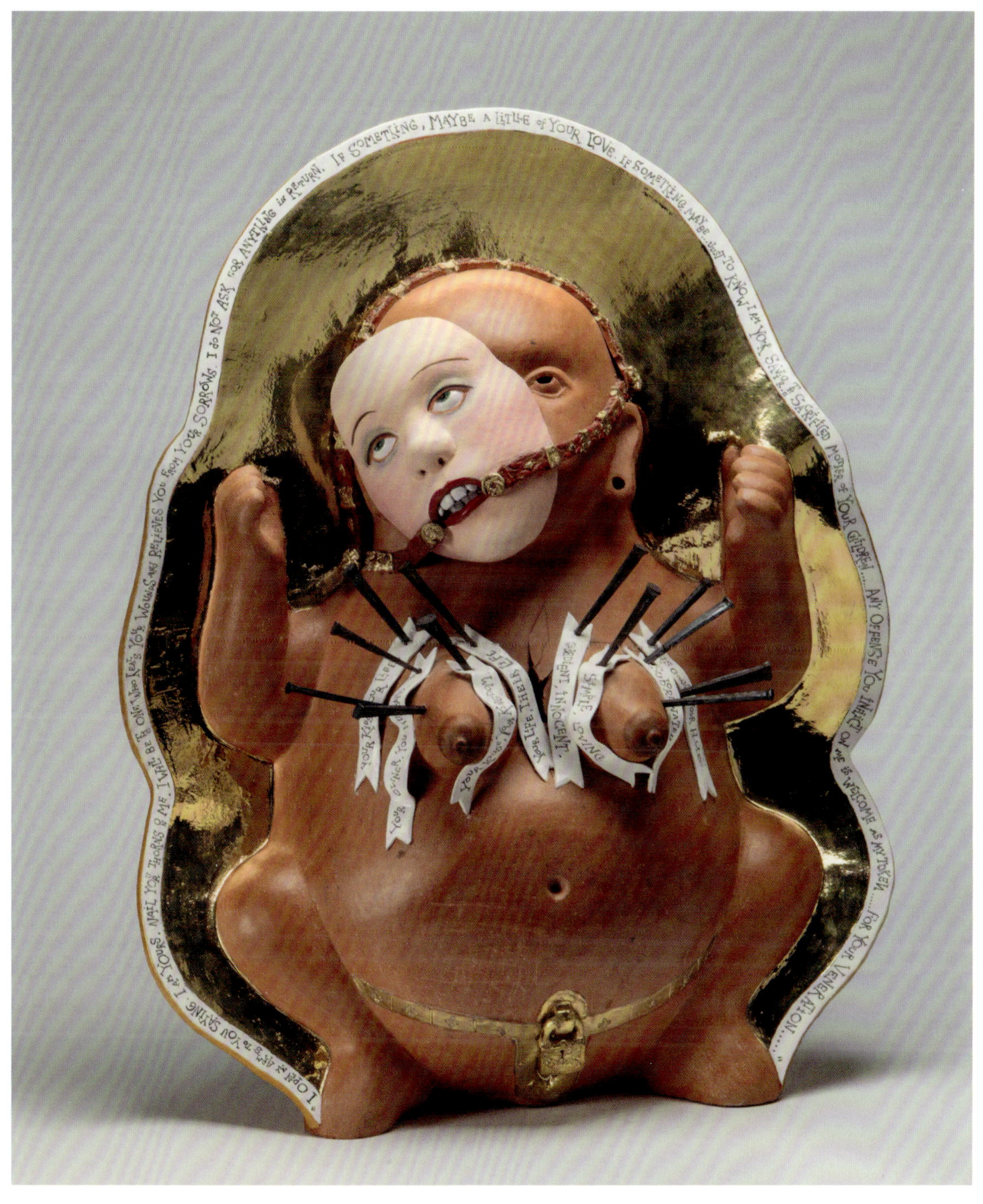

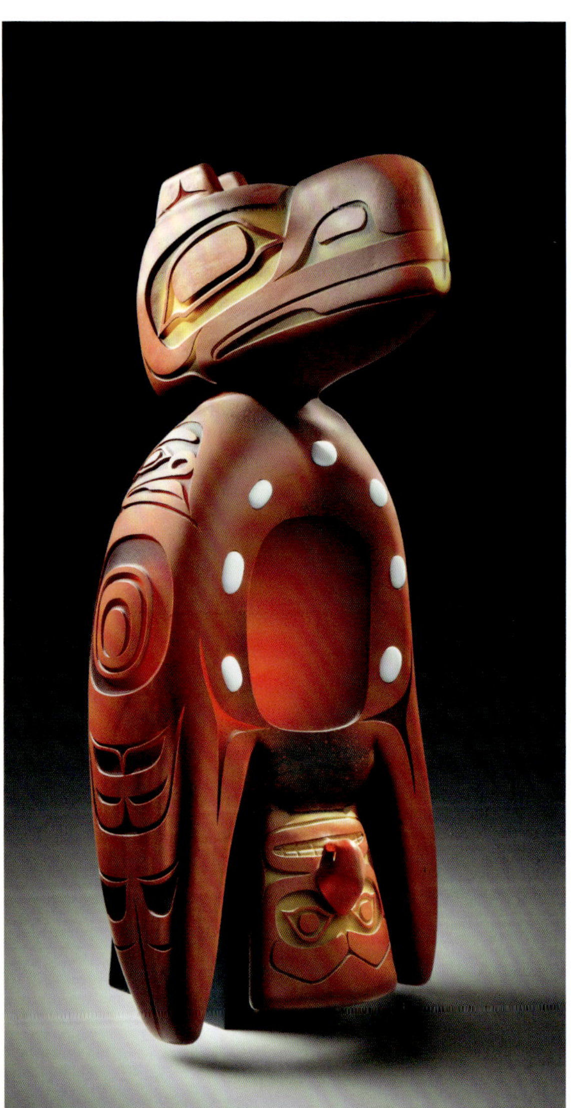

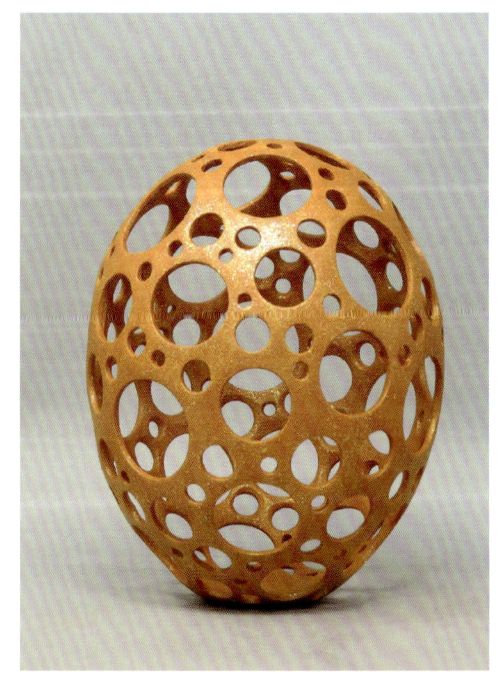

CAT. 132   Preston Singletary, *Thunderbird & Hawk*, 2011, blown and sand-carved glass, without mount: 15 ⅞ × 7 ⅜ × 7 ½ in.

CAT. 133   Hubert Candelario, *Perforated Golden Micaceous Orb*, 2020, micaceous clay, 6 × diam. 4 ¾ in. (irreg.)

CAT. 134   Vivian Wang, *Shanghai Tiger*, 2019, cast glass and stoneware with gemstones and gold leaf on steel base, overall: 31 ⅜ × 12 ⅞ × 14 ¾ in.

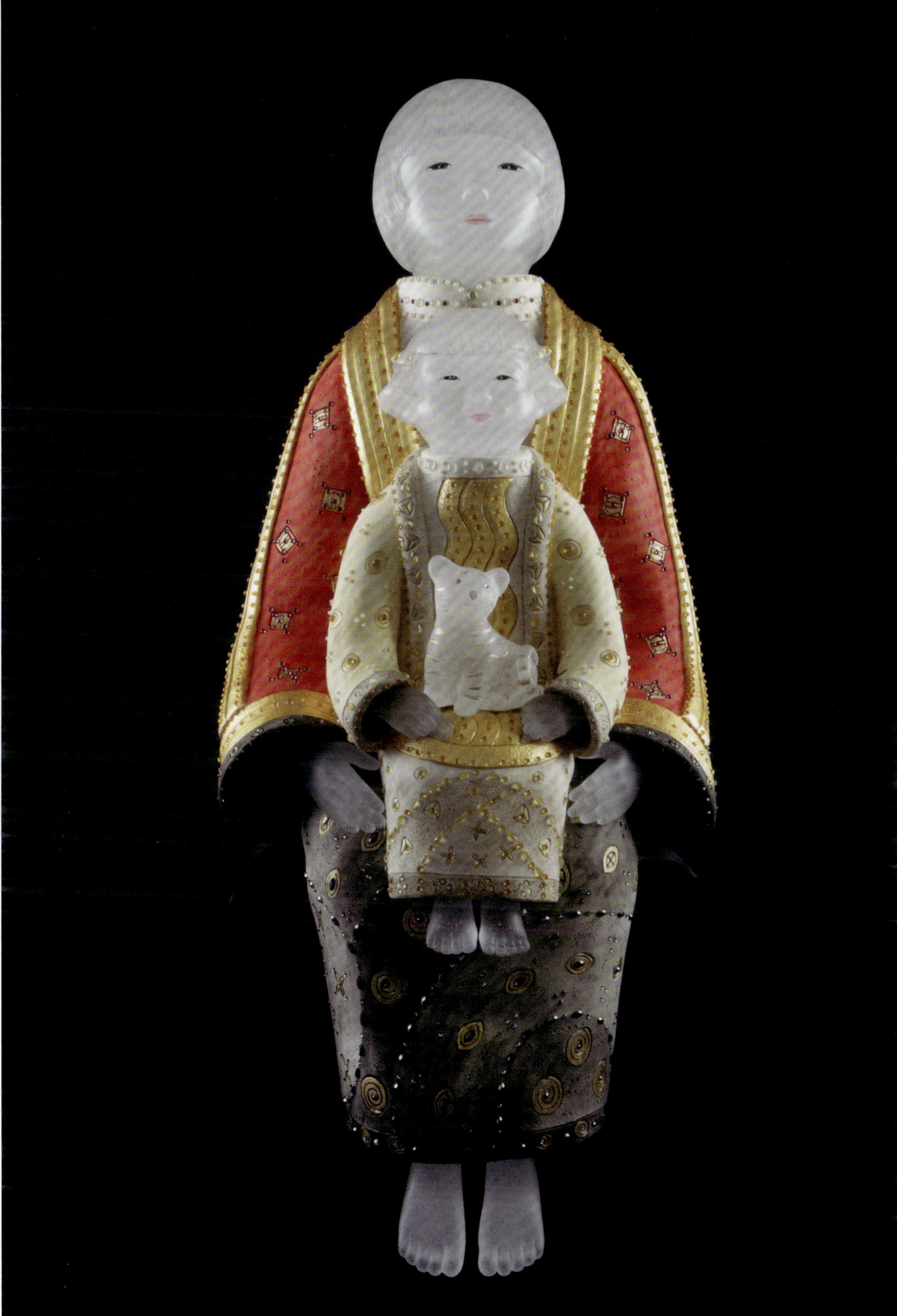

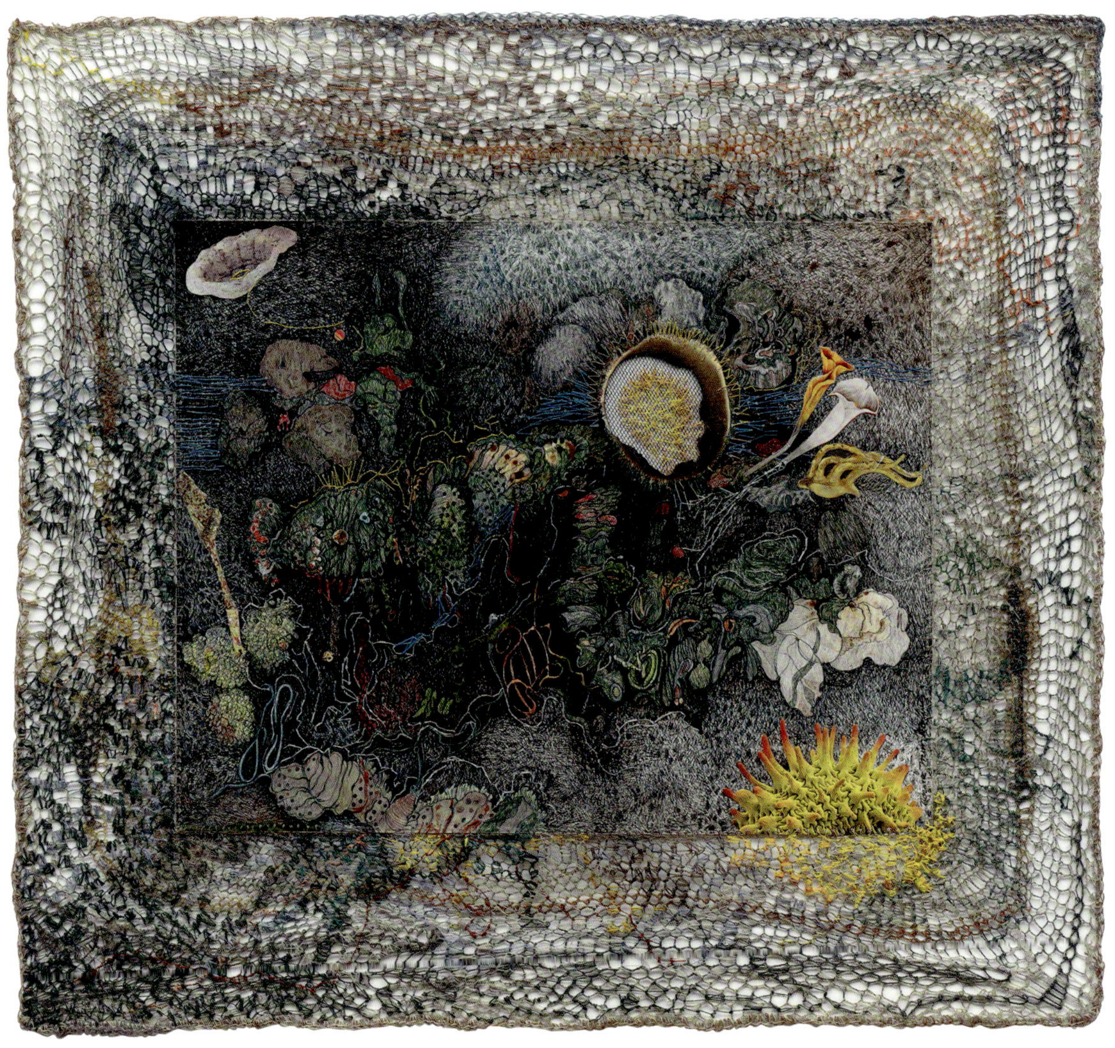

CAT. 135 Norma Minkowitz, *Goodbye, My Friend*, 2018, stitched drawing: pen and ink on paper with stitched and crocheted fiber and collage, 18 ⅛ × 20 ¼ in.

CAT. 136 Joyce Scott,
Yellow #4, 1998, cast and
blown glass with glass
beads, 11 5/8 × 10 1/8 × 5/8 in.

CAT. 137 Linda Sormin,
Ta Saparot (pineapple eyes),
2019, glazed ceramic with
found shards, glitter, and
gold leaf, 13 × 17 × 16 in.

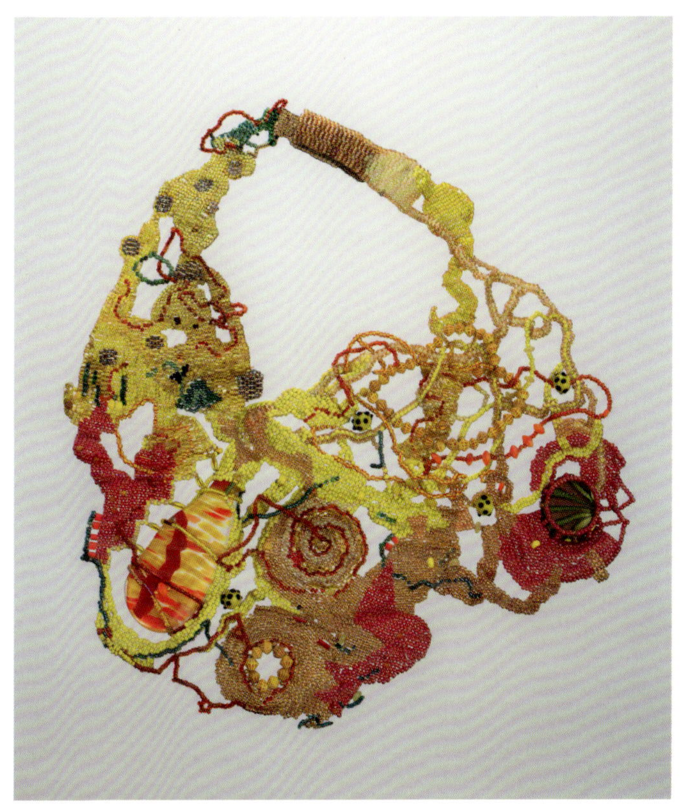

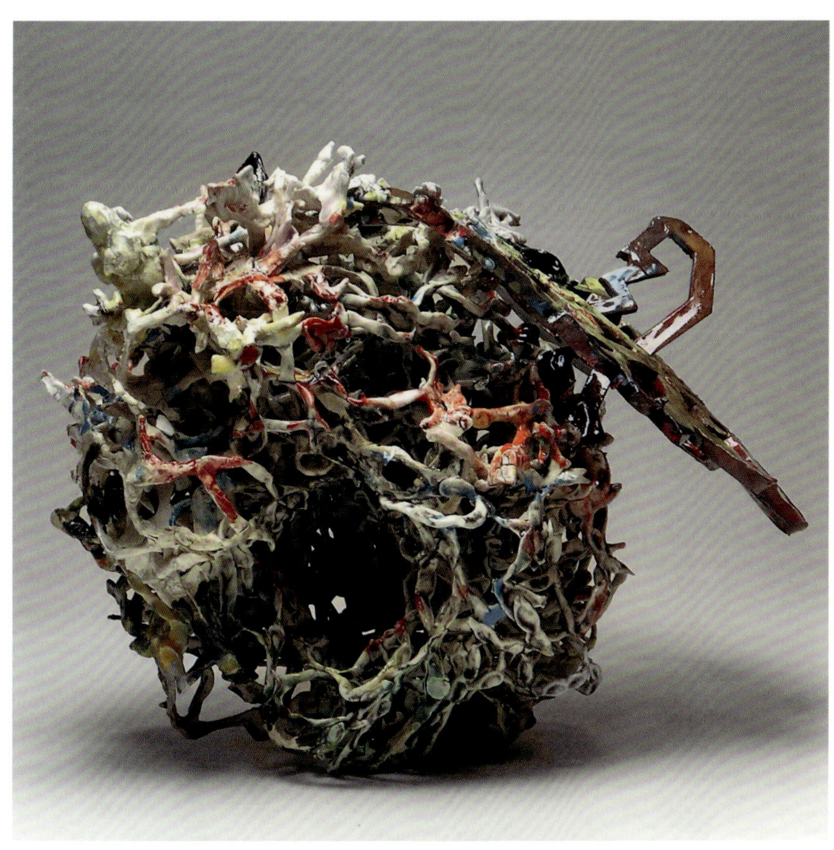

CAT. 138   Sharif Bey,
Louie Bones—Omega, 2017,
earthenware, vitreous
china, and mixed media,
55 × 55 × 3 in.

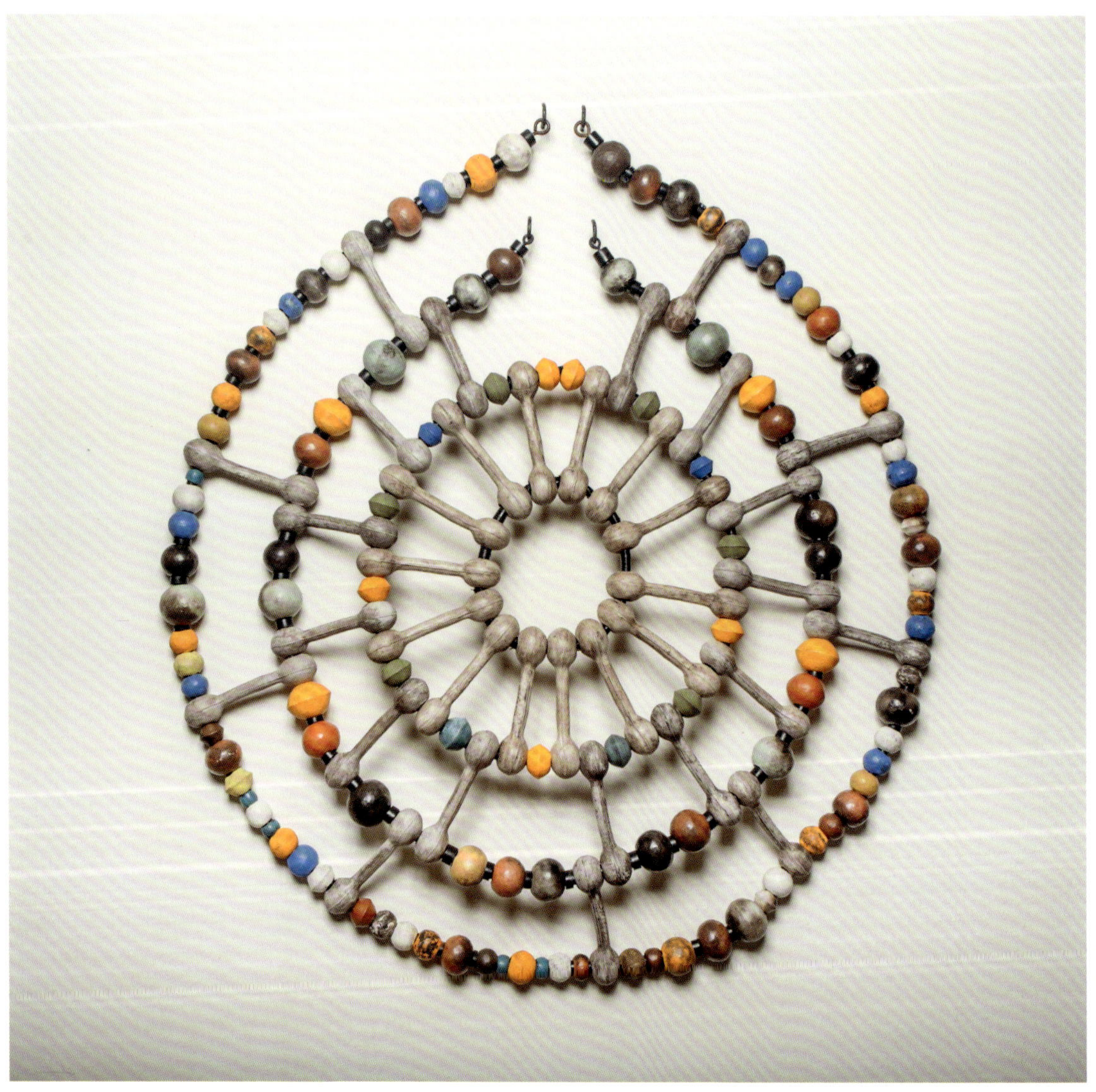

CAT. 139 James Bassler, *Jarrillan*, 2006, wedge-woven linen with indigo and natural dyes, 46 × 46 in.

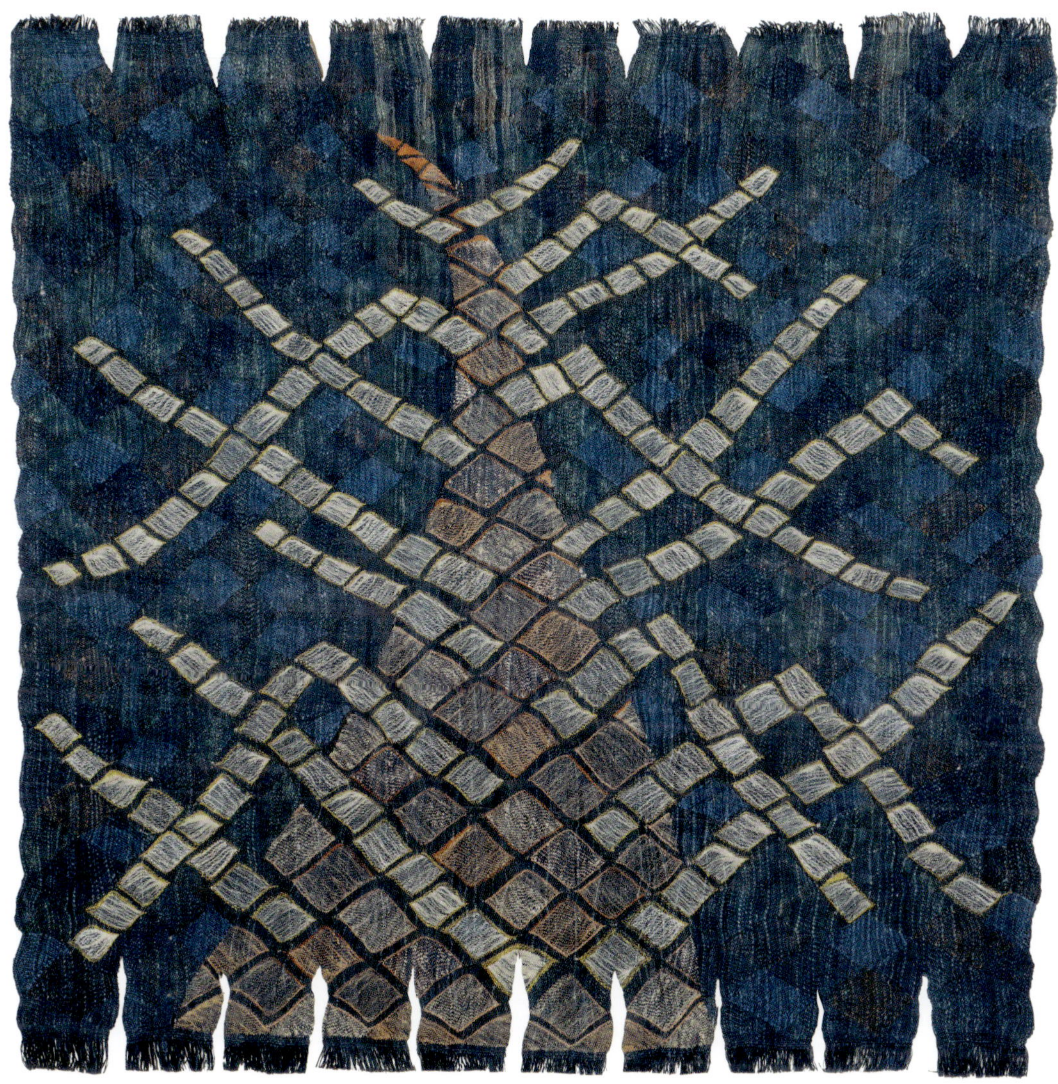

CAT. 140 Marvin Oliver,
Salish Clam Basket,
2008, blown glass
with etched image,
17 3/4 × 18 1/8 × 19 1/4 in.

CAT. 141 Preston
Singletary, *Safe Journey*,
2021, cast and sand-
carved glass on wooden
pedestal, chest:
14 7/8 × 27 1/8 × 16 3/8 in.,
lid: 3 7/8 × 27 1/2 × 16 7/8 in.,
pedestal: 45 5/8 × 28 3/8 ×
17 1/2 in.

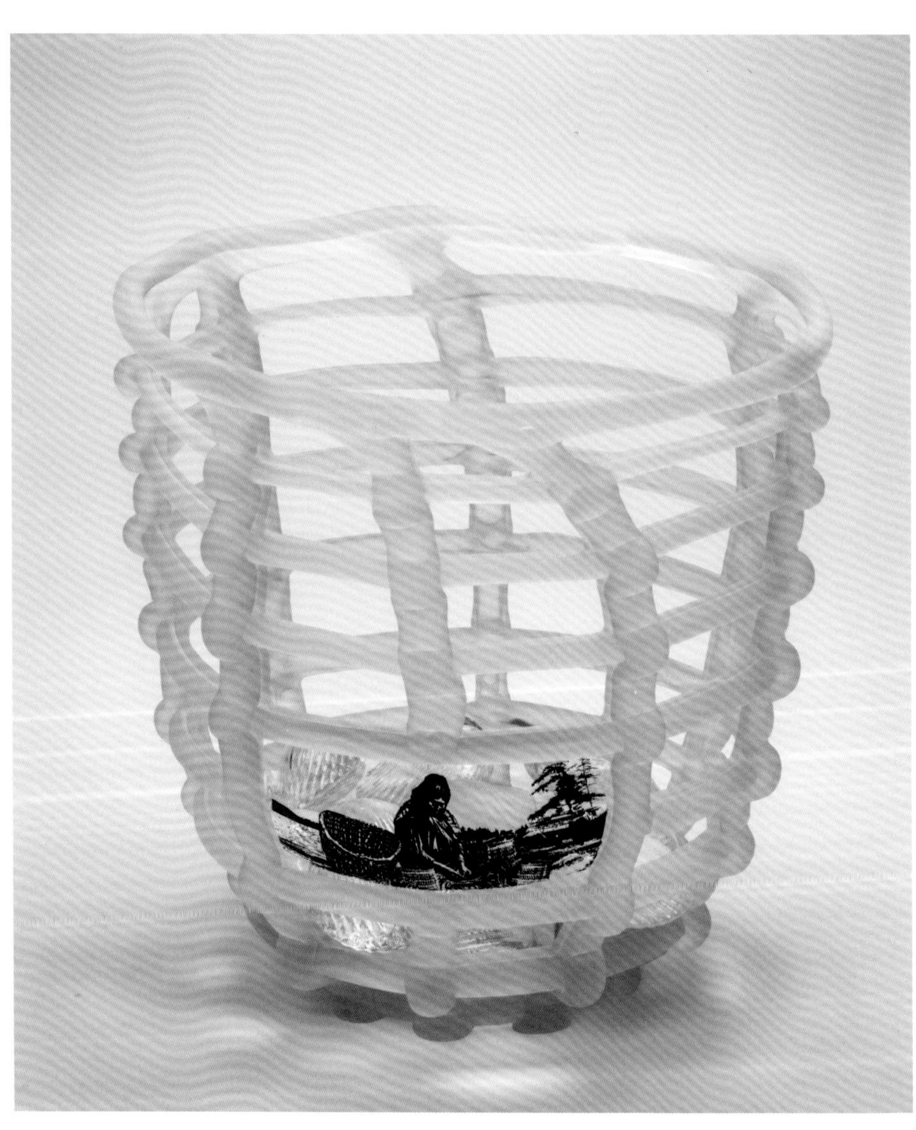

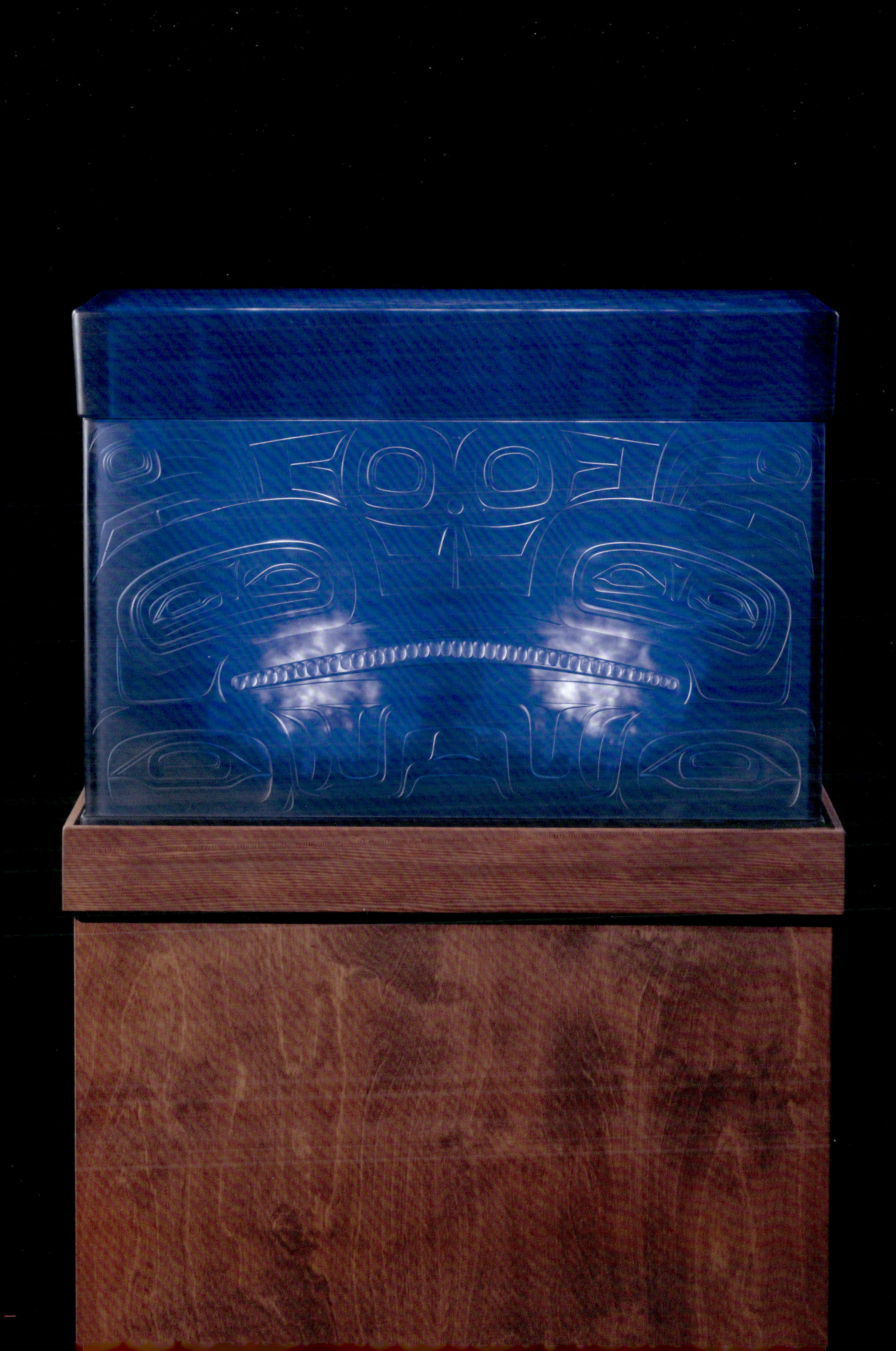

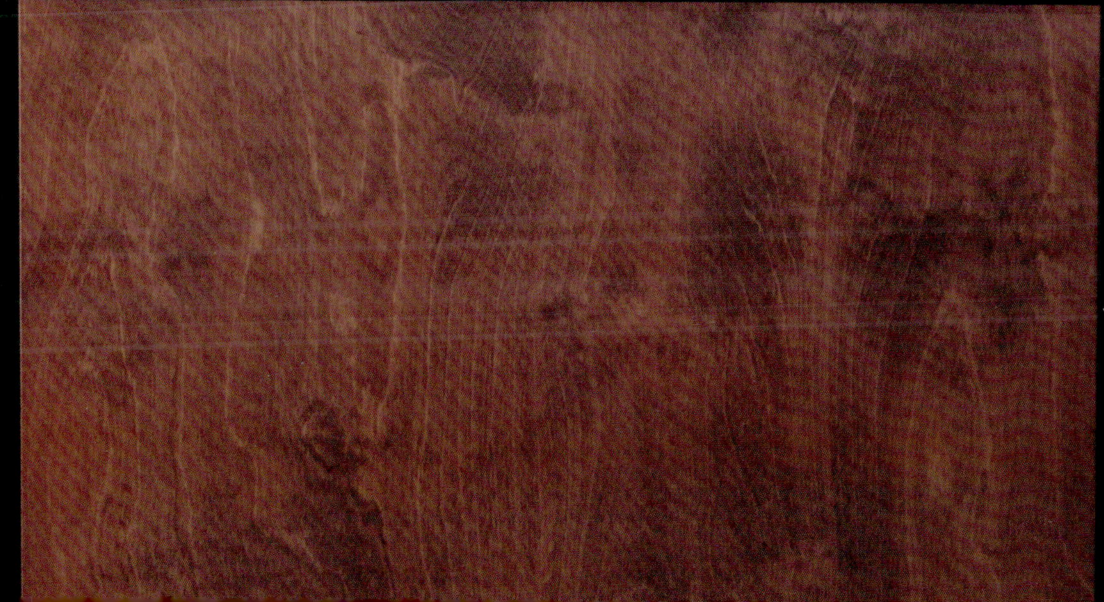

50TH ANNIVERSARY CAMPAIGN CHECKLIST

This checklist contains all works acquired as part of the Renwick Gallery's fiftieth anniversary campaign. The entries are arranged alphabetically by artist, then chronologically, then alphabetically by title. Dimensions are given in inches; height precedes width and depth. All works are in the permanent collection of the Smithsonian American Art Museum unless otherwise noted. Acquisition numbers have been provided for those available at the time of publishing.

Tanya Aguiñiga
b. San Diego, CA, 1978

Metabolizing the Border, 2018–20
analogue VR headset, breath distiller, sound amplifiers, Maglite border torch, "Saint Juan Diego and Our Lady" border cloak, water backpack, and huaraches made of blown, cast, and sculpted glass with rusted metal pieces of US-Mexico border fence, leather, and cotton twine; neoprene wetsuit, glass components made in collaboration with Pilchuck Glass School artisans, dimensions variable and designed to fit the artist
Joint museum purchase with the Cooper Hewitt, Smithsonian Design Museum through the American Women's History Initiative Acquisitions Pool, administered by the Smithsonian American Women's History Initiative
CAT. 28

Corey Alston
b. Mount Pleasant, SC, 1982

From Traditional to Contemporary, 2021
sweetgrass,
33 × diam. 33 in.
Gift of Carolyn L. Mazloomi

Olga de Amaral
b. Bogotá, Colombia, 1932

Montaña #13, 2001
handwoven linen with gold leaf and gesso,
60 × 77 × 1 in.
Promised gift from the collection of Robert and Sharon Buchanan
CAT. 95

Laura Andreson
b. San Bernardino, CA, 1902;
d. Los Angeles, CA, 1999

Bowl, 1939
earthenware with uranium glaze, 4 × diam. 11 7/8 in.
Gift of Forrest L. Merrill,
2021.90.2
CAT. 24

Rudy Autio
b. Butte, MT, 1926;
d. Missoula, MT, 2007

Jet Stream, 1989
stoneware with glaze,
35 3/4 × 36 × 26 in.
Promised gift from the collection of Colleen and John Kotelly

Carolyn Morris Bach
b. Lansing, MI, 1958

Untitled (Necklace), 2005
fine and sterling silver, copper, cow bone, fossilized ivory, ebony, and goat hair bristles,
16 1/2 × 5 1/2 × 2 1/2 in.
Gift of Sheldon Palley and children Lisa Palley, Donna Kass, and Kevin Palley in memory of Myrna Palley

Boris Bally
b. Chicago, IL, 1961

Tray, 2003
recycled traffic sign,
diam. 17 1/2 × 1 1/2 in.
Gift of Lloyd E. Herman, founding director and director emeritus of the Renwick Gallery (1971–1986),
2021.25.2

James Bassler
b. Santa Monica, CA, 1933

Jarrillan, 2006
wedge-woven linen with indigo and natural dyes, 46 × 46 in.
Gift from the collection of Clemmer and David Montague, 2021.61.1
CAT. 139

Garry Knox Bennett
b. Alameda, CA, 1934

Cubist, 2014
brass, Nevamar laminate, rock, and silver plating,
9 1/8 × 7 1/8 × 4 in.
Gift of Fleur S. Bresler,
2021.48.29

Lanny Bergner
b. Anacortes, WA, 1952

Celestial Body, 2005
bronze, brass, and aluminum, 63 × diam. 15 in.
Gift of Judith S. Weisman,
2021.62
CAT. 32

Guillermo Bert
b. Santiago, Chile, 1959;
based in Los Angeles, CA

Mapuche Portal #3,
from the series *Encoded Textiles*, 2014
wool with natural dyes; QR code to digital audio files of Mapuche Traditional Stories narrated by poet Graciala Huinao,
80 1/2 × 58 1/4 × 2 1/4 in.,
tapestry woven by Anita Paillamil, Mapuche weaver
Gift of Frances Spivy-Weber and Michael L. Weber, Denise M. Wynn, Michele A. Manatt and Wolfram Anders, and Donna M. Gottlieb
CAT. 107

Sharif Bey
b. Pittsburgh, PA, 1974

Louie Bones – Omega, 2017
earthenware, vitreous
china, and mixed media,
55 × 55 × 3 in.
Gift of Maureen Fennessy
Bousa and Edward P. Bousa,
2019.19
CAT. 138

Jerry Bleem
b. Chicago, IL, 1954

Ritual Language, 2002
found paper with
staples, wax, ink, acrylic
paint, and metallic foil,
8 × 21 3/8 × 12 3/8 in.
Gift from the collection
of Clemmer and David
Montague, 2020.76.1

Cynthia Bringle
b. Memphis, TN, 1939

Tea Pitcher, 2010
stoneware with salt glaze,
11 × diam. 8 in.
Gift from the collection
of Clemmer and David
Montague, 2021.61.2

Daniel Brush
b. Cleveland, OH, 1947

Diamond Egg (#90), 1991–93
24-karat gold and steel
with diamonds, overall:
2 × 1 1/2 × 1 1/2 in.
Gift of Fleur S. Bresler
CAT. 96

Bisa Butler
b. Orange, NJ, 1978

Harlem Hellfighters, 2021–22
pieced, appliquéd, and
quilted cottons, silk, wool,
and velvet, 109 1/2 × 156 in.
Gift of David Bonderman

Hubert Candelario
San Felipe Pueblo
b. Albuquerque, NM, 1965

*Perforated Golden
Micaceous Orb*, 2020
micaceous clay,
6 × diam. 4 3/4 in. (irreg.)
Museum purchase
through the Howard Kottler
Endowment for Ceramic Art,
2020.65
CAT. 133

Nick Cave
b. Fulton, MO, 1959

Soundsuit, 2010
fabric with beads and
sequins, 98 × 27 × 14 in.
Gift of Fleur S. Bresler,
2021.48.1
CAT. 91

David Chatt
b. Des Moines, IA, 1960

Love, Dad, 2012–13
glass beads and thread with
wooden table and thirty-year
collection of letters from the
artist's father, overall:
47 1/2 × 16 1/2 × 16 1/2 in.
Museum purchase through
the Kenneth R. Trapp
Acquisition Fund, 2021.18.1
CAT. 34

Dale Chihuly
b. Tacoma, WA, 1941
in collaboration with Seaver
Leslie and Flora Mace

*Ulysses Cylinder
"Wayfort,"* from the series
Irish Cylinders, 1975
blown glass, 10 × diam. 7 in.
Promised gift from the
collection of Colleen and
John Kotelly

Kelly Church
Ottawa and Pottawatomi
b. Allegan, MI, 1967

*Sustaining Traditions—
Digital Memories*, 2018
black ash and sweetgrass
with Rit dye, copper, vial of
EAB (emerald ash borer),
and flash drive containing
black ash teachings, overall:
9 1/2 × diam. 4 1/2 in.
Museum purchase through
the Decorative Arts
and Crafts Endowment,
2020.49A–B
CAT. 35

Sharon Church
b. Richland, WA, 1948

Oh No!, 2007
carved Castello boxwood
with enamel paints, lacquer,
14-karat yellow gold, old
European–cut diamonds, and
epoxy, 6 1/4 × 3 1/4 × 2 in.
Gift of Fleur S. Bresler
CAT. 118

Sonya Clark
b. Washington, DC, 1967
in collaboration with
The Fabric Workshop and
Museum, Philadelphia

Monumental, 2019
woven linen with madder dye
and tea stain, 180 × 360 in.
Museum purchase through
the American Women's
History Initiative Acquisitions
Pool, administered by the
Smithsonian American
Women's History Initiative,
the Luisita L. and Franz H.
Denghausen Endowment,
and the Kenneth R. Trapp
Acquisition Fund
CAT. 36

Richard Cleaver
b. Camden, NJ, 1952

Head and Shoulders, 2007
handbuilt ceramic with
freshwater pearls, garnets,
Swarovski crystals, carnelian
sapphires, bronze wire,
metal, gold leaf, and oil
paint, 11 1/4 × 7 1/2 × 4 5/8 in.
Gift of Robert and Sharon
Buchanan, 2021.41.3
CAT. 94

David Harper Clemons
b. El Paso, TX, 1973

The Weight of Deferred Gratification, 2019
sterling silver, stainless steel, brass, glass, and mahogany with corn, wild rice, and wheat, overall box, closed: 15 × 9 × 5 in.
Gift of the James Renwick Alliance in honor of the 50th anniversary of the Renwick Gallery and the 40th anniversary of the Alliance
CAT. 9

Lia Cook
b. Ventura, CA, 1942

Presence/Absence: Touches II, 1998
digital jacquard–woven cotton and rayon, 58 × 40 in.
Gift of Marc and Diane Grainer, 2021.77.2
CAT. 92

Michael Cooper
b. Richmond, CA, 1943

Modified, 2010
painted hard maple, steel, aluminum, pneumatic system, engine, and mechanics, 33 × 48 × 67 in.
Gift of Bannus and Cecily Hudson
CAT. 114

Cristina Córdova
b. Boston, MA, 1976

Araña, 2004
handbuilt ceramic with glaze and stain,
27 1/4 × 15 1/8 × 9 3/8 in.
Gift of Lorne E. Lassiter and Gary P. Ferraro, 2021.59
CAT. 93

Carolyn Crump
b. Detroit, MI, 1960

BLM-4, 2020
machine-quilted cotton with cotton thread and paint, 12 × 7 × 6 1/2 in.
Museum purchase through the Kenneth R. Trapp Acquisition Fund, 2021.15
CAT. 87

George Floyd, 2021
machine-quilted cotton with cotton thread and paint, 10 × 9 5/8 × 3 1/4 in.
Gift of Carolyn L. Mazloomi, 2021.64.1

Mermaid, 2021
machine-quilted cotton with cotton thread and paint, 10 × 8 7/8 × 3 1/2 in.
Gift of Carolyn L. Mazloomi, 2021.64.2

School Girl, 2021
machine-quilted cotton with cotton thread and paint, 10 1/8 × 9 1/2 × 3 1/2 in.
Gift of Carolyn L. Mazloomi, 2021.64.3

Frank E. Cummings III
b. Los Angeles, CA, 1938

Carousel: Age of Awareness, 1994
walnut and ebony with black onyx, 10-karat gold, and pearl rubellite,
16 1/2 × diam. 12 in.
Gift of Fleur S. Bresler, 2021.48.26

Rick Dillingham
b. Lake Forest, IL, 1952;
d. Santa Fe, NM, 1994

Large Silver Globe, 1978
reassembled raku-fired earthenware with glaze and silver leaf,
12 7/8 × diam. 15 7/8 in.
Gift of Robert and Sharon Buchanan, 2021.41.4
CAT. 31

Virginia Dotson
b. Newton, MA, 1943

Wood Bowl, n.d.
cherry with stain,
3 7/8 × diam. 8 in.
Gift of Dr. Joel Mulhauser, 2020.6

Ruth Duckworth
b. Hamburg, Germany, 1919;
d. Chicago, IL, 2009

Untitled (Mama Pot), 2007
stoneware, 20 × diam. 22 in.
Promised gift from the collection of Colleen and John Kotelly

Alicia Eggert
b. Camden, NJ, 1981

This Present Moment, 2019–20
neon, custom controller, and steel, 144 × 180 × 48 in.
edition 2 of 3
neon produced by Amy Enlow, fabrication assistance by Teresa Larrabee, Paolo Tamez-Buccino, Jaelyn Kotzur, and James Akers
Museum purchase through the Renwick General Acquisitions Fund, 2021.4
CAT. 37

Micah Evans
b. Cashmere, WA, 1975

Raphine, 2015
lampworked borosilicate glass, 11 3/4 × 7 3/4 × 9 3/4 in.
Gift of Fleur S. Bresler, 2021.48.27
CAT. 112

Dustin Farnsworth
b. Lansing, MI, 1983

The King Is Dead, 2015
basswood, poplar, and mild steel with polychrome, 56 × 20 × 18 in.
Gift of Fleur S. Bresler, 2021.48.28

Joe Feddersen
Colville Confederated Tribes, Okanagan and Arrow Lakes
b. Omak, WA, 1953

Horses and Deer, 2020
blown and sand-carved glass, 13 1/2 × 11 3/4 × 10 3/8 in.
Museum purchase through the Kenneth R. Trapp Acquisition Fund, 2021.34
CAT. 116

Jeremy Frey
Passamaquoddy
b. Indian Township, ME, 1978

Large Turquoise Urchin Basket, 2019
brown ash and sweetgrass, overall: 5 1/4 × diam. 11 1/2 in.
Museum purchase through the Kenneth R. Trapp Acquisition Fund, 2020.55
CAT. 14

Viola Frey
b. Lodi, CA, 1933;
d. Oakland, CA, 2004

*Untitled V Family
(Humpty Dumpty)*, 1995
handbuilt ceramic
with glaze, overall:
28 3/8 × 19 3/4 × 12 7/8 in.
Gift of Robert and Sharon
Buchanan, 2021.41.1

Susie Ganch
b. Appleton, WI, 1971

Drag, 2012–13
collected detritus and steel,
32 × 32 × 132 in.
Gift of the James Renwick
Alliance in honor of
Robyn Kennedy, 2021.81
CAT. 120

Mary Giles
b. St. Paul, MN, 1944;
d. Stillwater, MN, 2018

Metallic Horizon, 2013
waxed linen with hammered
tin and coated copper,
overall: 16 × 32 × 6 in.
Gift of Fleur S. Bresler,
2021.48.3

David Gilhooly
b. Auburn, CA, 1943;
d. Newport, OR, 2013

Eight Bean Stew, 1982
white earthenware with
glaze, 5 1/2 × 14 1/2 × 9 in.
Promised gift from the
collection of Colleen and
John Kotelly

Shan Goshorn
Eastern Band Cherokee
b. Baltimore, MD, 1957;
d. Tulsa, OK, 2018

Song of Sorrow, 2015
watercolor paper splints
with ink and acrylic paint,
overall: 9 × diam. 8 1/4 in.
Museum purchase through
the Kenneth R. Trapp
Acquisition Fund, 2021.32
CAT. 108

Donté K. Hayes
b. Baltimore, MD, 1975

Initiate, 2020
handbuilt black
stoneware, overall:
19 1/8 × 16 5/8 × 17 1/4 in.
Museum purchase through
the Kenneth R. Trapp
Acquisition Fund, 2021.5
CAT. 106

Carla Hemlock
Kanienkeháka (Mohawk)
b. Kahnawake, Quebec,
Canada, 1961

Our Destruction, 2019
wool stroud cloth with wool,
glass beads, Swarovski
crystals, and sequins,
34 1/8 × 30 5/8 × 7/8 in.
Museum purchase through
the Kenneth R. Trapp
Acquisition Fund, 2021.10
CAT. 88

Ron Ho
b. Honolulu, HI, 1936;
d. Seattle, WA, 2017

*Necklace Made for Patti
Warashina*, n.d.
silver, leather, and
Plexiglas with two wood
carvings by Julie Harrison
and one carved wooden
Japanese mask,
10 1/2 × 7 1/2 × 1 1/4 in. (irreg.)
Gift of Patti Warashina,
2021.86.1
CAT. 121

Lisa Holt
Cochiti Pueblo
b. Cochiti Pueblo, NM, 1980

Harlan Reano
Santo Domingo/Kewa Pueblo
b. Kewa Pueblo, NM, 1978

Untitled Pot, 2021
earthenware with acrylic
paint, 14 1/8 × diam. 13 5/8 in.
Museum purchase through
the Howard Kottler
Endowment for Ceramic
Art, 2021.96
CAT. 21

Timothy Horn
b. Melbourne, Australia,
1961; resides Provincetown,
MA, and Burlington, VT

Gorgonia 17, 2020
nickel-plated bronze and
mirrored blown glass,
49 × 72 × 12 in.
Museum purchase through
the Renwick General
Acquisitions Fund, 2021.80

Thomas Hucker
b. Bryn Mawr, PA, 1955
in collaboration with
Silas Kopf

Dearest Sally Chair, 2010
walnut, ash, and cherry with
marquetry, 32 × 20 × 20 in.
Gift of Fleur S. Bresler,
2021.48.12
CAT. 17

Katie Hudnall
b. Alexandria, VA, 1979

Nut Case, 2019
reclaimed wood with
found hardware and
fasteners, industrial felt,
and 178 acorns, closed:
40 × 30 × 20 in.
Museum purchase through
the Kenneth R. Trapp
Acquisition Fund, 2021.21
CAT. 8

Homei Iseyama
b. Japan, 1890;
d. Oakland, CA, 1975

Teapot and Cup, 1939–45
carved found slate, teapot
with lid: 4 5/8 × 6 7/8 × 5 in.,
teacup: 1 1/4 × diam. 2 in.
Gift of Aiko Iseyama and
Family, 2021.75A–C
CAT. 26

Janel Jacobson
b. Minneapolis, MN, 1950

#288 Friends, 1995
purpleheart and deer
antler with amber, gold
leaf, African blackwood,
and deer antler inlay,
4 1/4 × 1 3/4 × 1 3/8 in.
Gift of S. Fleur Bresler,
2021.48.17

#335 Rat, 2001
African blackwood with
black Plexiglas inlay,
1 5/8 × 1 1/8 × 1 1/16 in.
Gift of Fleur S. Bresler,
2021.48.21

#362 Night Stalker, 2003
boxwood with black
Plexiglass inlay,
3 5/8 × 1 5/8 × 1 1/4 in.
Gift of Fleur S. Bresler,
2021.48.15

*#405 Mouse & Pumpkin
Seeds*, 2007
Japanese boxwood,
1 11/16 × 1 1/2 × 1 1/2 in.
Gift of Fleur S. Bresler,
2021.48.20

#426 Juniper Toad, 2008
Ukraine juniper with
Baltic amber inlay,
1 3/8 × 2 1/8 × 1 3/4 in.
Gift of Fleur S. Bresler,
2021.48.14

#494 Long Bean Spoon, 2013
katalox, 6 1/8 × 15/16 × 7/16 in.
Gift of Fleur S. Bresler,
2021.48.18

*#505 Oak Savanna
Sentinel*, 2014
boxwood with acrylic
paint, gold and silver leaf
powder, and nail lacquer,
6 × 3 × 2 1/8 in.
Gift of Fleur S. Bresler,
2021.48.13
CAT. 22

*#510 Bean Pods & Peeper—
Netsuke*, 2014
boxwood with acrylic
paint and gold leaf,
4 7/8 × 7/8 × 7/8 in.
Gift of Fleur S. Bresler,
2021.48.16

#530 Between, 2015
boxwood,
2 1/2 × 2 1/4 × 1 7/8 in.
Gift of Fleur S. Bresler,
2021.48.19

Tony Jojola
Isleta Pueblo
b. Isleta Pueblo, NM, 1958

Orange Blown Vase, 2002
blown glass, 8 × diam. 7 in.
Gift from the collection
of Clemmer and David
Montague, 2021.61.3

Christine Joy
b. Ithaca, NY, 1952

Small Dark Cloud, 2012
willow and Rocky Mountain
maple with encaustic finish,
15 3/4 × 20 3/4 × 15 1/2 in.
Gift of Mary Anne Fray,
2021.55.2
CAT. 11

Nadine Kariya
b. Boise, ID, 1947

*Kingfisher Caught Between
Man's God and Mother
Nature*, 2015
sterling silver, 18-karat gold,
shakudō, carved boxwood,
melamine and tin images,
14-karat vintage snake,
diamonds, steel cut beads,
aquamarine, garnet, and
braided leather cord,
cord: approx. 18 in.,
pendant: approx. 6 × 10 in.
Promised gift from the
collection of Alida and
Christopher Latham

Susan Kavicky
b. Riverside, IL, 1953

Sitting, 2010
brown ash, fiberboard, and
oak, 15 3/4 × 19 × 12 3/8 in.
Gift of Mary Anne Fray,
2021.55.1
CAT. 111

Jim Kelso
b. San Mateo, CA, 1950

*Kinship of Cherished
Ephemerals*, 2014
verawood with shibuichi,
copper, and 18-karat gold,
13 3/8 × 4 1/8 × 1 3/16 in.
Gift of Fleur S. Bresler,
2021.48.22

Sharon Kerry-Harlan
b. Miami, FL, 1951

Portrait of Resilience,
from the *Flag Series*, 2020
machine-quilted, dye-
discharge fabric designed
by the artist and antique
quilt, vinyl, American flag,
and African print fabrics,
86 1/2 × 73 1/2 in.
Museum purchase through
the Kenneth R. Trapp
Acquisition Fund, 2021.35
CAT. 6

Chawne Kimber
b. Frankfurt, KY, 1971

still not, 2019
machine-pieced, hand-
quilted, hand-bound
mid-century fabric, quilting
cotton, and denim with
cotton sashiko thread,
71 1/4 × 69 1/8 in.
Gift of Nedra and Peter
Agnew in honor of the James
Renwick Alliance, 2021.83
CAT. 15

Basil Kincaid
b. St. Louis, MO, 1986

*Riverside Revival: Lift Every
Voice and Sing*, 2020
machine-pieced and hand-
stitched clothes from the
artist, donated clothes
and corduroy, old choir
robes from Black churches
in St. Louis, fragments of
vintage quilts, and Ghanaian
fabric and embroidery,
77 1/2 × 52 7/8 in. (irreg.)
Museum purchase through
the Kenneth R. Trapp
Acquisition Fund, 2021.50.1
CAT. 85

Joey Kirkpatrick
b. Des Moines, IA, 1952

Flora C. Mace
b. Exeter, NH, 1949

Bird Pages: Cooper Hawk,
ca. 2004–6
cast glass, 17 1/2 × 14 × 6 in.
Promised gift from the
collection of Colleen and
John Kotelly

Silas Kopf
b. Warren, PA, 1949

*Founding Fathers
Writing Table*, 2010
wood from historic estates
of George Washington,
Thomas Jefferson, James
Madison, Patrick Henry,
and James Monroe,
29 7/8 × 49 1/8 × 21 1/2 in.
Gift of Fleur S. Bresler,
2021.48.11
CAT. 16

Mariko Kusumoto
b. Kumamoto, Japan, 1967;
based in Lexington, MA

Seascape 1, 2021
polyester fabric,
12 × 13 ½ × 5 in.
Gift of the James Renwick
Alliance in honor of the 50th
anniversary of the Renwick
Gallery and the 40th
anniversary of the Alliance

Julia Kwon
b. Woodbridge, VA, 1987

Unapologetically Asian,
2020
Korean silk, cotton canvas,
muslin, and elastic,
overall: 5 × 14 × 1 ⅝ in.
Museum purchase through
the Kenneth R. Trapp
Acquisition Fund, 2021.1
CAT. 1

Karen LaMonte
b. New York City, 1967

Vestige (Pleated Dress),
2000
cast glass, 58 × 16 × 18 in.
Promised gift from the
collection of Hal and
Myra Weiss
CAT. 97

Dora de Larios
b. Los Angeles, CA, 1933;
d. Culver City, CA, 2018

Opera Singer, ca. 1960
stoneware with glaze,
18 ⅞ × 15 ⅞ × 8 ⅝ in.
Gift of Forrest L. Merrill,
2021.98.1
CAT. 128

Ron Layport
b. Elyria, OH, 1942

Wolf Spirit, 2011
turned and carved
maple with pigment,
16 ¼ × diam. 10 ⅞ in.
Gift of Fleur S. Bresler,
2021.48.10

Cliff Lee
b. Vienna, Austria, 1951;
active Kaohsiung, Taiwan,
and Stevens, PA

Lava-Glazed Vessel, 2011
porcelain with lava glaze,
12 ¾ × diam. 10 ⅝ in. (irreg.)
Gift of Fleur S. Bresler,
2021.48.5

*Yellow Lidded Lotus Vase
on a Pedestal*, 2021
porcelain, 13 ½ × diam. 9 in.
Gift of the artist in honor of
Nicholas R. Bell

Marilyn Levine
b. Medicine Hat, Alberta,
Canada, 1935; d. Oakland,
CA, 2005

RK Briefcase, 1981
stoneware and nylon
fiber with engobe,
stain, and glaze;
Plexiglass case, overall:
17 ¹³⁄₁₆ × 44 ¹³⁄₁₆ × 7 in.,
briefcase:
14 ½ × 17 ½ × 2 in.
Gift of the Jerome A. and
Deena L. Kaplan Collection,
2021.49.2

Mark Lindquist
b. Oakland, CA, 1949

Untitled, 1969–96
birch root burl,
7 ¼ × 14 × 9 ⅛ in.
Gift of Fleur S. Bresler,
2021.48.25

Meditating Vessel, 1972
white birch root burl,
3 ½ × 7 × 6 in.
Gift of Fleur S. Bresler,
2021.48.23

Melvin Lindquist
b. Kingsburg, CA, 1911;
d. Quincy, FL, 2000

Root Bowl, 1979
manzanita root burl,
7 ¼ × 13 ¼ × 8 ¼ in.
Gift of Fleur S. Bresler,
2021.48.24

*Sculptural Handled
Vase*, 1996
spalted hackberry,
10 × 7 × 6 in.
Gift of Jane and Arthur
Mason

Cynthia Lockhart
b. Cincinnati, OH, 1952

Created To Be Me, 2017
machine-pieced, machine-
stitched, hand-stitched,
hand-painted, and
dyed fabrics with found
objects, 42 × 50 in.
Gift of Sara M. and Michelle
Vance Waddell in honor of
Dr. Carolyn Mazloomi

Thomas Loeser
b. Boston, MA, 1956

With You in a Moment, 2016
honey locust and
found shovel handles,
120 × 35 × 21 in.
Gift of the artist, 2021.58
CAT. 113

Linda Lopez
b. Visalia, CA, 1981

*Blue/Purple Ombré
with Rocks*, 2018
handbuilt colored porcelain,
8 ¾ × 13 ½ × 5 ½ in.
Museum purchase through
the Howard Kottler
Endowment for Ceramic
Art, 2020.64
CAT. 126

Roberto Lugo
b. Philadelphia, PA, 1981

*Confederate Graffiti
Teapot 2*, 2015
porcelain with glaze,
china paint, and luster,
9 × 7 ¼ × 5 in.
Promised gift from
the collection of Marc
and Diane Grainer
CAT. 20

*Frederick Douglass and
Anna Murray Douglass
Vase*, 2021
glazed ceramic with
enamel paint,
30 ½ × 15 ½ × 17 ⅝ in.
Museum purchase
through the Smithsonian
Latino Initiatives Pool,
administered by the
Smithsonian Latino Center
CAT. 19

Juicy, 2021
glazed stoneware with
enamel paint and luster,
19 7/8 × 13 3/8 × 9 3/8 in.
Gift of the James Renwick
Alliance in honor of the 50th
anniversary of the Renwick
Gallery and the 40th
anniversary of the Alliance,
2021.68
CAT. 18

Lauren Mabry
b. Madison, WI, 1985

*Glazescape
(Green Shade)*, 2021
earthenware with slip and
glaze, 20 1/8 × 15 7/8 × 6 3/4 in.
Gift of Ted Rowland
CAT. 124

Jeannine Marchand
b. San Juan, PR, 1976

FOLDS CLXVIII, 2019
clay, steel, and wood with
painted wooden frame,
24 × 12 × 6 in.
Gift of Joseph P. Logan,
2021.99
CAT. 99

Wendy Maruyama
b. La Junta, CO, 1952

Patterned Credenza, 1990
painted poplar,
36 1/2 × 42 × 20 in.
Promised gift from
the collection of Colleen
and John Kotelly
CAT. 38

Sharon Massey
b. Winston-Salem, NC, 1977

*Touch (in the time of
corona)*, 2020
copper, 3 1/4 × 6 1/2 × 3/8 in.
Museum purchase through
the Kenneth R. Trapp
Acquisition Fund, 2021.33
CAT. 104

Judy Kensley McKie
b. Boston, MA, 1944

Leopard Chest, 1989
basswood with oil paint
and gold leaf,
33 1/8 × 49 7/8 × 18 in.
Promised gift from the
collection of Colleen
and John Kotelly

Rebecca Medel
b. Denver, CO, 1947

Framed Light, n.d.
knotted linen,
30 × 30 × 10 in.
Gift of Jane and Arthur
Mason

Shari Mendelson
b. Schenectady, NY, 1961

*Animal with Caged
Vessel*, 2019
repurposed plastic with
hot glue, resin, acrylic
polymer, mica, glass
frit, and monofilament,
13 3/8 × 8 5/8 × 6 5/8 in.
Museum purchase through
the Kenneth R. Trapp
Acquisition Fund
CAT. 98

Matthew Metz
b. Kendallville, IN, 1961

Tea Pitcher, 2018
black porcelain with salt
glaze, 11 × 9 × 8 in.
Gift from the collection
of Clemmer and David
Montague, 2021.61.4

Julie Anne Mihalisin
b. Gainesville, AL, 1962

Untitled Brooch, 1997
silver and glass,
2 3/4 × 1 1/2 in.
Gift of Lloyd E. Herman,
founding director and
director emeritus of the
Renwick Gallery (1971–
1986), 2021.25.1

Norma Minkowitz
b. New York City, 1937

Goodbye, My Friend, 2018
stitched drawing: pen
and ink on paper with
stitched and crocheted fiber
and collage, 18 1/8 × 20 1/4 in.
Gift from the collection
of Clemmer and David
Montague in honor of
Camille Cook, founder of
Fiber Arts International,
2020.76.2
CAT. 135

Katrina Mitten
Miami Tribe of Oklahoma
b. Huntington, IN, 1962

MMIW, 2020
cotton with ribbon, Czech
seed beads, bone, and shell,
overall: 4 3/4 × 41 1/8 × 1 5/8 in.
Museum purchase through
the Kenneth R. Trapp
Acquisition Fund, 2020.29.1
CAT. 2

*Ten Original Clans of the
Myaamia*, 2016
wool felt with Czech seed
beads, pony beads, brass
thimbles, polyester tassels,
satin ribbon, and cotton
liner, 41 3/4 × 22 × 3 1/2 in.
Museum purchase through
the Kenneth R. Trapp
Acquisition Fund, 2021.3
CAT. 115

Jiha Moon
b. Daegu, South Korea, 1973;
based in Atlanta, GA

Yellowave (black) 1, 2020
black stoneware with
underglaze and glaze,
11 1/8 × 7 1/2 × 5 3/4 in.
Gift of the Alturas
Foundation, 2021.50.2
CAT. 122

Debora Moore
b. St. Louis, MO, 1960

Cherry, from the series
Arboria, 2018
blown and sculpted glass
with natural boulder,
approx. 90 × 28 × 20 in.
Museum purchase through
the Luisita L. and Franz H.
Denghausen Endowment
with support from
Rebecca Benaroya
CAT. 117

Pink Lady Slipper Branch,
2005
blown and sculpted glass,
approx. 43 × 14 × 8 in.
Promised gift from the
collection of Jacqueline Urow

Gertrud Natzler
b. Vienna, Austria, 1908;
d. Los Angeles, CA, 1971

Otto Natzler
b. Vienna, Austria, 1908;
d. Los Angeles, CA, 2007

Vase, 1965
earthenware with glaze,
13 ½ × diam 4 ⅞ in.
Gift of Fleur S. Bresler,
2021.48.8

Bowl, 1968
earthenware with glaze,
3 ½ × diam. 6 ⅜ in.
Gift of Fleur S. Bresler,
2021.48.7

Marvin Oliver
Quinault/Isleta Pueblo
b. Seattle, WA, 1946;
d. Seattle, WA, 2019

Salish Clam Basket, 2008
blown glass with
etched image,
17 ¾ × 18 ⅛ × 19 ¼ in.
Gift of Sharon Karmazin,
2021.28
CAT. 140

Virgil Ortiz
Cochiti Pueblo
b. Cochiti Pueblo, NM, 1969

Pueblo Revolt 2180, 2018–19
coil-built white bentonite
clay with bee-weed (spinach)
paint, 14 ⅝ × diam. 12 ⅞ in.
Museum purchase through
the Kenneth R. Trapp
Acquisition Fund
CAT. 90

Jane Osti
Cherokee Nation
b. Tahlequah, OK, 1945

Tall Squash Pot, 2020
coil-built and pit-fired
earthenware, 18 ⅛ ×
diam. 12 ⅛ in. (irreg.)
Museum purchase through
the Richard T. Evans Fund,
2020.63
CAT. 23

Woody de Othello
b. Miami, FL, 1991

Covering Face, 2021
stoneware with glaze on
tiled base, overall:
47 × 21 ¼ × 21 ⅜ in.
Museum purchase through
the Kenneth R. Trapp
Acquisition Fund
CAT. 101

Marilyn Pappas
b. Brockton, MA, 1931

Nike with Broken Wings,
2002–8
cotton and linen with gold
thread, 66 ½ × 33 ½ in.
Gift of Fleur S. Bresler,
2021.48.2
CAT. 89

Kit Paulson
b. Hinsdale, IL, 1981

Lungs, 2020
flameworked borosilicate
glass, 12 ¾ × 9 ½ × 3 ⅜ in.
Museum purchase through
the Kenneth R. Trapp
Acquisition Fund, 2021.22
CAT. 5

Pencil Brothers

Ken Cory
b. Kirkland, WA, 1943;
d. Ellensburg, WA, 1994

Leslie LePere
b. Spokane, WA, 1946

Egypt, 1974
copper, champlevé
enamel, rosewood,
graphite on paper, and
glass, 4 × 4 × ¾ in.
Gift of Leslie LePere,
2020.77
CAT. 3

Kevin Pourier
Oglala Lakota
b. Rapid City, SD, 1958

Valerie Pourier
Oglala Lakota
b. Marine Corps Base Camp
Pendleton, CA, 1959

Monarch Nation, 2019
carved bison horn with
inlaid orange sandstone
and white mother of pearl,
3 ¾ × 3 × 11 ¾ in.
Museum purchase through
the Kenneth R. Trapp
Acquisition Fund, 2021.2
CAT. 84

Stephen Rolfe Powell
b. Birmingham, AL, 1951;
d. Danville, KY, 2019

*Lascivious Torrid
Cleavage*, 2003
blown glass,
41 ⅛ × 25 ⅛ × 14 ⅜ in.
Gift of Shelly, Piper, and
Oliver Powell, 2021.85
CAT. 125

Ken Price
b. Los Angeles, CA, 1935;
d. Taos, NM, 2012

Nounless, 1989
fired earthenware
with acrylic paint,
10 ½ × 14 ⅜ × 10 ⅝ in.
Gift of Colleen and John
Kotelly, 2021.63.2
CAT. 123

Ronald Rael
b. Conejos County, CO, 1971

Virginia San Fratello
b. Savannah, GA, 1971

Bad Ombrés v.2, 2017
six 3D-printed ceramic
vessels, overall:
23 × 51 × 35 in.
Museum purchase through
the Howard Kottler
Endowment for Ceramic Art
CAT. 29

Sheila Kanieson Ransom
Mohawk, Wolf Clan
from Akwesasne
b. Haudenosaunee (Iroquois
Confederacy), Northeast
Woodlands (NY), 1954

Pope Basket, 2021
sweetgrass and black ash
splints with commercial dye,
overall: 6 × diam. 10 ⅝ in.
Gift of Frances Dubrowski
and David Buente, 2021.79.1
CAT. 110

Ché Rhodes
b. Cincinnati, OH, 1973

Untitled, 2007
blown and cut glass,
4 pieces:
18 ½ × diam. 6 in.,
23 ½ × diam. 6 in.,
19 × diam. 9 in., and
22 × diam. 9 in.
Gift of Merrily Orsini
and Frederick Heath,
2021.57A–D
CAT. 33

Jon Eric Riis
b. Park Ridge, IL, 1945

*Heart of Gold,
Female #2*, 2002
tapestry-woven silk
with metallic thread;
custom mount, tapestry:
29 × 66 ⅝ × 2 ½ in.
Gift of the Jerome A. and
Deena L. Kaplan
Collection, 2021.49.1
CAT. 130

Richard Ritter
b. Detroit, MI, 1940

Untitled, from the
Triolet Series, 1989
solid cast and
furnace-worked glass,
8 ¾ × 9 × 8 ½ in.
Gift of Colleen and John
Kotelly, 2021.63.1

George Rodriguez
b. El Paso, TX, 1982

*Mexican American
Gothic*, 2019
stoneware with glaze and
underglaze, 84 × 60 × 30 in.
Gift of Alison and Glen
Milliman, Cynthia Sears,
and Michael J. Stein
CAT. 127

Joyce Scott
b. Baltimore, MD, 1948

Yellow #4, 1998
cast and blown glass
and glass beads,
11 ⅝ × 10 ⅛ × ⅝ in.
Gift of Chris Rifkin, 2021.60
CAT. 136

Birth of Mammy #4, 2004
blown glass and beads,
wire, thread, and wood,
23 × 12 × 9 in.
Gift of Sara M. and Michelle
Vance Waddell in honor of
Dr. Carolyn Mazloomi

Bonnie Seeman
b. Huntington, NY, 1969

Teapot with One Cup, 2011
porcelain and glass,
10 ¼ × 7 ¼ × 8 ¾ in.
Gift of Fleur S. Bresler,
2021.48.6

Kay Sekimachi
b. San Francisco, CA, 1926

Leaf Vessel, ca. 2012
big-leaf maple leaf and
kōzo paper with watercolor,
5 ½ × diam. 4 ½ in.
Gift of Fleur S. Bresler,
2021.48.4

Kay Sekimachi
b. San Francisco, CA, 1926

Bob Stocksdale
b. Warren, IN, 1913;
d. Oakland, CA, 2003

Marriage in Form, 1996
hornets' nest paper
and Pacific yew,
3 ¼ × 5 ¾ and 3 × 7 in.
Gift of Jane and Arthur
Mason

Aram Han Sifuentes
b. Seoul, South Korea, 1986;
resides Chicago, IL
for the Protest Banner
Lending Library

Otro Mundo Es Posible, 2017
felt and fusible web on
cotton; checkout card,
banner: 42 ⅞ × 42 ½ in.,
card: 4 × 6 in.
Gift of Jaimianne and
Anthony Jacobin in honor
of the James Renwick
Alliance, 2021.36
CAT. 86

Linda Sikora
b. Saskatoon, Saskatchewan,
Canada, 1960

Faux Wood Group, 2014–21
wood and salt-fired
stoneware with glaze,
ranging from approx.
8 × diam. 4 ¼ in. (vase) to
14 ¾ × diam. 14 in. (jar)
Museum purchase
with support from
Clemmer Montague and
the Kenneth R. Trapp
Acquisition Fund

Sally Silberberg
b. Syracuse, NY, 1945

Vessel, 1980
porcelain with glaze,
13 ¾ × diam. 6 ¾ in.
Gift of the artist, 2021.91

Black Striae, 1988–2019
porcelain on enameled
wooden base, without base:
11 ⅜ × 15 ¾ × 13 ¼ in.
Museum purchase through
the Richard T. Evans Fund

Preston Singletary
Tlingit
b. San Francisco, CA, 1963

Killer Whale Hat, 2002
blown and sand-carved
glass, 12 ¾ × diam. 18 ¾ in.
Gift from the collection
of Clemmer and David
Montague, 2020.76.3

Horizontal Frog, 2011
screenprint, 11 × 30 in.
limited edition
Gift of the artist

Shark Paddle, 2011
screenprint, 30 × 11 in.
limited edition
Gift of the artist

Thunderbird & Hawk, 2011
blown and sand-carved
glass, without mount:
15 ⅞ × 7 ⅜ × 7 ½ in.
Gift of Judy and Stuart
Heller, 2021.56
CAT. 132

Black Box, 2013
screenprint, 22 × 30 in.
limited edition
Gift of the artist

Safe Journey, 2021
cast and sand-carved
glass, chest:
14 ⅞ × 27 ⅛ × 16 ⅜ in.,
lid: 3 ⅞ × 27 ½ × 16 ⅞ in.,
pedestal: 45 ⅝ ×
28 ⅜ × 17 ½ in.
Museum purchase with
support from the James
Renwick Alliance in honor
of the 50th anniversary of
the Renwick Gallery and
the 40th anniversary of the
Alliance, and the Kenneth R.
Trapp Acquisition Fund,
2021.82A–C
CAT. 141

Vicki Lee Soboleff
Haida and Tlingit
b. Seattle, WA, 1964

Yellow Cedar Face Mask,
2020
yellow cedar and sinew,
overall: 4 × 5 5/8 × 3/4 in.
Museum purchase through
the Kenneth R. Trapp
Acquisition Fund, 2020.29.2
CAT. 82

Linda Sormin
b. Bangkok, Thailand;
resides New York City

*Ta Saparot
(pineapple eyes)*, 2019
glazed ceramic with found
shards, glitter, and gold leaf,
13 × 17 × 16 in.
Gift of Dorothy Saxe
CAT. 137

Robert Sperry
b. Bushnell, IL, 1927;
d. Seattle, WA, 1998

Ceramic Wall Mural "#988",
1991
stoneware with slip and
glaze; steel rim mounted on
plywood, 75 × 75 × 2 in.
Gift of Patti Warashina,
2021.86.2

Roy Superior
b. New York City, 1934;
d. Williamsburg, MA, 2013

Peace Missile, 1985
oak, walnut, laurel, and
hardwoods with brass
and music box, closed:
7 × 20 × 12 in.
Gift of Fleur S. Bresler,
2021.48.9
CAT. 109

April Surgent
b. Missoula, MT, 1982

Wave, 2021
cameo-engraved glass,
18 × 36 × 3/4 in.
Gift of Gwen and Jerome
Paulson in honor of the
James Renwick Alliance

Polly Adams Sutton
b. Waukegan, IL, 1950

Facing the Unexpected, 2013
western cedar bark, ash,
spruce root, and coated
copper wire, overall:
11 1/2 × 18 × 32 in.
Museum purchase with
support from Mary Anne
Fray and the Decorative
Arts and Crafts Endowment,
2021.52A–I
CAT. 12

Akio Takamori
b. Nobeoka, Japan, 1950;
d. Seattle, WA, 2017

Alice with Rose, from the
series *Alice/Venus*, 2009
stoneware with underglaze,
approx. 45 × 26 × 22 in.
Gift of the Jerome A. and
Deena L. Kaplan Collection,
2021.49.3
CAT. 129

Marlana Thompson
Mohawk, Wolf Clan from
Akwesasne
b. Cornwall, Ontario,
Canada 1978

*Ononkwashon:a
(Medicine Plants)*, 2020
black velveteen with
red flannel, Czech seed
beads, sweetgrass, sage,
and leather, overall:
5 × 51 3/4 × 1 7/8 in.
Museum purchase through
the Kenneth R. Trapp
Acquisition Fund, 2020.29.3
CAT. 83

Einar de la Torre
b. Guadalajara, Mexico, 1963

Jamex de la Torre
b. Guadalajara, Mexico, 1960
both active Baja California,
Mexico, and San Diego, CA

Ohio Goza y Mas, 2013
blown glass, resin
castings, and mixed media,
67 × 67 × 9 in.
Gift of Todd Wingate and
Steven Cason, courtesy of
the artists and Koplin Del Rio
Gallery, 2021.84
CAT. 4

Howard Ben Tré
b. Brooklyn, NY, 1949;
d. Pawtucket, RI, 2020

Wrapped Light #3/2, 2008
cast glass with gold leaf
and pigmented wax on
metal base, overall:
22 3/4 × diam. 8 1/4 in.
Gift of Wendy MacGaw,
2021.42
CAT. 30

Gail Tremblay
Mi'kmaq and Onondaga
b. Buffalo, NY, 1945

*When Will the Red Leader
Overshadow Images of the
19th-Century Noble Savage
in Hollywood Films that
Some Think Are Sympathetic
to American Indians*, 2018
35mm film from *Windwalker*
(1981), red and white leader,
and silver braid, overall:
15 1/2 × diam. 14 7/8 in.
Gift of Ms. Brenda Erickson
in honor of the James
Renwick Alliance, 2021.11
CAT. 13

M. J. Tyson
b. Morristown, NJ, 1986

Popular Devotion, 2020
devotional medals with
sterling silver and pewter,
19 1/8 × 10 1/2 × 1/2 in.
Museum purchase through
the Kenneth R. Trapp
Acquisition Fund, 2021.18.2
CAT. 105

**Consuelo Jiménez
Underwood**
b. Sacramento, CA, 1949

Run, Jane, Run!, 2004
tapestry-woven cotton,
linen, and other fabric with
barbed wire and caution
tape, overall: 120 × 67 5/8 in.
Gift of the Alturas
Foundation, 2021.51
CAT. 27

Herman Vandever
Diné (Navajo)
b. Prewitt, NM, 1964

*Natural Turquoise Buffalo
Pendant*, 2020
Morenci turquoise and
sterling silver, open:
2 ½ × 2 ⅞ × ¾ in.
Gift of Linda and David
Stout, 2020.57A–B

Kukuli Velarde
b. Lima, Peru, 1962;
based in Philadelphia, PA

*Santa Chingada:
The Perfect Little Woman*,
1999–2000
slip-cast ceramic and mixed
media, 25 × 18 × 11 ½ in.
Gift from the collection
of Clemmer and David
Montague, 2021.61.5
CAT. 131

Paul Villinski
b. York, ME, 1960

Comforter, 1994
found cotton gloves and
cotton thread, 88 × 75 ⅜ in.
Gift of the artist, 2021.70
CAT. 102

Dawn Nichols Walden
Ojibway descendant,
Mackinac Band of Chippewa
and Ottawa Indians
b. Vulcan, MI, 1949

Random Order XIII, 2006
cedar bark and roots
with beargrass, overall:
23 ¾ × diam. 14 ½ in.
(irreg.)
Gift of Robert and Sharon
Buchanan, 2021.41.2
CAT. 10

Jason Walker
b. Pocatello, ID, 1973

Los Comunicadores, 2006
porcelain with underglaze,
wire, and cement
23 ⅛ × 9 ½ × 10 ⅛ in.
Gift of Marc and Diane
Grainer, 2021.77.1

Vivian Wang
b. Shanghai, China, 1945;
based in West Palm Beach, FL

Shanghai Tiger, 2019
cast glass and stoneware
with gemstones and gold
leaf on steel base, overall:
31 ⅜ × 12 ⅞ × 14 ¾ in.
Gift of Aaron Schey—
Habatat Galleries Michigan,
2021.52
CAT. 134

James C. Watkins
b. Louisville, KY, 1951

Communion, 1998
raku-fired, double-walled
earthenware with glaze,
20 ¼ × diam. 22 in.
Museum purchase through
the Kenneth R. Trapp
Acquisition Fund, 2020.56
CAT. 7

Kurt Weiser
b. Lansing, MI, 1950

Many, Many, 2005
cast porcelain with
glaze and china paint on
bronze base, overall:
20 ⅜ × 19 ½ × 17 ½ in.
Gift of the Porter Family
CAT. 119

Betty Woodman
b. Norwalk, CT, 1930;
d. New York City, 2018

Pillow Pitcher, ca. 2012
earthenware with glaze,
21 ½ × 21 ⅞ × 21 ⅝ in.
Gift of the Jerome A. and
Deena L. Kaplan Collection,
2021.49.4

Nancy Lee Worden
b. Boston, MA, 1954;
d. Seattle, WA, 2021

Which Way?, 1989
silver, jasper, onyx,
typewriter keys, compass,
and steel ball chain,
30 × 5 × ½ in.
Gift of the Estate of Nancy
Worden, 2021.54.5

Exosquellette #2, 2003
copper, silver, bone, nickel,
wooden clothespin, steel,
glass eyes, and cotton cord,
28 × 12 ½ × 1 in.
Gift of the Estate of Nancy
Worden, 2021.54.2

Literal Defense, 2007
aluminum from cookware,
silver, copper and brass
rivets, plastic IBM
typewriter balls, glass
indicator lights, taxidermy
eyes, leather, and gold leaf,
24 × 13 × 5 in.
Gift of the Estate of Nancy
Worden, 2021.54.3

Luddite's Lament, 2011
copper, nickel, plastic
tubing, and silver,
15 × 10 × 1 ½ in.
Gift of the Estate of Nancy
Worden, 2021.54.4

*Sexual Harassment in
the Workplace*, 2018
silver, found gloves,
found purses, and plastic
flowers, 25 × 18 × 7 ½ in.
Gift of the Estate of Nancy
Worden, 2021.54.1
CAT. 103

Malcolm Wright
b. Minnesota, 1939

Buffalo, 2009
wood-fired brick clay,
9 × 11 × 9 ½ in.
Gift of the artist

gwendolyn yoppolo
b. Redwood City, CA, 1968

scoopbowl service, 2010
porcelain with
microcrystalline glaze,
bowl: 6 × diam. 14 ½ in.,
ten spoons:
2 × 5 ¼ × 3 in. each
Gift of Rebecca Anne Sive,
2021.74
CAT. 25

Wanxin Zhang
b. Changchun, China, 1961;
resides San Francisco, CA

Warrior with Color Face,
2009
high-fired stoneware
with glaze,
77 ¾ × 23 × 21 ¼ in.
Gift of David and Pamela
Hornik, 2021.72
CAT. 100

BERNSTEIN-CHERNOFF COLLECTION OF SCULPTURAL WOOD ART

All works are Gift of Jeffrey Bernstein, MD, and Judith Chernoff, MD

John Beaver
b. Santa Barbara, CA, 1963

3 Protruding Wave Bowl, 2011
alder and padauk,
3 × diam. 5 in.
2021.66.1
CAT. 45

Intersecting Waves, 2016
walnut and maple,
6 × diam. 8 in.
2021.66.2
CAT. 46

Dixie Biggs
b. Lafayette, IN, 1956

Duted Material, 2003
dyed palm and ziricote,
18 × diam. 11 1/4 in.
2021.66.3
CAT. 44

Sweet Dreams, 2010
painted sugar maple,
3 × diam. 4 in.
2021.66.4
CAT. 42

Sweet Spot, 2010
painted Jordan sugar maple,
7 1/2 × diam. 4 3/4 in.
2021.66.5
CAT. 43

Hunt Clark
b. 1969

Untitled Wood Sculpture,
2011
maple, 15 1/2 × 20 × 20 in.
2021.66.6
CAT. 52

Andy Cole
b. Beverly, MA, 1957

Hawaiian Six Pack, 2015
macadamia,
6 pieces: ranging from
7 3/8 × 12 1/4 × 10 5/8 to
1 3/8 × diam. 1 7/8 in.
2021.66.7
CAT. 65

Sharon Doughtie
b. Abington, PA, 1957

Four Winds, Two Poles, 2005
Norfolk Island pine,
3 × diam. 9 in.
2021.66.8
CAT. 72

Cindy Drozda
b. Missouri, 1958

Wooden Bowl #157, n.d.
eucalyptus gum burl
and desert ironwood
with 23-karat gold leaf,
3 × diam. 6 1/2 in.
2021.66.9
CAT. 47

*Pele (Hawaiian
Goddess of Fire)*, n.d.
Australian red mallee
burl and blackwood with
garnet in 14-karat gold,
15 4/5 × diam. 9 in.
2021.66.10
CAT. 48

Harvey Fein
b. Bronx, NY, 1940

Avelino Samuel
b. Coral Bay, St. John

Untitled, 2011
cocobolo, 10 × diam. 6 3/4 in.
2021.66.11
CAT. 58

Ray Feltz
b. Celina, OH, 1946

Ribbon Bowl II, n.d.
bloodwood, holly, and pink
ivory, 1 1/8 × diam. 3 1/2 in.
2021.66.12
CAT. 69

J. Paul Fennell
b. Beverly, MA, 1938

Untitled Vessel, 2004
carob, 5 × diam. 6 in.
2021.66.13
CAT. 50

Szechwan Serenity, 2013
African sumac,
11 × diam. 9 in.
2021.66.15
CAT. 49

Offering Vessel, 2015
ficus, 10 1/2 × diam. 9 in.
2021.66.14
CAT. 51

Ron Fleming
b. Oklahoma City, OK, 1937;
d. Boyd, TX, 2021

Echo, n.d.
spalted hackberry,
8 × 15 × 9 in.
2021.66.16
CAT. 74

Michael Hampel

*It's Not a House,
It's a Home*, 2007
English walnut,
11 × 13 × 12 in.
2021.66.17
CAT. 63

Stephen Hatcher
b. Colorado Springs, CO,
1953

Falling Blossoms, 2016
big-leaf maple, Gabon
ebony, and fiber veneer
with mineral crystal
inlay, rare-earth magnets,
resin, dyes, and lacquer,
6 1/2 × 7 3/4 × 6 1/2 in.
2021.66.18
CAT. 68

Louise Hibbert
b. Southampton, England,
1972

Cinachyra Box, 2000
sycamore and boxwood
with polyester resin and
acrylic ink, diam. 4 1/4 in.
2021.66.20
CAT. 80

Radiolarian Vessel VII, 2004
English sycamore with silver,
texture paste, and acrylic inks,
2 1/2 × 6 × 6 in.
2021.66.19
CAT. 79

Robyn Horn
b. Fort Smith, AR, 1951

Stone Circle, 2006
jarrah burl on steel base,
18 1/4 × 19 1/8 × 14 in.
2021.66.21
CAT. 66

Jerry Kermode
b. 1958

Untitled Bowl, 2007
redwood lace burl,
5 1/4 × diam. 18 3/4 in.
2021.66.22
CAT. 64

Pat Kramer
b. Honolulu, HI, 1949

Night Blooming Serious,
2003
Norfolk Island pine,
5 × diam. 15 ½ in.
2021.66.23
CAT. 41

John Mascoll
b. Barbados, 1951

Untitled Lidded Vessel, n.d.
royal palm and cocobolo,
overall: 17 ¼ × diam. 8 ¾ in.
2021.66.24
CAT. 54

Untitled Lidded Vessel, 2016
bleached chinaberry,
overall: 12 ¾ × 7 ¼ × 7 in.
2021.66.25
CAT. 56

Untitled Lidded Vessel, 2016
citrus, overall:
11 × diam. 4 ¾ in.
2021.66.26
CAT. 55

Hal Metlitzky
b. Johannesburg,
South Africa, 1946

Cyclone, 2012
yellowheart, Gabon ebony,
holly, imbuia, black walnut,
satiné, and old-growth
East Indian rosewood,
15 × diam. 21 in.
2021.66.27
CAT. 71

Connie Mississippi
b. Greenwood, MS, 1941

Midnight Mountain, 2001–4
Baltic birch plywood,
6 ½ × diam. 22 in.
2021.66.28
CAT. 39

Philip Moulthrop
b. Atlanta, GA, 1947

Mixed Mosaic, n.d.
pine, mimosa, oak, pear,
and cherry, 9 × diam. 13 in.
2021.66.29
CAT. 78

Mark Nantz
b. Queens, NY, 1969

Fusion, 2002
amboyna burl and ebony,
11 ⅜ × diam. 12 ¼ in.
2021.66.30
CAT. 40

Artifact Series, 2007
stabilized, dyed blue maple
burl and ebony with silver,
14-karat gold, steel, and
solvent-based aniline dye
suspended in liquid acrylic,
10 × 6 ¼ × 5 ⅝ in.
2021.66.31
CAT. 61

*Mottled Ebony Bowl
with Silver Inlay*, 2013
ebony with silver,
3 ½ × diam. 5 ¼ in.
2021.66.32
CAT. 60

Graeme Priddle
b. Lower Hutt,
New Zealand, 1960

Reflection, 2006
macrocarpa with
acrylic paint, 2 pieces:
14 ¼ × 4 ¼ × 4 in. each
2021.66.33
CAT. 81

Avelino Samuel
b. Coral Bay, St. John

Spiral Carved Vessel, n.d.
black olive, 8 ¾ × diam. 5 in.
2021.66.34
CAT. 57

Spiral Carved Vessel, 2006
mahogany,
12 ¼ × diam. 6 ¾ in.
2021.66.35
CAT. 59

Betty Scarpino
b. Wenatchee, WA, 1949

Inviolate Portal, 2007
ash, oak, and walnut,
16 × 14 × 3 ½ in.
2021.66.36
CAT. 53

David Sengel
b. Radford, VA, 1951

*Round Lidded Container
with Legs*, n.d.
Bing cherry with rose,
blackberry, and locust
thorns, 4 × diam. 3 ¼ in.
2021.66.37
CAT. 73

Koji Tanaka
b. Palo Alto, CA, 1984

Nagamé, 2013
African mahogany,
5 ¾ × 27 ⅞ × 2 ¾ in.
2021.66.39
CAT. 77

Uragaeshi (Inside Out), 2013
African mahogany,
6 ⅛ × 29 × 2 ⅞ in.
2021.66.38
CAT. 76

Curt Theobald
b. Cheyenne, WY, 1965

Eye of the Storm, 2013
butternut, maple, and
bubinga, 3 ½ × diam. 15 in.
2021.66.40
CAT. 70

Holly Tornheim
b. Ann Arbor, MI, 1948

Vessel II, n.d.
curly maple,
3 ¾ × 24 ⅜ × 5 ⅜ in.
2021.66.41
CAT. 67

Jacques Vesery
b. New Milford, NJ, 1960

*Makana Ka Na Hoku
(Gift of the Stars)*, 2006–7
cherry with 23-karat
gold leaf and acrylic paint,
2 ½ × diam. 5 in.
2021.66.42
CAT. 75

Andi Wolfe
b. Salem, OR, 1957

*When I Let Go of What
I Am, I Can Become What I
Might Be—Lao Tzu (Carved
Sphere, No. 2)*, 2008
redwood burl, diam. 4 in.
2021.66.43
CAT. 62

INDEX

IMAGE AND QUOTATION CREDITS

All artworks are in the collection of the Renwick Gallery of the Smithsonian American Art Museum unless otherwise noted.

Cover, pp. 2–3: Photo by Wiliam Perry / Alamy Stock Photo

p. 4, CAT. 117: Photo by Rozarii Lynch

p. 6, 8, CAT. 125: Photo by David Harpe

p. 12, Fig. 5, pp. 24–25, CAT. 95: Photo by Ron Blunt

pp. 22–23, CAT. 37, back cover: © Alicia Eggert, photo by Calen Barnum

Fig. 1: © 2015, Ehren Tool, photo by Gene Young

p. 17, CATS. 1, 10, 11, 17, 25, 26, 30–32, 34, 89, 92–94, 100, 105, 109, 110, 111, 119, 121–23, 129–31, 136, 139, 140, Fig. 6: Photo by Lee Stalsworth — Fine Art through Photography

CAT. 2 © 4/2020, Katrina Mitten, photo by Mildred Baldwin

Fig. 2: Photo by Dick Mowry, Smithsonian Institution Archives, acc. 11-009, image no. 72-1961-06

Fig. 3: Smithsonian Institution Archives, acc. 11-009, image no. 72-4407B

CAT. 4: © Einar and Jamex de la Torre, 2013, courtesy of the artists and Koplin Del Rio Gallery

Fig. 4, pp. 42–43: Photo by Bruce Petschek

CAT. 5: © 2020, Kit Paulson, photo by Lee Stalsworth — Fine Art through Photography

CAT. 6: © 2021, Sharon Kerry-Harlan, photo by Lee Stalsworth — Fine Art through Photography

CAT. 7: © 1998, James Watkins, photo by Lee Stalsworth — Fine Art through Photography

CAT. 8: © 2019, Catherine Hudnall, photo by Mary McClung

Fig. 7: Photo by Charlotte Raymond, Toshiko Takaezu papers, Archives of American Art, box 20, folder 14, image no. 10

Figs. 8–10, 12, 13, 17, 20: Photo by Gene Young

CAT. 12: Photo by Tom Grotta, courtesy of browngrotta arts

CAT. 13: © 2018, Gail E. Tremblay, courtesy of Froelick Gallery

CAT. 14: © 2019, Jeremy Frey, courtesy of Home and Away Gallery

CAT. 15: © 2019, Chawne Kimber, photo by Lee Stalsworth — Fine Art through Photography

CAT. 16: Photo by David L. Ryan

Fig. 11: © 2011, L. J. Roberts, photo by Gene Young

CATS. 18–20: © Roberto Lugo, photo by Dominic Episcopo, courtesy of Wexler Gallery

CAT. 21: Courtesy of Blue Rain Gallery

CAT. 22: Photo by Janel Jacobson

CAT. 23: © 2020, Jane Osti, photo by Lee Stalsworth — Fine Art through Photography

CAT. 24: Photo by M. Lee Fatherree, Oakland, CA

Figs. 14–16: © 2011, Margarita Cabrera, photo by Gene Young

CAT. 27: © 2004, Consuelo J. Underwood

CAT. 28: Photo by Gina Clyne

CAT. 29: Courtesy of Ronald Rael & Virginia San Fratello / Emerging Objects

CAT. 33: Photo by Bruce Miller

p. 97: Photo by Adam Field

pp. 99–100, 113: © Alicia Eggert, photo by Wesley Kirk of Vision & Verve

pp. 105, CAT. 35: © 2018, Kelly Church, photo by Richard Church (Pottawatomi and Odawa – Gun Lake Band)

p. 109: Photo by Nicholas Calcott

CAT. 36: Photo by Carlos Avendaño, courtesy of The Fabric Workshop and Museum, Philadelphia

p. 117: Photo by Michael Lou Bradley

Fig. 19: © 2014, Steven Young Lee, photo by Gene Young

p. 121: © Howard Lippin, San Diego Union Tribune via ZUMA Press

Fig. 21: © Association Marcel Duchamp / ADAGP, Paris / Artists Rights Society (ARS), New York 2021

p. 129: Photo by Guy Bishop, Courtesy of the Center for Art in Wood, Fleur & Charles Bresler Research Library

p. 133: Photo by Jovan Wilson

p. 137, CATS. 39–81: Photo by Mitro Hood

Fig. 22: © 2013, Judith Schaechter

pp. 170–71: Photo by Tim Brown / Alamy Stock Photo

CAT. 82: © June 1, 2020, Vicki Soboleff, photo by Mildred Baldwin

CAT. 83: © April 28, 2020, photo by Mildred Baldwin

CAT. 84: © Kevin Pourier, photo by Lee Stalsworth — Fine Art through Photography

CAT. 85: © 2021, Basil Alexander Kincaid, photo by Lee Stalsworth — Fine Art through Photography

CAT. 86: © 2017, Aram Han Sifuentes, photo by Lee Stalsworth — Fine Art through Photography

CAT. 87: © 2020, Carolyn Crump, photo by Lee Stalsworth — Fine Art through Photography

CAT. 88: © 2020, Carla Goodleaf Hemlock, photo by Stalsworth — Fine Art through Photography

pp. 182–83, CAT. 120: Photo by David Hale

CAT. 91: © Nick Cave, photo by James Prinz Photography, courtesy of the artist and Jack Shainman Gallery, New York

CAT. 96: © John Bigelow Taylor

CAT. 97: © Karen LaMonte, photo by Gabriel Urbanek

CAT. 102: © 1994, Paul Villinski, photo by Lee Stalsworth — Fine Art through Photography

CAT. 103: © 2020, Estate of Nancy Worden, photo by Rex Rystedt / Seattlephoto.com

CAT. 106: © 2020, Mindy Solomon, representative for Donté Hayes, photo by Mildred Baldwin

CAT. 107: Photo by Ronald Dunlap

CAT. 108: © 2021, Thomas Pendergraft

CAT. 112: Photo by Mercedes Jelinek

CAT. 115: © 2016, Katrina Mitten, photo by Lee Stalsworth — Fine Art through Photography

CAT. 116: © 2020, Joe Feddersen, courtesy of Froelick Gallery

CAT. 118: Photo by Ken Yanoviak

CAT. 124: Photo by the artist

CAT. 126: © 2020, Linda Lopez, courtesy of David B. Smith Gallery

CAT. 127: © Spike Mafford, courtesy of Foster / White Gallery, Seattle

CAT. 128: Photo by M. Lee Fatherree, Oakland, CA

CAT. 132: © Preston Singletary, photo by Daniel Fox / Lumina Studio

CAT. 134: Courtesy of Andrea Fisher Fine Pottery

CAT. 137: Photo by Brian Oglesbee, courtesy of Patricia Sweetow Gallery, San Francisco

CAT. 138: © 2019, Sharif Bey, photo by Nathan J. Shaulis / Porter Loves Creative

CAT. 141: © Preston Singletary Studio, photo by Russell Johnson

Image details and chapter openers

pp. 2–3: Renwick Gallery façade (detail), 2019

p. 4: Debora Moore, *Cherry* (detail; see CAT. 117)

p. 6, 8: Stephen Rolfe Powell, *Lascivious Torrid Cleavage* (detail; see CAT. 125)

p. 12: Olga de Amaral, *Montaña #13* (detail; see CAT. 95)

p. 17: Marilyn Pappas, *Nike with Broken Wings* (detail; see CAT. 89)

pp. 22–23: Alicia Eggert, *This Present Moment* (see CAT. 37)

pp. 24–25: Installation view of Leo Villareal's *Volume (Renwick)* (detail; 2015) suspended above the staircase in the Renwick Gallery

pp. 42–43: Installation view of Janet Echelman's *1.8 Renwick* (detail; 2015) in the Renwick Gallery's Bettie Rubenstein Grand Salon

p. 52: Bird's nest with eggs from Toshiko Takeazu's garden. Photo by Martha Russo, Toshiko Takaezu papers, Archives of American Art, box 22, folder 7, image no. 29

p. 97: Steven Young Lee working in the studio

pp. 99–100: Alicia Eggert with her work

p. 137: Andi Wolfe, *When I Let Go of What I Am…Lao Tzu (Carved Sphere No. 2)* (detail; see CAT. 62)

pp. 170–71: Installation view of visitors inside David Best's *Temple* (detail; 2018) in the Renwick Gallery's Bettie Rubenstein Grand Salon for *No Spectators: The Art of Burning Man* (2018–19)

pp. 182–83: Susie Ganch, *Drag* (see CAT. 120)

Quotation credits

p. 53: From *EVIDENCE* by Mary Oliver, published by Beacon Press, Boston. © 2009, Mary Oliver, used herewith by permission of the Charlotte Sheedy Literary Agency, Inc.

p. 82: From *Borderlands/La Frontera: The New Mestiza* by Gloria Anzaldúa, published by Aunt Lute Books, San Francisco. Copyright © 1987 by Gloria Anzaldúa.

p. 88: From *The Lathe of Heaven* by Ursula K. Le Guin, published by Scribner, a division of Simon & Schuster, Inc., New York. Copyright © 1971 by Ursula K. Le Guin. Copyright renewed © 1999 Ursula K. Le Guin. Originally published in *Amazing Stories* magazine.